ROLLS-ROYCE HER

The life and times of HENRY EDMUNDS

Pioneer, entrepreneur and 'Godfather of Rolls-Royce'

Paul Tritton

Historical Series No 38

Published in 2006 by the
Rolls-Royce Heritage Trust
PO Box 31, Derby, England DE24 8BJ

© 2006 Rolls-Royce Heritage Trust

2nd edition
Previously published as *The Godfather of Rolls-Royce* in 1993 by Academy Books

This book, or any parts thereof, must not be reproduced in any form without the written permission of the publishers.

ISBN : 1 872 922 33 3

The Historical Series is published as a joint initiative by the Rolls-Royce Heritage Trust and the Sir Henry Royce Memorial Foundation.

Previous volumes published in the Series are listed at the rear, together with volumes available in the Rolls-Royce Heritage Trust Technical Series.

Books are available from:
Rolls-Royce Heritage Trust, Rolls-Royce plc, Moor Lane, PO Box 31, Derby DE24 8BJ

Cover picture:
A portrait of Henry Edmunds aged 50.

Printed in 2006 by Océ

CONTENTS

	Page
Introduction	5
Foreword by Lord Montagu of Beaulieu	6
Foreword to the second edition	7
Acknowledgements	9
Prologue	12

Chapter one	The ironmonger's son	15
Chapter two	Adventures in America	34
Chapter three	Phonographs and telephones	52
Chapter four	'Improvements in electric lamps'	71
Chapter five	A family tragedy	89
Chapter six	Joseph Swan's negotiator	101
Chapter seven	Inventions and experiments	120
Chapter eight	A Royal command	139
Chapter nine	Power for the people	159
Chapter ten	'My association with Mr Rolls'	175
Chapter eleven	The first Royce motor car	195
Chapter twelve	Rolls meets Royce	221
Chapter thirteen	Side-slips and hill climbs	242
Chapter fourteen	Soirées and crises in Sussex	264

Family trees	296
Epilogue	297
Postscript to the first edition	302
Postscript to the second edition	325
The author	333

Henry Edmunds

INTRODUCTION

Henry Edmunds is motoring's forgotten pioneer, yet it was he who brought together the men who formed the most famous partnership in the histories of the motor car and aviation - the Hon. Charles Rolls, celebrated motor racing driver and balloonist, and Frederick Henry Royce, who would emerge from poverty to win fame as a designer of automobiles and aero-engines.

Thanks to Edmunds' foresight and persistence, without which their paths would never have crossed, Rolls and Royce founded an enterprise that brought honour and distinction to themselves and to their country. Who, today, can imagine a world without the luxury limousines that immortalize their names, or the Rolls-Royce aero-engines that have been so vital to the defence of freedom and to the development of civil aviation?

This biography of Henry Edmunds tells, for the first time, the full story of how, why and when the careers and aspirations of Rolls and Royce converged, their historic meeting in May 1904, the road tests of Royce's first car and many other fascinating events and adventures in the lives of motorists and motor engineers of the late Victorian and Edwardian eras.

Becoming 'the Godfather of Rolls-Royce' was, for Henry Edmunds, the culmination of an exciting career with few parallels in engineering history. As a young man he pioneered electric lighting, electric traction and telephony; became a friend of Thomas Edison, Joseph Swan and other eminent inventors and scientists; witnessed the first successful attempt to record sound; promoted Edison's Phonograph and Chichester Bell and Charles Sumner Tainter's Graphophone in Britain; introduced incandescent electric lighting into service with the Royal Navy and transatlantic liners; and persuaded the engineer in charge of London's City and Southwark Railway (now the City branch of the Northern Line) to operate electric locomotives. It thus became the world's first electrified underground railway.

This is a book that will be appreciated by all who are curious about the achievements (and failures) of the 19th century's inventors and pioneers of technology.

FOREWORD
by Lord Montagu of Beaulieu

No partnership in the history of car manufacturing is so internationally famous as Rolls-Royce - a name which today still signifies the best of British quality, long recognized after the death of the original participants. Fascination in Rolls-Royce by enthusiasts and historians the world over has resulted in countless books on Rolls-Royce cars but far fewer on Royce and Rolls, the latter who suddenly died in a plane crash near Bournemouth in 1910.

Part of the early success of Rolls-Royce was due to the marketing and organizational abilities of Claude Johnson, an early Secretary of the RAC and rightly recognized by his biographer as the hyphen in Rolls-Royce. Up to now there has been little known about the important missing link, namely the man who brought Rolls and Royce together. He was Henry Edmunds, one of those brilliant entrepreneur inventors of the Victorian Age, for whom Great Britain became renowned. Before organizing that historic meeting of Rolls and Royce in May 1904, Edmunds had been closely involved in the electrical field, including an early electric light bulb, the phonograph with Edison and electrical devices of all kinds. No doubt in the course of business he came upon Henry Royce, the electrical motor and crane manufacturer in Manchester who was experimenting in improving car design.

The rest is history and all motoring historians will be in debt to Paul Tritton for his excellently researched and written biography of a man, largely forgotten today, whose contribution to the early days of motoring deserves to be recognized. This book is a worthy tribute to the man who has rightly been described as the Godfather of Rolls-Royce.

Montagu of Beaulieu

FOREWORD TO THE SECOND EDITION

Henry Edmunds is the man who famously brought Charles Rolls and Henry Royce together, and the rest, as they say, is history. But how did that meeting come about; what were the circumstances leading up to that event in 1904, and what other related events were taking place in those times of great engineering development, and who was Henry Edmunds? Paul Tritton carried out a detailed investigation to piece together the events that led to that meeting, and his findings were published in *The Godfather of Rolls-Royce* in 1993.

When preparations for the centenary of that meeting were being made I was surprised to find that Paul Tritton's book was no longer available. I felt that the centenary year was an appropriate time to republish the book and, at the same time, make a valuable addition to the Rolls-Royce Heritage Trust series of books, so I decided to get the book back into circulation and make it available for all those interested in the early history of Rolls-Royce. Although the aim was to publish it in the centenary year, new evidence surprisingly came to light in July in the form of an inscribed silver matchbox, which was substantial confirmation that that fateful meeting really did take place on 4 May 1904. The story of the matchbox has now been added to the book and it is on display at the Sir Henry Royce Memorial Foundation, Paulerspury, Northamptonshire.

With the agreement of the author, who provided me with all the original material, the text and illustrations have been transposed onto computer and reformatted suitable for the Historical Series, and here is the result. I hope you enjoy reading it.

Roger Varney
June 2005

DEDICATION

To the memory of

Harriet Ames Fuller Claflin
(1895 – 1989)
of Providence, Rhode Island, USA

ACKNOWLEDGEMENTS

Many people and organizations who gave invaluable assistance while I was researching the life of Henry Edmunds have been mentioned in the main text of this book. My thanks to them for devoting so much of their time to answering my many and often quite complicated questions. I am especially indebted to Tom Clarke of the Rolls-Royce Enthusiasts' Club; to Michael Evans of Rolls-Royce plc, who is chairman of the Rolls-Royce Heritage Trust; to the late CW (Bill) Morton, who was an authority on the history of the Rolls-Royce motor car; and to David Preston of Rolls-Royce Motor Cars Ltd. I benefited immensely from their knowledge of the first Royce cars and the origins of Rolls-Royce. Michael and Tom kindly read and commented upon the first drafts of the chapters that discuss those subjects, but of course I am solely and completely responsible for any errors contained in the final text of these and indeed all other chapters.

Lt Col Eric Barrass, OBE, who was general secretary of the Rolls-Royce Enthusiasts' Club, and later chairman and a trustee of the Sir Henry Royce Memorial Foundation, took an interest in my project from the outset and published encouraging news of my progress in the RREC Bulletin as the manuscript gradually took shape.

Several members and relatives of the Edmunds and Howard families in Britain and the USA provided copies of photographs, some of which I have reproduced. Other relatives passed on vital information or sent me copies of letters and documents, all of which helped me fill gaps in my knowledge of Henry's career or reach what I hope are accurate conclusions about the more obscure periods of his life and activities. Bill Claflin of Providence, Rhode Island, and Michael Pritchard were especially helpful.

When the time came for me to seek a publisher for the first edition, Michael Worthington Williams, the motoring historian and journalist, and Michael Ware, curator of the National Motor Museum at Beaulieu, guided me into the publishing world. Their advice and suggestions undoubtedly prevented me from compiling a collection of rejection slips.

Lord Montagu of Beaulieu took a professional and personal interest in my research into Henry Edmunds' life, since Henry and his father, John Montagu, who was the 2nd Lord Montagu of Beaulieu, were fellow motoring pioneers and leading members of what is now the Royal Automobile Club. I frequently consulted Lord Montagu's biography of the Hon Charles Rolls (*Rolls of Rolls-Royce*: Cassell, 1966) while studying the period when Henry brought Rolls and Royce together. I was delighted and honoured when Lord Montagu agreed to write the Foreword to this book.

I spent many hours at the National Motor Museum at Beaulieu, where Philip Scott, Peter Brockes, Chris Gill, Lynda Springate and their colleagues willingly and promptly handled my many requests for copies of photographs and articles from Edwardian motoring magazines.

Investigating Henry Edmunds' work as a pioneer in sound recording and tracing his phonograph and graphophone apparatus were among the most fascinating aspects of my research. In addition to thanking those already mentioned I also acknowledge the help given to me by George Frow, and Frank Andrews (City of London Phonograph and Gramophone Society); Dr Derek A Robinson and Stephanie Millard (Science Museum, London); Benet Bergonzi and Peter Copeland (National Sound Archive, London); Gordon Bruce; Pamela Clark (Royal Archives): L Cohen (Institute of Physics, London); the Royal Society of Arts; Mrs I M McCabe (The Royal Institution); Mrs Leah S Burt (Edison National Historic Site, West Orange, New Jersey); Jane Langton; Dr D W Morley and Sarah Willcox (British Association for the Advancement of Science) and Robert Long (High Fidelity magazine) Great Barrington, Massachusetts.

Tony Freeman of Academy Books shared my enthusiasm for bringing the life and times of Henry Edmunds to the attention of a wider audience. As editor and publisher of the first edition of the book he shaped my 120,000-word manuscript into a marketable publication. He also interpreted and commented upon the meagre surviving financial records of the cameograph businesses; his comments are incorporated into Chapter 14.

For information on the companies with which Henry was associated while pioneering electric lighting and power I would especially like to thank Tony Jarram, Frank Pye, W A L Seaman (Tyne and Wear County Archivist) and Philip G Smyrk for sending me notes, documents and publications relevant to the histories of the Brush, Glover, Swan and Johnson Matthey companies respectively.

My wife Pat became a 'book widow' during autumn and winter weekends for several years while I was preoccupied with research and writing; she then took charge of the final, vital, tasks of collating the illustrations and compiling the index. John McPherson read the proofs and, in doing so, drew my attention to anomalies which (I hope!) I expunged from the final proofs.

My thanks also to: H A Mavor (Anderson Strathclyde Ltd); Harry Parkes (The Bath and Wells Diocesan Board of Finance); Bunny Austin and Peter Baines of the RREC; David Arscott and Robert Gunnell (BBC Radio Brighton); Margaret Cox (BBC Sound Archives); George Drake (Calderdale Industrial Museum); Caroline Dudley (Royal Pavilion Art Gallery & Museum, Brighton); Barry Greenwood (Rolls-Royce Motor

Cars Ltd); M.J. Mates and R M Morgan (BICC); Peter Mann and Ken Shirt (Science Museum, London); Margaret Payne (Blue Circle Industries Ltd); Jeremy Bacon; Doris Barron; Martha L Mitchell, Jennifer B Lee (Brown University Library); Charles Crossley; Kenneth A Lohf (Butler Library, Columbia University); Gail Plant (Cement and Concrete Association); R D Smith (Claremont, Haynes & Co); Ronald W Clark; A Dale; Horace C Dawson; Edward Riley (Evening Courier, Halifax); Mrs P J Emms (Electrical Times); Mary Edmunds; E Watkins (Brighton Area Library); Rev J Elsden; John Fasal; Harris E Howard; Lt Col J C E Harding-Rolls; W H Baker (Gwent County Council); M J Willis Fear (Greater Manchester Record Office); Manchester United Football Club; Roland Gelatt; M V Robertson (Guildhall Library, London); Brian Mee (Hawker Siddeley Group Ltd); Richard Knight (Holborn Library, London); W C L Gorton; the Hemel Hempstead Mail; Marian Griffith; Brian Butler, John Hargreaves, D M Hallowes (Halifax Antiquarian Society); The Providence Journal; Mrs E D P Symons (The Institution of Electrical Engineers); Mr W A Morris (The Institution of Civil Engineers); Dr Joan Leopold; Nancy Howard Landry; Lady Longford; Fionna Gibbon (Minet Library, Lambeth); E W Browning (Lambourne & Ridley [Reborers] Ltd); Miss G C Hanks, Aubrey W Stevenson (Leicester Museums and Art Galleries Service); Molly Howard Mears; Helen Pond Maccini; A B Marsh (LVLO Manchester); Andrew Helme (Monmouth Museum); H A Berry (Midland Hotel, Manchester); Tony Lyndon (Holiday Inn Crowne Plaza Hotel); Larry E Sullivan (New York Historical Society); Dr Richard Hills and Christine Heap (North Western Museum of Science and Industry, Manchester); D S Stonham (National Maritime Museum, London); D T Watson (Parsons Controls Holdings Ltd); W R Draper (Parsons Chain Company); Lord Ponsonby of Shulbrede; Francis James Dallett (University of Pennsylvania); Miss A B Buckley (Park United Reformed Church, Halifax); Rosalind-Anne Cole (The Patent Office); Lillian Payne. Christine Lamar and Marie F Harper (Rhode Island Historical Society); R N Eason Gibson (RAC Motor Sports Association); Dennis Miller-Williams; Anne-Marie Scott (Rugby Portland Cement Company Ltd); W F Boldison; J S G Pigott (Rolls-Royce Motors Inc); Roy Russell; Matt L Joseph (Society of Automotive Historians Inc.); Harry J Snyder; John Schroder; K A Blumenthal (Smiths Industries Ltd); London Borough of Hackney Library Services; R Winsby (Trafford Park Estates Ltd); Anna Girvan (United States International Communications Agency); John Physick (Victoria and Albert Museum); Conrad Volk; John R Moore (West Yorkshire Transport Museum); Miss M J Swarbrick (City of Westminster Archives Department); Freddie Whitelaw; Miss B Wilkins; and finally we must thank Roger Varney who was responsible for creating the second edition.

PROLOGUE

A black locomotive embellished with blue, white and vermilion stripes, a brass number plate and red buffer beams steamed across the Stockport Viaduct, high above the homes and factories of the busy cotton spinning town nestling in the steep valley of the River Mersey. It had been a long haul up from Crewe but the remaining few miles were downhill nearly all the way. The train gathered speed, adding its own contribution of steam and smuts to the industrial haze rising to meet the broken clouds drifting south eastwards over the North of England's premier city.

An occasional shaft of spring sunlight brightened the scene, sparkling on the gold letters 'L & NWR' on the sides of the carriages behind the locomotive. The train's travel weary occupants stretched, yawned, folded their newspapers, gathered their bags and umbrellas and moved towards the doors. The serious business of the day would soon begin.

There was little to indicate that two of the men who stepped on to the platform at Manchester's London Road Station a few minutes later, and jostled through the ticket barrier together, had much in common. The taller of the pair, clutching a 49 shilling first class return from London, was upright, alert and smartly attired in a dark suit. He had open, youthful features of the kind that, a dozen years later, would gaze forth from black framed portraits on the mantelpieces of countless families bereaved during the horrors of the Somme. He was, as his bearing suggested, a young Army officer - a captain in the Motor Volunteer Corps - but he was destined, not for battle, but for a sudden and early death on an aerodrome, in peacetime.

The man at his side was a greying, less agile, figure with a solemn, almost dour expression. A frequent visitor to Manchester, he strolled past the ticket inspector proffering a trader's ticket, such as were issued to regular travellers who ran businesses that provided the London and North Western Railway with valuable freight contracts. Although nearly twice the age of his companion, he would live to see the coming-of-age of the enterprise they were about to inaugurate. Today would see the successful culmination of his patient efforts to persuade the young man at his side to take a day trip to Manchester; it would also be an occasion that would change the course of motoring history.

As they stood on the forecourt and hailed a Hansom cab, the two men noticed that, despite Manchester's reputation for perpetual drizzle, it was a pleasant day; calm, dry, with intermittent sunshine. It was also a little warmer than when they had left London four hours earlier; the thermometer was now nudging 54 on the Fahrenheit scale. As always, the state of the weather was not far from the minds of those arriving in Manchester that day, but these two travellers had more important matters to think about.

Soon after leaving the station they arrived in the foyer of a nearby hotel to keep one of the most important appointments of their lives. Smiles of recognition passed between the older of the two men, and the person with whom they were to have lunch.

> *"Mr Royce"*, said Henry Edmunds, *"may I introduce you to Charles Rolls?"*

It was Wednesday 4 May 1904. The story of Rolls-Royce was about to begin, but for Henry Edmunds it was the last of a series of important meetings and introductions that he had arranged over a period of nearly 30 years.

Silver Street, Halifax, as Henry Edmunds knew it.
(Calderdale Museums Service)

Crown Street, Halifax, in 1854. No 2 Silver Street, where Henry was born in 1853, is on the extreme right. (Calderdale Museums Service)

CHAPTER ONE

The ironmonger's son

All was well with the world into which Henry Edmunds was born on 20 March 1853, at 2 Silver Street, Halifax, in the West Riding of Yorkshire. Only two years earlier, six million people had flocked to the Great Exhibition of the Works and Industries of all Nations at the Crystal Palace in London, where they admired the products and inventions that were the result of fifty years of unparalleled progress in science and technology. The first phase of the Industrial Revolution, the age of steam power and iron, was coming to an end; Britain was the world's leading industrial nation and there were even better times ahead.

Thomas Macaulay reflected the spirit of the era when he wrote: *'Numerous comforts and luxuries which are now unknown, or confined to a few, may be within the reach of every diligent and thrifty working man'*.

Halifax had been in the forefront of the Industrial Revolution. For many centuries sheep farming had been the main occupation of those who lived on the steep, spectacular, grass and heather clad Pennine hills enclosing the valley of the River Calder; in the villages nestling at the foot of the hills, the manufacture of woollen cloth was a flourishing cottage industry. Spinning and weaving were traditional hand crafts, but towards the end of the eighteenth century the power of the West Riding's tumbling rivers and streams was harnessed to drive textile machines. Later, waterwheels were superseded by steam engines, built from Yorkshire iron and steel and fed with local coal.

With so many essential raw materials available locally, and abundant sources of energy, the West Riding became the home of England's wool textile industry. Halifax, on the banks of Hebble Brook, a tributary of the Calder, was the centre for the region's 'piece trade', where local weavers sold their pieces of woollen and worsted cloth to wholesale traders. So important was the cloth trade to Halifax that anyone found guilty of stealing a piece worth more than 13½d was beheaded on a guillotine that stood in Gibbet Street, one of the main roads into the town. Thence arose the famous Thieves' and Vagrants' Litany: *'From Hell, Hull and Halifax, Good Lord deliver us.'*

By 1853 the town had attracted so many manufacturers, traders and mill workers that its population had reached 34,000 - three times that of 1800. This rapid growth led to overcrowding and poor sanitation, the blight of most industrial towns in the nineteenth century. Halifax's two leading manufacturers, John Crossley (who founded a famous carpet making company at Dean Clough Mill) and Edward Akroyd, resolved to alleviate these conditions and as a result of their efforts Halifax was endowed with model housing estates, almshouses, churches and public parks. Today, it retains many archetypal features of late-Victorian north country towns: handsome mills, a parish church by Sir George Gilbert Scott (*'on the whole, my best church'*), a town hall by Sir Charles Barry and, to the south and west, the fine residences of those who prospered during Halifax's heyday.

At the time Henry was born the Edmunds family had probably been established in the West Riding for about fifty years. His descendants recall elderly relatives saying that the family's roots were in Northamptonshire. The first 'Halifax Edmunds' seems to have been Henry's grandfather, Richard, who probably moved north in the late eighteenth century and married in the early 1800s. Richard had four sons: Frederick, Richard, William and Henry Edmunds Snr, who was born in 1823. He married Caroline Hatton, and when he registered the birth of their son Henry he described himself as an ironmonger. Later, he became the proprietor of a firm called Edmunds & Hookway, engineers and iron merchants. The Edmunds' first home was 'over the shop'; Silver Street was in the very heart of Halifax, near the town's mills and factories and even closer to the terraces of back-to-back houses where the mill workers lived. Henry Snr's customers ranged from the town's poorest people, whose purchases seldom amounted to more than a few penn'orth of nails, to wealthy industrialists requiring all kinds of expensive fixtures and fittings for their homes and factories.

Young Henry never knew his mother; she died on 26 May 1853, less than ten weeks after he was born. Just over a year later, on 1 June 1854, at Stainland Wesleyan Chapel, Henry Snr married Sarah Hannah Walker, daughter of Samuel Walker, woollen manufacturer, of Stannary House, Stainland. She and her stepson became very close and towards the end of his life he wrote of her with great affection:

> *'She was a true foster mother to me and I owe nearly everything to her kindly care and encouragement to do things for myself when a child. I was full of curiosity, even to cutting open a small pair of bellows to see where the wind came from. I was not punished for this but encouraged to think things out for myself.'*

Henry Jnr enjoyed a happy childhood, despite other sorrows that afflicted the family during the early years of his life. Between 1856 and 1860 his father and stepmother had four children - Edith, Alice Mary, William Milnes and Maria Louisa. William and Maria died in infancy; Alice lived until she was 24, only to die in childbirth.

After attending private schools in York and Sowerby until he was fifteen, Henry became a pupil of his father, who now described himself as a mechanical engineer and was, evidently, one of the most prosperous members of the town's business community. At about this time, the Edmunds family went to live at Southfield, a large house in Stafford Road, Skircoat, about a mile and a half from the centre of Halifax. As revealed by his boyhood experiment with the bellows, Henry was fascinated by mechanical contraptions, and a month before his eighteenth birthday he wrote to his godfather, Thomas Hunt, of The Holt, Middleton Cheney, Banbury, to explain the principles of a gas engine he had been studying. Mr Hunt replied:

> "I think I understand the working tolerably well but to my surprise I find we have one here in Banbury, at the printing offices of the Banbury Guardian, so I think I shall look in and ask to be allowed to see it. Again, allow me to thank you cordially for your excellent description, and to add how much pleasure it will afford me to hear of your success in whatever branch of business you undertake."

Southfield, Stafford Road, Skircoat.
(Author's collection)

Henry's pupilage lasted from 1868 to 1874 and left him well prepared to work 'on his own account' as an engineer and entrepreneur. On 15 April 1873, he and two associates, Joseph Arthur Wood, spinner, of Halifax and David Pitcairn Wright, of Wright & Butler, lamp manufacturers, of Birmingham, applied for patent protection for *'An invention for certain improvements in lighting and heating by the combustion of hydrocarbons or other volatile oils'*. Edmunds, Wood and Pitcairn received provisional protection, and their specification read as follows:

> 'The essence of our invention consists in inducing a current of air by the natural draught of a chimney to pass over or through hydrocarbon or other suitable volatile oil or spirit, or absorbent substances saturated therewith, by which the said current becomes impregnated with a gaseous vapour, which being conducted to a small escape orifice or orifices will then burn on the application of a light without the use of a wick, and continue to do so from the induced draught of the flue way or chimney, and whether used for the purpose of heating or lighting is capable of the most delicate adjustment, and may be adapted for the lighting or heating of the saloon or cottage, as well as for the generation of steam for marine, locomotive or fixed engines, or for cooking or heating purposes generally.
>
> By way of illustration we will describe our invention as adapted for ordinary table lamps, for which we use a vessel of any suitable material, with a supply mouth or other arrangement for charging, and with suitable internal arrangements by which air passage or passages, through or over the hydrocarbon or other volatile spirit or oil, or absorbent material saturated therewith, which air passage or passages terminate in this case in a reduced top end or contracted orifice or orifices, technically called the burner, around or near which a holder is formed for receiving the indispensable chimney. The air thus drawn by the draught of the chimney through or over the hydrocarbon ... becomes so strongly impregnated ... that it readily ignites and continues to burn by the upward draught of the chimney, which keeps up an active current through the body of the lamp. The same principle which applies to the description thus given of a lamp for lighting, may be with suitable appliances arranged and adapted for generating heat or steam; also for cooking, or for the many diversified forms that light and heat separately or co-jointly may be required.'

A.D. 1873, 15th April. N° 1355.

SPECIFICATION

OF

HENRY EDMUNDS, JUNIOR,
JOSEPH ARTHUR WOOD, AND
DAVID PITCAIRN WRIGHT.

LIGHTING AND HEATING.

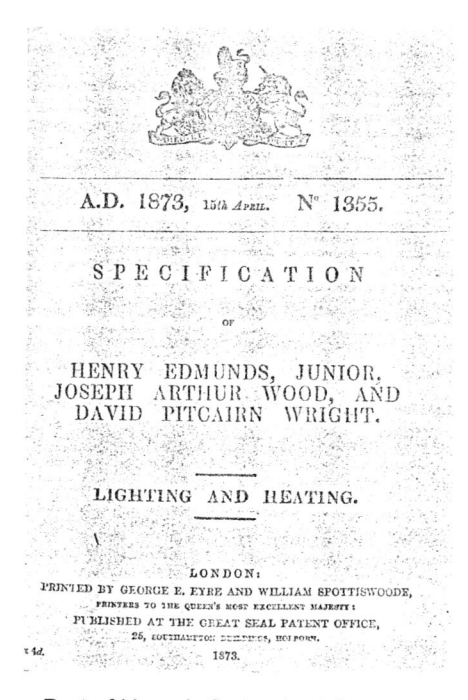

LONDON:
PRINTED BY GEORGE E. EYRE AND WILLIAM SPOTTISWOODE,
PRINTERS TO THE QUEEN'S MOST EXCELLENT MAJESTY:
PUBLISHED AT THE GREAT SEAL PATENT OFFICE,
25, SOUTHAMPTON BUILDINGS, HOLBORN.
1873.

Part of Henry's first patent document

This invention, and the description of the gas engine that so impressed his godfather, indicate that Henry was intent on making his own contribution to the future of heating and lighting and would, in his own way, help Macaulay's 'comforts and luxuries' become the property of the common man. In the years ahead he was to seek patent coverage for about one hundred and fifty inventions. In 1875, when 22 years old and no longer a pupil, he started to take a close interest in a new source of energy - electricity - and embarked on a series of experiments that would take him away from his home town and the family business and into the company of the early electrical pioneers. They were the first of many scientists with whom he was to be associated as they pioneered the electric light, the phonograph, the telephone, the motor car and other products of the second phase of the Industrial Revolution.

In the middle of the nineteenth century, Halifax owed much of its prosperity to the enterprise of the Crossley brothers, John, Joseph and Francis, who inherited Dean Clough Mill when their father died in 1837. Fascinated by science and engineering, they introduced steam power and many other new processes and inventions into their factory and donated much of their wealth to local charities and churches. Francis was the local Member of Parliament for twenty years and received a baronetcy for his public services. He took the senior role in the running of the business. When he died in 1872 most of his responsibilities were assumed by John, who also pursued a parliamentary career. One day in 1877 John went to Henry Edmunds Snr's warehouse to buy some zinc plates.

Henry Edmunds Jnr served him, and enquired: *"Would you, like them plain or amalgamated?"* John Crossley wanted the plates for an electric battery, probably one of the latest Voltaic cells or Galvanic piles. These contained zinc and copper plates immersed in diluted sulphuric acid, and produced a weak electric current when the plates were connected by a copper wire.

Before Count Alessandro Volta invented the battery in 1799, scientists could experiment only with static electricity. This produced violent sparks and shocks but nothing particularly useful. The Voltaic cell, however, generated what came to be called an 'electromotive force'. As early as 1802, Sir Humphry Davy had astounded the scientific world by passing the current from two thousand Voltaic cells between the tips of two pieces of charcoal to create a dazzling blue white light. But his invention, the arc-lamp, needed a simpler and more abundant source of electricity before it could become a commercial success. The zinc battery and the other types that followed found applications in the electric telegraph, small lamps and bells, and electroplating processes; John Crossley, presumably, had one or other of these devices and had called at Edmunds the ironmongers because the plates in his battery needed renewing.

Yet even though electricity had only a few practical uses at the time Henry Edmunds met John Crossley, exciting developments would soon be announced. More than 50 years had passed since Davy's former assistant, Michael Faraday, had discovered that an electric current could be generated in a copper wire by passing it across a strong magnetic field - a phenomenon known as electro-magnetic induction. The electric generators that Faraday built after making this discovery had limited applications because they produced a fluctuating current, but other scientists were able to develop Faraday's invention and build machines, which produced electricity cheaply and abundantly.

These 'dynamos', driven by steam engines, enabled electrical engineers to install far more extensive arc-lighting schemes than those that could be served by batteries. In 1841 the first arc-lamps for street lighting were installed in Paris. Eight years later London's first arc-lamp burned for three hours every night for two weeks on Hungerford Bridge. In the 1850s and 1860s, huge arc-lamps were installed in several lighthouses on the south coast of England. All these schemes were experimental, and one of the problems that still had to be solved was to provide the lamps with a constant supply - something that the inventions of Faraday's immediate successors failed to achieve.

Progress began to be made in 1865 when an Italian physicist, Pacinotti, designed a dynamo in which a bobbin of wire rotated between the poles of a magnet. This was improved by Z T Gramme, a Belgian electrician working in Paris. The Gramme dynamo was a continuous-current electric generator suitable for arc-lighting and for driving industrial machines, and after its introduction in about 1873 the development of electric light and power started to accelerate. But by now, despite the fundamental discoveries of Davy and Faraday, Britain had lost its lead in what was arguably the nineteenth century's most important branch of science; France had become the source of the best dynamos and arc-lamps and in the early summer of 1877 an important demonstration of the very latest type of lighting from that country was due to be held in London.

The event had a profound influence on Henry Edmunds' future; indeed, his career as an electrical engineer can be said to have started when he asked John Crossley whether he wanted plain or amalgamated zinc plates. As an MP, Crossley was one of several politicians who had been invited to attend the first demonstration in Britain of the 'Jablochkoff Candle', which had recently been used to illuminate various departments of the *Grands Magasins du Louvre* in Paris. Crossley was so impressed by Henry's interest in electricity that he gave him a ticket to the demonstration, which was due to be held at the East and West Indies Docks.

The promoter of the event, Paul Jablochkoff, had been a telegraph engineer in the Prussian army and, in 1871, director of the Moscow Kirsk telegraph lines. He resigned in 1875 in order to carry out research into arc-lighting and a year later settled in Paris. Originally he had merely been 'passing through' the city on his way to the American Centennial Exhibition in Philadelphia, but the attractions of Paris proved to be a greater lure to the 29 year old inventor. He abandoned his journey and joined the Breguet firm of scientific instrument manufacturers. After representing the company at an exhibition in London, Jablochkoff returned to Paris, where eight months later he invented a new type of arc-lamp - the first to have wide practical use.

Unlike its contemporaries, Jablochkoff's lamp did not need an expensive clockwork mechanism to keep the tips of the carbon conductors at the correct distance apart as they burned away. Instead, his 'electric candle' had two parallel carbon rods made from finely powdered coke or lampblack and separated by a layer of kaolin, a volatile, non-conducting substance. The 'candles' were supplied with alternating current, to ensure that the two conductors burned at the same rate; as they burned the kaolin melted, but enough remained beneath the arc to keep them apart.

Jablochkoff's arc-lamps were acclaimed as the brightest and simplest that anyone had ever seen. Furthermore, they worked in such a way that the failure of one lamp in the circuit would not extinguish others served by the same generator. One of Henry Edmunds' chief interests was the 'sub-dividing' of electric light in this way, and he eagerly looked forward to his visit to London. Forty years later, he retained a vivid impression of his experience and wrote:

> 'I lost no time in proceeding to London. At the docks I found a scanty concourse of people, met of course by Mr Jablochkoff, the inventor, and a Mr Applegarth. In a shed close by there was a semi-portable steam engine and an Alliance magneto alternating arc-lighting machine; and several so called Jablochkoff Candles. As the day faded and we were waiting for it to become sufficiently dark, Mr Applegarth suddenly announced that the pump, attached to the portable engine had broken down and it was not possible to repair it; he hoped to have a successful demonstration a fortnight later.' [1]

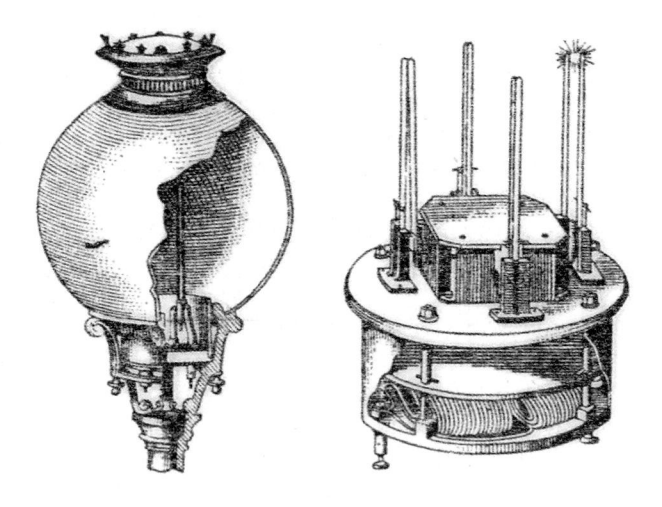

Jablochkoff candles. Left: a version with two carbon rods.
Right: a lamp containing four rods (with globe removed)

Henry had travelled two hundred miles to see the demonstration and was intensely disappointed by what had happened. Nevertheless, he had seen enough of the apparatus to gain some idea of how the arc-lamps worked. As soon as he arrived back home the same curiosity that had led him, as a young boy, to wonder where the wind in a pair of bellows came from, now induced him to make his own arc-lamp. He fashioned some gas-retort carbon into two sticks, separated them with

---

[1] *From Reminiscences of a Pioneer*, a series of articles Henry wrote for the *M&C Apprentices' Magazine* between 1919 and 1924. Unless otherwise stated, all the quotations in this biography that give Henry's personal accounts of events and experiences in his life are derived from these articles.

plaster of Paris, mounted them in a clamp, and connected them to all the batteries he could find: a collection of Grove cells and Bunsen cells. On stroking the tips of the carbons with another piece of carbon, he was delighted to see a small arc flash across the gap. He had created, on a small scale, the demonstration he had hoped to see in London.

Two weeks later, on Friday 15 June, Henry returned to witness what happily turned out to be a successful demonstration. The event was reported in the following week's issue of *The Engineer*:

> 'The experiments commenced soon after 9pm with the lighting of four electric lamps in the courtyard ... the lamps were arranged at distances of 45 ft from each other in one direction and 20 ft in the other. After the first few minutes the light was steady and that of one lamp was sufficient to enable small print to be easily read 20 yards away. After burning for a quarter of an hour the lights were extinguished and four gas lamps were lighted. The contrast, as can be imagined, was very great, the gas burning with what by comparison seemed a dull yellow light. The top storey of one of the larger warehouses was then lighted with three of the electric candles placed at considerable distances apart ... the light was most efficient. A portable light was afterwards carried down into the hold of a large vessel and sufficiency in that respect was fully demonstrated ... by the aid of these lights ... the loading and unloading of ships could be carried out at night. The carbon points exhibited will only burn for about an hour but Mr Jablochkoff arranges four of these candles in each lamp, and as one is consumed another is ignited by a simple switch arrangement so that the continuity of the light is hardly broken.'

The whole of the experiments were considered highly satisfactory and to indicate an important advance in the utilisation of electric light firstly as regards to the entire absence of clockwork and secondly, with respect to the divisibility of the stream of electricity which renders it possible to burn several lights with a single current. The simplicity of the Jablochkoff apparatus is most remarkable and as simplicity is generally the last character obtainable in an invention, we must credit the inventor with the ingenuity which alone could lead to the result obtained.

Recalling the demonstration more than forty years later, Henry said that Jablochkoff had also exhibited an experimental lamp in which a spark from a large induction coil caused a short piece of kaolin to become incandescent. This lamp was not as bright as the electric candle and attracted little interest. Henry, though, remembered it as the forerunner of the Nernst incandescent lamp, introduced in 1897.

While standing in the glow of the Jablochkoff Candles, Henry was accosted by a stranger, who asked: *"Have you seen anything of this kind before?"*

"Yes", replied Henry, *"I was here at the last demonstration, which was not successful, but I gleaned enough information to make an example for myself, which worked satisfactorily with the limited source of current at my disposal."*

The stranger pondered over Henry's reply. *"I would like to see more of you. Will you lunch with me tomorrow at the Palmerston Restaurant in Broad Street?"*

He then handed Henry his business card and disappeared into the darkness. Tilting the card towards the light, Henry saw that it bore no address, simply the name Richard Sigismund Karl Werdermann.

Richard Werdermann was one of the casualties of the age of invention in which the electric light became a practical reality. Born in Silesia in 1828, he served with a Prussian artillery regiment and later settled in Paris, where he worked as a civil engineer. While in Paris, Werdermann met Z T Gramme at the time he was developing the dynamo that was to provide the current for the 'second generation' of arc-lamps and some of the first electric motors. Fascinated by the prospect of electricity being transmitted over long distances to illuminate streets and buildings and drive machines, Werdermann had the foresight to purchase Gramme's English and American patents. At the outbreak of the Franco Prussian War he emigrated to England, where he promoted Gramme's dynamo and designed and built improved versions of it. Werdermann was the first to demonstrate the transmission of power by Gramme dynamos to Britain's Institution of Civil Engineers. Later, he showed the Postal Telegraph Office how a small Gramme machine could do the work of a complex of batteries and in 1875 organised a spectacular demonstration of arc-lighting on the roof of London's Charing Cross Hotel.

He also experimented with electric furnaces for melting refractory materials and with electric brakes for railway trains, and invented a semi-incandescent lamp. This gave out a soft, white light and was a partial answer to one of the main problems of arc-lamps: their overpowering brightness, which made them quite unsuitable for domestic lighting.

Werdermann died in September 1883, aged 55, leaving a widow, a son and three daughters. An obituary in *The Engineer* revealed how he failed to achieve the commercial success he deserved:

> 'Although very fertile in brilliant and ingenious ideas, Mr Werdermann was not a sufficiently shrewd businessman to reap

material benefits by his inventions. There was a certain childlike simplicity in his character, which made him look only to the successful carrying out of an invention and not to what it might bring commercially. He left the commercial parts to others and with the usual results, viz: very little benefit to himself; lawsuits, and interminable vexations which at last undermined his health. It is a fact, which redounds very much to Mr Werdermann's credit, and is characteristic of his scientific dignity and honesty, that last year when, during the electric light craze, inventors could ask and obtain their own price for their inventions, good, bad or indifferent, he would have nothing to do with limited companies.'

The plight of Werdermann's family after his death prompted Alabaster, Gatehouse & Co of 22 Paternoster Row, in the City of London, to launch an appeal for financial assistance. A partner in the company was quoted as saying: *"The deceased gentleman has, so far as can be seen prior to a complete investigation of his business affairs, left his family entirely destitute."*

One of Werdermann's brilliant and ingenious ideas was an arc-lamp which, from contemporary reports of the lighting devices and demonstrations of the 1870s, appears to have been similar in most respects to Paul Jablochkoff's 'electric candle'. Indeed, some accounts infer that Werdermann's and Jablochkoff's lamps were one and the same thing. What actually happened (according to *The Engineer*) was that Werdermann and Jablochkoff invented 'electric candles' simultaneously but independently, and that Werdermann sold his patent to Jablochkoff's company. (A similar 'coincidence of invention' occurred a few years later, when Joseph Swan in England and Thomas Alva Edison in America invented very similar incandescent lamps). Werdermann soon regretted handing the initiative for arc-lighting to Jablochkoff, whose demonstration in London in 1877 was soon followed by schemes in the *Avenue de l'Opera* in Paris and on the Thames Embankment in London.

That chance encounter between Richard Werdermann and Henry Edmunds on the dockside can, with the benefit of hindsight, be seen to be crucial to the formation of Rolls-Royce nearly thirty years later. That this should be so is one of history's quirks, but we now know that if Werdermann and Henry had not met, or if Henry had refused the invitation to join him for lunch next day - Saturday 16 June 1877 - it is unlikely that Henry's career would have followed a course that led him to become a friend of Charles Rolls and a business associate of Henry

Royce. Edmunds' meeting with Werdermann, and the more famous one between Rolls and Royce in 1904, are connected by a chain of events whose links are the relationships that Henry Edmunds developed with eminent scientists and electrical entrepreneurs from 1877 onwards.

Why Werdermann singled out Henry in the crowd under the Jablochkoff Candles will forever remain a mystery; no doubt the aspiring engineer turned this question over in his mind as he made his way along Broad Street to keep his appointment. At lunch, Werdermann told Henry a little about himself and explained that he had what he called 'a prior invention in the United States to that of Mr Jablochkoff', which would enable him to 'anticipate' the introduction of the Jablochkoff Candle in that country. It all sounded rather mysterious, but Werdermann probably meant that although he had sold certain rights in his invention to Jablochkoff, these did not include the American patents.

Werdermann suggested to Henry that as he seemed to know something about arc-lighting, he should proceed forthwith to New York, so as to arrive there when the American press published reports of the successful demonstration of the Jablochkoff Candles in London. Henry could then take advantage of the great interest that these reports would arouse, and introduce the Werdermann arc-lamp to a highly receptive market. Henry was to do all this at his own expense, but in return would receive half of whatever price he could obtain for the sale of Mr Werdermann's patents.

To anyone more experienced, or less impetuous, than young Henry, this proposition would have sounded like a confidence trick, but the reasoning behind it is easy to perceive. Werdermann, as we know, was to die in poverty only six years later and by 1877 he was probably very short of money. By now he was already working on a semi-incandescent lamp; we can imagine that he was devoting nearly all his time and capital to this venture, and hoping that it would at last bring him prosperity and security.

Across the Atlantic, rivals to Europe's inventors were achieving much publicity and some success for their electric lamps; Professor Moses Gerrish Farmer had exhibited a dynamo and arc-lighting set at the Centennial Exposition in Philadelphia, having previously found a way of 'sub-dividing' lighting into parallel circuits. Farmer's associate, William Wallace, a manufacturer of brass and copper wires, was developing arc-lamps and dynamos, equipped with Gramme armatures. The year 1877 was also the one in which Charles Francis Brush thrilled New Yorkers with an installation of arc-lamps in Madison Square and Union Square.

The Great Inventor himself, Thomas Edison, was rumoured to be ready to devote all his formidable talent and energy to the development of electric light, having, so he said, 'perfected' the telephone. Clearly,

America was seen as being both a threat to Europe's electrical innovators and a huge market for its lighting equipment; to Werdermann, success there would bring an end to his financial problems. Against this background, it is not surprising that he wanted someone to go to America on his behalf. Perhaps he had asked others to do so that summer, and they had refused? What is surprising is that Henry, without hesitating, agreed to go. After lunch he hurried home to Halifax to break the news to his father, who was naturally a little anxious about his son's sudden decision.

"Do you know anyone in America?", he asked.

"No", replied Henry, *"but an acquaintance of mine has recently returned from there, and I think he might give me an introduction."*

The introduction was to none other than William Wallace, whose parents had emigrated to America from Manchester, England - just across the Pennines from Halifax - about forty five years earlier, when William was seven years old. The acquaintance who gave Henry the introduction was a Mr Wood (perhaps Joseph Arthur Wood), who was related to the Wallaces. The way was open for Henry to make himself known to the American scientific community at a time of momentous discoveries.

Henry left England for America only eight days after meeting Richard Werdermann. He sailed from Liverpool on Saturday 23 June on the Abyssinia, a 3376-ton vessel owned by the British and North American Royal Mail Steam Packet Company (part of the Cunard Line). In an account of his 11-day voyage, written soon after he arrived in New York, Henry said that it had been *'a pleasant but rather rough passage'*, but he seemed more concerned about the lack of female companions:

A souvenir of an Atlantic crossing by the *Abyssinia*, the ship that took Henry to the USA in 1877

> 'We had very pleasant company all the way through but very few ladies, and we did not see much of them because of the bad weather. I, along with the purser and an Italian named Montavanna, got up a concert, the proceeds of which went to the poorest of the steerage passengers.'

That, and a few references to amusing himself by playing deck skittles and spotting ships, porpoises and whales, was more or less all Henry had to say about life on board the Abyssinia. However, a few weeks earlier William H Preece had travelled to New York on the same ship, in similar weather conditions to those experienced by Henry. Preece, then aged 43, was later to become Chief Engineer to Britain's Post Office and receive a knighthood for his work as a pioneer of electrical and wireless telegraphy; in 1877, though, he was still approaching the peak of his career, and was promoted to the position of Chief Electrician, having previously been the PO's Southern Divisional Engineer. On 13 April he and H C Fischer, Controller of the Central Telegraph Office in St Martins le Grand, London, set off for America to learn all about Professor Alexander Graham Bell's new 'speaking telegraph', or telephone, and Edison's latest improvements to the telegraph.

The sea was so rough during Preece's crossing that he was unable to write in his diary, but in a long letter to his wife Jane from the Fifth Avenue Hotel he gave a graphic account of what it was like to cross the North Atlantic in the 1870s. He found no fault with the service on board the ship ('a floating hotel') but noted that the vessel took 16 seconds to right itself when rolling in a storm. In these conditions, breakfasting was a matter of balancing a cup of coffee in one hand and securing your meat with the other. Dinner was even more trying: *'One of the funniest sights in the world is to see a whole dinner party trying to balance their soup plates. It is almost impossible to avoid either dipping your nose in hot pea soup or greasing your beard with the same.'* [2]

Preece's impressions of arriving in the New World were similar to those of the thousands of immigrants from northern and western Europe who had sailed past Sandy Hook and Staten Island before him:

> 'We found ourselves lying off a small Isle of Wight, studded all over with Swiss chalets and Florentine villas. We were in the Hudson River. On the other side was Long Island ... and before us was the magnificent bay of New York - a splendid, almost landlocked harbour large enough to anchor all the fleets in the

---

[2] *Sir William Preece, FRS*, E C Baker, Hutchinson, 1976

world. New York itself was just visible, its spires and towers filling up the landscape. How thankful we were to see it at last, and now that we were safe how little we cared for the dangers and troubles we had passed through. We landed at Jersey City ... after having been visited by the Quarantine Medical Officer and inspected by the Custom House gentlemen.'

From the deck of the *Abyssinia* Henry noticed that the harbour was *'crowded with river steamers, with everything in an uproar ... an excited waving of flags and firing of small arms ... and displays of rockets and fire crackers.'* William Preece, who began his voyage home from New York that day, witnessed the same sight. Henry had arrived, and Preece was departing, on the fourth of July: American Independence Day.

The *Abyssinia* docked in Jersey City, and after experiencing what he called *'the usual difficulties'* with the Excise officers, Henry and some of his fellow passengers took a steamer across the Hudson River to Manhattan Island. In 1877 this was the only way to get from New Jersey to the heart of New York City; in fact, all visitors to Manhattan, except those using the roads and railways that crossed the Harlem River at the northern tip of the island, had to travel by ferry.

Soon, though, bridges and tunnels would link Manhattan to the boroughs across the Hudson and East River; as his steamer approached the waterfront of what is now the lower West Side district Henry noticed, over on the opposite side of the island, the huge piers of the Brooklyn Bridge soaring into the skyline behind New York's tallest buildings, which were then a mere ten storeys high. The bridge had been under construction for seven years and would not open for another six, but it was already one of the engineering wonders of the world. Henry resolved to find an opportunity to make a closer inspection.

Like William Preece before him, Henry Edmunds booked into the Fifth Avenue Hotel, convenient for such attractions as Broadway and Madison Square Park; here, the torch-bearing right arm of the Statue of Liberty, which was all that its sponsor, Edouard Ren-de Laboulaye, had been able to afford to make in time for the American Centennial Exposition, was on show to the public. Though keen to start work on the job Richard Werdermann had given him to do, Henry decided to sample New York life first, a taste of which was offered as he sat down for his first breakfast in the city. The menu before him offered such delicacies as pickled tripe, mutton kidneys, broiled pig's feet, stewed oysters, fried smelts, English muffins and hominy. Henry's choice is not known but his meal would have set him up for a day's sightseeing, which he enjoyed in the company of the Miss Beaufords of Rock Island and a Mr Thiele.

They all went for a drive in Central Park (*'of very great extent, and tastefully laid out'*) and in the evening, after bidding goodbye to the Beauford girls, Henry and Mr Thiele attended a concert by an all-female orchestra.

Next day, Friday 6 July, Henry telegraphed William Wallace in Ansonia, Connecticut, having previously sent him the letter of introduction provided by Mr Wood. Wallace told Henry to come to Ansonia at once, so he hurried to Grand Central Station and at 3.00pm boarded a train on the New York Central Railroad. He changed trains at Bridgeport, greatly admired the scenery along the Housatonic valley, and arrived at Ansonia at 6.00pm, where he was met by William's brother, Thomas.

Tom Wallace was obviously expecting Henry to be much older, for he looked at him with some surprise and remarked: *"I have a boy of your age out in California."* Tom and Henry soon became close friends, and the young visitor from England was treated very hospitably by the Wallaces; he stayed at their home, and was given all the facilities he needed for making arc-lamps to Werdermann's design, and demonstrating Werdermann and Jablochkoff lighting systems. Work, though, took second place to sightseeing and while taking a buggy ride to White Hills with Tom Wallace on Saturday 14 July Henry was involved in an accident in which he nearly lost his life. This is how he described what happened:

> *'As we were crossing the [railroad] track, a locomotive standing on it at the time, the horse took fright and I was unable to hold him. Tom was thrown out, and I was thrown in such away that my legs wedged in the front wheel. I was unable to extricate myself and, if the carriage had not been very light, would no doubt have had my legs broken. As it was, the horse dashed on to the sidewalk, there being some wooden rails on one side and a lamppost on the other. The carriage was suddenly stopped, the shafts broke, and the horse was liberated. I was thrown violently to the ground and can't say why I was not killed. As it was I had some very severe bruises about the head and face, and the skin off many parts of my body, and I did not recover for a fortnight.'*

August, no doubt, was holiday time for the Wallaces, for in an account that Henry wrote while in the USA, entitled *Journal of a Run in America, June 23rd 1877 to December 3rd*, little is said about work or study that month. Presumably, William Wallace was taking a break from running his factory and developing new electrical apparatus; this gave Henry an opportunity to make a full recovery from his buggy accident by making a trip through New York State to Canada with a Miss Dickinson and a Miss Wallace (probably a daughter or niece of William). They travelled via New York City, leaving there on the Erie Railroad at 9.00am on Tuesday 7 August and arriving at Niagara at one o'clock the next morning.

Tired, despite the luxurious standard of his train, Henry checked in at the Cataract House Hotel, on the American side of Niagara Falls. After only a few hours' sleep, he was out and about, calling on a Mr Shepard to whom he had been given an introduction - for advice on the best places to visit in the area. In his *Journal* he described his day:

> *'The first impression of the Falls is rather a peculiar one ... [they] are very wide compared with their height, and the surroundings are rather flat. You do not at once realise their immensity but it rapidly grows on you, and the effect cannot but fail to produce a feeling of awe in any man.'*

After inspecting the American Falls, Henry and his lady-friends went to see the Canadian Falls, and were invited to visit 'the cave of the winds'. The misses Dickinson and Wallace declined. Never one to refuse a challenge, Henry entered a small dressing room where he donned waterproof clothing and thick felt shoes, then descended a circular staircase leading down the side of a cliff to the foot of the Falls. From here, he followed his guide across a narrow plank in front of the cascading water and climbed a flight of wet, slippery steps to the entrance to the cave. *'I shall never forget the utter feeling of helplessness and littleness that I then experienced'*, he wrote afterwards. *'We wended our way across a narrow shelf of rock with the water coming down in front of us in an immense column and which, dashing on the rocks beneath, produced a blinding spray of wind and water. It was a sight I would not have missed for anything'*.

Rejoining his companions, Henry went on to visit the Sister Islands before returning to Cataract House for dinner. Afterwards they took a drive to the Whirlpool Rapids, about a mile from the Falls, and crossed the suspension bridge into Canada, where, said Henry, *'I had great pleasure in welcoming my American friends to British soil'*. They all put on waterproofs and walked behind the wall of water, posing for photographs in their *'grotesque costumes'* before returning to their hotel.

Next morning, Henry enjoyed the 1877 equivalent of a Jacuzzi bath, fed by a powerful stream of water diverted from the Falls. The bath was, he said, *'a square kind of basin, about three feet deep, through which an immense stream of water rushes with great rapidity, and not knowing the strength of which, as soon as I got in, my feet were washed from under me and I was carried violently to the opposite end'.* Thus refreshed, Henry joined his companions and they all travelled by train to Toronto. They then temporarily parted company; the ladies rested while Henry took a boat trip across Lake Ontario to Kingston and returned to Toronto by the night train, arriving at 5.30am. It was now Friday 10 August, the day being spent visiting Toronto's university and other places of interest before it was time to join the night sleeper to Kingston.

Henry and the ladies had an exciting experience ahead of them when they left the train, for they had bought tickets for a journey on the steamer that made its way through the 'thousand islands' and down the rapids of the St Lawrence Seaway. *'We took our seats on the forepart of the boat and watched with almost breathless interest'*, wrote Henry. *'The ship behaved beautifully, for it was carried along by the immense volume of water through which they could only steer and otherwise were quite helpless'.*

Montreal was reached at about 6.00pm, and Henry and his friends immediately boarded a night-steamer for Quebec, arriving there at eight o'clock the next morning. They visited 'quaint houses and forts' and the Falls of Montmorency, and wandered through streets which reminded Henry of old English cities. It was a case of 'if this is Quebec, it must be Saturday', since that evening they all returned to Montreal, staying at the St Lawrence Hall Hotel. On Monday 13 August they left for Lake Champlain, staying overnight at Plattsburgh before taking a steamer to Fort Ticonderoga. A short railroad journey took them on to the head of Lake George, where they boarded a steamer for Fort William Henry. From here they went by stagecoach to Glens Falls, where they had to wait an hour for a train to Albany. While waiting, Henry struck up a conversation with a Miss Robertson from Washington DC; they exchanged cards and Miss Robertson said to Henry: *"If you are ever in Washington, do call on me"*. By now rather weary, Henry's party arrived at Albany late in the evening, taking staterooms on a steamer that took them down the Hudson River, arriving at New York early the next morning. It was Wednesday 15 August.

The noon train took them back to Ansonia, where they were greeted by William Wallace. Henry could not have timed his return more fortuitously, for within the next 12 days Mr Wallace was to receive several important visitors, all leaders in the development of electric light and power. They were Professor Chandler from Columbia College, New York; Dr Morton of the Stevens Institute, Hoboken; and Professor George F Barker of the University of Pennsylvania, who all arrived together, and Thomas

Edison, who travelled up to Ansonia a few days later. Edison was only 30 years old but was already world famous for his telegraphy inventions, and was approaching the height of his creative powers. He had recently reached a turning point in his career and set up a laboratory at Menlo Park, New Jersey, in order to work full time as an inventor.

Chandler, Morton, Barker and Edison had all come to Ansonia to see Mr Wallace's latest invention, the Telemachon, a dynamo and motor capable of transmitting electrical power over long distances. Henry met Wallace's distinguished guests, and by doing so took another step along the road that would lead him to Henry Royce's electrical factory in Manchester, England.

Professor George F Barker, one of the eminent scientists who befriended Henry in America in 1877.

CHAPTER TWO

Adventures in America

At the time of his visit to William Wallace in August 1877, Thomas Edison had carried out only limited research into electric lighting. In 1876 reports of arc-lighting schemes in Europe had inspired him to build his own experimental lamp, which he ran from a battery of 31 cells. But before he could make any significant progress one of his principal clients, the Western Union Telegraph Company, diverted his energies into finding new ways of transmitting multiple messages along telegraph wires. As was often the case in his career, one invention led somewhat unexpectedly to another, including a telegraph repeater. This was a device that enabled the dots and dashes of telegraph messages to be embossed on revolving paper discs, which became a recording medium from which the signals could be retransmitted down another line, at a rate of 200 words a minute.

During the summer of 1877, Edison had another idea. While experimenting with a telephone he noticed that the diaphragm in its receiver vibrated to the sound of his voice. Being hard of hearing, he could only test the strength of these vibrations by attaching a needle to the diaphragm and allowing it to prick his finger. He then wondered whether the sound waves striking the diaphragm could be recorded, via the pin, in the form of indentations on some kind of moving medium, such as a strip of paper or one of his telegraph repeater discs. Watched by his assistant, Charles Batchelor, he tested the theory by pulling a strip of paraffin impregnated paper under a pin attached to a diaphragm, while at the same time shouting *'Halloo'*. The paper was indented just as he predicted, and when he pulled it under another similar diaphragm he and Batchelor heard a distinct sound *'which'*, wrote Edison, *'a strong imagination might have been translated into the original Halloo'*. He jotted down the details of the experiment in his laboratory notebook, adding the comment, *'There is no doubt I shall be able to store up and reproduce automatically at any time the human voice perfectly'*. Yet he failed to foresee the most promising application for his discovery. All he wanted to do was to store and reproduce the sound of the human voice so that he could complement his 'telegraph repeater' with a 'telephone recorder, to record and retransmit telephone conversations'.

It is surprising that at this vital stage in his experiments, Edison found time to make the journey to Ansonia. He had a reputation for working day and night on a new idea, pausing only to snatch a few hours' sleep when he became exhausted. Had he realised that he was on the verge of making a talking machine with applications in entertainment and education, rather than telephony, he would probably have stayed on in his laboratory to develop a prototype capable of saying more than an indistinct *'Halloo'*. As it was, the attractions of William Wallace's Telemachon proved irresistible.

The reason why Edison made the journey is easy to deduce. The prospect of a cheap, clean and abundant form of energy to illuminate streets and buildings and drive industrial machinery was even more exciting than the invention of the telephone. Edison knew of the progress that was being made by Gramme, Jablochkoff and their contemporaries in Europe, and by Moses Farmer and William Wallace in America, and must have realised that sooner or later he would have to resume his research into the mysteries of electricity. The Telemachon was nothing less than an attempt to harness the power of the Niagara Falls and transmit it to distant towns and factories. The invention was not widely publicised until 1878, so in August 1877 Chandler, Morton, Barker and Edison were seeing it at an early phase in its development. Edison was most impressed by its possibilities and later, when it was ridiculed in the press, he sprang to its defence; during a long interview with a reporter from *The Sun* newspaper he announced that he had ordered a Telemachon. *"When it comes"*, he said, *"and I connect it with the neighbouring stream, I shall have no more use for steam, or for coal either"*. In the event, it was not the Telemachon that harnessed the power of Niagara Falls but George Westinghouse's huge hydroelectric machines some 15 years later.

When Henry Edmunds met William Wallace's eminent visitors he listened in awe as they talked of building powerful dynamos driven by waterfalls, and electric machines that would turn night into day in America's cities. Whether he had by now lost interest in the original purpose of his visit - to sell Richard Werdermann's patents - is not known, but it is likely that he was by now having doubts about his prospects of success. Soon after Edison went to Ansonia, Henry set off on another series of tours and visits.

The date of his departure, Monday 27 August, is important in the story of Rolls-Royce, for this was the day on which Charles Stewart Rolls was born. He was the third son of John Allen Rolls, first Baron Llangattock, High Sheriff of Monmouth and his wife Georgiana, daughter of Sir Charles Fitzroy-Maclean. Charles was born at the Rolls' London home, 35 Hill Street, in the heart of fashionable Mayfair in London. And since we have reached the point in history where one of Henry Edmunds' two most important future associates comes into the world, let us note what the second of them was doing at this time. Henry Royce, aged 14, was living in virtual poverty and working as a telegraph boy in Mayfair; it is quite possible that he delivered some of the congratulatory telegrams that Mr and Mrs Rolls received when the news of the birth of their son was announced.

Although Henry Royce's movements on 27 August were not chronicled, Henry Edmunds' were, for in his journal he related how he travelled to New York and, with William Wallace, went to the Union Square Theatre to see a performance of *Pink Dominoes*. Next day, Henry boarded the steamer *Vibbard*, bound for Albany, and this time was able to enjoy the scenery of the Hudson valley, which had been cloaked in darkness during his night-time trip down-river two weeks previously. A short ride on the railroad from Albany took him to Saratoga, where he stayed overnight at the Grand Union Hotel. After a day spent visiting the Geyser Spring and attending the races, Henry left Saratoga on the night train for Niagara. He stayed there for two days, enjoying the natural wonders of the area once again, but checking out of the International Hotel after only one night because a party of Knights Templars had taken all the best rooms. He spent the next night at the Clifton House Hotel, across the Canadian border.

On Friday 31 August a local resident in Niagara, a Mr Bush, invited Henry to a card party at his house. Henry had obviously taken in everything that William Wallace and Thomas Edison had said about the possibility of converting the power of Niagara Falls into electricity. Earlier that day he had calculated the millions of foot tons of energy that had tumbled wastefully over the precipice for centuries, and he told Mr Bush all about the Telemachon and another dynamo that Wallace had developed in partnership with Professor Moses Gerrish Farmer, of the United States Torpedo Station at Newport, Rhode Island. He wrote:

'*I prophesied that in a few years' time Niagara would be harnessed. Mr Bush was charmed with the delightful dream, but was evidently sceptical.*'

Henry left Niagara next day on the noon train and at dusk arrived at Windsor. Here he marvelled at the way in which the entire train was bodily shipped into 'a large species of ferry boat' for the last stage of its journey, across the Detroit River to Detroit. Henry spent the next three days in the company of a Dr Baldwin, a family named Leggitt and a Mr Flowers, and on Wednesday 5 September travelled on to Chicago, where he checked in at the Palmer House Hotel. Only six years earlier the city had been almost entirely destroyed by fire, but Henry could find no trace of the disaster and was amazed at how quickly the city had been rebuilt. In Detroit, Henry had enjoyed such cultural pleasures as a long literary discussion with Mrs Leggitt and an evening at the opera with Mr Flowers. In Chicago he passed his time more prosaically, visiting a water pumping station, a slaughterhouse in the stockyards and a machinery exhibition. After three days of this Henry moved on to

St Louis, to attend the opening on Monday 10 September of another big exhibition. He stayed at the Lindel House Hotel, where he befriended one of the young members of Cornelius Vanderbilt's family. Before visiting the exhibition he watched an eight-mile procession in which all the town's trades were represented, many of them by craftsmen who worked on wagons in the procession and distributed samples of their wares to the crowds lining the streets.

St Louis was the most westerly of Henry's destinations, and on Thursday 13 September he arrived in Cincinnati, where his host was a Mr Wilby, a friend of Mr Flowers. During his day in Cincinnati, Henry walked over the suspension bridge into Kentucky, watched the paddle steamers plying along the Ohio River, and visited a waterworks, a German beer garden and a flower show; he then caught the night train to Pittsburgh, where he arrived on Friday 14 September.

Pittsburgh reminded Henry of Sheffield, Birmingham and other centres of heavy industry back home, and he spent several hours in hot, noisy factories finding out how glass and steel shafts and tubes were made. Here, and in all the places he had called at since leaving Niagara Falls two weeks earlier, Henry had seen America at its best – highly organised industries and cities, sophisticated people. Soon, though, he was to see another face of America, which he found by taking a ride on the railroad running alongside the Allegheny River.

While staying at the Monongahela Hotel in Pittsburgh, Henry read a newspaper report of the discovery of a big 'gusher', from which huge quantities of oil and gas were spewing. Henry was anxious to see this phenomenon - oil wells were something new in 1877 - and on the advice of the hotel clerk he caught a 'way train' (a train that stopped at every station, and many places in between) to Parker, clearly a typical 'one horse town' of the period. His experiences there are best related in his own words:

> 'The train slowed down, and stopped. The car conductor shouted, "This is Parker". I seized my bag and stepped out. The train grunted, and moved on. There was no evidence of a station. Not even a platform. Around, it seemed a barren wilderness. Parallel with the line there flowed a sluggish, muddy stream, crossed by a rickety wooden trestle bridge. Night was falling, and there was not the least sign of any human habitation.
>
> Crossing the bridge, I was cheered to see some smoke rising in the distance. I was not so alone, after all! Presently I saw a man lounging against a post, with his arm in a sling. I asked: "Can you tell me the way to Parker?"

> "I guess you're a stranger", drawled the man. "Parker is over there." He pointed to a thin haze of smoke.
> "Is there a hotel there?", I inquired.
> "Not much hotel in this part of the world".
> I explained that I was a Britisher, and was curious to see the new spouter. I asked what he would advise.
> "Frisby is straight", he replied. "I guess you can't improve Frisby's. But don't tell anybody I put you on to Frisby's".'

In the distance, Henry could see a dirty house with the name 'Frisby' painted on it in large letters. He began to wonder whether he had been wise to make the journey but having come so far he plodded on, eventually arriving among a collection of ramshackle huts scattered alongside a deeply rutted road fringed by a sidewalk of loose planks. One of the huts had the appearance of a drinking saloon, and Henry entered. The scene and dialogue could have come from one of hundreds of movies of 70 years later:

> 'I saw a man seated, with his feet on the counter, smoking a long cigar. He said nothing, but stared at me.
> "Is this Frisby's?", I enquired.
> "It is so!"
> "Have you a visitors' book?", said I, remembering one's first duty on entering an American hotel.
> He fished out a dilapidated book and flung it on the counter. Evidently it had not been used for some time. I wrote 'Henry Edmunds, Halifax, England'. Frisby read the name, and seemed much surprised.
> "You're from Yew rope!", he exclaimed. "Here on business?"
> I said, "Not exactly", but that I was travelling about to see the country. He at once called out to a couple of grimy men, playing poker.
> "Allow me, gentlemen, to interdoose my friend Mr Henry Edmunds from England, who has come over to view this great country."'

After they had all taken a drink together, Henry was shown to his room it had a door in three of its walls and a small window over-looking the muddy street. It was not at all inviting:

> 'I wondered what the man had meant by saying 'Frisby is straight'. However, next morning after breakfast he appeared

clean-shaven and dressed in his Sunday best. He led me out into the street, where there stood a buggy drawn by two strong horses.

"Now Mr Edmunds", said Mr Frisby, "I've laid out the whole day to showing you all there is to be seen in this district". And I had one of the most interesting experiences of my life, witnessing the early development of the oil industry in Pennsylvania.'

Henry travelled for 35 miles along rough roads and through river-beds, past a seemingly endless vista of pipelines and derricks, dining at Butler Town before returning to Parker by the light of the gas flares that lit up the countryside for miles around. Next day, Henry left Parker on a narrow-gauge railway that crossed wild and rocky valleys on immense trestle bridges, some of them 200 feet high, and eventually stopped at a main-line connection for Pittsburgh.

Tuesday 18 September found Henry on the Baltimore and Ohio Railroad, en route for Washington. He checked in at the Ebbitt House Hotel and next morning called on Miss Robertson, whom he had met about four weeks earlier at Fort William Henry. Together they visited the city's patent office and museum and walked on to the Capitol. As they wandered through the various apartments and offices, Henry took a close interest in the lighting, heating and ventilation arrangements. In his Journal he wrote: *'The engineer very kindly explained all that he could to me and introduced me to the electrician, who showed me how all the gas was lighted up by electricity.'* (a rather cryptic comment that suggests that the building had electrically-ignited gas lamps).

Henry spent the next two days visiting the White House, the Treasury's bank note printing department and places of interest in the local countryside, including Cabin John Bridge. Then, on Saturday 22 September, he travelled on to Baltimore and Philadelphia, where he met Professor Barker and Mr and Mrs William Wallace. During the next nine days Henry enjoyed several interesting visits and introductions: he met Professor Leslie at the Zoological Gardens, toured the university, had lunch with Coleman Sellers, the machine tool manufacturer, and visited the Baldwin locomotive works. He was also given a personal demonstration of glass etching and stone-cutting by Mr Tilghman, who had invented a sand-blasting process and a saw that could cut through a seven-inch block of granite in an hour.

On Tuesday 2 October Henry returned to Ansonia, where he presumably spent at least part of his time studying William Wallace's electrical inventions and giving some thought to his future career. Eleven days later he went to Orange, New Jersey, to spend a week with some friends named Hemingway. New York City was Henry's next destination; he arrived at the Fifth Avenue Hotel on Thursday 25 October, and next day went to Columbia College in the hope of renewing his acquaintance with Professor Chandler. While Henry was waiting for Chandler, Professor Barker arrived and invited him to attend a meeting of the Academy of National Sciences, which had been in session at the college all that week. In his *Journal* Henry had only this to say about his day at Columbia College: *'I heard several very interesting papers read on the latest discoveries of science ... I had a most interesting time here'*, adding that after the meeting he had lunch with Professor Chandler, Professor Henry of Washington, Professor Draper and several other distinguished scientists. Luckily, he wrote a much fuller account in his *Reminiscences*:

> *'I was invited through Professor Chandler to make a demonstration ... of the Jablochkoff - Werdermann Lamp, the materials for which had been supplied to me by Mr. Wallace. With the aid of a small Gramme machine I proceeded to show to a New York audience, students of the college and some members of the press, this important development in the sub-division of the electric arc-light. The Jablochkoff Candle certainly did require some attention when running, and I was entertained the day following by a newspaper cutting which stated that 'A young Britisher, newly arrived from Europe, had shown ... a new light that, whatever its merits as an illuminant, appeared to take as much snuffing as a tallow dip. Nevertheless there was a great future for this wonderful invention. At present it was in its infancy and the public would hear more of it later on'.'*

This recollection of the event, written more than 40 years later, was more or less accurate, as the files of the *New York Daily Tribune* and the *New York Herald* verify. *The Tribune* carried this report:

> *'Yesterday's session was briefly interrupted at Professor Chandler's invitation to witness some experiments in the chemical lecture room. The Jablochkoff electric candle was exhibited. The current was supplied from a Wallace electro-magnetic machine driven by a steam engine. Judging from this exhibition it is safe to say that the Jablochkoff invention is superior to previous electric lights. It splutters less and does not often substitute darkness for light, as compared with ordinary arrangements from this source. Nevertheless it appears to have*

its own imperfections. It required snuffing about as often as a tallow dip. While it was working well its light was bright and steady. It is on the road to perfection but as yet not close to the goal.'

The *New York Herald* gave a briefer account:

'During the afternoon session, at the close of Professor Guyet's address, the members were invited down to Dr Chandler's lecture room to inspect a new electric light which was made by a small steam engine and rotating magnets, a simple process and a great improvement on other electric lights.'

The day after giving his demonstration, Henry visited the Celluloid Manufacturing Company in Newark, New Jersey, where Professor Chandler's friend, John Wesley Hyatt, was making the world's first mass-produced plastics wares: knife handles, brushes, combs and other forms of 'imitation ivory'. Henry concluded that the applications for the material were *'almost endless'*. He remained in New York City until Friday 2 November, spending his time visiting factories and scientific centres, including the Stevens Institute in Hoboken, where he dined with Dr Morton. Next came nearly three weeks of fairly intensive electrical experiments in Ansonia, followed by another but this time shorter tour that took him to factories in Hartford, Worcester, Boston and Springfield (where the American versions of the Rolls-Royce Silver Ghost and New Phantom would be built more than 40 years later). In Boston his host was Professor Barker's friend, Dr Waldo O Ross, who took him to Spurr's paper mills and the Smith Organ Works. On Wednesday 28 November Henry visited the American Screw Company's factory at Providence, Rhode Island, and the boiler works at Bristol owned by James Brown Herrishoff, designer of the beehive shaped coiled tube superheated steam boiler that powered the US Navy's first torpedo boat. Henry returned to Ansonia on Thursday 29 November and, according to his *Journal*, his final few days in America were uneventful. His final entry in his Journal reads: *'Monday, December 3rd, 1877. Came on to New York, stayed at the Fifth Avenue Hotel and said Goodbye to many of my friends before leaving.'*

But although he did not describe them in his *Journal*, Henry had another adventure while waiting to sail home from New York, and witnessed one of the most important scientific discoveries of all time.

John Augustus Roebling had but one ambition, and that was to build bridges. In 1831, after studying engineering at the Royal Polytechnic

Institute in Berlin, he emigrated to the USA, becoming the first person in that country to fabricate wire ropes. He established a wire factory in Trenton, New Jersey, won wide respect as a builder of suspension bridges and, in 1865, as soon as the American Civil War ended, submitted a scheme to Brooklyn's civic leaders to build a bridge across the East River to link New York City and Brooklyn. At this time, travellers between the two places had to endure a slow, uncomfortable and, in winter, dangerous ferry ride. Roebling's bridge, which would be twice as long as any in existence was opposed (naturally enough) by the ferry companies but also by many businessmen in Manhattan, who thought that it would take their trade away. Eventually, though, progress prevailed; in 1867 a group of investors formed the New York Bridge Company, with Roebling as its chief engineer. Construction of the Brooklyn Bridge began on 2 January 1870, but by now Roebling was dead. In July 1869, while he was surveying the location of one of the bridge's main piers, his right foot was crushed against a wharf by an incoming ferryboat. His toes had to be amputated (without anaesthesia) in an emergency operation at the home of his son, Washington Roebling. He later contracted a fatal illness, lockjaw.

Washington Roebling, who had been working with his father, took over as chief engineer of the project but in the spring of 1872 he was left partially paralysed after suffering from the bends while working in one of the pneumatic caissons in which the foundations for the bridge's towers were constructed. Washington was doomed to spend the rest of his life as an invalid, in constant pain, but a third member of the Roebling family was able to take over the project - Washington's wife, Emily, who had studied engineering and mathematics under her husband's guidance.

When Henry Edmunds first saw the bridge its two main towers had just been completed, and its first set of steel cables had been swung across the towers and fixed to their anchorages in Manhattan and Brooklyn. Secondary cables had been erected between the towers to support a walkway of timber slats, from which workmen gained access to various parts of the bridge. It was not until 1922, when the fifteenth chapter of his *Reminiscences* was published, that Henry's most daring and adventurous experience in New York in 1877 became public knowledge:

> 'Through my good friends the Wallaces... I was introduced to the Roeblings and managed to obtain a permit allowing me to cross from New York to Brooklyn on this aerial pathway. At noon I presented my pass to the man in charge of the entrance

from the New York side. He scanned it somewhat critically and remarked that it was the dinner hour, and that if I wanted to cross now, I must go by myself! It was a long climb up to the top of the first tower, but the view ... amply repaid one for the toil of getting there. On the Manhattan side I had a fine view of the Battery and the downtown houses, none of which at that period topped the spire of Trinity at the head of Wall Street in Broadway. Looking then across the river towards Brooklyn, one saw the various craft and many ferry boats, with their miscellaneous assortments of vehicles, including brewers' wagons. Then I ventured across. There was a strong wind blowing and the frail, swaying structure over which I had to walk was gently pendulating from side to side, and matters got worse as I descended towards the centre. My head began to swim. I was completely alone. I dared not turn back, and feared to go forward. I recollect well seeing the craft below, and wondered whether it would be my fate to fall down into the river among the traffic! Just then, however, on looking up towards the Brooklyn tower, I saw a man who was watching me steadily and beckoning to come on. Curiously enough, as I began to ascend I rapidly recovered my confidence, and eventually reached the summit of the Brooklyn tower. The man said, "You may think yourself lucky to have gotten across alive, especially with this wind blowing. Only the other day a sailor who had permission to cross laid flat down and we had to send four men to assist him over." The descent on the Brooklyn side was comparatively easy, providing I did not look down but kept my eyes straight to the vision in front. I have never forgotten that incident and would not repeat it today for the value of Brooklyn Bridge itself!'

In 1919, in the first instalment of his *Reminiscences*, Henry had revealed another hitherto forgotten incident that he had experienced in 1877:

'Before returning to Europe I called with Prof Barker one afternoon in November on Mr T A Edison, at his then small laboratory in Menlo Park. Prof Barker led the way, opening the door; in a dimly lighted interior we could just see Mr Edison and his assistant, working upon a small brass cylinder covered with tinfoil. Edison held up his hand dramatically. We halted. He slowly turned the cylinder with a handle, and an unearthly metallic voice, with a strong American accent, spoke out the

words 'Mary had a little lamb!' We had just arrived in time to hear the first reproduction of mechanically recorded speech, and that piece of tinfoil was the parent of the Phonograph, Gramophone and all similar recording machines.'

The laboratory at Menlo Park where
Henry heard Thomas Edison's first recording.

At first reading, this story is difficult to believe. Consider the background. A young and unknown British engineer accepts a rather risky business proposition and embarks, at his own expense, on a visit to America, where great advances are being made in electric lighting and telecommunications. In America, he meets several of the scientists and inventors responsible for this progress, including Thomas Edison and his friend and supporter, Professor George Barker. All this, of course, is entirely credible. But is it really possible that Henry arrived in Edison's laboratory at the very moment when he played back the first sound recording?

However, that startling paragraph from the first pages of Henry's *Reminiscences* is not merely an isolated example of what one might suspect to be a golden distortion of memory, excusable in someone approaching 70 years of age. In February 1922 Henry repeated his claim in a letter to the *Royal Society of Arts Journal*, and did so yet again in January 1927 in the following letter to a newspaper:

'I was in Mr Edison's laboratory with Professor Barker of Philadelphia when Mr Edison first recorded speech. In November 1877 I was in New York when Professor Barker called and suggested we should take the train to Menlo, New Jersey, to see

what Edison might be doing. We had both met him a few weeks earlier. When we arrived at the laboratory, a wooden building, we both saw Edison, surrounded by his assistants, who put up their hands to warn us something was happening. We walked carefully to the table on which was a curious looking instrument with a brass cylinder covered with tinfoil that seemed grooved with curious indentations on the groove, [and] a flywheel at one end of a steel shaft which, when we arrived, Mr Edison turned. Great was our astonishment when we heard the spoken words 'Mary had a little lamb'. Our astonishment was even greater than that of the other listeners, for evidently Mr Edison had spoken the words just before we entered the building and we had no idea what was coming. Thus we were just in time to be in at the birth of the Phonograph. I still have an original Phonograph sent me the year after by Mr Edison, which I treasure greatly.'

Thomas Edison with a Phonograph that he demonstrated to the American Academy of Science in April 1878.

To verify Henry's claim to have witnessed this historic event, it is necessary to compare his recollections with what is known about the invention of the Phonograph. For many years the date of the invention was considered to be 12 August 1877, but the evidence for this was a sketch of the Phonograph on which Edison wrote *'Kruesi - Make this - Aug 12/77'* (purportedly an instruction to John Kruesi, Edison's machine maker). However, researchers now agree that Kruesi was not instructed to make the first Phonograph until Thursday 29 November. On Tuesday 4 December, Charles Batchelor, one of Edison's principal assistants, wrote in his day book: *'Kruesi made the phonograph today'*. On Thursday 6 December Batchelor wrote: *'Finished the phonograph. Made model for the PO [US Patent Office]'*. This entry pinpoints the date of the invention; further proof is provided by the fact that on Friday 7 December Edison demonstrated the machine in the New York office of Frederick C Beach, editor of the *Scientific American*.

Thus far, then, we know that in early December, Henry Edmunds was in New York, saying goodbye to his friends before going home, while in Menlo Park, Edison and his assistants were working on the first Phonograph. Writing more than forty years later, Henry stated that he heard Edison's historic recording on a November afternoon, but this is something that can be excused as a distortion of memory. At the time he wrote his *Reminiscences*, Henry could not cross check his memory of events against the dates and details in his *Journal*, since he had temporarily mislaid it, otherwise he would have known that he was nowhere near Edison's laboratory on any afternoon in November; in any case, we now know, from information that has become common knowledge only in the past 30 or so years, that the first Phonograph was not made until early December. All this being so, how can the 'missing' days between 3 December, when Henry arrived in New York, and 6 December, when Edison first recorded sound, be accounted for? Surely, Henry would have been on a ship heading east across the Atlantic at the time the words 'Mary had a little lamb' crackled out of Edison's Phonograph?

A clue to what actually happened can be obtained by making a close analysis of Henry's *Journal*. It chronicles his journeys and social engagements, rather than his technical work; it also gives the impression of having been written day by day during his travels, or very soon after he completed them. The original manuscript, which has not survived, would have been in Henry's own handwriting, and we can imagine him sitting in trains, or in the lounge of his hotel, jotting down his schedule and descriptions in a notebook, the last entries being made after he checked in at the Fifth Avenue Hotel on 3 December. He then had his notes typed out, probably by one of New York's 'lady typewriters'. Her machine would most likely have been a Remington No 1, which had been in production for only three years and was one of the best selling models at the world's first typewriter shop at 4 Hanover Street,

New York. A typescript produced in 1877 would be a curious document to our eyes, since the typewriting machines of that period had only capital letters. Henry's 'typewriter' (the description 'typist' was not yet in common use) would have been regarded with about as much awe as the first word processor operators were 100 years later. She would not have been able to see the text as she typed it, nor would she have had the benefit of a back space bar when correcting mistakes. Sadly, Henry's typescript has not survived. He found it a few months before he died, edited it and at the same time wrote an unpublished Preface to his *Reminiscences*. In the process he revised many 'personal elements', which he thought would not interest present day readers, and then evidently discarded the original typescript. Henry's edited *Journal* does survive; we can only regret the loss of what might have been important, albeit personal, details and assume that the last entry in Henry's typescript (*'said goodbye to many of my friends before leaving'*) were the words he used in his original version. So what did happen? Was Henry's departure delayed after he had written his final words? And if so, can it be true that he was present in Thomas Edison's 'dimly lighted' laboratory on that very important afternoon?

A clue that helps us answer this question can be found in the sixth instalment of Henry's *Reminiscences*, among miscellaneous recollections of various visits he made to New York during his life:

'In 1877 I went one December night to a theatre in Broadway to witness the performance of the celebrated actress, Miss Mary Anderson, who was taking the part of Meg Merrilies in Guy Mannering. I believe this was her first appearance in New York; and I was much impressed, wondering why so charming a creature should wish to represent such a character as Meg Merrilies. After the theatre I returned to my hotel, where the clerk told me he had a card for me from Governor Howard, of the State of Rhode Island. I replied that I had not had the pleasure of knowing the gentleman; but was told he would call in the morning. Governor Howard called next day, and introduced himself. It appeared that he had been in New York and Philadelphia, and heard of me in connection with electric lighting. He was also introducing the telephone into Rhode Island. He knew Alexander Graham Bell, and many other pioneers of the movement. He was very anxious that I should go with him to Providence, RI, and meet some of his friends. I replied that it was my intention to sail on the following Wednesday for Europe and did not think I could alter my plans. However, he

persuaded me to postpone my return for a week. I had little idea at that time when I met Governor Howard, in such an apparently accidental manner, that the incident would have such a bearing on my subsequent career. As a preliminary I would say that it led to my introduction to, among others, Brown & Sharpe's well known firm of gauge makers; Mr Herreshoff, of Bristol, RI; the Providence Locomotive Co, the Armington & Sims Engine Co; Mr Wm Hochhausen, the inventor of the arc-lamp and arc-lighting machine; Col Hazard, one of the earliest founders of electric traction in the United States, [and] Mr Robt W Blackwell, an early tramway engineer, whose name was later associated with the insulating materials he later supplied to most of the electric railway and electric tramway systems in Europe.'

Henry's account of his movements in and around New York helps establish where he was at the time Edison's Phonograph was being built. Mary Anderson, then only 18 years old, had made her New York debut at the Fifth Avenue Theatre on Monday 12 November, earning enthusiastic reviews for her portrayal of Pauline in *The Lady of Lyons* and Juliet in *Romeo and Juliet*. One critic called her: *'The most beautiful woman I ever saw on the stage or, for that matter, off the stage.'* According to the *Annals of the New York Stage*, she played the withered gipsy crone Meg Merrilies in *Guy Mannering* every night from Wednesday 28 November until Saturday 1 December; on Thursday 6 December, Friday 7 December and Saturday 8 December; and on various nights between Monday 10 December and Saturday 15 December. The drama critic of the New York Herald saw one of her first performances as Meg Merrilies and on 30 November reported: *'In this part, Miss Anderson surpassed all her former efforts. Her beautiful contralto voice in the song held the audience breathless; the make up was wonderful.'*

We can be sure that Henry, seeking an evening's entertainment as his visit to America came to an end, would have read this review, or others in the same vein. Had he read the *Herald* on Sunday 2 December, he might also have seen this advertisement:

'Mr Stephen Fiske begs to announce the positively last three weeks of the brilliantly successful engagement of Mary Anderson; Monday, Tuesday and Wednesday nights and at the Saturday matinee as the lovely Greek girl Parthenia in Ingomar, Thursday, Friday and Saturday nights as the withered old gipsy crone Meg Merrilies, in which she has created such a furore. Seats may be booked for all the week.'

But which came first: Henry's visit to Menlo Park or his visit to the theatre and subsequent receipt of Governor Howard's message? Events that will be described in the next chapter confirm that Henry did witness a demonstration of the Phonograph at Menlo Park in December 1877; what remains to be discussed here is whether this was the first demonstration, or one of those that Edison, with his flair for publicity, may have staged for the benefit of the succession of visitors who flocked to his laboratory after the existence of his sensational 'talking machine' became public knowledge on 7 December. Edison himself wrote that the excitement he created at the office of the *Scientific American* attracted a crowd that *'got so great that Mr Beach was afraid the floor would collapse - the next morning the papers contained columns'*.

Had Henry visited Menlo Park after this event, it is beyond belief that then and forever after he would have been under the impression that the demonstration he witnessed was the very first. If, for some inexplicable reason, he had not read any of the newspaper reports that appeared on 8 December, Professor Barker would surely have told him the news? So we can either conclude that Henry's accounts of his afternoon in Edison's laboratory are accurate, or that he deliberately or unintentionally misled those who read his *Reminiscences* and other writings on the subject.

This author's opinion is that Henry *did* hear the Phonograph on 6 December. Whether, at the moment he and Professor Barker arrived, Edison was just about to play back his very first recording, will never be known - it is unlikely, though not impossible, that Henry and Barker timed their arrival so opportunely. In their book *The Edison Cylinder Phonographs 1877 - 1929*, George L Frow and Albert Sefl make the point that, while constructing the first Phonograph, Batchelor and Kruesi would themselves have recorded and repeated test phrases before presenting the machine to Edison. It seems fair to presume that later in that eventful day when the three men proved that the instrument really did work, they recorded their voices over and over again, calling in anyone who happened to be on the premises to share their excitement and witness their success; they may even have set up 'moments of discovery' to surprise visitors whose arrival was expected. Professor Barker, who must have known that Edison was about to prove that sound could be recorded, is unlikely to have set off on a trip to Menlo Park without having previously contacted the laboratory to make sure that Edison would be there to receive him. The great inventor may then have decided to give Barker a very special greeting!

So, having arranged the appointment, Barker met Henry and the two men set off on their journey. Menlo Park is only about 25 miles south west of New York, but was much more difficult to reach in 1877 than it is today. The Pennsylvania Railroad provided the only means of travelling there and back in one day, but the lack of tunnels or bridges across the Hudson River meant that there was no direct rail service. We know from Henry's own story that he went to Menlo Park by train and arrived there in the afternoon. The 1881 timetable (the oldest the present author has been able to locate) for the Pennsylvania Railroad shows that in order to travel from New York to Menlo Park, Henry and Barker would first have had to take a ten minute ferry ride from Des Brosses Street Terminal (the nearest one to the Fifth Avenue Hotel) or Cortland Street Terminal (further down town) to the railroad's Jersey City station. If the railroad service in 1877 was the same as that of the slightly later timetable, trains departed to Menlo Park at 1.12, 2.10 and 3.09 and arrived at 1.57, 3.00 and 4.04. Although Henry left no description of his rail journey, William Preece had travelled on the same route when he visited Edison about nine months previously and wrote this account:

'The railways here have no fences and they go bang through the streets of the towns. The whistles have the most horrid howls more like an elephant's trumpet than anything else. The stations have no names and there are no porters about. Everyone has to look for oneself. We nearly missed our station and as it was had to jump out while the train was moving ... the country we passed through was like home except that the hedges are mere wooden posts and rails.'

  Menlo Park itself would have reminded Henry of Parker, the 'oil rush' town he had visited in September; there were only a few farmhouses there, and a saloon with a billiard room near the railroad station. Edison's laboratory stood on a hill overlooking the railroad, and was a two-storey timber building with Edison's office, library and drawing office on the ground floor. Upstairs there was one, long room, with tables covered with instruments and experimental apparatus, and rows of shelves containing jars of chemicals and other materials. The building was illuminated by gas lamps, served by a gasoline converter, and it is not surprising that, in the gathering gloom of an afternoon only two weeks before midwinter's day, Henry noticed how 'dimly lighted' the room was.

  The Fifth Avenue Theatre's schedule now plays a part in this reconstruction of Henry's movements. His comment about Mary Anderson playing *'such a character'* as Meg Merrilies confirms that he saw her playing the old gipsy, and not the lovely Parthenia. When

Henry arrived in New York on 3 December, Miss Anderson was still playing Parthenia; she resumed playing Meg Merrilies on 6 December. Assuming that his visit to Menlo Park that day was a brief one (likely, since Edison was very busy) and that he managed to return to New York City in time, Henry could have gone to the theatre that evening; if not, he would have done so on one of the following two evenings. His meeting with Governor Howard would, therefore, have taken place on the morning of 7, 8 or 9 December - the first of these arguably being the most likely.

We can be sure that, after the excitement of a long visit to America and such an unexpected finale, Henry was anxious to hurry home and tell his friends in England all about his adventures and Edison's sensational invention. His comment to Governor Howard about intending to sail 'on the following Wednesday' suggests that he was due to leave on Wednesday 12 December. The *New York Times* of 13 December reported that the *China* had sailed for Liverpool and the *Alexandria* for Glasgow. Lloyd's List confirms that the *Alexandria* sailed on 12 December, and that on that same day the *France* left for Plymouth. Henry had probably booked a passage on one of these ships.

In order to sail from New York to Liverpool about a week later than he had originally intended he would have boarded the Cunard Line's *Algeric* on 19 December or the White Star Line's Royal Mail steamer on 20 December; both ships were bound for Liverpool, a convenient port for people living in the north of England. The steamships on the North Atlantic service in December 1877 took between nine and nineteen days to make the eastbound crossing, so Henry would not have arrived back in Halifax until after Christmas.

As he headed homeward, he reflected upon what he had learned and achieved in America. His efforts to sell Richard Werdermann's patents had not been successful; he had seen the progress that William Wallace was making in arc-lighting, and Wallace had told him that he and Professor Farmer had developed not only a new type of dynamo, but also a 'plate carbon' arc-lamp. This is thought to have been the first commercial arc-lamp made in the USA; it 'sub-divided' electric light and allowed a number of lamps to be run in series, and was patented on 18 December 1877 at about the same time as Henry finally set off back to England. However, Henry was not in the least dispirited. Wallace had been impressed by his interest and enthusiasm and had asked him to be his representative in Europe for the Farmer-Wallace electric light. Henry knew that 1878 was going to be a busy year.

CHAPTER THREE
Phonographs and telephones

The passengers on the ship that took Henry back to England in December 1877 were treated to some unexpected entertainment during their long voyage. Not only was he returning with news of the first talking machine and possibly prototypes of the latest arc-lamps; he also had two magneto telephones, designed by Alexander Graham Bell and made by William Wallace. Each of these consisted of a thin iron diaphragm placed near a permanent magnet, one pole of which was surrounded by a coil of copper wire. The two instruments were connected by a cable. Sound waves striking the diaphragms made them vibrate, creating fluctuating electrical impulses in the coils, which varied the current in the cable. The diaphragm in the instrument at the receiving end of the line then vibrated in sympathy with the diaphragm in the transmitter, thus reproducing the sound waves that had started the process. Henry and his companions amused themselves for hours with this simple apparatus, talking to one another from different parts of the ship along a cable 300 yards long - the first time, perhaps, that telephones had been used at sea.

Bell is the acknowledged inventor of the telephone, although others before him, notably Johann Philipp Reis, had been moderately successful in transmitting speech by electrical or mechanical methods. Bell's achievement was to make the first telephone capable of sustained articulate communications, and when he transmitted his first coherent message he used a phrase that has become almost as immortal as Edison's 'Mary had a little lamb'. On 9 March 1876, Bell had beaten his nearest rival by three hours in a race to patent his telephone. Next day, Bell and his assistant Thomas Watson were experimenting in their laboratory in Boston, Massachusetts; a telephone circuit had been rigged up between two rooms, and over it Bell spoke six words: *'Come here, Watson; I want you'*. The message was received and understood, and in July the Bell telephone was demonstrated at the Centennial Exhibition in Philadelphia in a display organised by Professor Barker. The telephone was one of the event's principal electrical exhibits, whose judges included Sir William Thomson, the future Lord Kelvin. Afterwards he described the demonstration that was arranged for his benefit:

'I heard it speak distinctly several sentences, first of simple monosyllables. 'To be or not to be' - marvellously distinct. Afterwards, sentences from a newspaper, 'SS Cox has arrived.' I failed to hear the 'SS Cox' but the 'has arrived' I heard with

perfect distinctness. Then, 'The Americans in London have made arrangements to celebrate the Fourth of July'. I need scarcely say I was astonished and delighted.'

Among those who took an interest in the invention was Governor Henry Howard of Providence, RI, who at one time considered investing in a company - proposed but never formed, that would have controlled Bell's patents. Providence did, however, become a centre of telephone research and development, largely as a result of his enthusiasm for the instrument; it was also the hometown of Bell's UK representative, Col W H Reynolds.

At the time of Henry Edmunds' visit to the USA, Bell telephones were already in regular use in Boston. The world's first private lines had been installed there in April 1877 at the home and office of Charles Williams Jnr an electrical engineer, followed on 17 May by the opening of the first telephone switchboard. This linked the offices of five clients of the Holmes Burglar Alarm Co. By coincidence, 17 May was also the day on which the telephone was first demonstrated to William Preece; he attended a lecture given by Bell, listened to the sound of an organ playing 32 miles away, and became *'simply lost in amazement ... at the simplicity of the apparatus employed in producing the phenomena'*. Two days later, Preece had a two hour meeting with Bell, noting afterwards: *'I hope to bring home with me a complete set to astonish the weak nerves of the Britishers'.*

Those weak nerves were tested by Bell himself in the autumn of 1877, when he demonstrated prototype telephones at the annual meeting of the British Association for the Advancement of Science. At about the same time, Col Reynolds was trying to persuade the British Post Office to adopt the telephone. R S Culley, the PO's Engineer in Chief, was not interested, saying that the uses for the instrument were very limited. Preece, on the other hand, urged Culley to obtain the rights to use and manufacture the instrument. His initial enthusiasm at this time, when he still had fresh memories of seeing the latest telecommunications developments in the USA, is in curious contrast to the views he expressed twenty months later, when he gave evidence to a parliamentary select committee that had been set up to report on whether local authorities should be allowed to adopt electric lighting schemes. The committee was concerned that electric cables would interfere with telephone lines. Preece was asked: *'Do you consider that the telephone will be an instrument of the future?'*. He replied: *"I think not ... the descriptions we get of its use in America are a little exaggerated. Here we have a superabundance of messengers, errand boys and things of that kind".*

The Bell telephone of 1876/7 used the same instrument, housed in an ebonite tube, for transmitting and receiving. The caller would speak into the tube and then hold it to his ear to listen to the reply. Fluent conversation was difficult and reception of speech, except over short distances, was poor. Callers often had to shout, and repeat themselves several times, in order to be understood.

As we have seen, the invention of the Phonograph stemmed from Edison's experiments with a telephone. Edison realised that the instrument needed to be made more powerful and in 1877 he achieved this by inventing the carbon microphone, which transmitted speech much more clearly, and at a far greater volume. Edison made several other improvements to the telephone, including fitting the microphone transmitter in a separate housing, an idea that led to the familiar 'candlestick' telephone set, consisting of a pillar with a carbon transmitter fixed to its top and a detachable receiver dangling at its side.

By the time Henry Edmunds arrived back in England with his Bell magneto telephone set, Edison's innovations had already made it obsolescent. Before leaving America, Henry had been given a letter of introduction to William Preece by Thomas Edison and, although it has not survived, it is reasonable to assume that its contents included details of Edison's most recent developments in telephony and his progress with the Phonograph. The fact that Edison was able to give Henry such a letter suggests that, between 6 December and the time he left New York City about a week later, Henry had at least one more meeting with Edison, or corresponded with him. The dramatic events at Menlo Park when the Phonograph was first played would surely have left no time during that day for Edison to consider helping Henry to meet Preece, yet they both had an interest in arranging such a meeting. Henry, the budding electrical engineer, would have had many reasons for wanting to meet one of the most eminent members of his profession, while Edison would have regarded Henry as an emissary who could tell Preece all about his latest ideas.

January 1878 found Henry setting up in business on his own account in London. He rented a small office at 57 Gracechurch Street, one of the thoroughfares that converge on the Monument to the Great Fire of London. His first commitment was to introduce the Farmer-Wallace arc-lighting system into Britain but he also hoped to become involved in promoting telephones and Phonographs; his recent meetings with Edison gave him an ideal opportunity to publicise his business and gain some valuable personal prestige - the kind of opportunity that every entrepreneur needs when launching a new venture.

By now, news that a 'talking machine' had been invented in America had filtered across the Atlantic, the 4 January issue of the English Mechanic having published a letter on the subject from Charles Batchelor, dated 9 December. More details were eagerly awaited and one of the first things that Henry did on settling in London was to contact Perry F Nursey, chief reporter on *The Times*, who subsequently devoted 30 column inches of his 17 January issue to an article on the Phonograph that began:

> 'Not many weeks have passed since we were startled by the announcement that we could converse audibly with each other, although hundreds of miles apart, by means of so many miles of wire with a little electromagnet at each end, yet we are on the point of realising some of the many advantages promised by the telephone. Another wonder is now promised us - an invention, purely mechanical in nature, by means of which words spoken by the human voice can be, so to speak, stored up and reproduced at will over and over again, hundreds, it may be thousands, of times. What will be thought of a piece of mechanism by means of which a message of any length can be spoken on to a plate of metal, that plate sent by post to any part of the world and the message absolutely re-spoken in the very voice of the sender purely by mechanical agency? What, too, shall be said of a mere machine by means of which the old familiar voice of one who is no longer with us on earth can be heard speaking to us in the very tones and measure to which our ears were once accustomed?'

Nursey concluded his very full account of the way the Phonograph worked with these words:

> 'Numerous applications suggest themselves but ... it is difficult to say with precision how they would work out in practice. In cases of depositions, it might be of the highest importance to have oral evidence mechanically reproduced in a court of justice. Authors, too, may be saved the trouble of writing their compositions. We should add that we are indebted for our information to Mr Henry Edmunds Jnr ... who has lately returned from a tour of scientific inspection in the United States and is interesting himself in Mr Edison's inventions.'

Henry was soon able to make even greater progress in his efforts to promote the Phonograph. On 1 February, William Preece was due to deliver a lecture to the Royal Institution of Great Britain, founded in

London in 1799 for the 'promotion, diffusion and extension of science and useful knowledge'. Its laboratory, library and museum in Albemarle Street were already world famous, and its weekly evening lectures were well-supported. Preece had decided to talk about the telephone but before he did so he was lectured on the subject by Henry Edmunds, who presented him with Edison's letter, showed him Wallace's magneto telephones, and put forward some ideas of his own:

> '*I took the opportunity of suggesting to Mr Preece that it would be worthwhile for the Post Office authorities to acquire the telephone patents which, I thought, at that time could be done for the sum of £30,000. Mr Preece replied that the telephone was an interesting instrument, but it was only a toy. The Government had recently taken up the Wheatstone ABC telegraph and had granted a pension to the widow of Sir Charles Wheatstone in recognition ... I expostulated with Mr Preece, telling him he should take wider views. Wheatstone's telegraph[3] could only be operated by someone who had had a few weeks' training, whereas anyone could take up a telephone and speak into it, not to mention the difference between spelling out words on an alphabet and actually talking. However, these points were not appreciated at that time ... the British Government, instead of acquiring the telephone rights for £30,000, had to pay several millions for them.*'

Preece's remarks to Henry Edmunds are further evidence of his ambivalent attitude to the telephone, for only four months had passed since he had urged R S Culley to buy the rights to operate and make the instrument. Only a month before Henry met Preece, Col Reynolds had offered the Post Office a forty per cent discount on Bell telephones, and the right to supply them to private subscribers at a profit. At this time, the Bell Telephone Company was advertising pairs of telephones on short and long circuits for £25 and £35 a pair respectively. Col

---

[3] Wheatstone's ABC telegraph was invented in 1860. An example in the Science Museum in London bears a caption that reads: 'Despite the success of Morse's code, Wheatstone maintained that the future of telegraphy lay in instruments which could be used by unskilled operators. As early as 1840 he had proposed ways of transmitting individual letters automatically. On these instruments the sending operator simply pressed the button corresponding to the desired letter and cranked the handle, sending electrical impulses along the wire, causing another dial to rotate until it indicated the transmitted letter.'

Reynolds' proposition had to be referred to the British Treasury, which did not sanction it until August 1878.

Toy or not, the telephone created considerable excitement at Preece's lecture. By February 1878 only a few public demonstrations had been held in Britain but in January, Bell and Col Reynolds had installed a private line at Osborne House, Queen Victoria's summer residence on the Isle of Wight, off the southern coast of England. This linked her apartments and a nearby cottage owned by Sir Thomas Biddulph. The two of them conversed over the line on 14 January, and it was then connected to Osborne House's telegraph line, so that the Queen could listen to a spoken message and a bugler playing the Retreat in Southampton, and an organ playing in London. One of the telephones used during this demonstration is on display at the Science Museum in South Kensington, London.

Preece had arranged a similar demonstration at the Royal Institution and a number of eminent people came to hear it, including Professor John Tyndall, the physicist, and Alfred Tennyson, the Poet Laureate. Preece reviewed the entire history of man's attempts to transmit sounds over long distances, culminating in Bell's latest achievements, and then conversed by telephone with a group of people who had gathered in Long's Hotel, a few hundred yards away in Bond Street. Someone there played a bugle; this was distinctly heard by Preece's audience, which by now had clustered around three telephones placed at various points in the auditorium.

Preece then announced that a connection had been made with the London & South Western Railway Company's telegraph line to Southampton, 80 miles from London, and that a bugler (perhaps the same one who had played for Queen Victoria a fortnight earlier) was waiting there to entertain them. According to Henry Edmunds, Preece said:

> "As the instrument is too feeble for you all to hear it, I will ask Mr Tennyson to kindly step up to the platform, and tell the audience what he can distinguish."
>
> The poet held the receiver to his ear for a few moments, and remarked gruffly: "I hear nothing!"
>
> Preece then listened for a moment and claimed: "I can hear The Campbells are coming." Glancing round the hall, he proceeded with his lecture and other demonstrations.
>
> A few days later, Preece met Henry and said: "Do you know, Edmunds, we had a most unlucky hitch the other night."
>
> "How so?", said Henry, "Everything went off splendidly."

"The bugler!", Preece replied. "The bugler at Southampton mistook the date, and did not turn up until the next evening. It was no wonder that Tennyson could hear nothing!"

Left: Professor John Tyndall plays back a recording on the Phonograph built with Henry's help for a lecture given to the Royal Institution on 1 February 1878 – the first demonstration of sound recording in Britain.

Right: William Preece records his voice on the Phonograph. (From the *London Weekly Graphic*, 16 March 1878)

Preece confided this story to only his close associates. The official explanation, as reported in the *London Weekly Graphic* and other newspapers was that *'Owing to the roar occasioned by the number of telegraphic messages being despatched around the country, the sound transmitted by the telephone was very feeble, so much so that none but Mr Preece could hear the bugle played at Southampton'*.

Preece, Henry Edmunds and others working in their field had no difficulty in understanding that vibrations in the air caused by sound waves could be made to induce vibrations in electrical and mechanical apparatus, which could then reproduce the original sounds, but many laymen found the idea difficult to grasp. When listening to the telephone they could hear a practical application of this scientific discovery but they could not see how sound waves and sensitive instruments interacted. To demonstrate the phenomenon, Henry set up an instrument called the Phonoscope at the Royal Institution after Preece's lecture. Henry is credited as having invented the Phonoscope. He probably did so while he was in America. Before he left England in June 1877 his knowledge of electricity would have been too limited, and in the few weeks before Preece's lecture he would surely have been too busy setting up his business to have had time to conduct electrical experiments.

The Phonoscope was an instrument in which the vibrations in sound waves were transformed into flashes of light. It consisted of a Gassiot vacuum tube, a Ruhmkorff high-tension induction coil, a Reis telephone transmitter and a platinum make-and-break 'interrupter' switch. The way it worked was described by one of Henry's associates, William Ladd, in an article he wrote for *The Electrician:*

> *'Sounds from the voice or other sources produce vibrations on the diaphragm ... which being in the primary circuit of the induction coil, induce at each interruption a current in the secondary coil similar to the action of a contact breaker ... therefore each vibration is made visible as a flash in the vacuum tube. This tube revolving all the time at a constant speed, the flashes produce a symmetrical figure like the spokes of a wheel as in the Gassiot star. The number of spokes or radii is according to the number of vibrations in the interrupter during a revolution of the tube and the number of vibrations being carried to any extent according to the sounds produced. The figures in the revolving tube will be varied accordingly. The same sounds always produce the same figures, providing the revolutions be constant. In case of rhythmical interruption being produced in a given sound as in a trill, most beautiful effects are noticeable, owing to the omission of a certain radii in the regular positions in the figure. The uses of this instrument are the rendering visible of sounds and showing the vibrations required in their production, and it forms a mode of confirming by sight an appeal to the ear.'*

The Phonoscope created much amusement and comment and today shows us the extent to which Henry's technical abilities had developed since he and two friends patented their gas burner less than five years earlier. The Phonoscope was evidently a precursor of the electronic valve, the development of which owed much to Sir William Crookes, who pioneered the study of the behaviour of radiant energy and electrical discharges in vacuum tubes. Henry would have been familiar with Crookes' work. While in America he might also have discussed, with the many scientists he met, the 'etheric sparks' that Edison had discovered in 1875, and the experiments that Professor Elihu Thomson had been conducting with Ruhmkorff coils since 1876. Edison had been on the verge of making the scientific discoveries that were to lead him into the world of electronics, and although at the time he met Henry Edmunds he had temporarily abandoned this line of research, he may have told his new acquaintance about his early results and shown him some of his experiments.

All this is conjecture. What is certain is that, at Menlo Park, Henry found out all he needed to know about Edison's most important invention to date, the Phonograph, and this fascinated Preece's audience at the Royal Institution more than the Phonoscope or even the telephone. Before the meeting (probably at the time he handed over Edison's letter and urged Preece to persuade the Post Office to adopt the telephone) Henry told Preece how Edison's recording machine worked. Preece was obviously impressed and asked Henry to help Augustus Stroh, his assistant, make a Phonograph. Henry quickly sketched out a set of drawings and by working day and night Stroh was able to complete, by 1 February, the first Phonograph to be built in Britain. Years later, Henry described the machine as having *'a clock driven revolving cylinder'*; if that was the case, it would have been more advanced than Edison's prototype, which was hand-operated. However, a contemporary sketch shows Preece cranking a handle to turn his machine's cylinder; the clockwork version Henry remembered would have been another Phonograph that Stroh made for Preece's second lecture on sound recording given to the Society of Telegraph Engineers on 27 February. The *London Weekly Graphic* described what happened at his first lecture:

> *'After remarking on the difficulty of knowing what to say under the circumstances, and that he should repeat something he had learnt years ago, Mr Preece spoke into the phonograph 'Hey, diddle, diddle, the cat and the fiddle,' very distinctly, and after waiting a minute or so the instrument was caused to repeat what he had said. The words were distinctly heard but the voice was very faint and an unearthly caricature. Professor Tyndall then made his way to the table and gave the phonograph a well-known quotation from the pen of Mr Tennyson, who was present, 'Come into the garden, Maud,' which was afterwards echoed to the satisfaction of the audience.'*

The occasion could not conclude without a contribution from the person who had brought news of the Phonograph to England, and enabled one to be built there before the first models arrived from America. Although photographs of Henry portray him as a rather solemn man, he enjoyed light music and poetry. Bending towards the Phonograph's mouthpiece, he sang:

> "Ho! Ho! Ho! He'll chuckle and crow.
> What? Marry old Margery?
> No! No! No!"

There were shrieks of delight when the song was played back. Henry left his own account of that memorable evening:

> 'William Preece was enthusiastically cheered and applauded; although no one there understood at that time what would be the future developments of the epoch-making inventions that had been described to them ... today we can barely realise what the world was like without telephones and gramophones. It is one of my greatest pleasures to recall that I was there... when speech recording and speech transmission were first publicly introduced to the English people.'

Perry Nursey was probably in the audience at Preece's lectures; if so they must have been the inspiration for a poem, dated 27 February 1878, that he dedicated to Henry Edmunds and which was, almost certainly, the very first of the hundreds of poems that would be written about the Phonograph and Edison. Nursey wrote:

> 'Now Adam, Noah, Melchisedec,
> And all their friends would laugh,
> Could they but visit earth again
> And hear the Phonograph.
>
> Sure Memnon, son of morning's voice
> Could not be more melodious
> Nor could old Stentor's roaring lungs
> E'er utter sounds more odious.
>
> The former's smooth as brooklet flows,
> The latter's harsh as medicine,
> But smooth or rough, like honour goes
> To Thomas Alva Edison.'

After the Phonograph and Phonoscope demonstrations at the Royal Institution, Henry became a minor celebrity in London's scientific community. On 27 February (the day when Preece delivered his second lecture on sound recording) he joined the Society of Telegraph Engineers, forerunner of today's Institution of Electrical Engineers, and started to widen his circle of associates in telecommunications and electric lighting, the 'sunrise industries' of the late 1870s. One of Henry's early acquaintances among the telephone pioneers of the day was Frederick Gower, who as a reporter on the *Star and Express* newspaper had covered a demonstration of the telephone given by Alexander Graham Bell in a stockbroker's ticket service office in Providence. Bell had come to the town to seek the support of newspaper publishers for his invention (this was probably the occasion when he first met Governor Howard). Gower was so impressed by the demonstration that on 31 March 1877 he organised a lecture during which he and Bell made a call over the telegraph wires to Boston, forty three miles away. This has been acknowledged as the first ever long distance 'phone call. Bell's activities in Providence led ex Governor Henry Lippitt to install the town's first commercial telephone system, between his bleach works and his downtown office. At about the same time, Gower decided to quit journalism for telephony. He designed an improved transmitter for what became known as the Gower Bell telephone[4] and with a Miss Kate Field arranged what was possibly the first transmission of music by telephone to a theatre audience over a telegraph line from Stratford upon Avon to the Gaiety Theatre in London.

Henry's own interest in music led him to build an instrument that embodied some of the features of the telephone and allowed tunes to be played through a receiver held to the ear. He glued a diaphragm to the bridge of a guitar and connected the diaphragm to the Reis transmitter and platinum switch that he had used in his Phonoscope. Between the points of the switch he fitted two strips of willow charcoal. The descriptions he left are rather vague but it appears that his device clearly amplified the sound of playing, singing and whistling some 50 years before the first practical electrical amplification of the guitar. Henry was now living in what he called a 'bachelor house' in Stoke Newington,

---

[4] A Gower Bell telephone circa 1881 is exhibited at the Science Museum in London. Its caption states that by 1881 the British Post Office had entered the telephone business in a small way, offering Gower Bell telephones for operation on lines previously used for ABC telegraph traffic. Its receiver, designed to evade Bell's patents, contained a magnet that was so heavy that listening tubes were fitted for the listener's comfort. Near this exhibit there is a Gower carbon pencil microphone of 1879, as fitted in the Gower Bell telephone.

and he invited William Preece to come and hear his invention. Preece listened attentively but turned to Henry and said: *"Edmunds! You are too late. Professor Hughes has shown me the draft of his lecture on an instrument he calls a 'microphone'. His lecture will be read in the next day or two. You must come and hear it."* Preece had noticed that Henry's 'guitar transmitter' and Hughes' microphone both relied on a resonating wooden soundboard to vary the pressure on carbon elements and thus cause fluctuations in an electrical current. Henry, alas, had built his microphone too late to gain any commercial benefit from it.

David E Hughes had achieved fame and fortune in 1855 by inventing a synchronised printing telegraph, used mostly on submarine telegraph cables between England and the Continent. The instrument's receiver contained a printing wheel, which rotated in synchronism with the character wheel at the transmitter. Characters were signalled by a single impulse whose timing made the wheel print the correct letter. Skilled operators could transmit thirty words a minute. In 1877 and 1878 Hughes and Edison were working, independently but on parallel lines, on a carbon transmitter to improve telephone communications. At around this time, rivalry between inventors was intense because huge fortunes were at stake; claims to have been the first to have come up with a particular idea, and accusations of patent infringement, were all too common, and a row of this kind was soon to develop between Edison and Hughes. Henry Edmunds, too, had a grievance.

While he was working on his transmitter, he was invited to breakfast at the Tavistock Hotel, London, by Louis John Crossley, the 36-year old son of Henry's friend, John Crossley, MP. Louis, who was one of the first members of the Society of Telegraph Engineers, had been experimenting with electricity and telegraphs since he was nineteen and had bought the first telephone to come into Britain[5]; he installed it at Dean Clough Mills, Halifax, in place of an alphabetical telegraph that he and the French electrician M Breguet had invented and were marketing with some success. Louis was concerned about the poor audibility of the telephone and was determined to find a way of improving its transmitter. During breakfast at the Tavistock, Henry drew a sketch of his transmitter on the back of an envelope and handed it to Louis. *"Some little time afterwards"*, Henry recalled ruefully, *"I learned that he had applied for patents for the Crossley Improved Telephone Transmitter. A company in Yorkshire took up his invention; I believe he received something like £15,000 for his improvements."*

---

[5] Source: *Crossleys of Dean Clough*, page 100, R Bretton, Halifax Antiquarian Society, 1950.

One of the first trials of the new transmitter took place at Square Congregational Church, Halifax, when the Sunday evening service was relayed to a church in Sir Titus Salt's model industrial village of Saltaire, eight miles away; *'the sonorous tones of Dr Mellor announcing the hymns and preaching ... and the singing of the congregation could be heard with equal distinctness.'* [6] On a later occasion, a line was run from the pulpit of Square Church to the telegraph office in Halifax railway station. Another of Dr Mellor's sermons was then transmitted along 36 miles of telegraph line to the Hunt's Bank, Manchester, office of Mr E C Warburton, the Lancashire & Yorkshire Railway Company's chief electrical engineer.

Later, the United Telephone Company, the sole proprietors of Bell's and Edison's master patents, bought Crossley's transmitter for £20,000. Whether he had already invented it at the time of his meeting with Henry Edmunds, or whether Henry gave him the idea for it, will never be known.[7]

Henry was in a highly creative mood in the months immediately following his visit to America, and he spent most of his time studying the behaviour of sound waves and how they could be converted into electrical signals. Other inventors had shown how sound could be passed along wires or captured on tin foil, but apparently no one had given much thought to how sound waves behaved under water. On 12 February, Henry patented what he called *'A mode of transmitting audible signals between places separated by water, without the aid of insulated cable wires'*. Henry did not give a name to his device; some called it an Aquaphone, and when about ten years later a more advanced type appeared (though not of Henry's design) the name Hydrophone came into common use.

Henry's invention consisted of an underwater electrically-controlled trembling bell, enclosed in a watertight box and connected to a battery installed in a signalling station on the shore or in a ship. The idea was that when the bell was rung to give a warning, or to transmit coded pulses of sound, vessels equipped with suitable receivers would be able to listen to, or record, the signals and take pre-agreed action. Henry calculated that the sound of such a bell would travel three or four times further under water than in the air, and saw many advantages for his device. The uses he had in mind included passing instructions between flagships and their fleets, and warning ships that they were

---

[6] Ibid

[7] A Crossley telephone, a curious box-shaped instrument with a mouthpiece and earpiece on its top and a lever with two positions, 'listen' and 'speak', can also be seen at the Science Museum in London.

sailing close to shoals and reefs - an aid that would be especially useful at night and in foggy weather. Bells and receivers could be attuned to various frequencies, enabling signals to be directed to individual ships among many.

One method of receiving signals required a boatman to dip one end of an oar in the water and hold the other to his ear! However, Henry later conceived a more sophisticated arrangement, employing submerged waterproof telephone receivers.

The Aquaphone was an idea that was ahead of its time. Nothing seems to have come of it, but in 1888 a similar system was tested in Brest Bay. The sound of a submerged bell, and the noise of the engine of the tug from which it was being operated, were heard on an underwater telephone receiver more than three miles away. In 1916, when the British merchant navy found itself defenceless against Germany's U boats, the development of hydrophones took a sudden leap forward; when used in conjunction with depth charges, it revolutionised naval warfare.

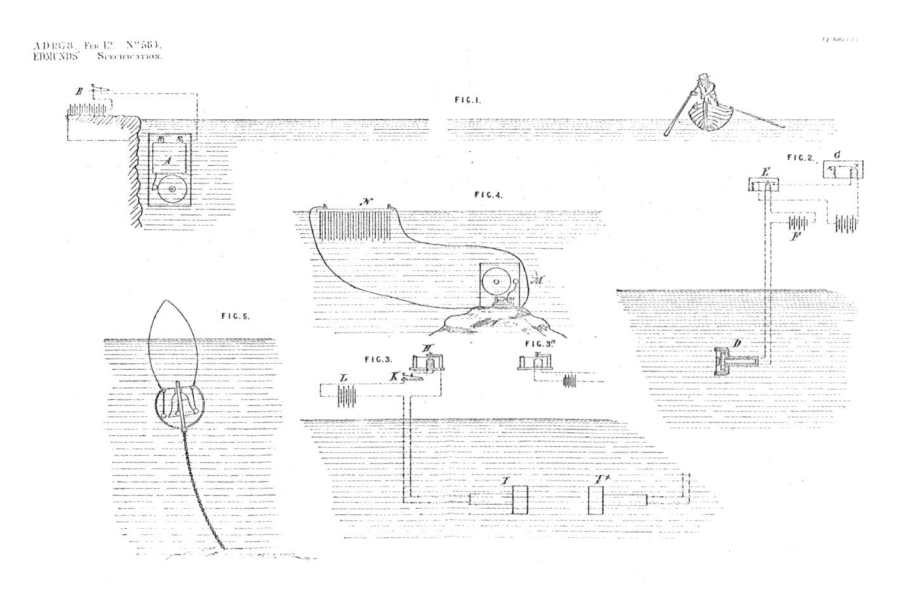

From Henry's specification for his Aquaphone.
Submerged electric bells transmit signals which, in one version of the invention, are heard by a boatman using an oar as a receiver (top right).

The 'guitar transmitter' and Aquaphone indicate that the inventions of Edison and Bell had a great influence on Henry in 1878, but two months after filing his patent application for his underwater signalling apparatus he turned his attention to a totally different new technology - the recovery of scrap and waste from industrial processes. The use of tinplate cans for preserving meat, fish, fruit and vegetables was now quite common but Henry had noticed that large mounds of scrap material accumulated around the factories where tinplate was made. He resolved to find a way of recovering tin and iron from this waste, and on 4 April he applied for a patent, which received only provisional protection for a centrifugal separation process, which he described as follows:

'The chief objective of this invention is to remove the coating metal of tin and terne plates in a rapid and economical manner, and thereby not only to recover the more valuable metal but also to bring the scrap iron into a fit state for working up again into plates. To this end I fuse the coating metal and by centrifugal action remove the same from the iron.'

Henry's process consisted of a cylinder, in which was placed a cage containing the scrap metal. In the centre of the cage there was a charcoal furnace, to heat and fuse the tinplate coatings on the metal. The entire apparatus rotated while the furnace burned, flinging the fused coatings on to the inside of the cylinder and leaving only clean iron in the cage. Other versions of the apparatus would, he said, recover scrap zinc, or separate wax 'from the scrap produced in the manufacture of what are known as paper ornaments for decorating fireplaces'.

Although unrelated to his experiments with electricity and acoustics, Henry's heated centrifugal waste separator reminds us that he was studying the whole subject of the generation and use of energy. Previous examples of his work in this field being his interest in gas engines in 1871 and his improved oil burner of 1873. Nothing came of Henry's endeavours to recycle scrap metal; it was another of the many ideas that he failed to develop, and was merely a temporary distraction from his main activities in early 1878, which were the promotion of electric lighting systems and the desire to become involved in the commercial exploitation of Edison's latest inventions, particularly the Phonograph.

Having helped Augustus Stroh build a replica, Henry was anxious to obtain an original Phonograph. He wrote several letters to Edison, urging him to despatch one at once, and in the Edison archives at West Orange, New Jersey, there is a copy of Edison's reply, dated 12 February and written on the letterhead of Edison's Electrical Pen and

Duplicating Press, the first duplicating process to employ a wax stencil (it was later promoted as the Mimeograph by A B Dick). In his letter to Henry, hurriedly written and lapsing occasionally into 'telegramese,' Edison said:

> 'A few days after you left I made arrangements with Mr Theodore Puskas for Telephone and Phonograph on the Continent, he paying for the patents. His arrangements did not include England. However he arrived in England some six days ago and Telegraphs if he can sell Phonograph patent, and I telegraphed 'yes' if price is satisfactory to me; that was two days ago. I have heard nothing since, but may do so at any moment. He is stopping at the Langham Hotel and has pair Telephones and 2 Phonographs. I have shipped Mr Preece a Phonograph, which left on City of Montreal. I will send you one immediately it is done; I am sorry that I could not have done something through you as you have been so kind. However I will put you in the way of something good presently and should Puskas fail in his negotiations you might then come in to it, but as it stands my telegram commits me.
>
> In this country phone is booming and they are making applications on every side to different things. Await arrival of your machine and I will send you all the points for good lecture, with amplified tracings of the Lord's Prayer and other things. 475 feet is the distance attained now by using sheet copper and speaking loud. The astonishing thing about the whole thing is the great difference it makes whether the machine is turned by hand or by controlled mechanism, with the latter the thing is perfect. I have dictated more than a dozen letters and Mr Batchelor copied them perfectly without knowing previously their nature. Attempts to do this with the hand turned machine was comparatively a failure; although to persons who heard it dictated it was plain. The Times article is first class and I thank you very much.
>
> PS You might call on Puskas and you may do something with the Russian patent. Puskas is a good man and a gentleman.'

Theodore Puskas, Edison's foreign patent lawyer, had made too much progress for Henry to have any chance of obtaining a licence to exploit the Phonograph patents in Britain - the London Stereoscopic Company was the successful applicant - but Henry was still keen to do what he could and, on 26 February, he wrote to Edison:

> '... I am sorry you cannot put the Phonograph into my hands commercially but I am pleased you will let me lecture and exhibit scientifically. I have promised to read a paper before the Society of Arts. I am only waiting your notes, diagrams and Phonograph, which I hope you will send off per first steamer, or else write me definitely when they will be here, as the Soc do not wish to postpone the paper any longer than can be helped I have written a good deal of a paper already, and shall now wait till I hear from you. I am glad you were pleased with the article in The Times. It caused quite a sensation here in England. Please keep me posted up as to all improvements and new inventions. I shall be pleased to do all I can for you in introducing them here.'

The day after Henry wrote this letter, William Preece delivered his lecture to the Society of Telegraph Engineers. He demonstrated three machines. One of these was another copy of Edison's original Phonograph, made by W Pidgeon. The second was an improved model, sent over by Edison, which recorded and played back through a single diaphragm and was equipped with a heavy flywheel to control the cylinder's rate of rotation. The third machine, also a 'single diaphragm' type, was the clockwork version constructed by Augustus Stroh, referred to previously. Its motor was driven by a falling weight and controlled by a speed governor.

After receiving Henry's letter of 26 February, Edison replied cordially on 12 March:

> 'Friend Edmunds! I see Preece exhibited your tube experiment at the Royal Institution. One of my assistants leaves for England on the 16th and carries with him 2 small Phonographs. I will instruct him to go with you and assist you when you deliver your lecture ... since you left I have the articulation perfect, reproducing whispers... Carbon Telephone has passed a severe test under WUTel [Western Union Telegraph] auspices; worked 720 miles and other wires at noon when traffic was going on. 100 miles it works long and perfect - 2 cells of battery at each end only used. Many improvements have been made in last 3 weeks.'

Henry was somewhat annoyed that, on 12 March, Edison had still not despatched the Phonograph promised four weeks earlier. On 2 April he wrote again to Edison:

> *'... your assistant, Mr Adams... dined with me yesterday. I was much surprised to find you had not sent me a Phonograph as promised in yours of February 12th. As I explained [to] Adams, it puts me in a very awkward position with the public scientific men here, to whom I showed your letters. However, if you would kindly send me one per first mail it will make it all right. Also I should be pleased if you will kindly put something else in my way as soon as you have something good, for I am sure I can introduce here for you in the best manner, both among scientific and business men. What have you done with respect to the Electric Light that is a subject of great importance just now. Please write me soon and let me have Phono at once.'*

Clearly, Adams - probably James Adams, one of Edison's most skilled craftsmen, but a chronic alcoholic - had turned up empty handed. No other letters from Henry to Edison have survived to tell us exactly how the saga of the long-awaited Phonograph ended but Henry did eventually receive the machine, sometime during 1879. Its subsequent fate and present whereabouts will be revealed in a later chapter. One other letter from Edison to Edmunds has survived. Dated 26 May 1878, it was written when Edison was under the impression that William Preece, to whom he had shown his carbon microphone, had passed on his secrets to David Hughes. The letter is a long, rambling complaint about an article on Hughes' microphone that had appeared in *Engineering* and a lecture that Preece had given:

> *'I am very much grieved at the Hughes article ... that Mr Preece should announce before the BA[8] my discovery of the variation of resistance of carbon and other semi-conductors by pressure and the same fact published and broadcast for over two years and within the last 6 months of the great success of my carbon telephone and Adams in England with the apparatus it is incomprehensible that the article should appear giving the credit to Hughes. It is not co-invention because after a thing is known all over the world for two years its sudden re-invention is clear stealing. Months ago your telegraphic journal published and illustrated my pressure relay - all of the experiments of Hughes made by me two years ago incidentally to the perfection of my telephone. The Wheesy sound of his device was the*

---

[8] The 'BA' is the British Association for the Advancement of Science. Edison probably meant to refer to the Royal Society, which was given details of Hughes' microphone on 8 May 1878.

great difficulty that I had to eliminate. The grating of wires when disturbed does not give articulation and his statement that certain substances are sensitive to sound is all bosh and is refuted in the very same article ... any disturbance of the connecting junctions must increase or decrease the pressure. In my English patent the whole thing is shewn - it is a notorious fact in this country that G W Phelps, Supt of the WUTel shops, was the inventor of the Hughes apparatus so it is only his second attempt. I telegraphed the Engineering about it and have sent them the papers. I am afraid I bore you with this but I cannot help it as it is rather rough to work two years to discover a fact and then have it stolen without comment, especially in England where I want to stand well. If you will do what you can to set this matter right I will reciprocate in such a way that you will not regret it.'

There was not much that Henry could do, and in any case the controversy eventually died away. A colourful character by the name of Colonel George Gouraud, a veteran of the American Civil War, became Edison's agent in Britain and as Henry no longer had any prospect of benefiting from the astounding inventions that were emerging from Menlo Park he gradually lost touch with Edison. Most of his energies went into electrical engineering, a field that Edison was soon to re enter with renewed vigour. In the race to bring electric light and power to the people, Henry would find himself in the curious position of working closely with some of his American friend's fiercest rivals.

CHAPTER FOUR

Improvements in electric lamps

The party of English and American visitors to the Universal Exhibition had returned to the *Hotel de Lille et Albion* for dinner. It was late June and Paris was typically hot and stifling; after walking around the *Palais de l'Industrie* for several hours everyone was tired, hungry and thirsty. Henry Edmunds and his friend Tom Wallace took their places at the long dining table and waited, rather impatiently, for the table d'hôte to be served.

Tom complained that he had a raging thirst, so Henry ordered a bottle of claret and some soda water. Tom drank copiously, to the obvious envy of the young English girl sitting next to Henry. She turned to her father and remarked: *"I really must have something to drink before I eat anything."* Overhearing this, Henry passed her the claret and soda siphon. Later that evening, as the visitors relaxed after their meal and shed some of their weariness, the girl's father came over to Henry and his friend, thanked Henry for his courtesy, and remarked that he represented one of the companies taking part in the exhibition. Tom Wallace had been very impressed by what he had seen that day and commented that the display of platinum on the stand of Johnson, Matthey & Co was the most important of all the exhibits. *"That is most gratifying"*, said the stranger, *"for I am John Scudamore Sellon, one of the partners in that firm"*.

John Scudamore Sellon

As we shall soon discover, by sharing his claret and soda with Miss Sellon, Henry Edmunds initiated a chain of introductions that helped Thomas Edison obtain supplies of a rare metal that was vital to his latest research project and led to the foundation of arguably the most important of all the companies that pioneered electric lighting in Britain; but first, Henry's presence in Paris must be explained.

One day in the middle of June 1878, Tom Wallace called unexpectedly at 57 Gracechurch Street. He had arrived at Liverpool Docks the previous day, taken the boat train to London and checked in at a hotel conveniently close to the City and Westminster. At midday he went to see Henry, who immediately offered to take his friend sightseeing and started to work out a schedule. *"Wait a moment, Edmunds"*, said Tom, *"let me tell you what I have done already. I have seen Westminster Abbey, St Paul's Cathedral and the Tower of London"*. It is only lunchtime, thought Henry, so that's not bad going - even for an American globetrotter!

Tom was the second American tourist Henry had met that summer. The first was Governor Howard, who had been appointed by President Hayes as an assistant commissioner to the Universal Exhibition and instructed to report on the various textile exhibits displayed there. Howard was accompanied by his wife Catherine and son Charles, 19, a graduate of Brown University, Providence, in the class of '78. While en route to Paris they stayed in London for a few days and on 14 May Henry called to see them at their hotel. In his diary, Howard noted: *'I accompanied him down the street and went about with him from 12 o'clock until 4.30, when I took the underground railway to come back to this hotel'*.

This meeting renewed Henry's acquaintance with one of America's most influential civic leaders and industrialists; on the other hand, Tom Wallace's visit enabled Henry to forge a closer relationship with those in London who were not letting America's electrical pioneers win all the honours. The Universal Exhibition, though, was not devoted entirely to electrical inventions and it is unlikely that Henry would have visited it, but for Tom's keenness to see everything the world of science had to offer.

Henry and Tom's visit to Paris took place around 24 June. We know this because at midnight on that day, Tom wrote a letter to his wife, which Henry somehow managed to see some fifty years later. He quoted from it in his *Reminiscences*, calling it *'an instance of the joie de vivre experienced in a first visit to the French capital'*:

> *'If I had legs that never grew weary, feet that did not get tired and sore, eyes that could look day and night without aching, a brain that would keep every impression distinct and separate, the arms of Briareus, the pen of an angel, assisted by Mephistopheles, I might feel like trying to express what never can be told: the story of Paris life, of Paris itself, its gaiety, beauty, intellectuality, frivolity and sensuality. Read the most extravagant story that is written, listen to the most impressionable tale that was*

ever spoken, and conclude that the half has never been told. Aladdin's garden would be dull and tame compared with the Champs Elysées, and Mahomet's Paradise cold and cheerless beside the Jardin Mabille.'

Although distracted by Paris's other attractions (temporarily, we will assume), Tom and Henry knew that the exhibition that was the purpose of their visit was taking place at an important period in the advancement of science. In 1878, competition was intensifying among the inventors on both sides of the Atlantic who hoped to be the first to introduce a reliable incandescent electric lamp, even though some scientists still doubted that this was possible and agreed with Professor Silvanus P Thompson, the eminent physicist, who had said: *'Anyone who tries to invent an incandescent electric light is doomed to failure'*. Arc-lamps were by now in common use, but were so bright that they could be tolerated only outdoors, in such places as streets, markets and railway stations. Their other disadvantages were that they consumed large amounts of electricity, required frequent adjustment, and were mostly wired 'in series' which meant that if one lamp failed or was switched off, all the others served by the same generator went out. If electricity was to be used to illuminate homes and offices, lamps that would emit a soft glow instead of a fluctuating glare were needed. Developing lamps of this type, and finding a simple way of wiring them to their generators 'in parallel', so that any lamp in a circuit could be switched on or off without affecting the rest, became a quest called *'sub-dividing the electric light'*.

The answer to the first part of the problem lay in 'electrically-induced incandescence', first demonstrated by Humphry Davy at the Royal Institution in 1802. In that year he not only discovered the phenomenon of the electric arc, he also showed that a platinum wire or carbon rod became hot and glowed when an electric current was passed through it. The discovery had no immediate practical use, because the illuminants oxidised and soon burned away, but from about 1840 various scientists found ways of making the illuminants last longer by enclosing them in a glass globe. These first electric light bulbs contained either a partial vacuum or an inert gas, the aim being to isolate the illuminant from oxygen and thus prevent it from burning. At that time, no one managed to develop the idea to the stage where incandescent lamps could be produced commercially but in the 1870s there was a resurgence of research, thanks largely to two important innovations. These were the electric dynamo, a much more convenient and powerful source of electricity than batteries; and Herman Sprengel's mercury vacuum pump, which (as Sir William Crookes had found when experimenting with his radiometer) could remove air from glass globes more efficiently than any previous machine, producing a vacuum equivalent to one millionth of an atmosphere.

Most of the inventors who triggered off the new wave of experiments into incandescent lighting regarded platinum as one of the most promising materials for the manufacture of illuminants. It had a higher melting point than any other metal, which was important because the hotter the temperature of the illuminant, the brighter the glow. Two of the experimenters, Moses G Farmer in America and Joseph W Swan in England, were resuming research which they had abandoned for several years while pursuing other interests, but with the notable exception of Swan, none of incandescent lighting's veterans or newcomers was a match for Thomas Edison, who until now had taken only a brief interest in the problems of improving the electric light.

His future supplier of platinum, Johnson Matthey, had its head office in an old Georgian house at 74-79 Hatton Garden, London, from where it conducted its business as a refiner of gold, silver and platinum and manufacturer of platinum apparatus. The firm's success, and the impact of its display at the Universal Exhibition, was largely attributable to the technical skills and business acumen of J S Sellon, whose uncle, Percival Johnson, had founded the business in 1817.

Sellon had joined the company as an apprentice in October 1851 and became a partner in 1860, when Johnson retired. Refining and fabricating platinum, an extremely scarce metal, was one of Sellon's specialities, and in 1872 he negotiated a contract that enabled the firm to buy the Russian Imperial stock of platinum. The material was in demand for making boilers for the concentration of sulphuric acid and apparatus for producing pure oxygen. Platinum filaments had been partially successful as illuminants for experimental incandescent lamps, and in 1874 the material was found to be suitable for making conducting or 'lead in' wires to carry the current through the seal in the stem of the glass globe or bulb.

Edison, no doubt, wished he could have attended the Universal Exhibition but he had accepted an invitation to join Professor Barker and a group of other scientists on an expedition to Rawlins, in the Rocky Mountains, to observe the total eclipse of the sun on 29 July. He then enjoyed a vacation - his first for seven years - in California and did not return to Menlo Park until the end of August. Among the papers awaiting his attention was a report on the Exhibition from Grosvenor P Lowrey, general counsel to the Western Union Telegraph Co, who had much to say about a splendid display of Jablochkoff candles in the Avenue de l'Opera, wired up to the latest Gramme dynamos. Nearer home, Charles F Brush and Moses Farmer appeared to be about to achieve commercial success with their arc-lights and both Lowrey and Barker urged Edison to resume his experiments with electric lighting.

He was finally inspired to do so on 8 September, when he and Barker went to Ansonia to see a demonstration of William Wallace's new 500-candlepower arc-lamps, powered by an eight horsepower dynamo that Wallace and Farmer had designed. Although impressed, he remained convinced that the lighting of the future would be in the form of incandescent, not arc, illumination. Turning to Wallace, he said: *"I believe I can beat you making the electric light. I do not think you are working in the right direction"*.

September 8th was also Tom Wallace's first opportunity, since returning to America, to tell Edison about Johnson Matthey's display of platinum in Paris. At about this time, Edison started pasting various references to platinum in his scrapbooks, which are now preserved at the Edison National Historic Site at West Orange, New Jersey. One of the books contains several pages extracted from Johnson Matthey's exhibition brochure, which Tom Wallace probably handed to Edison while telling him about his visit to the company's stand and his meeting with John Sellon. Johnson Matthey's own records show that the company supplied samples of platinum to Edison and subsequently sold large quantities of platinum wire in the USA. No documents have been found to prove that these large orders came from Edison but it seems safe to assume that they did. At that time there was only one local producer of platinum and he was J Bishop of Philadelphia, who made only crucibles and small ware. Henry Edmunds was sure that, thanks to Tom Wallace, Johnson Matthey supplied a large variety of metals and alloys to Edison and some of his rivals. Two of these, William E Sawyer and Hiram S Maxim, abandoned platinum illuminants because they burned out soon after they became incandescent, but Edison thought he could overcome this problem with a thermostatic regulator, which he patented on 5 October 1878. Two weeks later a syndicate of capitalists, among them Lowrey, J P Morgan and the richest man in America, W H Vanderbilt, formed the Edison Electric Light Company (a forerunner of today's General Electric Company) to provide Edison with $300,000 of finance for his research. Within a few days Edison's representative in London, James Adams, who had an office at 6 Lombard Street, was in touch with Johnson Matthey, enquiring about the price of platinum.

Edison persisted with his experiments with platinum illuminants for about a year. During this time he made several discoveries that were to be crucial to his future success. He found that incandescent lighting systems containing illuminants offering low resistance to the passage of electric current would require copper mains cables of such thickness and volume that no one would be able to afford to wire up even a few rows of houses. He discovered that a bulb containing a vacuum protected the illuminant more reliably that one containing an inert gas, and that by heating the illuminant while the air was still being pumped out of the bulb, he could dispel the traces of various gases and vapours that had previously become trapped in the bulb and caused the illuminant to melt or burn. In April 1879 he patented his first high resistance platinum lamp which, he calculated, would consume only a fraction of the amount of current required by low resistance types and require only one hundredth the amount of copper cable. Soon he was claiming that he had just about solved all the problems of incandescent lighting, and telling the newspapers that existing sources of platinum would not be able to meet all his demands when the lamp went into mass production. This sparked off a 'platinum rush' all over North America but in November 1879 Edison patented a high-resistance, high-vacuum lamp with a carbon illuminant, which was as efficient as, but cheaper than, his platinum lamp. For a while the precious metal remained in demand for making lead in conductors, only to be supplanted by a metal alloy.

Edison's total commitment to incandescent lighting allowed him no time to continue his correspondence with Henry Edmunds. By the time of the Universal Exhibition, Henry had given up any hope of becoming involved in promoting the Phonograph, which was now being overshadowed by other scientific novelties. However, he had other irons in the fire and sometime in 1878 he and William Ladd, who had an office in Beak Street, London, became partners in Henry's efforts to introduce the Farmer-Wallace arc-lighting system. Ladd, it seems, provided the facilities to store, assemble and rig up the machines, while Henry found the customers and planned the installations.

When he returned to England in December 1877, Henry brought back what he said was the first Farmer-Wallace arc-lighting machine. Details of its subsequent use in Britain are sketchy, but it appears that it was not until Henry teamed up with Ladd that any progress was made. In October 1878, when it became known that Thomas Edison was using Farmer-Wallace dynamos in his experiments, two British technical journals reported that Messrs Ladd & Co had introduced an improved version of the Farmer-Wallace machine and lamp. On 25 October *The Engineer* said: *'The Wallace lamp is really a modification of the Jablochkoff Candle. The latter has vertical carbons separated by kaolin. The one we are now considering has horizontal carbons separated by a non-conducting stratum of air. It is hardly possible to devise a simpler arrangement'*. Next day, *The Electrician* carried a similar report, commenting: *'The lamp can be hung anywhere and with suitable carbons gives a good steady light'*.

Obviously, the development of an improved machine infers that the original one had certain faults. In trials at the Benjamin Franklin Institute in Philadelphia, the first version was found to lack sufficient power but on 2 November *The Electrician* was able to announce that Farmer and Wallace had made several modifications, and described the new improvements in these words:

> 'The machine consists of two uprights on which, and at right angles to the uprights, are placed two masses of soft iron surrounded by coils, the whole thus forming two horseshoe electric magnets. These magnets have their opposite poles facing each other and constitute the field magnets. Between the poles are two sets of 25 smaller magnets fixed to a shaft, which revolves between the arms of the horseshoe magnets by means of bands at both ends. As the shaft revolves some 800 times a minute, the rotating magnets cut the fields 1,600 times a minute. A commutator is used for continuous current but arrangements are made to utilise the alternate currents.'

This, then, was the 'Mk 2' Farmer-Wallace dynamo. Henry himself left a more detailed description of its lamps than had been published in *The Engineer* and *The Electrician*.

Mr Wallace...had produced not merely a new type of dynamo...but also a method of sub dividing the electric light, or rather running a number of lamps in series by means of plates of carbon some 9-in long and 3-in or 4-in wide ... supported in a rectangular frame. The lower plate was held rigidly, while the upper could be lifted by a rod connected to the armature of a magnet. When the current passed through the electromagnet it pulled up the rod and so lifted the upper plate of carbon, thus striking an arc between the two pieces. The arc travelled along the edges of the carbons until so much was consumed that the arc failed, when the electromagnet immediately became active again, and struck a fresh arc.

Probably after, rather than before, the new dynamo became available, Farmer-Wallace 'in series' arc-lamps fed by direct current were installed at the Great Eastern Railway's new London terminus at Liverpool Street. According to Henry, this scheme was carried out in 1878 and was *'the first example of public lighting in this country by arc-lamps in series, with direct current'*. St Enoch's Station, Glasgow, is usually acknowledged as having been the first railway station in Britain to be illuminated by electricity (Crompton arc-lamps were installed there in September 1879) but if Henry's recollection is to be relied upon, a slight revision of the history of electric lighting is required. There is no doubt that Henry had a hand in the Liverpool Street scheme. He recalled that, afterwards, he received 'numerous inquiries from all over the country'. *The Electrician* kept its readers up-to-date with progress and later was able to report:

> 'So satisfied have the Great Eastern Railway Co been with the electric light at their Liverpool Street terminus that they have increased the number of lamps from 16 to 31. Three of the new lamps are outside the station, one being close to Liverpool Street, the second at the foot of the approach to the main line, and the third on the approach to the suburban booking offices. The system is also extended into the booking offices and instead of being confined as heretofore to the main platform, has now been carried to the suburban platforms also.'

This report appeared on 21 August 1880; but between the time the first lamps were erected at Liverpool Street and the time the scheme was extended, Henry faced disaster. Here, in his own words, is what happened:

> 'A consignment of Farmer-Wallace machines was received from America. They were unpacked, and put under test, but to our horror they yielded no current at all. We could not make out what was wrong with them, and Mr Sellon directed me to lose no time in seeing Mr Wallace and learning the reason. Our little organisation was overwhelmed with orders but we had nothing to deliver: and we could not understand the behaviour of the machines sent us.'

Having been disappointed at not obtaining any commercial rewards from the Phonograph or the telephone, Henry now feared that success in electric lighting was about to elude him.

Henry's recollection that John Sellon 'directed' him to hurry to America to find out what was wrong with the Farmer-Wallace dynamos suggests that, towards the end of 1878, he and William Ladd recognised that they lacked the entrepreneurial flair needed to give their electric lighting venture any chance of success. Henry's enthusiasm could not compensate for lack of commercial experience - it was, after all, less than a year since he had set up his business in Gracechurch Street. Ladd had the engineering resources that Henry needed, but perhaps they both saw Sellon as someone with the management experience, drive and capital to turn ambitious ideas into sound business ventures. This is probably why Henry and Ladd became partners of John Sellon in an arc-lighting venture formed soon after Henry met Sellon at the Universal Exhibition in Paris.

By the autumn of 1878 Henry had moved his office to Ladd's premises in Beak Street. Soon afterwards they set up a small demonstration room at 78 Hatton Garden, next door to Johnson Matthey, and before long they were working closely with Sellon to try and develop an improved arc-lamp. A delightful description of the conditions in which Henry and his colleagues worked is given by Donald McDonald in the first volume of his history of Johnson Matthey:

> *'One can imagine the scene in those narrow offices, further confined by the fact that for security reasons the wooden shutters had to be put up nightly at 6 pm, effectively and hermetically preventing any access of fresh air. Originally the operations were lit by naked fish tail gas burners in the Victorian gold fish bowl of translucent glass, belching out hot gases tainted with sulphur and soot and turning the rooms into suffocating gas chambers long before the task was done.'*

The conditions in which the electric lighting pioneers themselves had to work were their best incentive for succeeding in their experiments. Only three years were to pass before Sellon, assisted by St George Lane-Fox and H A Kent, replaced the gas lamps in their offices with incandescent electric lamps but in the late 1870s, despite the optimistic news emanating from Edison's laboratories, many inventors, Henry Edmunds among them, were still busy trying to improve arc-lighting.

One problem that had yet to be solved entirely satisfactorily was that of keeping the arc-lamps alight while their carbon elements gradually burned away. This required a method of automatically regulating the gap between the tips of the elements.

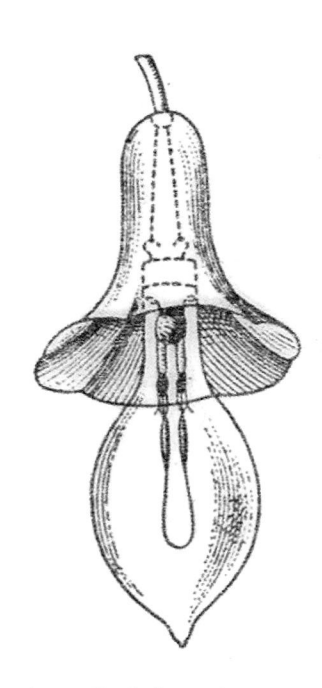

Lane-Fox's incandescent electric lamp, circa 1881

Clockwork mechanisms, and kaolin separators of the kind developed by Paul Jablochkoff for his 'electric candle', were two of the methods employed but Sellon, Ladd and Henry came up with another idea and on 15 November 1878 they applied for a patent for their 'Improvements in Electric Lamps'. In the preamble to their application, this is how Sellon and Henry described their invention:

'The object ... is to provide a simple and efficient means for establishing and maintaining the light of electric lamps, whether used singly or in groups. In order to render unnecessary the mechanism heretofore employed for retaining or sustaining the carbon points in the desired position, we propose to insert the carbons in guides in which they will move freely and bring their extremities into contact with fixed rests carried by brackets or other supports connected rigidly with their respective guides and forming portions of the circuit. These supports will convey the currents to or from the carbon points, and will sustain the weight or pressure of the carbons. By making these supports of iridium or similar heat-resisting metal they will not suffer from the heat of the electric arc. These carbon points may be set at an incline or parallel to each other, and in each case provision is made for establishing the light. When the carbon points are set at an incline, the guide for each of these points is pivoted to a fixed support, and is capable of rocking thereon to put its carbon in or out of contact with the carbon of the fixed guide. When the lamp is out of use, the carbon points will be in contact, and the circuit will be unbroken at that point. In order to open the circuit and produce the electric arc, an electro-magnet is placed within the circuit and in such a position to act upon the pivoted carbon guide, and rock it on its fulcrum as soon as the current is established. By this arrangement the lamp will be lighted immediately the circuit is employed; the electro-magnet then acting to part the carbons and produce the arc. If from any accidental cause the light is extinguished the circuit will be broken, and the electro-magnet becoming inoperative, will allow the rocking carbon to complete the circuit, by which means the current will be re established and the lamp re-lighted.'

They called their invention an 'elastic lamp' and a drawing attached to their specification shows the two carbons fitted into the lower halves of two slim metal tubes arranged in the shape of a V, the tips of the carbons protruding from the bottom of the tubes. 'Propelling springs' (like those in propelling pencils, invented 15 years earlier) in the tops of the tubes pushed the carbons downwards and held them in contact with their fixed rests or supports. The version with parallel carbons was more compact, and described thus:

'Their guides [are] fixed and the carbons resting upon or pressing against the retaining or sustaining points will always

preserve the same relative position with respect to each other, their distance apart being determined by the arc desired to be produced. To provide for the lighting of this modified form of lamp, we fit the lamp with a contact piece which, when in position, will close the circuit through the carbon points. This contact piece is by preference carried by a hinged keeper which is operated on by an electro-magnet placed within the circuit. When the current is established, the electro-magnet acting on the hinged keeper will draw back the contact piece and the arc will then be formed. Should however the light be accidentally extinguished, the circuit will be broken, and the electro-magnet as in the first example ceasing to act, the contact piece will, under a spring or other pressure, fall into position between the carbons and thus restore the circuit. The arm of this contact piece may carry a crossbar which on one or both of the carbons failing, will come into metallic contact with parts of the lamps connected with opposite poles of the electric generator, and thus close the circuit, leaving the other lamps in the circuit unaffected.'

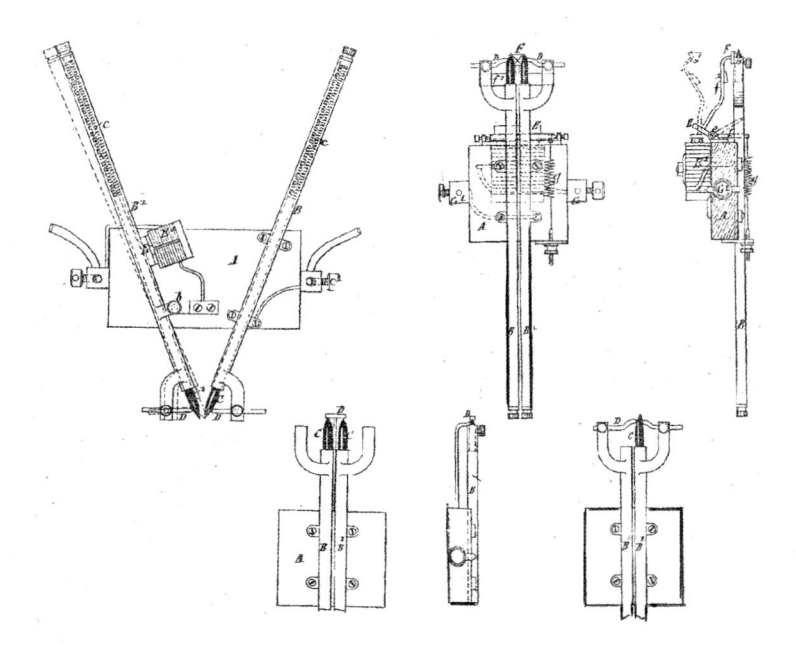

From Sellon, Ladd and Edmunds specification for an 'elastic lamp'.
Propelling springs control the carbon points.

Ingenious though it undoubtedly was, the 'elastic lamp' exemplifies the complexity of controlling arc-lamps. Fortunately, in a few years' time electric lighting became so much simpler, with the invention of incandescent lamps which could be turned on and off by flicking a switch and replaced within a few seconds when their illuminants burned out.

By 1879 Henry and Sellon were experimenting with incandescent lamps as well as arc-lamps, using platinum, iridio-platinum, osmium and other rare metals. They were given an opportunity to demonstrate the progress they had made when William Preece delivered another of his lectures, this time at the Royal Albert Hall. Edward, Prince of Wales, was the chairman of the meeting. His brother Alfred, Duke of Saxe Coburg Gotha, was in the audience, and they had all come to see an impressive array of electric lighting, including Jablochkoff Candles and the latest arc-lamps of Colonel R E B Crompton, V L M Serrin, and Ernst Werner von Siemens and his brother Wilhelm. Henry demonstrated a set of ship's lamps, which he claimed could not be extinguished by wind or water. The lamps were illuminated by incandescent iridio-platinum wires and switched on when Preece gave a signal, but the Duke soon pointed out Henry's lack of knowledge of naval matters, which had led him to identify the lamps incorrectly:

> *"You must remember, Edmunds, that the port light is to the left and is red, like port wine. The starboard light is green, and to the right."*

Nevertheless the Duke was very impressed by the lamps. The occasion was, claimed Henry, Britain's first public demonstration of incandescent lighting, but arc-lamps were still the only forms of electrical illumination in commercial use. However promising Henry's experiments with incandescent wires may have been in 1879, his main problem that year was to establish the cause of the failure of his consignment of Farmer-Wallace dynamos. On arriving in New York, Henry was met by William Wallace who explained that he had been experimenting with a new type of insulation material, soluble glass, for the dynamo's wires. Previously he had used shellac. Glass insulation had worked well in the dry air of the USA but the combined effects of the sea voyage and England's damp climate had caused it to fail. Wallace was anxious to do everything he could to help Henry.

> *"I don't want you or your little company to suffer in pocket or reputation through my errors"*, he told Henry. *"Cable to Europe to have the whole lot sent back."*

"But how", asked Henry, *"will we fulfil our orders if we have no dynamos?"*

"I shall give you an introduction to Mr Charles F Brush of Cleveland, Ohio", said Wallace. *"He has been developing the running of arc-lamps in series, and he has solved the problem in a better manner than I have. I will give you full credit for my machines that have failed, and I will leave you to make your own arrangements with Mr Brush."*

Brush, 30 years old, was at this time on the threshold of a brilliant career as an electrical pioneer, having previously worked in the iron business after graduating as a mechanical engineer at Michigan University. He built his first dynamo in 1876, his first arc-lamp a year later. His inventions were now being built under contract by the Telegraph Supply Company of Cleveland, in return for a royalty. By the time Henry Edmunds met him, Brush had developed a system of wiring lamps 'in series', so that if one went out the rest stayed alight. For more than a year his lamps had been illuminating Broadway in a highly spectacular manner, much to the concern of Thomas Edison's financial backers, who were beginning to wonder whether the *'wizard of Menlo Park'* (as one newspaper had described him) would ever be able to perfect the incandescent system that he had been publicising so enthusiastically.

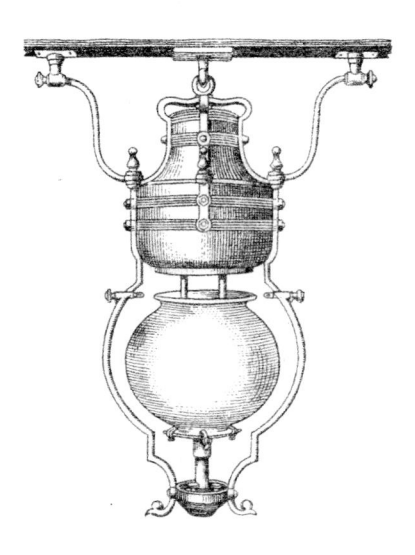

Brush arc-lamp, circa 1880

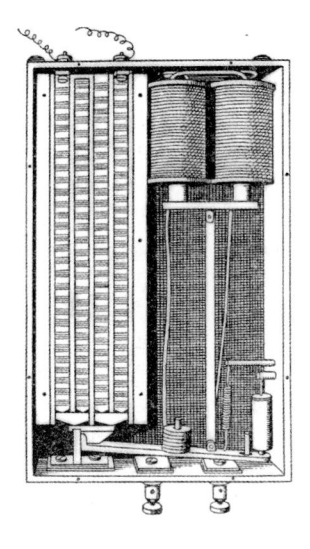

An automatic regulator for Brush arc-lighting, circa 1880

In Cleveland, Henry inspected Brush's lighting system. It was, he said afterwards, *"truly a marked improvement upon anything that had been done before. He had copper-plated his carbon rods and thus immensely improved their conductivity. Instead of the flickering uncertainty of the Farmer-Wallace lamps, as the electric arc jumped about between the two plates of carbon, there was now a steady glow. The arc was kept in one place and the copper plating so reduced the resistance of the carbon that less power was required to maintain the light."*

Henry offered there and then to be the British agent for the system but a week earlier Thomas J Montgomery, one of Brush's representatives, had sailed for Europe to exhibit a number of dynamos and lamps. Henry decided to hurry back to London and negotiate with Montgomery, but before sailing for home he called on two inventors, Hiram S Maxim in Bridgeport, Connecticut, and William E Sawyer, who at that time were serious rivals to Edison in the race to 'sub-divide' the electric light. Maxim, who will reappear in this story some years hence, when the careers of Henry Edmunds and Henry Royce start to converge, had already made incandescent lamps with platinum and graphite illuminants. In 1879, after experimenting for a while with arc-lamps and electric generators, Maxim was busy developing incandescent lamps again, and would soon start producing a high-resistance type with a carbon illuminant essentially similar to Edison's lamp. William Sawyer showed Henry his new low-resistance lamps, which had replaceable carbon illuminants sealed in nitrogen-filled bulbs. Henry thought the lamps were expensive and inefficient, but later realised that they pointed the way to the coming incandescent lamp.

Henry also took the opportunity to renew his friendship with Thomas Edison, probably after meeting Maxim and Sawyer. *'At that visit'*, Henry wrote, *'I learned that Mr Edison was making experiments with metallic wire incandescent lamps. This was confirmed by Messrs Johnson Matthey, who told me of the large variety of metals and alloys with which they had supplied him'*. Henry's visit was also his opportunity to collect the Phonograph that Edison had promised to send him more than a year earlier. It was, said Henry, *'a heavy, ponderous machine, chiefly made of cast iron, with a brass cylinder, turned by hand, and steadied by a large fly-wheel'*.

When he returned to London, Henry wasted no time in meeting Thomas Montgomery and taking him to Hatton Garden, where he introduced him to John Sellon and William Ladd and explained the problems they had been having with the Farmer-Wallace dynamos. Arrangements were immediately made to import Brush's high-tension direct constant current dynamo into Britain, and thus enable Henry and his associates to honour their contracts. At about this time, British patents were being filed for Brush's dynamo and a simplified arc-lamp that he had invented to work with it. This contained a negative carbon fixed to the base of a holder, and a positive, upper, carbon carried on a rod surrounded by a loose metal ring. When the current to the lamp was switched on, an electromagnet raised a metal 'finger' which lifted one side of the ring, causing it to tilt, grip the rod and raise the upper carbon so that an arc could be established between it and the negative carbon. This 'self regulating' feature enabled as many as 50 arc-lamps for street lighting to be installed 'in series', and no doubt was recognised by Edmunds, Sellon and Ladd as being superior to their 'elastic lamp'. This lamp was almost certainly the one selected for the Liverpool Street Station scheme: certainly, Brush and not Wallace arc-lamps were used there, even though the dynamos, initially at least, were the Farmer-Wallace types that were to develop faults in their insulation.

After meeting Thomas Montgomery, Sellon quickly gathered a group of financiers and others together to acquire the British patent rights to Brush's inventions. In December 1879 they formed the Anglo-American Electric Light Co Ltd, with offices at 74 Hatton Garden. Montgomery, Sellon and Ladd were appointed directors. Henry Edmunds was made Chief Engineer. One wonders whether it was his inexperience in business matters, or an inability or reluctance to put up some money for the new enterprise, that lost him a seat on the board of directors.

The Chairman of the AAELC was Sir Henry Whatley Tyler, KT, of Wyvenhoe Hall, Colchester, Essex, who during a long career in business and politics was Chairman of the Westinghouse Brake Co and the Rhymney Iron Co, Deputy Chairman of the Great Eastern Railway and Member of Parliament for Harwich. It was probably Tyler who persuaded the GER to install arc-lighting at Liverpool Street Station; he certainly hastened its introduction in other ways, for on 12 July 1879, *The Electrician* reported that he was having electric lamps rigged up at Wyvenhoe Hall. He was even credited with having invented a form of incandescent lighting:

> 'He employs ... a substance such as carbon, platinum or other material ... which in offering a certain resistance to the passage of electric current, however produced, becomes heated so as to give out light or heat, and these substances he encloses within another substance ... constituting a casing of a refractory nature such as German glass, rock crystal, glaze, fire-clay or steatite, which shall either be sufficiently transparent to allow of the light of the incandescent charcoal or other substance passing

through them, or shall themselves be rendered incandescent by the heat of the interior substance and shall thus constitute the means of affording light. By such refractory outer casing the carbon or other material forming the conductor is prevented from burning away or being destroyed, while it allows the passage of a continuous current and facilitates the employment of a greater number of lights on one circuit than heretofore.'

The credit for being the first person in Britain to install electric lighting in his home is usually given to R E B Crompton, who started manufacturing Gramme generators and Serrin lamps at Chelmsford, Essex, in 1879, having previously imported them from Paris. Crompton, regarded by some as the 'father' of the British electric lighting industry, installed battery-powered arc-lamps at his home in Porchester Gardens, London, in December 1879 but it is possible that by then Tyler's lights had been working for several months.

Under Tyler's leadership the AAELC prospered and in 1880 it was reconstituted as the Anglo-American Brush Electric Light Corporation, with a capital of £800,000 in 80,000 shares of £10 each. Tyler remained as Chairman, with Sellon as Deputy Chairman. A 14,000 sq ft factory, called Victoria Works, at 112 Belvedere Road, Lambeth was purchased from Powis Western Ltd and equipped with 85 lathes, 35 drilling machines and 12 milling machines. The firm had four main activities: making and selling dynamos, lamps and carbons for lighting systems capable of illuminating up to 12 arc-lamps of 6,000 candle power each from one dynamo; selling Brush patents overseas; leasing lighting systems supplied by central generators; and carrying out contracts for corporations, public services and private firms and individuals. During its first year of trading the company sold £350,000 worth of apparatus, the buyers including the Admiralty (which purchased a lighting system for HMS *Inflexible*, as we shall see later), the Royal Arsenal at Woolwich, the Barrow Shipbuilding Co and the Great Western Railway. The next two years saw tremendous progress. Victoria Works became a power station (arguably London's first) and supplied current to street lamps in the surrounding area, and the company won medals at the Paris Electrical Exposition of 1881. In that year, two electrical pioneers who were to become famous in their own right joined the company: Emil Garke, who later formed the British Electric Traction Co, and William Morris Mordey, inventor of soft iron stampings for transformer windings.

Surprisingly, Henry Edmunds resigned from the AABELC soon after it was formed although he was, he claimed, the company's Chief

Engineer, if only for a few months. In the north of England, Holden's Mill in Bradford and Bright's Mill in Rochdale had been among the first industrial concerns to introduce Brush electric lighting. Henry, who had probably been responsible for installing these systems, decided that he wanted to move back to his hometown of Halifax and become the AABELC's agent in Yorkshire. By now, St George Lane-Fox had developed a reasonably efficient incandescent lamp which, thanks to the efforts of John Sellon, was introduced commercially in England by the AABELC. This enabled the company to offer a complete range of equipment: dynamos, arc-lamps for open spaces and factories, and incandescent lamps for use in the home and in offices, theatres and clubs. Henry Edmunds had every reason to hope that, with the sole rights to sell Brush and Lane-Fox systems in one of Britain's most prosperous regions, his future when he returned to Halifax would be just as bright as it would have been if he had stayed in London.

Henry also had another reason for returning home. He had fallen in love.

Annie Wayman, Henry's first wife

Park Congregational Church (now Park United Reform Church), where Henry and Annie were married.

CHAPTER FIVE

A family tragedy

On Wednesday 2 June 1880, Halifax's Park Congregational Church was crowded with members and friends of two of the town's most well known families. Outside, spectators lining the streets cheered and clapped as, a few minutes before eleven o'clock, Annie Wayman and her father Thomas Wayman, JP, a wool stapler and former Mayor of the town, arrived from their home at The Grove accompanied by four bridesmaids, and walked in procession along the carpeted path to the church door.

    They entered the building to the sound of the march *Silver Trumpets* played by the organist, Mr Leah. At the communion rail they were joined by the bridegroom, Henry Edmunds, and welcomed by the pastor, Rev J R Bailey. The wedding ceremony was brief, simple and traditional; everything went according to plan, except for a slip of the pen by the church's registrar, who on the marriage certificate entered Annie's age as 32 instead of 23 - an error which went unnoticed then, and has never been corrected. Henry and Annie left the church to Mendelssohn's Wedding March, ducked under a hail of rice, and rode at the head of a convoy of nine flower-decked carriages to their wedding reception at The Grove. They left Halifax that afternoon for a honeymoon in the Lake District and Scotland. When they returned, they set up home at 5 Heath Villas (below), a large detached house with, at the front, an impressive carriage drive providing access to Heath Gardens and thence to Manor Heath and, at the rear, a 'tradesmen's entrance', reached via a tree-lined cul-de-sac branching off Free School Lane.

The Edmunds family's delight at the homecoming of Henry and Annie was overshadowed by the deaths of his half-sister Alice Mary at the end of June and of her baby daughter, also named Alice Mary, a few weeks later. Henry registered the child's death and helped arrange her funeral. At about this time Annie became pregnant and this encouraged Henry to look to the future. He was busily occupied with schemes for introducing electric light and power to Yorkshire, and taking a close interest in all the latest developments in lighting. To quote Matthew Josephson, one of Edison's biographers, the quest was on to invent 'the first practical and economical electric light for universal domestic use'. Lane-Fox had come fairly close to producing what was needed, but one cannot help thinking that even though Henry Edmunds had more knowledge than most people of Lane-Fox's progress, he had an inkling that his friend Thomas Edison would ultimately lead the field. That, indeed, was what happened, but not before the world had witnessed one of the most remarkable coincidences in the history of science - the simultaneous creation, by two inventors working completely independently, of a lamp that is the true precursor of those that we buy today for a few pence or cents, and plug or screw into sockets around the home with scarcely a thought for those who first patented them.

Edison, of course, was one of the inventors, but he did not start to take a sustained interest in electrically-induced incandescence until that day in September 1878 when he told William Wallace: *"I believe I can beat you making the electric light"*. Long before this - indeed, since before Edison was born - a quiet and unassuming Englishman, Joseph Swan, had been working along the lines that Edison was to follow.

Swan first became interested in electricity when he attended a lecture on arc-lighting given in the shipbuilding town of Sunderland, in north east England, in 1845. Swan was at that time a 17 year old apprentice with a firm of chemists and druggists; he began devoting much of his spare time to studying his new subject and became convinced that, of all the methods and materials the lighting pioneers had experimented with until then, incandescent carbon illuminants enclosed in glass bulbs were the most promising. He realised that thin, flexible but strong illuminants were necessary, and succeeded in making them from strips of carbonised paper. However, he was defeated by the problem of creating a high vacuum in the glass bulbs - the exclusion of residual oxygen being essential in order to prevent the illuminant from burning and disintegrating once it had been heated to the temperature at which it became incandescent.

In 1860 Swan reluctantly concluded that he could make no further progress with incandescent lighting. He spent the next 17 years working on the other inventions for which he became famous, including processes for making photographic prints and typographic half-tone blocks, but in 1877 his interest in lighting was re-awakened by Sir William Crookes' Radiometer, an instrument consisting of four-pivoted discs sealed in a glass sphere. The discs, black on one side, reflective on the other, rotated when exposed to a source of light or heat. Crookes had used Hermann Sprengel's mercury vacuum pump to create the required high vacuum within the sphere, and Swan realised that the same method could be used to evacuate glass bulbs for carbon incandescent lamps. Within a short while, Edison too was experimenting with Sprengel pumps while working on platinum and platinum alloy incandescent lamps, and for a period of nearly two years he and Swan were running virtually 'neck and neck' in the race to make the production of incandescent lamps a commercial reality. Despite the greater reliability and longevity of the lamps they produced with the aid of Sprengel pumps, they both discovered that residual vapours and gases remained in the illuminants. These were released into the vacuum when the lamps were first switched on, causing the illuminants to deteriorate and the bulbs to blacken. Edison, like Swan, soon found that this fault could be prevented by flashing the lamp while the bulb was being exhausted; this made the illuminant incandescent and caused it to release its residual gases, which were then extracted before the bulb was sealed.

In 1880 Swan and Edison completed the pioneering phases of their research. The Englishman patented his methods for removing residual gases, and for making more efficient carbon illuminants from 'parchmentised' cotton threads or 'filaments' - cotton treated with diluted sulphuric acid. Edison abandoned metallic illuminants in favour of carbon and on 1 October, at Menlo Park, manufactured his first commercially produced light bulbs. Swan had been releasing details of his research with 'cotton filament' lamps to the public since June but it was not until the beginning of 1881 that his lamps went into commercial production at the Benwell, Northumberland, factory of his newly-formed Swan Electric Lamp Company.

Swan heralded the manufacture of his lamps by delivering a lecture entitled 'Electric Lighting' to the Newcastle upon Tyne Literary and Philosophical Society on 20 October. When he reached the end of his talk, the 70 gas jets illuminating the lecture room were turned off and, after a momentary pause, 20 of his own lamps were switched on. This was the first time a public building in Europe had been illuminated with incandescent electric lighting, and the event was widely reported in the national and provincial newspapers. Henry Edmunds read an article about Swan's lecture in the *Leeds Mercury* and with characteristic impetuosity immediately despatched a telegram to Swan in which he asked whether he could come to Newcastle to see the new invention and discuss the possibility of becoming a partner in Swan's new venture. They met at Mawson & Swan, the firm of druggists and chemists where Swan had served his apprenticeship and later become a partner of his employer, John Mawson. Henry left this account of their discussion:

> 'I was surprised and delighted to see the showroom illuminated by a number of glass bulbs. This was my first view of what has developed into the incandescent electric light system of today. Mr Swan was much interested in hearing of my experiences in America, and before I left him I had arranged with him a partnership in his foreign patents in connection with electric lighting. Mr Swan told me that, when he saw Crookes' Radiometer ... it occurred to him that this was the vacuum or state of exhaustion necessary to make the electric incandescent lamp practicable ... It is late in the day now to discuss who was the original inventor ... in this country it was Mr Swan, but it was developed in America quite independently by Mr Edison ... by my arrangement with Mr Swan I became a pioneer in the introduction of the Swan incandescent lamp.'

One of the first private houses to be illuminated with Swan's lamps was that of Sir William Spottiswoode, president of the Royal Society, Britain's oldest scientific society. One evening in early 1881, Sir William Thomson and Captain John Fisher, RN (the future Admiral Lord Fisher of Kilverstone) dined with Spottiswoode. Fisher, who had joined the navy at the time of the Crimean War (when he was only thirteen years old) had recently been given command of HMS *Inflexible*, which was then being fitted out at Portsmouth prior to entering service as the greatest battleship of her day, with thicker armour plating and bigger guns than any other afloat. Fisher wanted the latest and best equipment for his ship. In 1879, HMS *Dreadnought* had been lit by two arc-lamps. In 1880 the Oregon Railway and Navigation Company's new Pacific Coast liner SS *Columbia* had been equipped with 115 Edison incandescent lamps and four dynamos (driven by the ship's engine); it also had a Maxim headlight fitted in the focus of a parabolic reflector, which directed a cone of light far out to sea. We can be sure that Fisher had been taking a close interest in these maritime applications for the electric light, and while he was dining with Spottiswoode in the glow of six of Swan's incandescent lamps he decided that this was the type of lighting he wanted for *Inflexible*.

HMS *Inflexible*, the first ship of the Royal Navy
to be equipped with incandescent electric lighting.
(The National Maritime Museum, London)

A few days later Fisher sought Swan's advice on the subject. By now, Henry was employed as Swan's salesman or agent, receiving a commission of five shillings for every bulb he sold, but no salary. The bulbs retailed for 25 shillings (£1.25) each - a very high price in 1881 and several times their present day cost. Henry, therefore, had the opportunity to earn a considerable amount of money if he could secure large orders from government departments, factory owners and anyone else to whom the safety and convenience of incandescent electric lamps justified their premium price. Fisher's enquiry was one of the first that Henry followed up, and he set off for Portsmouth carrying a shallow box containing a quantity of precious bulbs, carefully wrapped in cotton wool. The bulbs had thick glass stems, about three-quarters of an inch in diameter, and were three inches long, with platinum lead in wires formed into a loop at one end. Here, in Henry's own words, is a description of what happened after he arrived at the dockyard:

> '*I was met by Captain Fisher, who took me over the Inflexible and invited me to lunch at his club; he had arranged for a demonstration in a shed in the dockyard, which had been darkened for the purpose. It had suspended two parallel bare*

copper wires by strings from the ceiling, passing outside to a searchlight dynamo driven by a semi-portable engine, controlled by signals between two Bo'suns, one inside the shed and the other out. These seamen communicated by whistle, and the speed of the engine was carefully adjusted, so that the incandescent lamps ran brightly without being distressed. At that period we had no fuses, no voltmeters, no ampere meters and practically no switches, and it required no little care to get proper adjustment.

At last we got our lamps to glow satisfactorily; and at that moment the Admiral was announced. Captain Fisher had warned me that I must be careful how I answered any questions, for the Admiral was of the stern old school and prejudiced against all new fangled notions. The Admiral appeared, resplendent in gold lace, and accompanied by such a bevy of ladies that I was strongly reminded of the character in HMS Pinafore, 'with his sisters, and his cousins and his aunts'.

The Admiral immediately asked if I had seen the Inflexible. I replied that I had.

"Have you seen the powder magazine?"

"Yes, I have been in it."

"What would happen to one of these little glass bubbles in the event of a broadside?"

"I do not think it would affect them."

"How do you know? You've never been in a ship during a broadside!"

I saw Captain Fisher's eye fixed upon me, and a sailor was despatched for some guncotton. Evidently everything had been ready prepared, for he quickly returned with a small tea tray, upon which was a layer of gun cotton, powdered over with black gunpowder. The Admiral asked if I was prepared to break one of the lamps over the tray. I replied that I could do so quite safely, for the glowing lamp would be cooled down by the time it fell amongst the gun cotton. I took a cold chisel, smashed a lamp, and let it fall. The company saw the light extinguished, and a few pieces of glass fall on the tray. There was no flash, and the gun powder and gun cotton remained as before. There was a short pause, while the Admiral gazed at the tray. Then he turned and said to Fisher: "We'll have this light on the Inflexible".'

And that was the introduction of the incandescent light into the British Navy.

HMS *Inflexible* was a ship that took a long time to prepare for service. Although launched in April 1876 she was not commissioned until July 1881, nor completed until October of that year. She was originally fitted with arc-lamps, for on 29 May 1880 *The Electrician* reported that *'the trial of the Brush light on the Inflexible has proved satisfactory, and it is decided to use the light for the mast head and bow lights of iron-clads. Portsmouth Dockyard will also be illuminated by the Brush light. Each light gave out about 2,000 candles, at a cost of about 2d per hour'*. The installation of incandescent lamps to supplement or perhaps replace the Brush lamps appears to be one of several improvements that Fisher insisted upon when he arrived at Portsmouth to take command of *Inflexible* in January 1881. He quickly became exasperated by the attitude of his superiors, who seemed intent on preventing him from having the ship fitted out as he wanted her to be. The Admiral, who Fisher described as being *'prejudiced against all new fangled notions'*, was, evidently, Rear Admiral the Hon Fitzgerald Foley, Admiral Superintendent of the Dockyard. During his first inspection of his new ship, Fisher asked Foley if a bridge could be erected forward, to aid navigation. Foley refused, saying the ship was in all respects ready for sea. Fisher would not accept this and made a direct approach to the Admiralty who not only approved his request but also ordered that *'all Captain Fisher's requests are to be complied with, and anything he considers necessary is to be done'*.

Henry's account of his demonstration at Portsmouth was published in the second instalment of his *Reminiscences*, in October 1919. He sent a copy to Lord Fisher, who by coincidence was at that time writing his own memoirs and working on a chapter in which he described some of his arguments with those in high places who had opposed his ideas. Fisher replied to Henry, saying: *"... I remember it all - specially your very lucid exposition. I'll have you in my second book as a Pioneer!"* He kept his word and recalled the event as follows:

> *'Yesterday I heard from a gentleman whom I had not seen for 38 years, and he reminded me of a visit to me when I was Captain of the Inflexible. I was regarded by the Admiral Superintendent of the Dockyard as the Incarnation of Revolution. What upset him most was that I asked for more water closets and got them. This particular episode ... was that I wanted the incandescent light ... I wrote to Mr Swan ... and he sent down the friend who wrote me the letter I received yesterday, Mr Henry Edmunds, and we had an exhibition to convert this old fossil of an Admiral Superintendent.'*

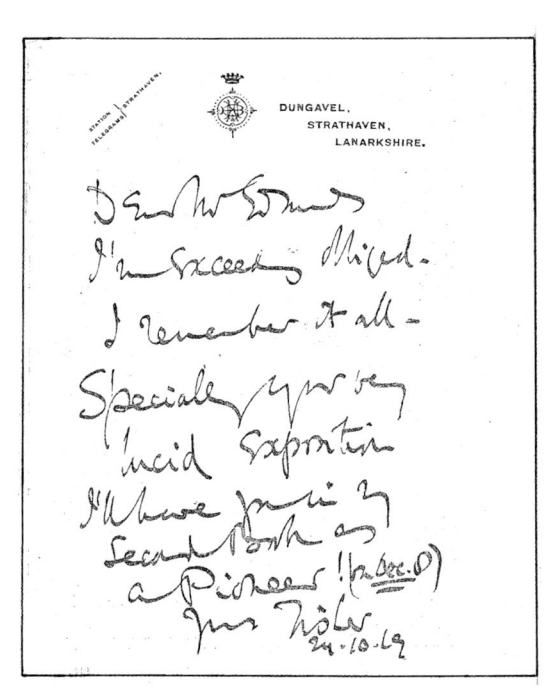

Admiral Lord Fisher to Henry Edmunds: *'I remember it all ...'*

    It has to be admitted that the suspicion of Fisher's superiors to new fangled inventions such as electric lighting was to some extent understandable. One day, an earth leakage from the Inflexible's 600-volt AC dynamos gave the coxswain a severe shock when he touched an arc-lamp. Sir William Thomson was visiting the ship at the time, probably a few days after his and Fisher's lamp-lit dinner with Sir William Spottiswoode. Thomson inspected the cable feeding the arc-lamp and said he had found *'a nasty little leak, but not likely to be dangerous to life'*. At that moment the cable slipped through his fingers and he touched a bare wire. The shock made him leap in the air and deliver a second diagnosis: *'Dangerous. Very dangerous to life. I will mention this to the British Association'*. Thomson was lucky not to have been electrocuted; soon afterwards, a stoker was killed by a similar short circuit. Following an inquiry into this incident, the voltage in battleships' electrical systems was reduced to 80 volts. Insulation of electrical equipment was in those days very unreliable, as Henry himself knew from his experiences with the Farmer-Wallace dynamos in 1879, and when the *Inflexible* eventually entered service, the field magnets in one of her dynamos developed an earthing fault shortly before she was due to call at several Italian ports. As there were no materials in the ship's stores suitable for insulating the new wiring that had to be fitted to the dynamo, a silk dress that had been lent to one of Fisher's lieutenants for a fancy dress ball was cut into strips and bound around the wires.

Henry's success in selling incandescent lamps to the Royal Navy marked the beginning of a brief but eventful association with Joseph Swan. Their relationship can be traced through the minutes of the directors' meetings of the Swan Electric Light Company. The first reference to Henry is made in a report of a meeting held on Tuesday, 22 February 1881. This took place shortly after what Henry described as *'the most eventful week of my life'*, during which he not only introduced incandescent lamps into battleships, but also into the Merchant Navy. The Inman Steamship Company, which had installed arc-lamps aboard its liner *City of Berlin in 1879*, chose Swan lamps for its latest ship, *City of Richmond*, which in June 1881 became the first liner equipped with incandescent lighting to cross the Atlantic. The installation of the lamps was supervised by Henry. During that eventful week early in 1881, Henry went from Portsmouth to W D & H O Wills' tobacco factory in Bristol, where he and Dr Silvanus P Thompson, the company's electrical consultant, gave a demonstration that later resulted in Swan lighting being installed in the factory. Only a few years earlier, Thompson had regarded the attempt to invent an incandescent electric lamp as a waste of time!

City of Richmond, the first liner equipped with incandescent lighting to cross the Atlantic. (The National Maritime Museum, London)

Henry was present at the directors' meeting on 22 February, and instructed to proceed with negotiations with Wills on the understanding that they, and not Swan's company, should pay for experimental work. Henry also reported on the progress he was making with the owners of Alnwick Castle, in Northumberland, who were planning to install incandescent lighting. He also urged Swan to open an office in London, run by his own staff, rather than have an agency there. The question of Henry's working relationship with the Swan company was also discussed; he was requested, for the first but by no means last time, to submit weekly reports of his work, these to arrive at the office by Monday morning. The terms of his business agreement with Swan were also presented to the directors, some of whom had already seen it. Evidently, Henry's expenses had not been fully agreed; the directors decided against discussing the subject until they had had more time to think about it.

March 1881 found Henry busy helping Swan sort out several technical problems, one being that of making the glass globes for the lamps. Only one glass blower with sufficient skill was available Fred Topham, who worked for Charles H Stearn of Birkenhead. Stearn read an advertisement for Crookes' Radiometer and became one of Swan's collaborators, developing a way of creating high vacua for experimental lamps. Topham alone could not produce all the globes required for commercial production; eventually glass blowers from the Thuringian district of Germany were recruited, and trained by Topham, but before this happened Henry was evidently trying to solve the labour shortage, for on 3 March the directors read a letter in which he reported that he had engaged 'another' glass blower. He also said that he hoped to have a Brush generator and gas-engine running that day at Rock Ferry, presumably for a demonstration. The small scale of Swan's production can be gauged from a footnote in the minutes, recording that one hundred and five lamps were made during the previous week!

Henry, it appears, was an enthusiastic representative for the company but like many in his profession he was rather slow in keeping his paperwork up to date. At their meeting on 14 March the directors instructed the company secretary to number all the letters sent to Henry and ask him to *'give particulars of his negotiations in each case, referring to each by number... and to enter up such particulars against the copies of letters'*. At the same meeting, the possibility of exhibiting at the forthcoming Paris Electrical Exposition, an event that would have a great influence on the future of the electric light, and on Henry's own career, was discussed and provisionally approved.

On Saturday 19 March, Henry attended what was to be his last meeting with the directors for several months. He was at that time negotiating with Messrs Graham, Muir and Smith on the question of forming a syndicate to run an electric lighting company in Glasgow. Similar negotiations between Henry and 'various gentlemen' in Sheffield, Banbury, Halifax, Leeds and Bradford were also in progress and he was asked to provide a formal report on all these matters for full discussion by the directors on 22 March. At this meeting, Henry's report on the Glasgow scheme was discussed. It appears that the syndicate was interested in setting up a lighting contracting company and manufacturing Swan lamps under licence, a proposition that caused some concern among the directors. The Glasgow businessmen were seeking to make a profit corresponding to a 50 per cent 'mark up' on the cost of Swan lamps. Swan and his colleagues considered this to be 'quite unreasonable' and proposed instead a royalty of five shillings per lamp. The directors decided not to take the matter any further until Mr Smith wrote to them giving his views *'fully and distinctly'* of the nature of the proposed company and the *'names and standing of the gentlemen he would propose to associate with him'*.

Henry's remuneration following any arrangements made with other parties in Glasgow or elsewhere was also discussed, and the secretary was instructed to write to him as follows:

> *'Your report was read at the meeting of directors held today and after considering its contents, especially the portion referring to the Glasgow scheme, I was instructed to communicate to you that Mr J W Swan was requested to write to Mr Smith asking him to put in writing the details of his proposals ... I was further instructed to say to you that if this scheme is realised, your claim to remuneration would be fairly considered; but that the feeling of the Board is that such propositions are, in the present state of the business, rather premature and embarrassing and should not be encouraged, they being beside rather outside the scope of our agreement with you.'*

When the directors met again two weeks later they heard that Henry had not replied to the letters they had sent him, or forwarded copies of any orders he had received. Clearly somewhat exasperated by his failure to communicate, they devised a form, which was to be attached to each letter they sent to him; this form contained a blank space in which he was to write his response. Several letters and forms were posted to Henry after this meeting, and again on 31 March, but by now Annie Edmunds was nearing the end of her confinement and Henry was preoccupied with domestic affairs. During the last week in March he wrote to Annie, telling her all about his business meetings and demonstrations and saying that he hoped to arrive home on the evening of Saturday 2 April. He said he looked forward to meeting her at The Grove, her parents' house, where he would tell her all about his experiences. But when he arrived at Halifax railway station, he immediately realised that all was not well:

> 'I was met by a cousin, who seemed strangely agitated. As I hailed a cab, he asked where I was going.
> I replied: "To my father in law's house".
> He said: "Have you not received our telegram?"
> "No. Why?"
> "Do you not know that your wife was prematurely confined last night?"
> I was stunned. I drove home at once, to find my dear young wife insensible. Her mother, nurse and doctor were there - but all in vain - she quietly passed away. I never told her.'

CHAPTER SIX
Joseph Swan's negotiator

Annie had given birth to twins, Claud Henry and Dorothy Annie, but after suffering puerperal convulsions for 15 hours she died of exhaustion. She was buried in a double grave that Henry purchased in the borough cemetery at Stoney Royd; evidently he intended to be buried beside her when his time came, but soon after her death he moved away from Halifax and gradually severed his connections with the town. He returned regularly to visit his father and stepmother while they were still living at Southfield but when they retired and went to live at South Bank, a house in Cheadle, Cheshire, the link between Halifax and the man who was to become 'the Godfather of Rolls-Royce' was finally broken.

Annie's grave in Stoney Royd Cemetary, Halifax

Annie's grave can be found beside one of the steep paths that meander between the thousands of vaults and memorials, some humble, others ostentatious, that mark the last resting places of the generations that saw Halifax grow from a small town into a major industrial centre. Her grave is covered by a stone slab and surmounted by a cross, on the plinth of which the inscription chosen by Henry ('He giveth his beloved sleep') is still legible. Nearby are the graves of other members of the Edmunds family, including Henry's half-sister, Alice, and her baby daughter, whose deaths the previous year were still fresh in the memories of those who gathered round Annie's graveside on the day of her funeral in the early spring of 1881. From the cemetery, high on a steep wooded hillside, all the places associated with Henry's life in Halifax can be seen. To the north-west is the busy town centre, where he was born and grew up. Immediately beyond Silver Street, where his father had his ironmongers shop, is Dean Clough Mill, where the Crossleys made their fortune. Further to the west is Lister Lane Cemetery, where Henry's mother lies buried near the graves of various members of the Crossley family, including John Crossley, MP and Louis John Crossley. To the south-west of Stoney Royd just beyond the Huddersfield road, are Heath Villas and Stafford Road, Skircoat among tree-lined suburban streets which peter out into windswept lanes leading to remote moorland villages such as Stainland, once the home of Henry's beloved step-mother, Sarah Hannah, who is also buried at Stoney Royd.

One of the first people to send his condolences to Henry was Joseph Swan, who more than anyone else helped Henry rebuild his life. *'Come to us at Newcastle for Easter'*, Swan wrote. *'There is nothing like work to relieve you in your great trouble, and there is much work to be done'.* Easter fell two weeks after Annie's death, and on or about 16 April Henry set off to take up Swan's invitation.

During Henry's absence, Swan had received an enquiry from The Cunard Steam Ship Company, whose liner *Servia* was being fitted out in Glasgow. Having only recently sold Swan lamps to the Royal Navy and the Inman Line, Henry was confident that he could persuade Cunard to follow suit for their new liner, which was designed to carry a greater number of first-class passengers across the Atlantic than any other ship in service. Incandescent lighting would give the ship a distinction that few others could match, but when Henry met Cunard's Mr John

Servia, the luxury transatlantic liner that was equipped with incandescent lighting as a result of Henry's efforts.
(Stewart Bale Ltd)

Burns in Glasgow he was told that the company had considered electric lighting, but had decided to fit oil lamps instead. Burns was unaware of Swan's recent sales to other shipbuilders. *"Why haven't our people told me about this?",* he asked. Henry explained that the matter had been overlooked because of his recent bereavement. Burns summoned a colleague, Captain Watson, and said: *"Show Mr Edmunds over the Servia and then report to me."* The outcome was an order for Swan lamps for the liner, which had the distinction of being the biggest vessel to be launched since Isambard Kingdom Brunel's *Great Eastern* in the 1850s, and the first large steel-hulled liner to operate across the Atlantic.

Throughout the summer of 1881 Henry was busy selling Swan lamps and arranging installations and demonstrations. The minutes of the company's board meetings contain numerous references to his work[9]. On 3 June he attended a meeting to explain the difficulty he was having in quoting prices for 'store lamps' (ie spare lamps) for HMS *Inflexible.* The directors decided to supply lamps in three classes: 'first lamps', complete with sockets, for 25 shillings each; 'store lamps' without sockets for ten shillings each; and 'renewals' (new lamps exchanged for old ones) for five shillings. At the same meeting, Henry reported that when she returned from New York the *City of Richmond* would be fitted with a No 7 Brush generator, one or two arc-lamps and 'the Swan lamps to the fullest capacity of that machine'. The liner had, in fact, arrived in New York a few days earlier, equipped with Swan lamps in its main saloon and staterooms. *The Electrician* reported that the lamps had worked well during the voyage:

> *'The light is described by those who observed it ... as very steady and mellow, not subject to fluctuation or accident, easily managed and very brilliant. The six lamps in the main saloon rendered the apartment as light as day, enabling passengers to read at any point.'*

Henry also told his directors on 3 June that the managers of the Inman Line wanted to meet him to discuss lighting for another liner, *City of Rome,* under construction at Barrow. This meeting resulted in an order for 100 lamps for the saloon and 150 lamps for the drawing rooms, smoke rooms, state rooms and the captain's and officers' cabins. However, the engine room and upper and lower steerage were illuminated with Siemens alternating current arc-lamps.

---

[9] Minutes of Directors' Meetings 1881 1884, Swan Electric Light Company, Tyne & Wear County Council Archives Dept., ref 1101 / 486.

On 10 June the directors accepted a quotation that Henry had obtained from John Sellon for a year's supply of platinum. The material would not have been required for the manufacture of illuminants since it had already been found to be unsuitable for this purpose. Instead, it would have been used as conductors or 'lead-in' wires. Platinum was ideal for this purpose because of its heat-resistance; it also had the same coefficient of expansion as glass and therefore would not crack the lamp bulbs when they were heated and cooled.

On 14 June the board approved the terms on which Henry had offered lamps to the Inman Line for the *City of Richmond.* It was at about this time that he started trying to exert a stronger influence on the company's prices and policy. As previously mentioned, he had an arrangement whereby, in lieu of a salary, he received a commission of five shillings on each lamp. However, some time in 1881 he told Swan that the lamps should be retailed for five shillings each if they were to be a commercial success.

"Then what will become of your commission?", Swan asked Henry. That, replied Henry, was a matter for negotiation. The terms of their new agreement are not known but the price of lamps was reduced, not only in order to widen their market but also because more economical manufacturing methods evolved; initially, production was geared to making lamps for demonstrations, experiments and prototype installations but when full-scale manufacture was commenced, unit costs came down.

A rather incomplete picture of the new agreement that Henry wanted can be gleaned from the minutes of the directors' meetings held in July and August. On 1 July the company's solicitor, R S Watson, reported that Henry had suggested that the firm should open an office in London, with Henry as manager, paid by salary. Henry, however, was still in arrears with his paperwork and the company secretary was instructed to respond as follows:

> *'The directors would prefer to deal with the question of your re-engagement after they have received your Accounts, as in the absence of this it is impossible to ascertain the result of the work that has been done hitherto.'*

During the next two weeks Henry submitted some kind of statement but on 14 July he was called before the board and told that no arrangement could be considered until the accounts had been 'fully furnished'. By the next meeting, held on 2 August, the matter had been resolved and Henry was sent a cheque for £500. We do not know exactly what the sum covered; part of it may have been commission owed to him for his sales during the previous months, but reimbursements for expenses may also have been included.

Whatever Swan may have thought of Henry's tendency to be late in submitting reports, and his efforts to enhance his position in the company at inopportune moments, he obviously admired him for his organisational ability and confidence in incandescent lighting. These qualities led to Henry being made responsible for managing the Swan company's exhibits at the Paris Electrical Exposition.

Held at the Palais de l'Industrie in the Champs-Elysées from 1 August to 15 November 1881, the exhibition was the world's first comprehensive display of electric lighting and was described by the London *Times* as *'greater than anything that has ever been seen'*. There were 1,767 exhibitors and all the major inventors and manufacturers of electrical lighting systems and generators attended or were represented, including the four pioneers of incandescent lighting who had succeeded in putting their inventions into commercial production: Joseph Swan, Thomas Edison, St George Lane-Fox and Hiram Maxim. On one night, 29 August, a total of 1837 electric lights, 1500 of them incandescent, were in operation. One of the thousands of visitors was William Preece, who commented afterwards on the *'vivid impression that the great blaze of splendour made on the minds of visitors entering the building. There can never be anything like it again'*.

Swan's lamps, which were the first to be switched on, were to be seen not only on the company's stand in the main exhibition hall but also in the congress room, the telephone room, the refreshment room, the offices of the British Commission, and the British Post Office Pavilion. The refreshment room had three chandeliers, one consisting of numerous brass arms holding clusters of small bulbs in blue crenelated bell-glass covers. But the lamps in the congress room were the most spectacular. In the centre of the room were eight brass coronae, suspended from the ceiling and each supporting 20 lamps. Around the walls there were 16 festoons of crimson cord, each festoon carrying 20 bulbs. The lamps emitted light equivalent to that of 10,000 candles but could be regulated to create only a faint glow if required. *Engineering,* one of the journals that covered the exposition, commented on *'the beauty of the illumination and the simplicity of the apparatus'* and on the *'charming taste with which the installation has been carried out under the able superintendence of Mr Henry Edmunds'*.

Henry installed two different types of generator to supply current to the lamps in the congress room. Although Edison had developed a complete lighting system of lamps, dynamos and distribution cables (and by now had bought a site in New York City for his first central generating plant) Swan had followed a different policy and had concentrated solely on perfecting his lamps. This meant that he had to buy his dynamos from other companies. One of these was the Anglo-American Brush Electric Light Corporation. Henry remained an agent for Brush dynamos during the time he worked for Swan and with the help of Thomas Montgomery installed two Brush high-tension direct current machines at the Paris Exposition. Montgomery paid for all the work involved in setting up the Brush equipment, and one Saturday morning Henry received a cablegram from Montgomery in New York informing him that £1,000 had been credited to his account at Drexel Harje's bank in Paris. Henry needed the money immediately to pay his workmen, so he hurried to the bank, which was about to close for the day, only to be told by the manager that he could not withdraw the money unless he could prove his identity.

Henry produced his visiting cards, and letters addressed to himself, but the manager would not accept them and asked him to fetch someone who could identify him. Henry had no time to do this but suddenly remembered that the linen shirt he was wearing carried a tab bearing his name. He offered to remove his waistcoat and show the tab but the manager replied that this would not be necessary; he was now satisfied, and Henry could have the money. That evening, as he dressed for dinner, Henry remembered the incident and looked at the tab on his shirt. It bore the name of Charles Brush's nephew, F C Phillips, who was occupying the room next to Henry. The hotel laundry had mixed up their linen.

The Brush dynamos that Henry installed at the exhibition supplied current to the Swan lamps festooned around the walls. Two Siemens generators were also installed, one for the suspended coronae in the congress room, the other for the chandeliers in the refreshment room. Elsewhere, Henry connected Swan's lamps to Faure batteries. This reliance on other inventors' generators was noted in a review of the exhibition in *The Electrician:*

> '*The effective manner in which Mr Edison's rooms are lighted is equalled by the manner in which Mr Edmunds ... has lighted the rooms in his charge. The exhibit of Mr Edison differed in some essentials from Mr Swan's. The former has aimed at giving a system complete, a system that will compare favourably and compete successfully with gas. The latter has given us a lamp. Excellent it may be but it still forms but one important part of a system. Mr Edison has considered his lamps in his design*

of machine, and his machine in the design of his lamps. He also has a method of mains and insulation, of compensating the various resistances in the circuit, and measuring the current used by a householder. It can hardly be expected, then, that lamps dependent on machines taken at random will be equally good at all points as those designed as part of a system, yet we doubt if any observer would deliberately give an opinion as to the superiority of the one over the other.'

As was the custom at exhibitions in the nineteenth century, diplomas and medals were awarded to the best exhibits. At the Paris Exposition the judges had no difficulty in deciding that the first prize, the Diploma of Honour, should go to Thomas Edison for his magnificent exhibit of a complete electrical system, which included 500 lamps each of 16 candle-power, his steam-driven Jumbo dynamo (named after P T Barnum's famous elephant) and all manner of accessories and controls. His policy of designing and building all the equipment required for generating and distributing electricity and regulating lighting installations had given him an unassailable advantage over his competitors. He also received the French Legion of Honour and various medals. He was not present to receive his prizes personally. Joseph Swan was one of the first to congratulate him.

Swan was not entirely outclassed. Like Edison, he was awarded the Legion of Honour; he also received a gold medal, as did various manufacturers of dynamos and arc-lamps, including the AABELC, R E B Crompton and the British Electric Light Company. Later, several of the companies who exhibited in Paris became involved in the great 'patent battle' of the 1880s, when Swan and Edison each claimed that the other had infringed his patent rights, and Edison sued (or threatened to sue) other rivals, such as Hiram Maxim, William Sawyer and Albon Man, who, he claimed, had stolen his inventions. Edison and Swan settled their argument out of court and merged their interests into the Edison & Swan Electric Light Company. Ediswan, as the new concern was called, soon monopolised the incandescent lighting market and while doing so sued the AABELC, which had acquired the rights to manufacture Lane-Fox's incandescent lamps. Ediswan successfully claimed that the AABELC was infringing Edison's patents and the company had to stop making incandescent lamps.

Edison's and Swan's new form of lighting was soon accepted by the public, although there were those who were suspicious of it or did not understand how it worked. For their benefit, notices like this started appearing in electrically illuminated hotel rooms in the 1880s:

> This Room Is Equipped With
> **Edison Electric Light.**
> Do not attempt to light with match. Simply turn key on wall by the door.
> ———
> The use of Electricity for lighting is in no way harmful to health, nor does it affect the soundness of sleep.

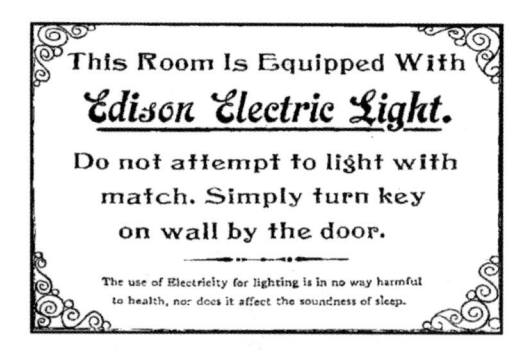

This room is equipped with EDISON ELECTRIC LIGHT. Do not attempt to light with match. Simply turn key on wall beside door. The use of electricity for lighting is in no way harmful to health, nor does it affect the soundness of sleep.

The Paris Exposition was the public's first opportunity to compare Edison and Swan lamps under the same roof, and we can be sure that Henry Edmunds found time to acquaint himself with the progress that his American friend (and now business rival) had made during the two years that had passed since their last meeting. More details of Henry's activities are contained in the letters that Swan wrote home to his wife, Hannah, nearly every day during the many weeks he attended the exhibition.[10] Swan had special letterheads printed for the occasion, on which Henry is named as *Ingéniour Gérant*. On 21 September, Swan wrote to Hannah, saying that he had spent the morning with Henry, who was unwell:

> 'The chief theme of my conversation with him was taking additional safeguards against fire. I obtained promises from him that every precaution would be exercised and safeguards introduced.'

Swan's concern was timely. When he returned to the exhibition a fire broke out in one of the galleries. It was not serious but it showed how hazardous electrical apparatus could be in those days. Next day, Swan again wrote of his fears about safety:

> 'The scare we got ... last night ... has left a very strong impression on me and I feel that we are sailing too near the wind in the matter of safety. I will try and see Mr Edmunds tonight and convey my feeling to him. I have already had a long talk with him on the subject ... but I fear that unless I speak again, and more strongly, no action will be taken in the matter.'

---

[10] Letters from J Swan to his wife 1881, Tyne & Wear County Council Archives Dept., ref 1101 / 1058 1064.

Henry, we assume, complied with Swan's instructions when, a day or two later, he recovered from his illness and resumed his duties. Certainly, Swan's exhibits were unscathed by fire during the three months over which the exhibition was held. Henry's own account of his work in Paris contains stories of many incidents and adventures, beginning with the way in which he arranged Swan's display:

> 'Special fittings were designed by Messrs Faraday & Sons, of Berners Street. I remember telling Mr Harold Faraday that I wanted fittings that could not be mistaken for gas, or oil, or candles, or any other of the old-fashioned methods of illumination. I expected something quite different. Hundreds of small spherical lamps were made at Newcastle, with platinum loops, which were hung on to spring hooks, as a lamp-holder, to which were attached the insulated wires. To display these, Messrs Faraday designed a fairy-like structure of light lacquered brass. This was arranged to support small yellow silk-covered wires in festoons, to show that no tubes were in evidence to suggest gas. From these depended glass globes about 2½ inches in diameter, for these were the kind of lamps then used; and the whole structure was extremely decorative and effective for exhibition purposes. I took over to Paris from Yorkshire several men whom I could trust to look after the installation and the running of the lamps; a very necessary precaution in those days, for a fire would have damaged our future business most seriously. Since then I have often wondered how we escaped accident, considering the primitive nature of all our apparatus and the general ignorance of the most elementary principles of electrical engineering. I believe a providence looks after children; and at that time we were in a very juvenile stage. We had no protecting devices, such as fuses, our cables had very doubtful insulation; and we were in a temporary building, constructed of lath and plaster, with flimsy wooden partitions and framework.'

Henry befriended a Frenchman, Maurice Simon, who supplied various items of equipment that Henry, as a stranger to Paris, would otherwise have had difficult in finding. Simon also introduced Henry to M Garnier, the architect responsible for Paris's Grand Opera House. Garnier told Henry that he wanted to illuminate the building with electric lighting. It was an experiment that helped herald the end of the romantic but dangerous lighting of theatre by gas lamps. Arc-lamps had already been installed in the Theatre Bellacour in Lyons and Her Majesty's Theatre in Carlisle, England and at the end of December 1881 Swan installed 1,158 lamps in London's Savoy Theatre. Now, following Henry Edmunds' meeting with Garnier, there was a chance to show opera lovers what incandescent lighting could do. Henry quickly put the idea to the organisers of the Paris Exposition, who agreed that the Opera House should be regarded as an annexe of the exhibition. The necessary permits were issued. By 23 September Joseph Swan had become involved in planning the lighting scheme and on that day he took advantage of a 'spare and quiet moment' to write to his wife and give her the news:

> 'Did I tell you that it was settled that we were to light the interior of the Grand Opera House? Edison, Lane-Fox and others are to light parts of the building also. I do not know which of us has the best part, for there are splendid opportunities for effective lighting in several of the rooms and staircases, besides that which we have seen in the Opera itself.'

The necessary equipment for Swan's scheme was in short supply, which meant that it took several weeks to complete the installation. On 20 October Swan wrote to Hannah:

> 'Still here! And very tired of it ... young Mr Stevenson has arrived with 400 lamps for the Opera but we have not yet got the necessary engine power to utilise the lamps and complete the lighting. There are two steam engines on the way from Dieppe... Mr Edmunds' father, uncle, sister and cousin are here.'

Eventually, Swan's lamps were installed and from an account that Henry wrote we can learn how the various lighting companies collaborated in what was, for the 1880s, a highly ambitious scheme. Siemens Bros provided generators capable of running 500 or 600 lamps, their cables being supplied by Messrs Menier, Latour et Lecarrier, the firm that had fitted gas lighting in the Opera House, helped install the electrical equipment. Hiram Maxim's company provided the footlights. Illuminating the stage itself was comparatively simple but in the auditorium the electricians were obstructed by a huge gas-lit bronze chandelier hanging from the ornate ceiling. The Theatre's manager insisted that this should remain in position as a stand-by. *"An interesting example of the new light struggling to assert itself in the face of the existing gas illumination"*, commented Henry, who went on to describe the problems he and his fitters faced:

> 'One could only work during certain limited hours, passing through mysterious trap doors in the ceiling. The electric lamp bulbs had to be carefully attached and wired, so that they would be in their proper electrical circuit, as well as suitably supported under these trying conditions. You may be sure that it was an anxious time for me. I wanted to make a good and effective show ... but we had to contend with limited materials and the want of experience among those who were at work on the installation. Therefore I was immensely relieved when it was found that everything was satisfactorily arranged for the night of the performance, the opera presented being *Guillaume Tell*. When the public flocked in they found the building flooded with a new light, of unwonted brilliance; and the whole performance went through without the slightest failure of the new illuminant; and with no occasion to fall back on gas.'

Paris's incandescent electric lighting displays attracted worldwide publicity, helped by the constant press coverage given to the preparations for the event, the exhibits themselves and the visits of various VIPs, including the Prime Minister of France, Léon Michel Gambetta, Edward, Prince of Wales, and Princess Alexandra. Henry was on duty on Swan's stand at the time of the Royal visit, and was presented to Prince Edward by Lord Crawford. The Prince complimented Henry on the lighting of the British section of the exhibition and asked him to explain the principles of incandescent lighting to Princess Alexandra, who had never seen it before. Henry had with him a few 'fairy lamps' of the kind that Swan had supplied to Richard d'Oyly Carte for the premiere of Gilbert and Sullivan's *Iolanthe* at the Savoy Theatre. After explaining how the lamps worked, Henry presented one of them to the Princess as a souvenir.

A less sophisticated visitor to the exhibition was King Kalakaua of Honolulu, who summoned Henry to his suite at the Hotel Continental and asked him to explain the mysteries of electric lighting. Although it had a few Jablochkoff Candles in its courtyard, the hotel had no general electrical supply; Henry could only show the king a few lamp bulbs and try to explain how they worked:

> 'The dusky monarch viewed the bulbs with great amazement, and was greatly perplexed to understand how they could become filled with light when attached to a couple of wires. He was further amazed that I could not there and then make the bulbs glow, as he had seen in the exhibition. It was not easy in those days to explain electric lighting, even to those who were more or less

> *familiar with electricity as applied to telegraphs ... and therefore the reader will appreciate the impossibility I felt in explaining the most elementary ideas to people ... whose knowledge of English was limited and whose native language had no word to explain the simplest idea in science or mechanics.'*

Premier Gambetta, had no difficulty in understanding the principles of Swan's lamps and their many applications. He paid several visits to the exhibition and initiated a demonstration that Henry gave to officers of the French Navy at Brest. Henry conducted experiments similar to those that he had performed for Captain Fisher at Portsmouth, and did his best to explain, in his halting French, the lighting scheme that had been installed on HMS *Inflexible*. Henry's workmen, who accompanied him to Brest, found it almost impossible to converse with the Frenchmen; Eli Bates, a great friend of Henry's and possessed of a broad Yorkshire accent, complained several times that he wished he could meet someone he could understand, and who could understand him! Nevertheless their efforts were rewarded and the French Navy placed 'considerable orders' for Swan lamps. Soon afterwards, Swan established a factory in Paris.

The contract with the French Navy was one of several that Henry negotiated while following-up enquiries received during the exhibition. One of Swan's objectives was to sell the patent rights to his incandescent lamp to foreign electrical companies. Henry was involved in this project but from a letter that Swan wrote to his wife on 22 September it is evident that little progress was being made:

> *'None of the foreign patents are sold yet. Mr E says he has had offers but did not feel free to accept as the sum offered - £40,000 for France - did not reach the amount that Mr Montgomery had named as the minimum. There is a 'serious' enquiry from Spain. I am perhaps unreasonably impatient that with all the enquiries, nothing is settled.'*

The reference to Montgomery shows that at this stage in his efforts to find international markets for his invention, Swan was establishing close links with the AABELC in London and Charles F Brush in America. This was all part of the making and breaking of agreements and joint venture that occurred between manufacturers of lamps, generators and distribution systems in the year before the evolvement of the two firms that began to dominate the electrical industry from the 1890 onwards: General Electric in the USA (whose 'ancestors' included Edison's and Brush's companies and the General Electric Company in Britain).

Swan's disappointment at the lack of progress in selling his patents was again evident in a letter he wrote on 21 October, in which he said: *'The patent business is all in a perfectly unsettled state. No sale has been made yet anywhere'*. However, he commented that the *'Spanish business looks very like going off'*. This was a reference to developments in Barcelona, where the local municipal council was considering installing electric lighting, even though it had only recently started to build a gasworks. Henry was promptly despatched to Barcelona to negotiate with a group of businessmen who were interested in buying Swan's Spanish patent rights. Before Henry set off he asked R S Watson to write a memorandum reviewing the position of the various parties who had an interest in the sale of Swan's patents. Luckily this document, written in Paris and dated 19 October 1881 has survived, enabling us to reconstruct the chronology of an important phase of Henry's career and that of Joseph Swan.[11]

The memo reveals that Swan's English patents had already been sold to the Swan Electric Light Company by the time Henry appeared on the scene. At this time Henry and Thomas Montgomery were associates at the AABELC. Henry introduced Montgomery to Swan, who as we know had a promising electric lamp but needed dynamos for his first schemes. Montgomery had sold Charles Brush's patents in England to the AABELC, and because of his experience in negotiations of this kind Swan made him responsible for selling his foreign patents. Montgomery was to receive half the purchase money paid to Swan for each sale, but had to pay his own travelling and other expenses, including those for *'any exhibition he might make of the lamps and all remunerations to sub-agents and persons employed by him'*. Montgomery's appointment was for two years, and he was instructed personally to visit all the capitals of the European Continent and the USA 'as soon as practicable' with the object of selling the foreign patents.

At the time the agreement was drawn up, Swan already expected to take part in the Paris Exposition. Faced with immediate and exceptionally heavy expenses, Montgomery argued that this event did not come within the scope of their agreement and offered to pay them on condition that they would be refunded to him from the proceeds of his foreign patent sales. Montgomery also offered to pay the expenses of all persons employed to help sell the patents except Henry Edmunds, who had already been appointed manager of Swan's exhibits in Paris.

---

[11] *Swan papers*, Tyne & Wear County Council Archives Dept, ref 1101/486.

In August, shortly before the exhibition opened, Montgomery went to the USA to sell Swan's patents there. The outcome was the formation of the Swan Incandescent Electric Light Company of New York, which later granted a manufacturing licence to the Swan Lamp Manufacturing Company of Cleveland. Montgomery appointed Henry to act as his agent for the sale of foreign patents in all other countries except Austria, Australia and New Zealand. Watson's memorandum also explains in detail two other projects in which Henry was involved: the lighting of the Opera House, and the manufacture of Swan lamps in France and Belgium:

> 'Mr Edmunds was requested to show the practical working of the lamps by undertaking to light the great chandelier ... Mr Swan was asked by him whether he objected to this and he consented to do it and Mr Montgomery agreed to it, subject to Mr Swan's approval. Finding that there were certain legal difficulties in the way, Mr Swan withdrew his consent and wired that the lighting was not to go on. The point raised was the following. According to French law ... a patentee who introduced into France articles manufactured in a foreign country and similar to those covered by his patent, forfeits all his rights. The Minister of Agriculture and Commerce may authorise the introduction of models of machines required for the patenting in France of an invention already patented elsewhere. Under this exemption ... the exhibition has been held and the lamps reintroduced into it. The minister was requested to sanction the lighting of the Opera but refused to do so for more than two days. He has however extended this permission for such time as may be necessary to try the experiment. It is a grave question as to whether the minister has not exceeded his powers in this matter, but as Mr Edison and Mr Maxim, as well as the Brush company, are all lighting under the same authority the danger to the patents has been diminished. This point must be carefully attended to before other exhibitions of the light are made.'

To illustrate the strictness of French patent law, Watson cited the experience of the Singer company, which patented its sewing machines in France and indeed made them there. However, the company made the machine's cases in the USA and imported them into France whereupon it was held that, in so doing, it had invalidated the machine's patents!

Watson then went on to review the question of manufacturing Swan lamps in France and Belgium. There was, he said, a considerable demand for the lamps in those countries, and in France local manufacture would help in the sale of the French patents, though this was a question of general policy that Montgomery, rather than Swan, would have to consider. In Belgium, lamps could be imported but local manufacture must begin within 12 months of the lamps being used commercially in any other country:

> 'The question of the manufacture of lamps is only incidentally concerned with Mr Edmunds' department, as he will have sufficient to attend to in the sale of patents, but as [he] will require many of the lamps, and as it is part of the arrangement with Mr Montgomery, it is well that he should know exactly what Mr Swan is willing to do. Mr Swan has formed a small manufacturing staff who can attend to the whole manufacture; that is, they can, amongst them, make all the parts of the lamp, can exhaust it and can install it. M de Waele, a large timber merchant in Antwerp, wishes to have fifty Swan lamps in his works at once ... the staff will proceed to Antwerp ... install the lamps and begin the manufacture of other lamps in premises supplied by M de Waele. In the meantime M Simon offers to find suitable premises in Paris for the manufacture of the lamps there. These premises should be fitted up under the advice of Mr Edmunds, who could probably spare Mr Mackenzie to see that the work is rapidly, thoroughly and economically carried out. M Simon offers to attend to the mercantile part of the French business, and it is probable that an arrangement to this effect could be made with him.'

It is clear from the memorandum that the decision to manufacture in France was not taken without a great deal of thought:

> 'If the patents could not be sold without it there would still be the question [of] whether it was worthwhile to do it and whether it could be properly carried out. The difficulty of any private person carrying on manufacture and installation would be great... The danger of arousing litigation is also to be considered. The other owners of incandescent lights would find you first in the field and wish to check your progress. It is no doubt wise policy on the part of incandescent lighters not to fight each others' patents if it can be avoided. The simple commencement of proceedings (whether they were carried on or not) would be sufficient to check the sale of the patent indefinitely. The great

> and exceptional difficulty arises from the fact that you can in most countries import and install lamps without invalidating the patent: you cannot do so in France. Mr Swan may say 'I am advised by Mr Edmunds and Mr Simon that this course must be taken in order to sell the foreign patents, therefore it belongs to Mr Montgomery'. Mr Montgomery will reply 'But you let me bind myself to make exhibitions of the light and, unless you manufacture, I cannot make them in France for I have no right to manufacture'. It is quite clear that the manufacture must not be permanent.'

The memorandum said that Simon had received an offer of £40,000 for the French patent rights but had rejected it because it was below the lowest price that Montgomery had set.

> 'The offer ... should have been accepted ... the plan adopted should have been to say that as his (Simon's) principals were in England and America, he would be obliged by the delay of a day in order that he might lay the application before them ... it is scarcely probable that a better offer will be made at present.'

Henry's negotiations to sell the Spanish patent rights were also criticised:

> 'The proposed sale ... has raised a question upon the construction of the agreements between Mr Swan and Mr Montgomery which had better be settled at once. It arises thus. Mr Edmunds agreed, if the transaction were carried through, to pay the Engineer of the Marquis de Campo £1,000. He explained this to Mr Swan and asked him if he was willing to accept £9,000 for the patent. Mr Swan agreed to do so, but he objected to any payment being made to the Engineer. Mr Edmunds sold the patent to the Marquis for £10,000 and agreed with the Engineer to give him the commission he asked. He now proposes to treat the sale as one for £9,000; that is, to deduct the commission paid to the Engineer before any division. But this is manifestly contrary to the spirit and letter of the Agreement. By them, Mr Montgomery is to receive one half of the receipts, less all expenses and commissions. The only exception is the ... exhibition in Paris. Mr Swan has nothing whatever to do with what commissions are paid or to whom. He could not refuse his assent to the payment of any commission, for Mr Montgomery has to pay it, he has

> not. The only thing that concerns him is the full price actually obtained for any patent. He is indeed to be consulted before a sale is made ... but if, after he has agreed to any special sum, a larger sum is obtained, he is entitled to receive the clear half of such larger sum ... Mr Montgomery is bound to tell him the true sum actually agreed upon and one half of that true sum belongs to Mr Swan. The very high commission given to Mr Montgomery is clearly to cover all expenses. It would be as reasonable to contend that Mr Swan was bound to accept the minimum prices arranged between him and Mr Montgomery tentatively when the detailed Agreement was entered into, as that he must accept a price named to him by Mr Edmunds before a sale but which proved to be less than the sum actually obtained.'

To illustrate the importance of the principle under consideration, the memorandum gave a detailed example:

> 'Mr Edmunds asks Mr Swan whether he will accept £20,000 for the Austrian patents, and he replies in the affirmative. Mr Edmunds, having to pay £5,000 in commission, asks and obtains £25,000 for the patents. Mr Swan would surely be entitled to £12,500, not £10,000. Or suppose that Mr Edmunds, finding the French patents hanging a little, asked Mr Swan to take £20,000 for them and he agreed to do so, but Mr Edmunds sold them afterwards for £40,000. He would not seriously contend that Mr Swan should only have £10,000 and Mr Montgomery £30,000. In every case of the sale of a foreign patent some commissions will have to be paid. Whether the payments are small or large is a question for Mr Montgomery and him alone. All that Mr Swan has to do with is the true amount actually obtained, and he is entitled to have a clear half of that.'

Having dealt with the complex question of commissions, the memorandum set out the way in which future foreign patent sales were to be negotiated. This was to be done by following-up the enquiries and correspondence generated during the Paris Exposition and by making personal visits to the countries where patents had been obtained:

> 'I suggest that Mr Edmunds should at once have his entire correspondence properly tabulated in a book specially prepared for the purpose, the several letters being entered under the heads of the different countries, and a proper digest being

made of each. When this is done it will be seen at a glance which countries should be visited first, and Mr Edmunds will go to them with the best kinds of letters of introduction. He will be furnished by Mr Swan with a Power of Attorney enabling him to enter into the necessary Agreement for Sale ... I suggest that he should take with him also another book containing the best selection of newspaper extracts bearing upon the Swan lamp, and that he should have sufficient specimens of the lamps always with him, so as to show what actually can be done with them on the spot.'

Henry was further instructed that any agreement should be put into writing, and no guarantee given of the validity of any of Swan's patents:

'This should not practically interfere with the sale of the patents ... the reasons for such a stipulation are manifest. We have something to sell which we believe to be of value ... we are not willing to have hanging over us for ten, twelve or fourteen years, nor even for one year, the possibility and uncertainty of legal proceedings over which we should have no control, and which might be brought on by injudicious action upon the part of the purchaser, or might even be brought about by his direct collusion.'

Watson recognised that because they were unable to offer guarantees, they might have to accept a lower price for their patents than they would wish. Nevertheless, Henry was left in no doubt that the conditions of sale 'must be strictly adhered to'. Watson went on to say that as much 'cash down' as possible should be obtained, and that any deferred cash payments were to be properly secured with the guarantee of a respectable bank:

'The most important of all things is prompt and decisive action. In such matters delays are not only dangerous but disastrous. Every help which Mr Swan or the writer can afford Mr Edmunds will always be at his service, but he must remember that the end he should have in view is not manufacturing or selling lamps, still less making exhibitions of them, but the speedy disposing of the patents. That can only be achieved satisfactorily by well considered measures, promptly taken.'

Armed with Watson's memorandum, which with its accompanying Power of Attorney document ran to 13 foolscap pages, Henry and Maurice Simon travelled from Paris to Barcelona to complete the negotiations with the group of businessmen who called themselves the Spanish Electric Society. They were met at the railway station and escorted to the Hotel des Quatre Nations, where they were entertained to dinner before enjoying an evening at the opera house. Next day, Henry and Simon and their hosts sat down to discuss the sale of Swan's patent rights. The earlier proposed agreement that had so displeased Watson seems to have been scrapped, for in the Swan company's archives in Newcastle-upon-Tyne there is a copy of a contract in which Henry agreed to sell Swan's Spanish patent and 100,000 lamps to the Spanish Electric Society for the sum of £50,000.[12] The evening after the deal was completed, Henry entertained his clients at a farewell banquet at his hotel. Early next morning, as he prepared to leave the hotel to catch a train to Paris, he asked for his bill, only to be told by the proprietor of the hotel that his clients had paid for his accommodation and for the banquet as well.

His work in Paris done, Henry returned to England and for a while continued to work for Joseph Swan. In December he was involved in a trial installation of Swan lamps and Brush generators at the House of Commons; he also bought 200 Swan lamps for his father's shop at a discount of 20 per cent. Presumably, the family business was now trading in electric lighting equipment as well as ironmongery. In February 1882 Henry asked if 51 of the lamps could be renewed without charge; Swan agreed to renew 25. At about this time 50 fully paid up shares in the Swan company were transferred to Henry, who a few weeks later applied to become Swan's agent for Yorkshire and Lancashire. The company's directors decided not to appoint an agent for the time being.

As winter gave way to spring in 1882, more interesting ventures and a new romance were in the offing for Henry. He was also about to face some unexpected business problems at the very time when, thanks to the success of the Paris Exposition, electrical engineers were hoping to make their fortunes.

---

[12] *Swan papers* Tyne & Wear County Council Archives dept., ref 1101/486.

CHAPTER SEVEN

Inventions and experiments

In the afterglow of Paris, London staged its own electrical exhibition. It was held in January 1882 in that symbol of the enterprising spirit of the British Empire, the Crystal Palace. This amazing glass and iron building, originally erected in Hyde Park for the Great Exhibition of 1851, had for nearly 30 years dominated the southern suburbs of the capital from the summit of Sydenham Hill, and now became the stage on which Thomas Edison's associate, Edward H Johnson, presented spectacular displays of incandescent lighting before an invited audience that included the omnipresent Prince of Wales. To demonstrate how safe the lights were, Johnson wrapped glowing bulbs in his handkerchief and smashed them while holding them in his hands. Edison, with his shrewd blend of genius and showmanship, was beginning to dominate the electric light business and while the exhibition was still in progress the Edison Electric Lighting Company opened the world's first central generating station for incandescent lighting, at 57 Holborn Viaduct in the heart of London. Two-thousand lamps, on the streets and in local shops, offices and the City Temple church, were supplied with current generated by Edison's second and third Jumbo dynamos, driven by two Babcock and Wilcox water-tube boilers. Although the company was American-inspired, it was financed with British capital and owed much of its success to the expertise of two British technical consultants, Dr John Hopkinson and John Ambrose Fleming.

Electric lighting in Britain reached the peak of its first boom in early 1882. Although Edison's central station in London was now attracting all the publicity, the Anglo-American Brush Electric Light Company had led the field until then because it was able to offer systems consisting of Brush dynamos and either Brush arc-lamps or Lane-Fox incandescent lamps. Lighting companies could obtain operating licences from the AABELC for either system and the AABELC's success is evident from its accounts, which show that its annual turnover surged to £200,000 in 1882, from only £80,000 in 1881. On 28 January Sir Henry Tyler presented an encouraging report when the shareholders gathered at the Cannon Street Hotel in the City of London for their annual meeting:

> 'We had a very fine display at the Paris Exhibition, which did us great credit... To show you that our Brush system is really an assured success I may mention the number of lamps and machines sold up to the present time. In England we have sold

220 dynamos and 2,711 arc-lamps, but in the USA where they have been longer at work, where coal is dearer and where there is more opening for rapid development for such a system, we have sold 850 machines and 12,457 arc-lamps. We are sometimes told that the arc-light is going out of fashion and that the incandescent light is to take its place but if, as I believe, 10,000 arc-lights have been sold during the past year, I think that there is a good deal to be done in the same direction in other countries besides America. Arc-lighting is more adapted for open spaces, streets, factories and the large manufacturies of all descriptions, while incandescent lighting is more adapted for domestic purposes, theatres, clubs and buildings of that description, and I believe there is a great future for both of them.'

That great future was about to be postponed. The British government, ever anxious to control and regulate new technologies, decided during 1882 that the time had come to impose some restrictions on the growth of the electric lighting industry. Unfortunately, in doing so it retarded its progress and allowed other countries to gain technical and commercial advantages. Readers familiar with the history of motoring will see this as another manifestation of the attitude that spawned the 'Red Flag Act' and other absurdities which discouraged the development of high performance motor cars in Britain, giving car manufacturers in France and Germany an advantage from which they quickly gained commercial benefit.

The 1870s and 1880s saw the birth of 'municipal trading' and the growth of state-owned public utilities. A precedent was set in 1870 when the Tramways Act gave town councils the power to pass by-laws regulating the operations of tram owners. At about this time, councils started buying gasworks and waterworks, and the government purchased, for £10 million, the plant and businesses of the various telegraph companies and gave the General Post Office the monopoly in telegraphy. From about 1879 onwards the government and its civil servants started to consider ways in which the electricity supply industry should be regulated. Certainly, some controls were necessary, if only to avoid a free for all in the digging up of streets for mains cables. A parliamentary select committee was formed to consider whether it was desirable to authorise local authorities to adopt schemes for lighting by electricity. The committee's deliberations ranged far and wide, extending at one point into the future growth of the telephone industry. Expert witnesses were interviewed by the committee, and it was at one of these sessions that William Preece uttered his famous gaffe (referred to in a previous chapter) about there being such a *'superabundance of messengers [and] errand boys'* that the telephone would not be *'largely adopted'* by the British general public.

After exhaustive hearings and debates, parliament passed the Electric Lighting Bill, which became law on 12 August 1882. From this date, companies wishing to supply electricity from a central generating station had to obtain a licence or 'provisional order' from the Board of Trade. The licences ran for only seven years, the provisional orders for 21 years. In both cases, applications by local authorities were given precedence over private companies. Local authorities were also empowered to purchase compulsorily the generating stations of the private companies when the provisional orders expired. The price paid to the company was to be determined solely by the value of the plant, with nothing extra for goodwill or current or future profits. When the Bill was passed, prospective investors in electrical companies immediately took fright. When J A Fleming told Edison about the new legislation he exclaimed, *"They've throttled it!"*. How right he was. In America the electrical industry surged ahead and the power station companies were soon paying out dividends of 6 to 14 per cent. In Britain the AABELC's performance speaks for itself; its profit slumped to zero by the end of 1882 and most of its associated regional companies were liquidated.

The speed with which the recession hit the firm is evident from a report published in *The Electrician* on 28 July, only two weeks before the new legislation took effect. The report concerned a visit of 130 members of the Society of Engineers to the AABELC's lamp works in Belvedere Road, Lambeth, and dynamo factory in Borough Road and ended with the comment: *'The company is just now extremely busy - in fact quite unable to execute orders fast enough'*. Most of the firm's £200,000-worth of sales in 1882, which included 8,700 lamps, had been achieved during the first half of the year but from August onwards manufacturing suffered, leading to many redundancies in the workforce of 800. The company had to survive as a contractor, installing and maintaining electrical equipment. In 1888 the Electric Lighting Act was amended to extend to 42 years the period covered by the provisional orders. The investors returned but by then Britain's overseas competitors, especially in America were the leaders in electrical generation and distribution, and in the development of lamps and electrical equipment.

During the first six months of 1882 Henry Edmunds was busy working for Joseph Swan and the AABELC and running his own business in Halifax. On 1 July *The Electrician* reported that he had designed and registered a new form of safety plug for incandescent lamps. Henry was well aware of the lack of plugs and other accessories for Swan's lamps and had evidently been giving the matter a great deal of thought since returning from Paris. The press report described his plug as follows:

> 'The only safety plug in the market was that devised by Mr Edison and not only were they [sic] far from perfect in operation or appearance, but unattainable by those who wish to use any system but the Edison. Instead of lead wire which oxidises and is eaten away by exposure, Messrs Edmunds employ tin, lead or other metal foil, so attached to an insulating substance that neither heat nor damp will loosen it and of such bulk that it will carry enough current for one lamp but little more. In the numerous installations made by Messrs Edmunds these appliances are extensively employed and are now coming into general use with those companies who do most of the incandescent lighting in this country.'

When the prospects of the British electrical industry took a sudden nosedive, Henry made his third visit to America, to help Thomas Montgomery set up a joint lamp manufacturing venture for Joseph Swan and Charles Brush. The Swan Incandescent Electric Light Company was formed to introduce the Swan lamp into the USA in 1882 and at about this time Brush bought Swan's US patents. Production of Swan lamps began in Cleveland, home of the Brush Electric Company, a few years later. The venture was never a success but Henry's visit did result in his having another fortuitous meeting with ex-Governor Henry Howard, after which he embarked on another series of unplanned meetings and introductions that changed the direction of his life and career.

Sometime in the summer of 1882, probably during August, Henry arrived in New York and checked in at the Fifth Avenue Hotel. By coincidence, Howard was also staying there; at breakfast next morning he was very surprised to see Henry, and told him that he had heard of his work at the Paris Exposition and his success in selling electric lamps to the Royal Navy for the *Inflexible*. Howard invited Henry to visit him and his family in Providence and meet some of the local industrialists. Soon, Henry was once again boarding a train at New York and settling down for the five and a half hour journey which took him through the countryside bordering Long Island Sound, past the creeks and coves of Narragansett Bay and into the busy city, which would soon become his second home.

Rhode Island is the smallest of the United States and is part of New England, where immigrants led by the Pilgrim Fathers settled in the seventeenth century. One of the immigrants was Thomas Howard, born in about 1643. He was the forefather of a large family, which gave Rhode Island several of its leading lawyers, politicians and industrialists, including Judge Jesse Howard, who in 1825 married Mary King. (Mary's maternal grandfather, Nicholas Mathewson, had served with the Revolutionary forces during the American War of Independence). Jesse and Mary Howard had two sons, Henry and Albert Crawford, and a daughter, Abby Alice. Both sons distinguished themselves in many ways.

Albert Howard, the youngest, set up his own mercantile business at the age of 17; five years later he embarked on a career in banking. During the American Civil War he served as a captain in the 11th Regiment of the Rhode Island Volunteers, later being promoted to the rank of lieutenant-colonel. He became a member of the Legislature of Rhode Island in 1873 and later served two successive terms as Lieutenant-Governor of the state, under Governor Van Zandt. In 1853 he had married Ellen Murray, from South Waverly, Pennsylvania, but by the time he began his first term of office Ellen had died, leaving him with two daughters, Alice and Ellen Murray, and three sons, Albert Harris, Henry Augustus and Jesse Wayland.

Henry Howard also gained useful experience in business early in his career and in 1848 began studying law in the office of Governor W W Hoppin. He was called to the Bar in 1851, the year in which he married Catherine, daughter of ex-Governor Elisha Harris, a lineal descendant of Roger Williams, the founder of Rhode Island. Henry practised as a lawyer in Providence until 1858, when he opened the New York City office of Elisha Harris's Harris Manufacturing Company, which owned several cotton mills in Providence. Harris died suddenly in 1861 and within a short time Henry Howard was appointed president of the company. He soon became one of the leading figures in Providence's business community, his particular interest being the application of new scientific inventions to manufacturing and communications. He was also a founder and president of the Providence Telephone Company, and president of both the Pintsch Gas Company (which made a system for illuminating railway trains with compressed gas) and the Armington & Sims Engine Company. He was associated in various capacities with many other concerns and inventors, including the Brown & Sharpe Manufacturing Company (which built America's first linear dividing engine and universal grinding machine), the Providence Locomotive Company, James Brown Herreshoff (inventor of the 'beehive' tubular steam boiler and designer of the boiler and hull of the US Navy's first torpedo boat), William Hochhausen (inventor of arc-lamps and generators), and Colonel Hazard and Robert W Blackwell, electric traction and tramway pioneers.

Through Armington & Sims, Howard was associated with Thomas Edison's early central electricity generating stations in America. The first of these, in Pearl Street, Manhattan, was opened on 4 September 1882, after an almost disastrous trial-run two months earlier when it proved impossible to synchronise the two Porter-Allen steam engines that drove the station's generators; the fault was due to the engines' ineffectual governors. To quote Edison, *'one engine would stop and the other would run up to a thousand revolutions; and then they would seesaw'*. An eyewitness reported: *'The engines and dynamos made a horrible racket, and the place seemed to be filled with sparks and flames of all colors'*. On another occasion, Henry Edmunds came across a less spectacular but equally conspicuous failure of a steam engine to work in harmony with its dynamo, when he noticed that every 'beat' of the engine was being reproduced as a rhythmic fluctuation in the brightness of the lamps served by the dynamo. Edison's problem was solved by a talented engine designer, Gardiner Sims, who developed an engine with a mechanical governor controlled by centrifugal force; two of these engines were built for Pearl Street in 1882 and soon afterwards another four were installed. Edison was well pleased, saying *"I fail to see what improvement in its mechanism can be suggested. They have a higher economy than any other automatic cut-off engine I have tested"*. He ran one of the engines non-stop for 16 days 17½ hours and afterwards found it to be in first-class condition, no readjustments being required. The achievement is reminiscent of that of the Rolls-Royce Silver Ghost twenty-five years later, when the car was driven for a distance of 15,000 miles, during which it had to make only one involuntary stop; this was to allow a petrol tap to be opened, after it had been shaken shut during a journey over a bumpy road. After the trial, Royal Automobile Club observers certified that the car was *'in all respects in perfect running order, and in exceptionally good condition'*. Sims and Henry Royce, with their similar standards of reliability, would have had much in common, even though one drew his power from steam, the other from internal combustion. After becoming Edison's salvation at Pearl Street, Armington & Sims engines were installed in cotton mills in Rhode Island; they were of particular interest to Henry Edmunds and his contemporaries because they were the only automatic high-speed engines that could drive dynamos by means of a belt attached to their fly-wheels.

During the years leading up to the time when he started supporting the latest inventions, Howard also found time to pursue a political career. He was a founder of the Republican Party in 1856 and in that same year was elected to represent the town of Coventry in the state Legislature. He became Governor of Rhode Island in 1873 (coincidentally, the year when a financial panic caused a recession in the state that was to last for six years) and was re-elected unopposed in 1874. He declined an invitation to serve for a third term in 1875 but remained prominent in public life as well as in business, his experience in both fields being called upon in 1878 when, as President Hayes' assistant commissioner at the Universal Exposition in Paris, he prepared a detailed report on the textile exhibits.

Despite the recession, the late 1870s and early 1880s were years of great change and progress in Rhode Island. Before the American Revolution, molasses was the cornerstone of its economy; it was imported from the West Indies and either exchanged for English-made goods or distilled into rum, some of which was bartered for slaves from Africa. Modern industry had been introduced into the state in 1786, when a cotton spinning company was established in Providence; the Pawtuxet Valley, abundant in water power, became the centre of Rhode Island's cotton industry, which in turn became the state's major employer. When Henry Edmunds visited Providence in 1877 and 1882 he would have noticed a strong resemblance between day-to-day life there and in the textile-producing towns in his native West Riding of Yorkshire and the neighbouring county, Lancashire. The population of Providence had quadrupled, to 105,000, in only 20 years; water power in the mills had been supplanted by coal; one million tonnes were being landed at Providence docks every year, five times the amount imported in the late 1850s. Horse-drawn trams clattered through streets crowded with factory workers. But by 1882 glimpses of modern America could already be seen; the Rhode Island Electric Lighting Company, Providence's first electricity company, had been formed, heralding the day when new industries - principally jewellery manufacture and metal production - as well as the cotton mills would depend on electric light and power, and when electric traction in the shape of trolley buses would supersede the horse-drawn trams.

The growth of commerce around Providence required improvements in communications and, as we have already seen, Henry Howard at one time considered in investing in the Bell telephone. He abandoned that particular idea, telling Bell that he suffered from heart disease. Presumably, he thought he might be risking his health by making a direct investment in what he may have regarded as a venture that would require much of his time and energy; he already had many business and political commitments. Nevertheless, Howard was confident that the telephone would become indispensable and formed the Providence Telephone Company. His son, Charles Taylor Howard, who had recently graduated from Brown University with the degree of Bachelor of Philosophy, joined him as assistant secretary. In 1881 Charles became secretary and treasurer; he remained with the company when it merged with the New England Telephone and Telegraph Company and became a vice-president in 1925, a year before he retired.

Providence's telephone pioneers played an important role in developing Bell's system. Important technical improvements were made to Bell's telephone at Brown University in the city by John Peirce, a professor of chemistry. Peirce was a relative of the Howard and a direct descendant of Roger Williams. His interests extended to physics and mathematics, his studies in these fields leading him to invent several improvements in duplex and quadruplex telegraphy. Peirce and two colleagues, Professor Eli Whitney Blake and Dr William F Channing, followed Bell's experiments with great interest and, at around the time when Bell and Thomas Watson were having their first telephone conversations, Peirce and his colleagues, assisted by a group of students, decided that they too would try and improve the instrument. Their activities annoyed Bell, who suspected that the university team's interest in telephony was not merely academic. However, 'the experimenters', as Bell patronisingly called them, were able to convince him that they were working solely in the interests of science, with no thought of commercial gain; by early 1877 two of the students, James H Earle and John J Greene, were conversing over a line strung between their rooms in Hope College. Later, Earle and his roommate, James L Wells, constructed a phonograph of their own design and played a recording of *Mary had a little lamb* (no doubt inspired by Thomas Edison) over a telephone line between two rooms.

Peirce was particularly critical of Bell's telephone because its transmitter and receiver weighed more than ten pounds and were housed together in an oblong metal box. A short length of tubing protruded from the box; the user spoke into this when transmitting, and held it to his ear when listening, a clumsy arrangement that led to a notice being fixed to the instrument: *'Do not try to listen with your mouth or speak with your ear'*. Inside the box, a diaphragm of gold-beater's 'skin', glued to a metal armature, crudely reproduced whatever 'conversations' the users were able to sustain while trying to point the appropriate part of their anatomy towards the tube.

'The experimenters' had two objectives: to improve the quality of the telephone's reception, and to design what we would today call an 'ergonomically efficient' transmitter and receiver, portable and easy to use. Blake improved the sound quality by redesigning the diaphragm and making it from ferrotype plate; Peirce came up with the idea of a funnel-shaped mouthpiece, and worked out the optimum depth, curvature and width of its aperture. From this the team evolved a 'hand telephone', housed in a much smaller box than Bell's. When the prototype was installed at Rowland Hazard's house on Williams Street in the late winter or early spring of 1877, listeners in a study at the end of the long hall were amazed to find that they could recognise the voices of individual callers at the reception room just inside the front door. By now 'the experimenters' were sometimes abreast, sometimes ahead, of Bell's own developments. Soon after the demonstrations at Williams Street, William Ely, one of Blake's physics students, suggested an improvement in the design of the magnet assembly that created the telephone's current. Ely's 'bar magnet' receiver produced a clearer and more distinct tone than any of its predecessors and could be fitted within a separate hand-held mahogany housing, which Peirce called the 'butter-stamp' receiver after its shape. The first pair of these receivers was despatched to Bell before being seen or used by anyone outside Peirce's group. Bell later claimed that he had been working on parallel lines and had made a similar hand receiver a few days before he received the ones from Brown University; credit for the invention remained a matter of controversy for some years. One of the first authors of a book on the telephone, George B Prescott, claimed in 1879 that Bell had not given sufficient credit to Peirce and his colleagues.

When he arrived in Providence in the late summer of 1882, Henry Edmunds would have heard all about the city's latest developments in telephony and electrical engineering from the Howards. Henry would later resume his own experiments with the telephone but for the time being his main concern was to help Thomas Montgomery establish a factory for Swan lamps. Joseph Swan had told Henry that when made in large quantities, the lamps could be produced at a cost of about two shillings each. Until this could be organised in America, Charles Brush's new Swan Incandescent Electric Light Company was naturally anxious to import the lamps as cheaply as possibly, especially as they were subject to a very high *ad valorem* import duty. Henry took 2000 lamps to America, which were invoiced at cost price. On arrival at New York, Henry had to declare their value to the Customs officials, and show them the invoice. They, of course, knew the price at which Edison's lamps were being sold in the USA and immediately objected that Swan's lamps could not possibly be manufactured for the amount shown on the invoice. The lamps were held at the docks 'pending enquiries', while the Customs department asked the US Consul in Yorkshire to check Swan's prices. The consul went to a retail shop and bought six lamps, for which he paid five shillings each. The price on Henry's invoice was in the region of two shillings per lamp, and the Customs officials decided to confiscate the entire consignment. Thomas Montgomery intervened, but he could only secure the release of the lamps by agreeing that they should be valued at five shillings each, and by paying a duty of 33.3 per cent on that price. Henry wrote afterwards: *'The crushing duty levied upon imported lamps made it necessary for us to start manufacturing ourselves with as little delay as possible, because rival lamps were being put on the market before ours.'*

Despite the urgency of the situation, it was not until 1885 that Swan lamps went into production in Cleveland.

Henry's visit to the USA was only a partial success; introducing Swan's lamps proved to be more difficult than he had expected, but when he returned home sometime in September 1882 he had concluded arrangements to introduce Hochhausen arc-lamps and Armington & Sims engines into England. He also returned as a married man.

Henry's bride was Ellen Murray Howard ('Nelly' to her family and close

Mr Albert G Howard requests the pleasure of your company …'

An invitation to the wedding of his daughter Ellen and Henry Edmunds.

friends). She was 26 years old and the youngest daughter of Albert Crawford Howard. In March 1881 Mary Alice, Albert's first daughter, had married Arthur Whitman Claflin, whose family owned a medical supplies company on Acorn Street, Providence. Now, just 18 months later, Ellen too was leaving home, and leaving Rhode Island, after what must have been a whirlwind courtship. From Henry's *Reminiscences* we know that he met Ellen at Henry Howard's house; but we do not know when they met. It is possible that they were introduced during Henry's first visit to Providence, in 1877. He returned to America in 1878, when problems arose with the Farmer-Wallace generators but, although we know that on that occasion he travelled as far north of New York as Bridgeport, Connecticut, to meet Hiram Maxim, we do not know if he went on to Providence, to renew his friendship with the Howards, or whether any members of the Howard family came down to see him while he was in New York. But whatever happened in 1877 or 1878, no romance developed between Henry and Ellen and in 1880 he married Annie Wayman. Whatever the circumstances of their first meeting, Henry and Ellen were married in Providence on 7 September 1882;

and although she belonged to a distinguished local family and had a wide circle of friends and relations, no notice or report of her wedding appeared in the *Providence Journal,* the city's principal newspaper. Nor were any of Henry's family likely to have been present; so far as we know, he had travelled to America alone. Who, one wonders, was his Best Man: Thomas Montgomery, perhaps, or one of the first friends he made in America, Thomas Wallace? Three weeks after their wedding, Henry and Ellen arrived in England. On 28 September his grandmother, Mary Hatton, wrote to him from 8 Northampton Park, London:

> *'I am very pleased to have to congratulate you and your beloved wife upon your safe arrival in England. I trust for many years to come you will be very happy in each other's love and the married duties that are already devolved upon you. As I hear you are coming to town on Saturday will you kindly bring your dear Nelly, your sister Edith and Miss England with you on Sunday afternoon next, to take tea about 6 o'clock, and have one more peep at your fading grandmother.'*

'Will you kindly bring your dear Nelly ... to take tea'.
An invitation to Henry from his grandmother, Mary Hatton.

Henry and Ellen probably lived in lodgings in the weeks immediately after they arrived in England, but sometime during the first six months of 1883 they bought or leased a house in Streatham, in the southern suburbs of London. They called their house Rhodehurst. At about the same time as the Edmunds settled in Streatham, Joseph Swan and his family moved to Lauriston, a new house in Bromley, a few miles from Streatham. By now Swan and Edison had resolved their differences over patents and formed the Edison and Swan United Electric Company. Swan had also developed an improved non-fibrous filament for his lamps (an idea that later led to the invention of artificial silk) and had opened a factory at Ponders End, on the northern outskirts of London, which was manufacturing more than 10,000 lamps a week. We do not know if Henry benefited from Swan's long-awaited commercial success, but it seems unlikely that he did. Characteristically, in 1883 Henry was again embarking on new ventures. On 10 April he applied for a British patent for an invention described as *'Improvements in electric lamps and in the electric circuit connections and devices for same'*. His application states that he was at this time temporarily living in New York City. Ellen was by now more than six months pregnant, and it seems likely that she stayed at home while Henry was engaged in various electrical projects, including we presume the experiments that preceded his patent application. This was granted on 10 October and covered a number of devices for insulating electric cables, installing circuit fuses and switching incandescent lamps on and off. We know from Henry's own remarks that he was very conscious of the lack of fuses and other means of preventing fires and short-circuits in electric lighting installations, and clearly this provoked him to draw up his own ideas.

Despite his continuing interest in incandescent lamps, Henry was looking for an opportunity to launch the Hochhausen arc-lamp in Britain. He did not have to wait long. An International Fisheries Exhibition was due to open at South Kensington in May 1883 and in March the organisers decided to illuminate the exhibition galleries by electricity, and remain open until 10.00pm every day to allow the lighting to be seen to its best effect. Davey, Paxman & Co of Colchester won a contract to install six engines with a combined horsepower of nearly 700 to drive the various exhibitors' dynamos and lights. Immediately after he returned from America, Henry set to work to organise a display of six Hochhausen lamps, mounted on a tall mast. This was, Henry claimed, the first example of 'central lighting' in Britain. The exhibition was opened by the Prince of Wales, but not before the organisers had experienced the kind of hiatus that usually precedes such an occasion. *The Electrician* reported:

> 'To the surprise of those of us who had seen the buildings and grounds two or three days before, the Exhibition was practically complete in all its details. The electric lighting department is the most backward and Messrs. Davey, Paxman & Co. will have to work hard to get all their engines ready. This is not their fault. On the opening day one engine was at work, driving a Siemen's dynamo which supplies current to a considerable number of Swan lamps in the Prince of Wales Pavilion... the lamps are 20 candle power and have the great resistance of 95 volts, requiring a current of 0.6 amps.'

In July the Prince of Wales made a second visit to the exhibition, accompanied by other members of the Royal family. Henry wanted to improve the way in which his lamps were suspended, and while on his way to South Kensington with some special fittings, supplied by Waygood of Hatton Garden, the dog-cart in which he and two of his mechanics were travelling was involved in an accident. Here is his own account of what happened:

> 'A slight shower of rain had made the road slippery. A two-horsed bus was taking in passengers at the corner of Sloane Street and just as our vehicle was about to pass, the bus pulled out into the roadway, throwing our dog-cart against a passing brougham and completely overturning it, throwing us all into the roadway. The two mechanics were badly hurt. The driver escaped without injury. I was thrown against the wheels of the omnibus, and only missed going underneath it by clinging to the brake. I was dragged a little distance before the omnibus stopped, and then struggled to my feet. A lady called out: "Won't someone take this gentleman to the hospital?" I replied: "I must get to the Exhibition". "Look at your arm", she said; and for the first time I noticed blood streaming down my arm. The limb was dressed at St George's Hospital, and for some weeks I was laid up at home.'

According to *The Engineer* the exhibition contained *'one of the most interesting displays of electrical plant ever got together ... nothing so complete, so efficient or of equal magnitude and value has ever been shown under one roof in Great Britain'*. Davey, Paxman & Co's six engines drove 40 dynamos of various types, and because the lighting displays allowed the exhibition to remain open until late in the evening, more than 2.6 million people had attended the event by the time it closed at the end of October.

After the exhibition one of the Hochhausen lamps was sent to Blackpool; as a result Henry met Michael Holroyd Smith, another Halifax-born engineer and inventor. Smith, aged 36, was at this time pioneering electric tramways. In December 1882 he had written to the *Halifax Courier* criticising proposals to build a cable-hauled tramway in the town. *'Why waste power hauling eighty tons of steel rope?'*, he asked. *'Why not employ electricity as the motive power?'* In 1883 Smith built three experimental narrow-gauge electric tramways. The first of these was driven by a Siemens D3 dynamo that acted as an electric motor, and drove the wheels of a truck. Next, Smith wanted to test the idea of collecting the current for his tramcars from a central conduit running parallel to the rails. Louis John Crossley, who by now had a well-equipped private electrical laboratory at Moorside, his home at Skircoat Green, allowed Smith to build two tracks, one about one hundred and fifty feet long, the other twice that length, in the grounds of Moorside, the current for the cars being provided by Crossley's Gramme dynamo and Smith's Siemens D3. If, as is likely, Henry visited Halifax at the time of these experiments he could not have failed to see them and may perhaps have assisted: his parents' house, Southfield, overlooked Moorside. The experiments were successful and Smith moved to Blackpool, where the city council was considering building an electric tramway along the busy seafront.

Smith, whose work in Blackpool established him as a distinguished pioneer of electric trams, suggested that Henry should introduce his traction system into the United States. Soon after meeting Smith, Henry went to Rhode Island and discussed the idea with Robert Blackwell, but Blackwell maintained that the system that he had already chosen was superior. However, it was as a result of meeting Smith and Blackwell that Henry took a professional interest in the progress of electric traction, and quite by chance became involved in a controversy over the type of locomotives that should run on London's first 'tube' railway, the City of London and Southwark Subway. This incident, like so many others in Henry's career, occurred quite by chance.

On 23 July 1883, Ellen gave birth to a son, Howard Maurice; the event was announced in *The Times* and soon afterwards a man named Henry Husson called on Henry at Rhodehurst and asked him whether he was the Mr Edmunds who in 1877 had been elected the first president of the North of England Cyclists' Association. Henry confirmed this, and Husson explained that, as secretary of the Liverpool Cyclists' Club, he had attended the association's first annual meeting, held in Harrogate in

1877 while Henry was in the USA. The two men reminisced about their cycling days and Henry Edmunds recalled that the first bicycle he rode was a machine weighing 130 pounds ('as strong as a farm wagon') that Herbert Crossley had purchased in Paris in the early 1870s. A few years later, in Coventry, Henry bought a machine which had a front wheel 48 inches in diameter; he once rode this from Halifax to York, a distance of 40 (very undulating) miles; this was a remarkable achievement in the 1870s. When Halifax's first cycling club was formed, Henry became its captain, and took part in many long-distance runs.

Henry Husson was a nephew of Sir Henry Tate, the wealthy sugar merchant and art patron. Husson introduced Henry Edmunds to Sir Henry, whose home, Park Hill, on the north side of Streatham Common, was virtually 'round the corner' from Rhodehurst. The two men shared a common interest in electric lighting (Park Hill was one of the first mansions to be lit in this way) and in later years Henry often acknowledged the encouragement that he had received from Sir Henry in the days when it was not easy to persuade property owners to install this new form of illumination. During one visit to Park Hill Henry met James Henry Greathead, who had developed a tunnelling machine called 'the Greathead Shield', which was being used to bore the underground tubes for the 'City and Southwark'. The world's first underground railway, the Metropolitan, had been built in London in the early 1860s in 'cut and cover' tunnels, the construction of which involved digging huge trenches, laying the rails, and placing roofs above the tracks so that roads or houses could be built above the railways. The trains were steam-powered and equipped with condensers, which allowed them to run from one open section of track to the next without emitting steam or smoke. That, at least, was the theory! But when the need arose for railways that could burrow deep beneath streets and buildings, and reach the heart of the city, a construction method that would not create havoc on the surface was required; so, too, was a non-polluting form of traction.

The Greathead Shield solved the first problem. Powered hydraulically, it bored through the London clay, unseen and unheard from the streets above. As it progressed, it left behind a series of cast-iron rings which lined the tunnel, the space between the rings and the sides of the tunnel being filled with liquid cement which was forced into place by compressed air.

London's first bored tube (as distinct from 'cut and cover') railway, the 'Tower Subway', ran under the River Thames between termini near the Monument and London Bridge Station. Its tunnels were bored by a precursor of the Greathead Shield, invented by Peter William Barlow.

Rhodehurst, Henry and Ellen's first home in Streatham
(Author's collection)

Park Hill, Streatham, where Henry met James Henry Greathead
(Author's collection)

The railway had cable-hauled carriages but as these could carry only twelve people at a time, the subway's capacity was too small to allow it to recover its capital and running costs; the service ceased on 23 December 1870, after operating for only four months. In the mid-1880s work began on the more ambitious 'City and Southwark' scheme, which ran from King William Street, north of the Thames, to Southwark and on to the Oval and Stockwell. Greathead, who had been Barlow's contractor on the 'Tower Subway', was made chief engineer of the new scheme and for it he developed an improved version of Barlow's shield. But despite the fact that, by the time work began, Magnus Volk had opened Britain's first electric railway at Brighton, the 'City and Southwark' was planned as a cable railway.

Greathead had been impressed by the cable tramways built on Clay Street Hill, San Francisco, and Highgate Hill, London, and was sure that a similar traction system would work equally well underground. Henry Edmunds thought otherwise; when he met Greathead he enthused about the developments he had seen in Rhode Island and urged him to consider electric locomotives. As a result of this conversation, Henry said afterwards, the scheme for cable haulage was abandoned. The announcement that electric traction was to be used instead was made by the chairman of the promoting company, Charles Grey Mott, at a shareholders' meeting and reported in *The Electrician:*

> *'The chairman ... said that the question of the best method of working the line, and the nature of the power to be used, had for some time exercised the special consideration of the directors. It was essential that whilst the trains should be very frequent and the transit rapid, the cost of running and maintenance should be kept as low as possible. In many respects, the system of endless cable should be the best, but it had certain disadvantages in its application to the working of the line, which it was not easy to overcome. After much careful consideration the directors had arrived at the conclusion that electrical force, conveyed by continuous conductors, offered the best solution to the difficulty and would give a motive power at once reliable and economical.'*

Today's network of deep-level railways under London stems from the success of the world's first electrified tube railway, the 'City and Southwark'. Other promoters soon came forward with plans to extend 'the tube' to other parts of London. But the opponents of electric traction were reluctant to admit defeat, and employed covert methods to try and prevent it being adopted for the new schemes, as Henry himself recalled:

> 'The question of London traffic was then agitating many minds, and a select committee of the House of Commons was sitting on the subject. I was approached by a powerful representative of the London underground railways and asked if I would accept a retaining fee to state before the committee that from my observations, I was of the opinion that electric traction was not sufficiently developed to render it suitable for their railways in place of the steam locomotives then in use. About the same time, a firm of solicitors sent me a retaining fee of fifty guineas. On my asking what they wished me to do for it, they replied that I was to keep away from the select committee, lest I might be asked to give evidence in support of the opposition to electric traction and I might be asked to state that it was not sufficiently developed for railway work!'

Despite the problems created by the Electric Lighting Act of 1882, the 1880s became an era of exciting progress in electrical engineering, once the ability of the mysterious new force to move vehicles as well as provide illumination had been proven. This created opportunities for entrepreneurs to set up factories to make the vast range of ancillary equipment - wires, cables, switches, lamp-holders, connectors and so forth - demanded by companies who were now introducing electric light and power on a scale that, only a few years earlier, would have been unimaginable. Among those entrepreneurs were Walter Twiss Glover, formerly a manufacturer of machines for braiding the steel hoops of crinoline dresses, and Frederick Henry Royce, who had invested £20 (probably his entire savings) to set up a small factory in a back street in Manchester, where he hoped to make his way in the world as an electrical and mechanical engineer. With customary good fortune, Henry met Glover and Royce at a time when they both needed the kind of encouragement and practical help that Henry was able to offer.

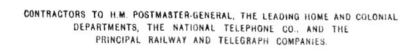

The cover of Glover's price list for 1893

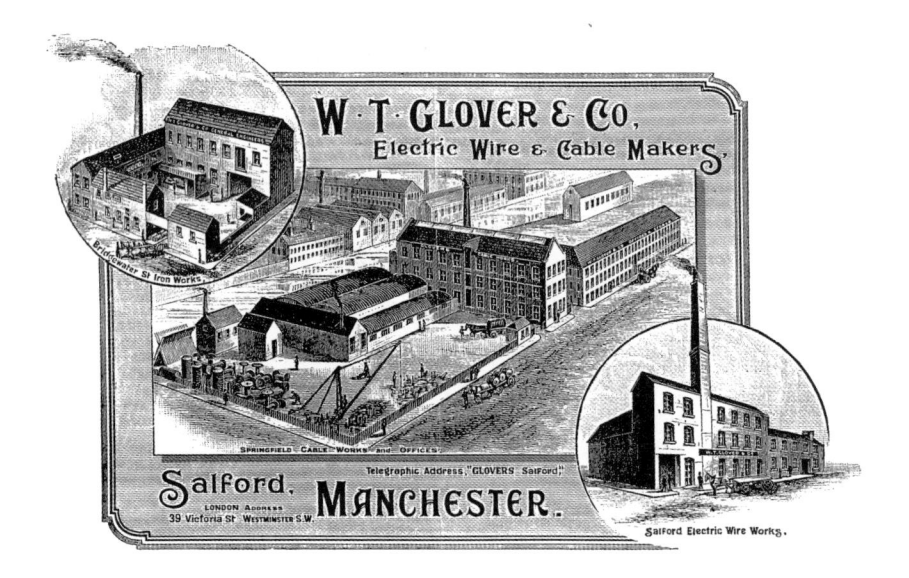

Glover's factories in Salford
[*From Glover's Centenary, 1868 - 1968* (BICC Cables Ltd)]

CHAPTER EIGHT
A royal command

In 1868, when he was only 22 years old, Walter Glover founded the Bridgewater Street Iron Works in Salford, on the western outskirts of Manchester. There he made machinery for the city's booming cotton industry and ran an agency for yarn and cloth traders. In the 1870s he met George T James of Nottingham, who had invented various machines for making cotton braids and cords. One of the machines had been adapted to apply braid to crinoline dressmakers' hoops and to the lead wires from which hair curlers were made. Glover wanted to use this machine to apply silk and cotton to electrical conductors, so he formed a partnership with James and established a second company in Bridgewater Street, the Salford Electric Wire Works. Initially, about twenty men were employed making cotton-covered and braided insulated copper wires, but soon a demand developed for insulated cables and cable-making machines.

Walter Twiss Glover
[From *Glover's Centenary, 1868-1968* (BICC Cables Ltd)]

In 1880 Glover opened another factory, the Springfield Lane Cable Works, and started producing conductors insulated with up to three layers of rubber and covered with waterproof tape and cotton braid. One of his first customers was Henry Edmunds, who in 1881 was looking for a firm to make special flexible insulated wires and cables for Joseph Swan's display at the Paris Electrical Exposition. Henry was considering winding cotton spirally on to the conductors but Glover persuaded him that it would be much better to braid them, and offered a selection of colours and patterns from which Henry was soon able to find exactly what he wanted. In 1882 Glover won a silver medal for his wires and cable-making machinery at the electrical exhibition at the Crystal Palace; in 1885, at the International Electrical Inventors' Exhibition, he won gold and silver medals.

By this time Henry had parted company with Joseph Swan, John Sellon and his other friends and associates of the early incandescent lamp era. His work with Swan and Sellon in particular had given him valuable experience, and there was a time when he and Sellon seemed to have a promising future as co-inventors. Their patented *Improvements in electric lamps*, described earlier, were followed by a patent for *An improved mode of regulating electric currents*, a provisional patent for regulating the current supplied to iridium incandescent lamps, and a provisional patent for generating electricity. Why Henry parted company with Swan and Sellon is not known but his visit to the USA in 1882 and his marriage mark another important change in the direction of his life and career. For the next few years he worked in London as an electrical consultant and agent and by 1884 had an office at 2 Victoria Mansions, London SW, in an area favoured by consulting engineers. He was now pursuing various ideas, applying for (and in some cases obtaining) patents on several more inventions. None of these appears to have been of any commercial value, although a few of them are of unusual interest.

His *Improvements in electric lamps and in the electric circuit connections and devices for same* have already been mentioned. This patent covered various domestic incandescent lamp fittings. These included a new type of switch, activated by twisting the base of the lamp; a method of wiring chandeliers and electroliers into electrical circuits; and a way of converting gas-lit imitation candles in chandeliers into electric imitation candles - an interesting example of how traditional styles had to be maintained, despite the introduction of new sources of illumination.

This patent application and its reference to Henry's sojourn in New York, is the only evidence we have that Henry returned to the USA in

1883. Another application suggests that during the next two years he made another visit, for on 25 August 1885, he and Charles T Howard were the 'communicators' for a patent application by J Y Johnson of 47 Lincoln's Inn Fields, London, for a toll telephone, described as *'a telephone that cannot be used for communication until a specified coin or token has been deposited in the instrument'*. This idea pre-dated the world's first coin-operated call box, installed in Hartford, Connecticut, in 1889.

The toll telephone venture with Charles Howard may indicate that in the mid-1880s Henry was still hoping to become a telephone pioneer in Britain. Electrical engineering remained his principal interest however, and on 18 January 1886, he and a Mr W T Goolden applied for, but subsequently abandoned, a patent on a method for generating and utilising electricity. Little is known about Henry's brief partnership with Goolden. In 1885 Henry's name disappears from the London Post Office Directory's entry for 2 Victoria Mansions and is replaced by one for a firm named Edmunds and Goolden. From 1886 to 1888 the premises were occupied by a business called Goolden and Trotter and in 1889 by W T Goolden & Co. This firm moved to Woodfield Road, London, in 1890. In 1887 Henry reappeared in the directory at 10 Hatton Garden, and filed three more patent applications in his own name and one for electrical circuits in partnership with W T Glover.

The Hatton Garden office, close to Johnson Matthey's premises, was not only Henry's address but also the London office of W T Glover & Co, as Glover's various wire and cable businesses were now called. Henry became a director of the company in 1886, invested substantial sums of money in it during the next few years (£1000 in January 1887 and £5000 in September 1889) and remained with the firm for the next 25 years, during which time he helped it become one of the world's leading manufacturers of power and electric traction cables.[13]

After taking up his appointment, Henry continued to live in London but spent much of his time at the cable factories in Salford. Henry Royce was by now established as an electrical manufacturer at Hulme, only a few miles away in the inner suburbs of Manchester. If Henry Edmunds had not taken the opportunity to join Glover it is unlikely that he would ever have placed himself in a position from which he was able to bring Royce and Rolls together. But once he had decided to become Glover's partner it became inevitable that, sooner or later, he would meet Royce.

---

[13] In 1944 Glovers assisted in the manufactured PLUTO, the Pipe-line Under The Ocean for the supply of fuel across the English Channel for the Allied Invasion Forces after the D-Day landings in World War II, a vital ingredient to the success of the invasion.

To understand how and why that meeting eventually came about, it is useful to know the circumstances that resulted in Royce coming to Manchester not long before Henry Edmunds arrived there.

In childhood, Royce had experienced desperate poverty and deprivation, as a result of the ill health and early death of his father, a flour miller; but thanks to a generous aunt he became a premium apprentice at the Great Northern Railway's New England Works in Peterborough. For three years she managed to find the £20 annual premium but in November 1880 she ran short of money and Royce had to seek work elsewhere. Although he lacked the qualifications a full apprenticeship would have given him, he had acquired some mechanical skills and was determined to make his way in the world. For a year he worked for a firm of machine tool makers in Leeds, and sometime in 1881 he became a tester with the Electric Lighting and Power Generator Company at Bankside, on the Thames in London. He was paid twenty-two shillings a week. At about this time the firm was attempting to recover from a disastrous loss of £4,000 on a contract to illuminate part of the City of London with French Lontin arc-lamps, and had acquired the British patent rights to Hiram Maxim's incandescent lamp and Edward Weston's arc-lighting system. The firm was renamed the Maxim Weston Electrical Co. Maxim had shares in its parent company, and after the Paris Electrical Exposition he went to Bankside to see how his patents were being used. In his autobiography, published in 1915, he described working conditions in the factory (conditions that must have appalled Henry Royce):

> 'I had never seen anything like it in my life. The place was unspeakably dirty, everything was so out of order that we were tripping over copper wires everywhere; the windows were so thick with dirt that they admitted little light; and the few men at work were burning gas out of the open end of the pipes without any burner. In walking about the place I saw a high-priced Brown and Sharp's milling machine. It was all smothered with dirt and appeared to be in a very dilapidated condition. The roof was leaking and the machinery had been rained on and was slightly rusty in places ... I think about four or five men were employed. Two of them appeared to be working on arc-lamps ... it required only a very small quantity of work to keep these two men fully employed.'

Royce may have been one of the men Maxim observed. Fifty-one years later, Royce reminisced about his time at Bankside for his friend G R N Minchin:

> 'We were once exhibiting our system of arc-lighting at the Guildhall in the City, where we also had a set of 33 accumulators under the care of Monsieur Emile Faure ... From these accumulators we were exhibiting electric lamps burning under water, which, naturally, was novel in those days. The glass tank aquarium had a mixed variety of fish swimming in it. It was said that these were not wisely selected because a quarrel arose and most of the smaller fish jumped out during the exhibition and we had great trouble putting them back. Many people thought that it was the electric light that was to blame for this! Our chief experimental electrician, Mr (afterwards Sir) Hiram Maxim, turned his thoughts to his famous gun and neglected our electrical works so much that the company failed.'

We can imagine how relieved Royce must have been when, towards the end of 1882, he was appointed first (or chief) electrician to a subsidiary of the Bankside company, the Lancashire Maxim Weston Electric Co, and put in charge of a scheme to illuminate a number of streets and theatres in Liverpool with 1600 arc-lamps. The scheme began on 24 March 1884 (three days before Royce's twenty-first birthday) and although it was fairly successful it ceased after only two months; Royce's employer was bankrupt, leaving him out of work but sufficiently confident of his abilities as an electrical engineer to consider setting up his own business.

His partner in this venture was Ernest A Claremont. Where and when Royce met Claremont is not known, but a clue to Claremont's career prior to his decision to become Royce's partner can be found in a chapter on engineers in *Contemporary Biographies,* published in 1899, which states that Claremont trained at the Brush Electrical Engineering Co and subsequently worked at Cordner, Allen & Co in Wandsworth, London. The reference to Brush Electrical Engineering is not quite correct; this company did not exist at the time Claremont began his career, but was formed in 1889 through the amalgamation of the Anglo-American Brush Electric Light Corporation, the Falcon Engine and Car Works Ltd and the Australian Electric Light Power and Storage Co Ltd. Claremont was born in 1864 (he was a year younger than Royce). The Brush company in existence at the time he was a young trainee was the Anglo-American Brush Electric Light Corporation, (AABELC), established in 1880. It is safe to assume that this company was Claremont's first employer and it is entirely possible that his first few months with the firm, and Henry Edmunds' brief period of employment there, overlapped, and that it was then that they first became acquainted. Perhaps, at the very beginning of his career, Royce's future partner was offered advice and guidance by Henry Edmunds.

As neither Royce nor, apparently, Claremont had any earlier connection with Manchester, it seems likely that they met in London. When he joined the Electric Lighting and Power Generator Co, Royce found lodgings in the Old Kent Road, attended lectures at the London Polytechnic, and went to Professor William Ayrton's evening classes in Finsbury and to some of his demonstrations of accumulators at the City & Guilds of London Institute. Royce's lodgings and Bankside were not far from the AABELC's factory in Lambeth. Claremont's training must have required him to attend evening classes and electrical demonstrations. The two men were not worlds apart during their time in London; it is also possible that not only did Royce first meet Claremont there in the early 1880s, but that Henry Edmunds met both of them during the same period. Whatever the background, Royce and Claremont became partners in 1884, soon after the demise of the Lancashire Maxim Weston Electric Light Co, and they are unlikely to have gone into business together unless they had known and trusted one another for some time. With a capital of £20 Royce founded the business F H Royce & Co, electrical and mechanical engineers, making arc-lamps, filaments, lamp-holders and bells. Claremont joined him soon afterwards as a partner, putting another £50 into the business. Within two or three years they were able to take on more employees and the precursor of today's Rolls-Royce companies was becoming well established.

In 1887 there occurred an event that certainly brought an upsurge of work for Glover & Co and probably had an equally beneficial effect on Henry Royce's new enterprise, although no documentary proof has been found to confirm this. The occasion was the Manchester Jubilee Exhibition, one of many events held all over the British Empire to mark the fiftieth anniversary of the accession of Queen Victoria. Glover took a stand at the exhibition and also won a contract to supply copper cables and wires for the entire site. The weight of the copper used amounted to ten tons. In an advertisement featuring this achievement the company proudly boasted:

> 'This quantity, if drawn into a wire of No 36 gauge, would reach a length equal to the circumference of the earth.'

The exhibition grounds were illuminated with 500 Brush arc-lamps, forming what was stated to be the largest lighting scheme that had ever been installed in Europe. As former employees of the company that pioneered Brush lighting in Britain, Henry Edmunds and Ernest

Claremont would have taken great interest in the use of Brush lamps on such a large scale, and it is possible that some of the electrical accessories required for the scheme were made locally, in F H Royce & Co's factory at No 1A Cooke Street, Hulme. Sometime in its formative years the company added dynamos to its range of products, and it is possible that Royce was inspired to diversify in this way after inspecting the wealth of modern electric lighting equipment that lit up the Jubilee Exhibition. He told his biographer, Sir Max Pemberton:

> *'In dynamo work, in spite of insufficient ordinary and technical education, I managed to conceive the importance of sparkless commutation, the superiority of the drum-wound armature for continuous current dynamos and [F H Royce & Co] became famous for continuous current dynamos which had sparkless commutation in the days before carbon brushes. While at Liverpool from 1882 to 1883 I conceived the value of the three-wire system of conductor in efficiency and economy of distribution of electricity and also, afterwards, the scheme of maintaining a constant potential at a distant point. Both of these I successfully applied. In the early days I discovered and demonstrated the cause of broken wires in dynamos through the deflection of the shafts by weight and magnetism.'*

Carbon brushes were introduced in 1888, so obviously Royce's dynamos were in production by then. The 'three wire system' was invented in 1882 by Thomas Edison, who first used it at Sunbury, Pennsylvania, in a town lighting scheme. It consisted of two 110-volt dynamos connected in series to give a potential in the main circuit of 220 volts. Dr John Hopkinson, the Edison Electric Light Company's consultant, has been credited as the co-inventor of the system, and indeed its English patents were owned jointly by him and Edison. The fact that Royce knew about the system as early as 1882 shows how rapidly the latest American improvements in electrical engineering were adopted in England. Royce's application of the system demonstrates how receptive he was to these ideas and provides us with an early example of one of his lifelong credos, 'take the best and make it better'. Henry Edmunds' influence on Royce's first steps as a designer and manufacturer of electrical equipment can perhaps be detected here; Edmunds was in as good a position as anyone to bring Thomas Edison's and Charles Brush's latest patents to Royce's attention, and help him decide which of the new developments in electrical engineering offered the most scope for the skills and talents of Royce's small, enthusiastic and hard-working team in Cooke Street.

The year 1888 saw Henry Royce beginning to prosper as an electrical manufacturer and Henry Edmunds establishing useful contacts for W T Glover & Co from his new London office; his neighbours there included Hiram Maxim, who retreated to 57D Hatton Garden to concentrate on designing his machine gun, after becoming disillusioned with the way the Maxim Weston Electric Company was being run. Another engineer on the verge of fame was also working in Hatton Garden at about this time; in a workshop on the top floor of No 57B, Sebastian Ziana de Ferranti had started making alternators, arc-lamps and meters of his own invention, and within a few years would design and build, at Deptford, the first of London's large-scale power stations.

Henry Edmunds, though less talented than Royce, Maxim and Ferranti, had many ideas and schemes that he was anxious to nurture to success. In addition to helping Glover run his cable company he was about to become involved in yet another extraordinary incident in the development of a long-forgotten invention. Ten years earlier, he had been present when the words 'Mary had a little lamb' had hissed and crackled from its mouthpiece, to the astonishment of those privileged to be present in Thomas Edison's laboratory at such an historic moment. Now, new life was to be breathed into the 'talking machine' and Henry Edmunds was to play an important role in its revival.

In October 1878 Thomas Edison had abandoned further work on sound recording so that he could devote all his time to developing a cheap and efficient electric lamp. However, other inventors saw just as bright a future for the 'talking machine'. Among those who became interested in sound recording was Alexander Graham Bell, whose invention of the telephone had won the French government's $10,000 Volta Prize. Bell used the money to set up the Volta Laboratory in Washington DC to carry out further research into sound and acoustics. In 1881 he decided that his next project would be to improve Edison's Phonograph. He was assisted by his cousin, Chichester A Bell, a chemical engineer, and Charles Sumner Tainter, a scientist and instrument maker. Together they carried out a complete review of the way in which the Phonograph worked. Edison's crude needle and diaphragm, his fiddly, fragile tinfoil and his jerky, hand-cranked cylinder would forever have confined the instrument to the playroom but the Bell cousins and Tainter had better ideas. In trying to find a new way of recording and reproducing sound they experimented with jets of air, water and even (100 years before the invention of laser-activated compact discs) beams of light. None of these methods was satisfactory and eventually they developed a 'floating' reproducing stylus, which followed the grooves in the recording more accurately than Edison's rigid needle.

In searching for a better recording medium than tinfoil, Bell and his team chose a wax compound. At one stage they stepped ahead of their time and considered recording on wax discs, even specifying them in their first patent application for their improved sound recording machine, but when the machine finally appeared its records were cylindrical in shape and made of wax-coated cardboard. The cylinders were rotated at a more or less constant speed by a foot-operated treadle, similar to those fitted to the sewing machines of the day. The recording stylus cut a spiral groove in the wax, and as it did so the vibrations created by the sound waves engraved a pattern of perpendicular vibrations or 'hills and dales' in the base of the groove. Sound reproduction was clearer than that of Edison's Phonograph, but quieter, so the recordings had to be listened to through a kind of stethoscope.

The new machine was called the Graphophone (neatly reversing, phonetically, the name Edison had chosen for his 'talking machine') and was patented in May 1886, but before its inventors announced it to the public they sent a prototype to Edison, hoping that he would make further improvements and become their partner in a joint venture to launch the machine commercially. They acknowledged that Edison was the true inventor of the 'talking machine'; said that they wanted to co-operate, not compete, with him; and offered to turn all their work over to him, bear all the costs of experimental work, and invest capital in the venture, in return for a fifty per cent interest in the enterprise.

Edison was furious and accused the Bell cousins and Tainter of stealing his invention. Examining the prototype they had left with him, he declared astonishment that it had been granted a patent, since in his eyes it contained nothing new except the improved stylus. The patent had, in fact, been applied for on 27 June 1885, so Edison and his legal staff had had plenty of warning of its imminent introduction. After rejecting the Bell cousins' offer of a joint venture, Edison at last set to work to make his own improvements to the Phonograph. From now on he gave the impression that he had always intended to resume work on sound recording after he had developed the incandescent electric lamp. Whether or not that was so, during the next two years he made up for lost time and on 16 June 1888, he unveiled the prototype of his 'Perfected Phonograph'. A famous photograph taken at the time shows the dishevelled, fatigued inventor slumped behind the prototype after he and his assistants had worked for five days and nights to get it to work satisfactorily. Ostensibly the Graphophone and the redesigned Phonograph were identical, although there were important differences in their details. Edison's cylinders were made of solid wax, were thicker than those of the Graphophone, and could be shaved smooth to erase previous recordings and allow new ones to be made. Because the groove was only one-thousandth of an inch deep the cylinders could be re-used many times; Graphophone cylinders could be recorded upon only once. The Phonograph recorded by forming impressions or indentations in the cylinder's groove, whereas the Graphophone actually cut material from the groove. And to drive the cylinder when recordings were made and played back, the Phonograph had an electric motor.

In 1887, while Edison was still struggling to regain his lead in the field of sound recording, the Bells and Tainter sold their interest in the Graphophone to the American Graphophone Company, which had its headquarters in Washington DC and regarded the government departments there as a ready-made market for dictating machines; the Graphophone seemed ideal for this purpose.

It was at this time, when an open conflict between Edison and his rivals seemed inevitable, that Henry Edmunds decided to revisit some of his old haunts and his business associates and relatives in the USA, and while there see if there were any new ideas that he and Walter Glover could introduce into Britain. But sometime in 1887, probably before he went to America, Henry and Ellen enjoyed a holiday in Northern Ireland. They were the guests of W A Traill, who at Portrush had promoted and built one of the world's first electric railways, to take tourists to the famous Giant's Causeway promontory on the Antrim coast. Since meeting Michael Holroyd Smith and Robert Blackwell some years earlier, Henry had been taking a close professional interest in electric traction. He found the Giant's Causeway Railway especially interesting because it derived its power from the River Bann. This reminded Henry of the time in 1877 when he had listened to Thomas Edison and William Wallace discussing the possibilities of hydro-electricity, and had prophesied to a sceptical Mr Bush that within a few years the power of Niagara Falls would be harnessed. During his visit to America in 1887, Henry revisited Niagara Falls and quite by chance met Mr Bush again:

> 'I was walking over the suspension bridge when an elderly man approached. He looked hard at me and exclaimed: "Why! You are the young engineer who told me ten years ago about lighting the Falls. It's all come true, and I've lived to see it".'

We do not know if one of Henry's reasons for returning to the USA was to discover more about the imminent renaissance of the 'talking machine', but he arrived there at an important stage in the Graphophone's development. The Bell cousins and Tainter had just, or would soon, sell their interest in the machine to the American Graphophone Company but its foreign rights had not yet been disposed of. Somewhat brazenly, the company asked Colonel George Gouraud, Edison's British agent, if he would like to head a British agency for the Graphophone, but when Gouraud sent a cablegram to Edison from London asking for his approval he was told: *'Have nothing to do with them. They are [a] bunch [of] pirates'*. Edison's response was despatched on 1 August 1887. Soon after this date, Henry Edmunds went to Washington, where he was introduced to Tainter by Philip Mauro, a patent agent (and soon to become Bell-Tainter's attorney). Evidently Tainter and the Volta Laboratory still retained some control over the Graphophone's promotion, for Tainter was able to appoint Henry as his European representative. It was not until the summer of 1888 that the Graphophone and Edison's new Phonograph were shown to the American public. Meanwhile, Jesse H Lippincott, a millionaire manufacturer from Pittsburgh, had invested $200,000 in the American Graphophone Company and become its sole licensee, with exclusive rights to promote the machine in the USA. Lippincott had also bought the patent rights to Edison's Phonograph for $500,000 and formed the North American Phonograph Company to sell the machine. The Phonograph rapidly went through three stages of improvement in 1887 and 1888, culminating in the Perfected Phonograph, embodying a battery-powered electric motor to turn the cylinder and a governor and flywheel to regulate the cylinder's speed. The Graphophone's lack of an electric motor was not quite such a disadvantage as may appear, since the primitive battery that drove Edison's machine had a life of only fifteen hours.

This, then, was the state of the art when the Graphophone was introduced into Britain. In July 1888 Henry made another visit to America; on 3 August *The Electrician* announced:

> *'We hear that Mr Henry Edmunds ... is bringing some Graphophones back from the States and will probably read a paper on the Graphophone before the British Association.'*

Formed in 1831, the British Association for the Advancement of Science has, as one of its objectives, the dissemination of popular knowledge of science. It holds its annual conferences in various British Commonwealth countries and British provincial cities, the venue in 1888 being Bath, the most celebrated of Britain's spa cities. Before the conference opened, Henry demonstrated the Graphophone at his London office, which was now at 10 Hatton Gardens, in some ways repeating his triumph of 1878, when he brought news of Edison's tinfoil Phonograph to England. A reporter from *The Electrician* went along to Henry's office to find out about the new instrument:

> 'On the day of our visit a phonogram had just been received from Mr Chichester A Bell ... his voice is well known to us and was instantly recognised as soon as the machine was set in motion. Owing to rough treatment in the post the cylinder had been quite bent out of shape and we were agreeably surprised to find that in spite of this, only one or two words out of a long letter were slightly indistinct ... The machine is driven by a treadle ... the work required to drive it is much less than for a sewing machine and a small electric motor may of course be used if desired. The inventors, however, are of the opinion that it is better dispensed with so long as primary batteries have to be used as the source of energy and we have no doubt that such of our readers as have used primary batteries to drive electro-motors will agree with us.'

The reporter described how the rotation of the cylinder and the movement of the recording or reproducing stylus along the wax surface (for pauses in dictation or transcription) could be halted by pressing a small lever: 'a very much simpler arrangement than the one used for the same purpose in Edison's new phonograph'. Another great advantage was that, once properly adjusted by the makers, the Graphophone needed no further attention, whereas Edison's machine had to be adjusted every time a cylinder was put on and therefore could only be used satisfactorily by an expert.

The British public had its first opportunity to compare the two latest talking machines on 6 September 1888, at the Masonic Hall, Bath, where papers on the Graphophone and the latest Phonograph were presented by Henry Edmunds and Colonel Gouraud respectively. Henry began his presentation by reviewing the history of man's first attempts to record and transmit sound. He then spoke of his visit to Edison's laboratory at the time the tinfoil Phonograph was invented; of his efforts to promote the machine in Britain in 1878; and of Edison's subsequent abandonment of the Phonograph until provoked into resuming his work by news of the progress that had been made at the Volta Laboratory. In a statement that would not have been well received at West Orange, New Jersey, where Edison had recently relocated his laboratory, Henry said:

> 'All praise accorded to Mr Edison and his agents for the 'improved Phonograph' is fairly due to Mr Charles Sumner Tainter and his associates.'

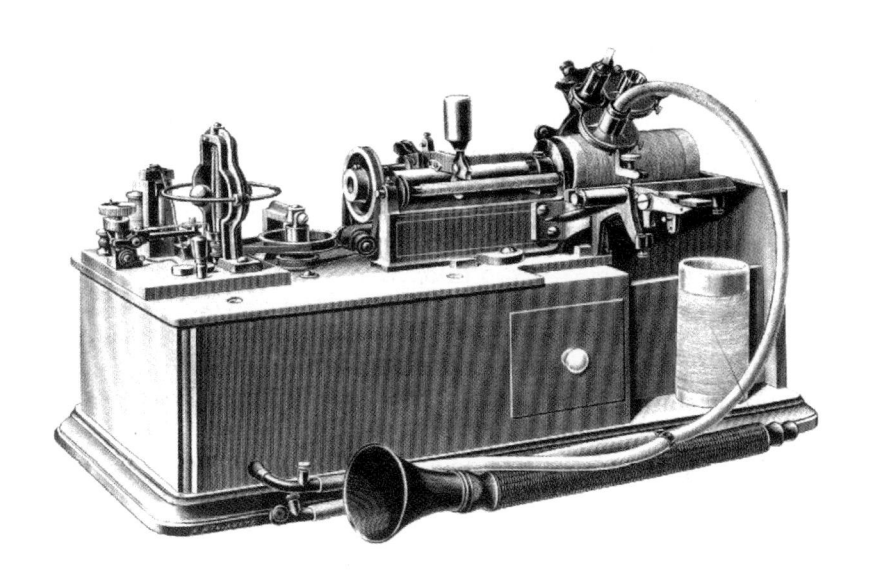

Edison's wax cylinder Phonograph, demonstrated to the British Association's conference at Bath. (From *Engineering*, 14 September 1888)

Henry explained the Phonograph and its uses in more detail:

> 'The Graphophone as shown here is propelled mechanically. The whole has been designed to attain the best results with the fewest parts and absence of skilled attention. There is no electricity. An ordinary treadle ... rotates a speed governor. This by a leather belt communicates a constant speed to the rotating wax cylinder. A diaphragm of mica carrying a steel graver, called the recorder, is mounted in a metal holder which by means of a revolving screw traverses the wax cylinder, cutting a fine thread 100 to the inch. A mouthpiece attached to a flexible tube carries the sound vibrations to the diaphragm, which causes the graver or style [sic] to cut into the wax a series of depressions more or less frequent, and varying in depth according to the sounds producing the vibrations. These undulations, while so slight as to be barely perceptible, can, nevertheless, produce in the diaphragm of the reproducer similar vibrations to the original sounds and give back, not once, but indefinitely, the words or sounds which were first recorded ... Great economy has been found in the use of a cardboard cylinder coated

with wax instead of solid wax cylinders. They are more easily handled, less liable to fracture, and much lighter for postage, besides being cheaper than notepaper, when the saving of time in writing is considered. The very simplicity of the instrument startles us ... its introduction into everyday life marks a new era. Truly the unlimited reproduction of the human voice in speech and song is a most wonderful achievement. When we consider its marvellous adaptability to modern life, there seems to be no limit to its powers. A child may work it and communicate to those who love it, its childish prattle; or preserving the small cylinder refer in after life to how it spoke. Business men may carry on negotiations, recording each word spoken, preventing misunderstandings as to what was said ... the stenographer may read his notes to it, leaving it to dictate to others to write them out.'

Henry also suggested how a Graphophone could be attached to a telephone, to allow *'fleeting words to be recorded for future reference'*. He had, in fact, on the day before his lecture, filed a patent application for such a device. At about this time, he and Walter Glover formally set up their Graphophone agency; the Glover papers in the North West Museum of Science and Industry in Manchester contain an entry dated September 1888, which reads:

'Started on Graphophone account. Took out patents in colonies. Sold half interest to Sydney Morse account for £1,000. Paid Volta Graphophone Co, Washington £4,086.'

While at Bath, Henry attended a lecture on atomic theory by Sir Frederick Bramwell, the British Association's president, and listened to Lord Kelvin, Professor Silvanus Thompson, William Preece and Sir Oliver Lodge discuss such subjects as 'the true nature of electricity'. He also met John Glaisher, the pioneer balloonist and founder of the Royal Meteorological Society. Glaisher showed a keen interest in sound recording and may have been among the many members of the association who recorded their voices on Henry's Graphophone.

Three months after the Bath meeting, Henry became a member of the Royal Society of Arts, a learned society founded in London in 1754 to promote the practical arts and sciences. Its pioneering work had already included the Great Exhibition of 1851 (the world's first international exhibition) and the advent of a practical method of recording and reproducing sound was of considerable interest to its members. On the day he was elected a member, Henry delivered a lecture on the Graphophone to the society and commented upon the reaction the instrument had received since he first showed it at Bath:

> *'I have been much interested to note the enormous diversity of uses that have been suggested. Physicians ask for it in order that when returning home late at night they, without any fatigue, may simply speak into the machine as to the condition of the patient visited and suggest the necessary treatment. It is also suggested that residents in Bournemouth or Nice need not come to London to consult their medical men but can send samples of their cough by Graphophone, thus indicating the improvement or condition of their lungs. Blind people may also through the medium of their ears avail themselves of avenues of instruction and amusement to which their eyes have been so long closed. The small tradesman who cannot afford to have his own bookkeeper, and has not time during the press of business to put down the verbal orders he receives, or the sales he is making, can incidentally speak to this instrument, recording each transaction, and leisurely take off the words thus spoken later in the day, entering them into book form. Connected to the telephone the other day, I was enabled to record the words spoken and to recall afterwards that which I had forgotten in the hurry of the moment, viz. whether I had made an appointment to meet a friend at London Bridge at six minutes past five or five minutes past six.'*

Henry left five Graphophones in the RSA's library for a few days, so that members could examine them at their leisure.

In the aftermath of the British debut of the Graphophone and the improved Phonograph, Henry Edmunds and Colonel Gouraud achieved a great deal of publicity for their machines. Gouraud put the Phonograph on display at the Crystal Palace and persuaded William Gladstone, Lord Tennyson and Robert Browning to record their voices; but it was Henry who had the greatest success in recording the voices of the famous, even though at the time he was not allowed to publicise the fact. Here, from his *Reminiscences,* is his own account of what happened:

> *'After the Bath meeting, my offices in Hatton Garden were thronged with persons of all grades of society, all astonished with the new Gramophone [sic]. Its fame even reached the ears of Royalty and the aged Queen Victoria expressed a desire*

to have a demonstration at Balmoral Castle. I could not go myself but my friend and solicitor, Mr Sydney Morse, took an instrument to Scotland and had the honour of showing it to the delightful old lady. Abandoning the usual Royal reserve, Her Majesty expressed her unqualified delight; so much so that Mr Morse was emboldened to request the Queen to speak a few words into the Gramophone. As is well known, Queen Victoria strongly objected to autograph hunters and all that sort of folk; and now she was asked to give, not merely a specimen of the Royal signature, but a record of a Royal voice! However, her admiration of the new invention overcame her scruples; and Mr Morse exhibited to me a small black cylinder with a few spiral lines traced upon it, containing the record of the voice and speech of the celebrated Queen. He declared that that was his most cherished possession; and would pass it to his children as his chiefest treasure.'

The world's sound archives, notably the British Library's National Sound Archive and the BBC Sound Archives, contain recordings of many voices of members of the British Royal family, including Queen Victoria's cousin, the Duke of Cambridge, who in 1888 recorded a message to Thomas Edison on a Phonograph cylinder. The earliest authenticated surviving recording of a reigning monarch is one of King George V, made in 1923. The most obvious omission from the archives is a recording of the voice of Queen Victoria. On 8 August 1898 (ten years after Henry received his 'Royal Command') she did record a message on a cylinder for Emperor Menelik of Abyssinia but instructed that it should be destroyed after it had been played to him. When the cylinder was delivered to the Emperor he stood to attention and welcomed it with an artillery salute; a few days later, the cylinder was returned to the Queen's agent in Abyssinia, Captain Harrington, and was immediately *'broken into pieces, as promised'*.[14] Menelik had been highly honoured. In 1897 the Queen had been asked by the Edison Bell Phonograph Corporation to make a recording to commemorate her Diamond Jubilee, but the company was told that she had previously declined all similar invitations and would not make an exception in this case. Further invitations in 1899 and 1900 were also refused. Henry Edmunds's revelation, in the early 1920s, that Queen Victoria had been persuaded to record her voice in 1888, the year after her Golden Jubilee,

---

[14] *The Letters of Queen Victoria.* Third Series, Vol III, G E Buckle (Ed). John Murray 1932.

did not encourage anyone to try and find the 'small black cylinder' with its 'few spiral traces', or discover more about the occasion on which the recording was made, but many years later, while researching the Queen's life for her book, *Victoria R.I.*,[15] the Countess of Longford, found out about it and wrote:

> 'What the Queen called 'treats', including professional theatricals, became plentiful after the Jubilee... a gramophone [sic] was brought to Balmoral by Mr Morse and after the household had recorded whistles and German jokes Her Majesty spoke a few words. Mr Morse was warned not to tour the country playing them.'

Queen Victoria and the Graphophone on which she recorded her voice in 1888. The small box among the cylinders above the Graphophone bears Henry Edmunds' name and address (From a montage by Tony Freeman).

---

[15] Weidenfield and Nicholson, 1964

Lady Longford's source was a letter written by the Queen's private secretary, Sir Henry Ponsonby, to his wife, from Balmoral on Wednesday 29 August 1888. The full transcript of the relevant passage from Sir Henry's letter gives the precise date and almost the precise time on which the first sound recording by a reigning monarch was made:

> *'A man friend of Miss Bauer came here yesterday with a graphophone. It is different from Edison's Phonograph and has been made by Bell ... and some others and is very ingenious – no electric or magnetic currents - simply worked like a sewing machine with a treadle. Little cylinders revolve which a little machine marks with your voice - and the contrary return your voice thro' a pipe into your ear -only one can really hear it - but it is very curious. Wernher spoke in German, Edwards whistled and I laughed my 'Coachman's laugh' - it was most extraordinary the clear way this was reproduced as often as one liked. The Queen said to me at dinner "heard your hearty laugh this evening". This was 6 hours afterwards and he says it will keep for years. HM spoke into it - but we told Mr Morse he must not go round the country reproducing the Queen's words.'*[16]

'Wernher' may have been Julius or Derrick Wernher, guests of the Queen; 'Edwards' was almost certainly Fleetwood Edwards, a member of her household.

The *Court Circular* for 29 August reported: *'Mr Sydney Morse had the honour of exhibiting the graphophone before the Queen and Royal Family'*. Assuming that dinner was served at eight o'clock on the 28th, then there is no doubt that the first Royal recording was made at about 2.00 pm that day - a little post-luncheon amusement, no doubt.

With two sources to rely on, we can see that Henry's memory failed him when he implied in his *Reminiscences* that the Graphophone was demonstrated to the Queen *after* the British Association's meeting. We do not know why he personally did not take the Graphophone to Balmoral, but Sydney Morse was an ideal deputy. As we know from the Glover papers, he was about to purchase an interest in Henry Edmunds and Walter Glover's Graphophone agency. He was at this time 34 years old and embarking on a distinguished career. He represented various electric lighting companies in London, and became associated with the promotion of many tramways and light railways. But what were more important than his business activities, so far as his visit to Balmoral

---

[16] Published by gracious permission of Her Majesty the Queen, RA Add. A.36.

was concerned, were his connections with the Royal family. In the letter quoted above, Sir Henry Ponsonby described him as a friend of Miss Bauer (Fraulein Ottillie Bauer, German governess to Queen Victoria's children and later her Letrice). Sydney's wife Juliet Mary (nee Tylor) and his mother-in-law Isabella Tylor (nee Tindall) are believed to have been ladies-in-waiting in the Royal household at some time, possibly to Queen Victoria's fourth daughter, Princess Louise, who in 1871 married the Marquis of Lorne, the future 9th Duke of Argyll. Neither Mrs Morse nor Mrs Tylor are mentioned in the Royal Archives' list of the Princess' ladies-in-waiting (the list is incomplete) but Mrs Tylor was a friend of Madame Rollande, who was French governess to Queen Victoria's children from 1847 until 1859. The Royal Archives contain a number of letters from Madame Rollande to Mrs Tylor and her husband Albert. One of them refers to a present of doves that Princess Alice, Queen Victoria's second daughter, sent to Juliet Mary and her brother Edward, so it seems that the Royal family and the Tylor family were on friendly terms when their children were young. The friendship continued after Juliet married Sydney Morse, and in the Royal Archives there is also a significant letter to Princess Louise from Fraulein Bauer. In early 1907 Juliet and Sydney Morse dined with Princess Louise. Soon afterwards, Juliet wrote to Fraulein Bauer to tell her about the occasion, and on 15 March Fraulein Bauer wrote to Princess Louise, saying:

> 'Mrs Morse wrote to me after she and her husband had dined with you, but said that unfortunately your wish to hear the voice of the dear Queen had been a disappointment. After so many years this is not to be wondered at, especially as great improvements have no doubt been made to the instrument since then. I remember very well that visit of Mr Morse to Balmoral, after he had received the Queen's permission on our journey there to bring the Phonograph.'[17]

Fraulein Bauer should, of course, have called the instrument a Graphophone but by 1907 all recording machines were becoming known as Phonographs or Gramophones, their future generic names. Fraulein Bauer appears to have been under the impression that Sydney Morse had asked the Queen whether he could take the Graphophone to Balmoral. If so, Henry Edmunds' account of the sequence of events that preceded the Royal recording is incorrect in another detail, though not

---

[17] Published by gracious permission of Her Majesty the Queen. RA Add. A 17 /1043.

in substance. The one firsthand account of the occasion that everyone would like to read is, of course, one by Queen Victoria herself. It is highly like that she wrote about Sydney Morse's visit to Balmoral, and the amusement she derived from the Graphophone, in her famous journal, but as is well known this was transcribed after her death by her youngest daughter, Princess Beatrice, who then destroyed the original. When making her transcription the Princess omitted various passages; perhaps one of them was an account of Sydney's visit?

Although Henry Edmunds's efforts to launch the Graphophone in Britain generated great interest and publicity, he soon lost what proved to be his last chance to gain any lasting benefit from becoming a 'talking machine' promoter and pioneer. But what became of the recording apparatus that he demonstrated during those exciting years? Where is the Phonograph that was built, with his help, for William Preece in 1878? Where are the tinfoil recordings that were made by Preece, Professor Tyndall, Alfred Tennyson and Henry himself? Where are the Graphophones he demonstrated to the British Association, the Royal Society of Arts, and Queen Victoria? Where are the wax-coated cylinders used by Henry and Sydney Morse while demonstrating the Graphophone - cylinders on which Sydney recorded the voices, whistles and laughter of the Queen and those who were with her at Balmoral on 28 August 1888? Attempts to answer the most important of these questions will be described later.

CHAPTER NINE
Power for the people

The year 1888 was the beginning of a period in which Henry Edmunds failed to obtain a financial return on several inventions that might have made him a rich man, but succeeded in establishing W T Glover & Co as a world leader in the manufacture of electricity cables. From now onwards his career was that of a company director and he embarked on fewer independent entrepreneurial ventures.

Underwater telephony provides an example of Henry's missed opportunities. While he was busy launching the Graphophone in Britain, the French Navy was achieving excellent results with a Hydrophone which was identical in principle to Henry's patented 'mode of transmitting audible signals between places separated by water' of 1878, described in Chapter Three. The French experiments were reported at about the time that the first articles on the introduction of the Graphophone and the British Association's meetings in Bath were published in the British press. Henry was now too busy to resume his work on underwater telephony and other inventors took over where he had left off; it is unlikely that he had given much thought to the subject for many years and doubtful whether he gave even a moment's consideration to getting back into the field to help the British Admiralty keep pace with France's progress.

In sound recording and reproduction, major changes in the marketing of the Phonograph and Graphophone outside the USA were imminent in the last few months of 1888, following the acquisition by the North American Phonograph Company of the sole US rights to both types of machine. Had he been able to persevere with the Graphophone, Henry might eventually have become more than merely a forgotten pioneer of sound recording in Britain, for he would surely have been in a position to bid for rights to the machine that superseded cylinder players. This was the disc-playing Gramophone, demonstrated to the Franklin Institute in Philadelphia by its inventor, Emile Berliner, on 16 May 1888, only 12 days after Alexander Graham Bell and Charles Tainter's Graphophone was patented. Henry met Berliner in America in 1889 but by the end of that year, because of other commitments, he and Walter Glover sold their interests in the Graphophone to The Graphophone Syndicate, which had been registered in London on 14 February 1889 with a capital of £100,000.

This abrupt cessation of Henry's Graphophone enterprise was due to a sudden decline in the health of Walter Glover in 1889, following a bereavement. For several years Henry had to run W T Glover & Co virtually single-handed; Walter died in Northampton on 27 April 1893 but it was not until 1895, when Godfrey B Samuelson became a director of the company, that Henry was able to delegate some of his responsibilities.

Sydney Morse seems to have sold his interest in the Graphophone at the same time as Henry and Walter sold theirs; Sydney, too, had extra demands on his time, for the Electric Lighting Act of 1888 was now freeing the electrical supply industry from the restrictions imposed by the original act of six years earlier. As we have seen, one of the provisions of the 'ill-advised' (according to Professor J A Fleming[18]) Electric Lighting Act of 1882 was that any local authority granting a provisional order allowing a company to install a public electricity supply could, when the Order expired 20 years later, purchase compulsorily the company's plant and works at their 'book value', without taking goodwill or current or future profits into account. This deterred investors to such an extent that although 64 orders were granted under the Act, none of them was put into operation. In the USA, no less than 120 electric lighting companies were established during the early and mid-1880s. The new Act of 1888 allowed companies to provide a public electricity supply for 42 years before local authorities could purchase them compulsorily and required the purchase price to be the 'fair market value'. There was an immediate and rapid growth of electrical supply schemes and, by January 1889, more than 50 central generating stations were in operation or under construction in Britain. The introduction of new legislation designed to encourage companies to apply for operating licences and orders would inevitably have created more legal work for Sydney Morse; certainly, Henry Edmunds lost no time in attempting to benefit from the boom in demand for electric light, and we can imagine that Henry Royce and Ernest Claremont, too, began to win more orders for their electrical accessories at this time.

One of the projects carried out at W T Glover during the rapid advance of electrical engineering technology in the late 1880s was the production of power and traction cables that could be installed underground. The copper conductors of these new cables were insulated with oil-impregnated jute wrappings and sheathed overall with lead; Glover's factory was one of the first to install plant for making this type of cable, the forerunner of paper-insulated high voltage cables. The patent for the sheathing was owned by Henry. While developing lead-sheathed cables, he and Walter Glover became interested in designing and manufacturing extrusion presses both for sheathing cables and making

---

[18] *Fifty Years of Electricity: Memories of an Electrical Engineer*, p53. Iliffe & Sons Ltd, 1921.

lead tubes. Glover Patent Lead Presses became widely used by other cable makers and lead pipe manufacturers, not only in Britain but also in Norway, Sweden and on the Continent. The company embarked on other diversions from the electrical field at this time. Glover presses were adapted to produce patent glazing strips, and a glazing department was formed to carry out contracts all over the country. Another successful venture was the development of a double ram horizontal press to make lead waste pipes. Ventures, which failed to become commercially viable, were an electric time clock, a prepayment meter and a toll telephone (probably the one described in the patent application that Henry and Charles T Howard filed in 1885).

Electric traction was one of the new technologies of the late 1880s, but the cables for power distribution still had to be transported with the aid of an older invention – steam traction.
[From *Glover's Centenary, 1868-1968* (BICC Cables Ltd)]

Another of Henry's ventures was an electrical distribution system, which he patented in 1887 and first described publicly in a paper presented at the British Association's meeting in 1888, a few days after he and Colonel Gouraud demonstrated the latest recording machines. The 'Edmunds system', as it was called, was different in every essential respect to any previous form of electrical distribution. Henry described it thus:

'A number of groups of cells which we will call the local batteries are placed at different points or centres where supply is required in a district, each battery having its individual number of cells according to the voltage required locally, and the amount of current to be supplied. Unlike the Brush method these local batteries are electrically distinct and independent of each other and of the charging main, neither is there a duplicate set

> *to be charged ... but instead we employ an additional group within each of the local batteries (which we will term the main batteries), a number of cells of which are a divisor of the number employed locally - generally one third. Such a system lends itself to many purposes. For instance, in the working of railroad switches and signals electrically, a distributor at each block station would enable a whole line of rail, say 200 miles, to be supplied from one source, the pressure on the main being only a small fraction of the sum of the local pressure. Or in electric tramway work, a charge main ... would supply a number of points en route, which in turn would each independently of the other supply large volume low pressure currents locally, saving risk of breakdown and consequent interruption of traffic. But more particularly it is useful in detached house and suburban lighting, for it solves the problem of giving each house its own individual supply of electricity continuously day and night, totally independent of continuous or regular working at the local station or of interference from other work on the same circuit, being at the same time absolutely safe from the danger of shock and, above all, supplying electric light at a reasonable cost.'*

Two months later Henry presented a similar paper to the Society of Telegraph Engineers but, according to *The Electrician* of 30 November 1888, his system *'did not lead to any lively discussion. The compliments which were paid to the ingenuity of the inventor were doubtless both sincerely meant and thoroughly well deserved but there was an unmistakable feeling that as yet the time had hardly arrived for a recognition of the system as a practicable and commercial method of distribution'.*

The main criticism voiced by the society's learned members was an almost total absence of figures in Henry's proposals, especially for the electrical 'distributor' required in every house. Some members thought that this could not be made for less than £50 or £60 a piece (a large sum of money in 1888); if so, there was no point in discussing the system's chances of working satisfactorily or the advantages of its method of intermittently charging its batteries.

A few months before Henry described his system to his sceptical peers, the Cadogan Electric Lighting Company of London (registered in March 1887) began supplying electricity to parts of Chelsea, Kensington, Brompton and Knightsbridge. Its managing director was J S Sayer. Henry was a director and probably one of the company's founders; his involvement in the business would certainly have had Walter Glover's approval and perhaps his financial support as well, since any scheme to distribute electricity to residential and commercial districts would have obvious benefits to a manufacturer of cables. The Cadogan company employed the 'Edmunds system' and had a generating station at 91 Manor Street, near the River Thames in Chelsea - a convenient location not only for the delivery of coal and removal of ashes by barges, but also for supplying current to London's most fashionable and wealthy districts. The station was designed to supply high-tension current to 50,000 lamps and was praised by *The Electrician* as being *'one of the best designed and most spacious buildings which has yet been erected in this country for the purpose of central station electric lighting'*. Each of the company's customers or 'consumers' had a storage battery with between eight and 64 cells, divided into four groups. Each cell had a capacity of 700 ampere-hours and at any one time three of the groups of cells were available for use and connected in parallel to the consumer's load. The fourth group was connected to the company's seven-mile long charging main, which linked all the consumers 'in series' to the generators. Each consumer's 'distributor' had a motorised switch which every two minutes disconnected one group of cells from the charging main and connected another. The power station was equipped with three steam engines and three generators, two or three being run in series according to demand. By dusk all the batteries were more or less fully charged and ready to illuminate the premises in which they were installed.

For some months after the generating station started operating, arguments about the merits (or otherwise) of the 'Edmunds system' continued in the technical press. Its critics were chiefly concerned about its cost, one of them commenting: *'At the moment we must be pardoned if we regard the system rather as a brilliant tour de force than as a substantial addition to the resources of electrical engineering'*. The company never had many customers and in 1893 was taken over by the Chelsea Electricity Supply Co, which was backed by Callender's Cable Co, the Electric Power Storage Co and the Electric Construction Co. Instead of providing each of its consumers with a group of rechargeable batteries, the Chelsea company installed battery substations for each area it served. The substations were charged in series, and at times of heavy demand all the batteries could discharge to the supply mains simultaneously.[19] This arrangement was more efficient than the one designed by Henry Edmunds, and the Chelsea company prospered where Cadogan had failed.

---

[19] *A History of Electric Light and Power,* R Bowers, Peter Peregrinus 1982.

The failure of the 'Edmunds system' to become a viable form of electrical distribution did not in any way diminish Henry's inventive flair. During the 1890s he registered no less than 72 applications for electrical patents, including one (subsequently abandoned) for electric tramways and vehicles. The early years of the decade were marked by two sad events in his life, the death of his stepmother, Sarah, in October 1891, and of Walter Glover two years later. Henry was also involved in business and domestic changes of address at this time. In 1893 W T Glover & Co opened a second London office, at 39 Victoria Street, near the Houses of Parliament, but retained 10 Hatton Garden for another two years; also in 1893, the company purchased for £1800 the land and buildings in Springfield Lane, Salford, that it had rented since 1880. Sometime in the early 1890s Henry and his family moved from Rhodehurst, home since their marriage in 1883. According to street directories of the period they lived at Rhodehurst until 1889 or 1890 and at 71 Upper Tulse Hill, near the junction of Streatham Hill and Brixton Hill in Streatham, from 1894. In the interim they may have lived at 38 Hamilton Road, London SW19; a 'Henry Edmunds' is listed at that address in 1891. Henry and Ellen remained at 71 Upper Tulse Hill for 19 years; he is listed at that address in all the street directories published during that time, but for some reason his name is given as 'Henry Antron Edmunds' in 1894. This was the first and only indication that Henry had, or assumed, a second forename; other allusions to 'Antron' occur later in this story.

In 1893 members of W T Glover & Co visited Italy, Switzerland, Germany and Malta in pursuit of new contracts. They now had important new products to offer to world markets. One of these was a 'flexible coal cutter cable', patented by L B Atkinson and called the 'Atkinson trailer'. This was the forerunner of all flexible cables for the mining industry. Under Henry's direction another innovation, paper-insulated cables, was being promoted at this time. The insulating compound with which the paper was impregnated was called Diatrine; more than a century later the company was still receiving orders for 'Diatrine cables', particularly from abroad, even though the name had not been used for years. The various improvements in cable manufacture pioneered at W T Glover & Co, and the increasing demand for all kinds of wires and cables for telephones, electric lighting and power transmission, meant that the Springfield Lane works were constantly being modernised and expanded, but out on the streets the firm's gangs had a problem; they were looking for an easier way of threading cables through underground conduits. Years later, Henry described what happened:

'It was usually done by 'rodding'; that is to say, wooden rods were provided with screw sockets at either end. A rod was passed into the pipe and then another screwed on to it and pushed further; and so on until the first rod appeared at the other end of the tube. One of the engineers proposed to overcome these difficulties by making use of ferrets. He thought the animal might be fitted with a collar, to which a cord could be attached, and in running through the pipe he would pull this cord with him. Unfortunately the co-operation of the ferrets could not be relied upon. The ferret would be put into one end of the tube, and an expectant man stood at the other end with a piece of meat to reward it. Very often the ferret did not appear, and on passing a rod into the pipe to find out where he was, it would be found that the animal had crept halfway through and then gone to sleep. The sporting instincts of the ferret were invoked and a rat put in first, in expectation that the creature would follow it. This was not a success; and, to crown it all, it was found that the ferret, when it felt the cord dragging it, simply set to work and gnawed it off.'

In an attempt to solve the problem Albert Harris Howard, one of Henry's brothers-in-law, invented an electric trolley with flexible wheels mounted above and below its chassis. The wheels gripped the top and bottom of the conduit as it travelled along, pulling the cord behind it. The idea was only a partial success and the cable layers often had to resort to the tedious task of 'rodding'.

Ever-increasing quantities of copper were required, and Henry found that the firm's suppliers, Thos Bolton and Sons of Longmoor, Staffordshire, virtually had a monopoly in the material. At Henry's suggestion his friend Fred Smith of Halifax set up a copper mill; from this evolved the London Electric Wire Company & Smiths Ltd.

On one of his overseas trips, Henry met William Preece in Malta and the two men were entertained by Mr Portelli, a representative of the Eastern Telegraph Company. Although they were old friends, Henry and Preece did not see eye-to-eye on the future of the telephone service in Britain. Preece believed that it should be owned and controlled by the government, while Henry advocated free enterprise. Preece had been one of the principal witnesses for the Crown when the Edison Telephone Company of London fought the General Post Office's claim to have the right, under the Telegraphy Act, to control all public telephones. The Crown won the case and offered licences to telephone companies in return for a ten per cent royalty on their receipts. In 1893, as the GPO's Engineer-in-Chief, Preece was arguing for the full public ownership of the telephone system. In Malta, Henry tried to dissuade him:

> *'Preece... admitted the 10 per cent royalties were of great importance to the government. But he believed, under the control of the GPO, the profits would be much larger and the service much better, especially in regard to trunk calls. I ventured to call his attention to the fact that, since the GPO had controlled the telegraphs in the United Kingdom there was a marked absence of new inventions and improvements in apparatus and accessories in telegraph work. No new English patents were forthcoming, though before the GPO control (in 1870) the English were in the van of telegraphic progress; now they were in the rear. I pointed out to him that a monopoly controlled by government officials was apt to be strangled by red tape. There was no competition, which is the life of business, either in public or private affairs. Preece admitted the truth of this but naively remarked that most new telegraphic inventions were now coming from the United States. I replied, "Just so! The USA telegraph services are run by public companies, for the benefit of the shareholders, which can only be obtained by good service to the public". Preece admitted the justice of my remark but said with some pride, "You must not forget that in England, since we took control, you can send a telegram of twelve words anywhere in the United Kingdom, even from John o' Groats to Land's End, for sixpence". "Yes", I said, "but where it is useful to the public, it is profitless to the government".'*

In 1911 (two years before Preece died) the GPO finally succeeded in gaining complete control of the national telephone service. Arguments of the kind that Henry had put to Preece in Malta won popular support 90 years later when British Telecom, into which the Government had 'hived off' the GPO's telecommunications operations, was de-nationalised.

In the mid and late 1890s, and at the turn of the century, events occurred which had a major influence on the convergence of the careers of Henry Edmunds, Frederick Henry Royce and the Hon Charles Rolls, and on the expansion of Edmunds' and Royce's businesses. Within a few miles of their factories, the Manchester Ship Canal, which had been under construction since 1887, was completed in January 1894 and opened four months later, on 21 May. This led to the development of a vast complex of docks for ocean-going vessels almost in the heart of Manchester, and the creation at nearby Trafford Park of the world's first industrial estate. Royce won a large contract to install electric arc-lights along many miles of the waterfront, and in the warehouses (completing all arrangements in a few weeks', according to one account). Royce also manufactured worm drives and screw wheels for the docks' lock gates. Faced with an increasing demand for their company's products and services, Royce and Ernest Claremont realised that a substantial injection of capital was required, to finance new plant and an extension to the factory and enable the workforce to be expanded. On 20 June 1894, F H Royce & Co became a limited company, F H Royce & Co Ltd, with Royce as managing director and Claremont as chairman and joint managing director, and shares were offered to the public.

In 1898 Henry Edmunds and Godfrey Samuelson found that they too needed to raise new capital to finance their business plans, so W T Glover & Co also became a limited company, W T Glover & Co Ltd, with a capital of 200,000 £1 shares. Henry was appointed chairman and managing director. At about this time H P Holt and W P J Fawcus (who was soon to succeed Henry as the company's chairman) joined the board of directors. In March 1899, Royce and Claremont sought another £30,000 in share capital and at the same time changed the name of their company to Royce Ltd. By now, Glover was Royce's main or perhaps sole supplier of cables; collaboration between the two companies became even closer when Claremont became a director of W T Glover & Co Ltd and Henry Edmunds became a shareholder in Royce Ltd. The arrangement appears to have been the result of a deal whereby Henry exchanged some of his shares in Glover for a block of shares in Royce Ltd, in 1899 or a few years later. The story of both firms at this time is one of mutual prosperity; although documentary proof is lacking, there can be little doubt that W T Glover & Co Ltd supplied cables to Royce for the Manchester dock lighting scheme and purchased electrical equipment from Royce when, a few years later, it won the exclusive right to supply electricity to all the streets and premises in Trafford Park. To handle such a large undertaking Glover formed a separate company, the Trafford Power and Light Co Ltd.

By now the cable making industry was growing so quickly that Henry Edmunds decided that the time had come for those who controlled it to work together on matters of mutual interest. On 10 January 1900, 20 of them met for dinner at Dartmouth House, 2 Queen Anne's Gate, which had become Glover's third London office. Twenty-three years later, Henry wrote:

> *'I used occasionally to meet Mr George (later, Sir George) Sutton and Mr James Taylor. We were friends and yet competitors ... and we found that a friendly conversation was often useful in regard to questions of contracts, especially in connection with the demands of the Post Office and the National Telephone*

Company. I arranged with my board to have a dinner. I proposed the health of my various guests and took the opportunity of telling them that I thought it was desirable that we as a group should try to live off the public rather than off each other, in which sentiment I found there was complete unanimity.'

Today, talk of 'friendly conversations on questions of contracts' and 'living off the public, rather than each other' would create suspicions that a cartel was being formed to fix prices and share markets but Henry considered that his group, which became the Cable Makers' Association, was important to the industry's future:

'The mistake frequently made is that people in the same business are apt to have so much jealousy of each other that they overlook the great advantages that may accrue to each and all by seeing how they can collectively deal with commercial problems to much better advantage than by each confining himself to his own interests. The purchasing public is better served. Manufactures are standardised and foreign competition can be dealt with collectively to greater advantage than by the individual alone. We the chiefs of the electrical cable industry met at the Round Table. We employed this to show that all were equal, though the older firms looked patronisingly at the younger ones.'

Among those at the dinner were Robert (later, Sir Robert) K Gray of the Silvertown Cable Company and a future president of the Institution of Electrical Engineers; Alexander Siemens of Siemens Bros; and Thomas (later, Sir Thomas) Callender, founder of the firm that became British Insulated Callender's Cables (BICC). Everyone present gave Henry his autograph, probably on the back of a menu; the signatures were reproduced in his *Reminiscences* and show that others present included Ernest Claremont, A H Howard (who became a director of Glover in 1900), Godfrey Samuelson and W P J Fawcus. Another of the autographs is that of Claude Johnson. Could this be Claude Goodman Johnson, who later became Charles Rolls' and Henry Royce's partner (*'the hyphen in Rolls-Royce'*). It seems unlikely; there is little or no resemblance between the rather immature handwriting of the Claude Johnson who wrote his signature for Henry in 1900 and the authenticated signature of Claude Goodman Johnson found in Rolls-Royce Ltd's archives.

Autographs of some of the founders of the Cable Makers' Association.

Third signature from the top: 'Claude Johnson'

An authentic signature of 'Claude Goodman Johnson' from the Rolls-Royce archives

Nevertheless, it is tempting to suppose that *the* Claude Johnson was present at the cable makers' dinner and that he was prevented from writing his usual assertive signature because of a sprained wrist! If that theory is correct, Johnson was in strange company; in 1900 he was secretary of the Automobile Club of Great Britain and Ireland (forerunner of the Royal Automobile Club) and so far as is known he had no professional interest in electrical cable manufacture, then or at any future time. However, Henry was by now a member of the Automobile Club and would have been well aware that Johnson had considerable flair as an organiser and publicist; perhaps he was invited to the dinner to offer advice on how the Cable Makers' Association should be run, or was even regarded as a prospective secretary?

All through the 1890s Henry had kept abreast of the latest developments in science and engineering, by visiting exhibitions and attending meetings of professional and learned institutions. He had been an associate of the Institution of Electrical Engineers since 1879 and in 1897 he was elected a member of the Royal Institution; his proposers were Joseph Swan, James Crichton Browne, Dr John Hopkinson and F A Abel. In 1899 he joined the Institution of Civil Engineers. Meanwhile, in November 1896, another novelty had started to appeal to his imagination - the automobile. Years earlier, as a result of meeting Robert Blackwell and Michael Holroyd Smith, he had become interested in electric traction; the invention of the internal combustion engine and the pioneering efforts of Karl Benz in Germany in 1886 would not have escaped his notice, but Britain was ten years behind the times in motor car development. For Henry Edmunds and many of his contemporaries, the only form of personal mechanical transport they could afford at that time was the bicycle but on 14 November 1896, the long-awaited Light Locomotive Act that raised the speed limit from 4 mph to 12 mph came into force, the occasion being marked by the famous Emancipation Run from London to Brighton, organised by the Motor Car Club, a predecessor of today's Royal Automobile Club,

Both Henry Edmunds and Claude Johnson witnessed the event, but had yet to meet; Johnson, then 32 years old and chief clerk at the Imperial Institute, cycled halfway to Brighton with the convoy and therefore pedalled, no doubt somewhat breathlessly, past Henry, who had made his way to Brixton Hill to watch the cars go by. Henry Royce, we can be sure, was not there, since it would be some time before he took an interest in automobiles, but Charles Rolls, then a 19-year-old undergraduate at Cambridge, was *almost* present. He had set off from Cambridge in his Peugeot, intending to take part in the run, but the car's back axle broke and Rolls and his passengers were forced to abandon their journey. But for that accident, the 'hyphen in Rolls-Royce', 'the Godfather of Rolls-Royce' and Rolls himself would all have been within a few yards of one another on that important Saturday morning in motoring history. It would be several years yet before all three became acquainted.

The sight of those primitive motor cars making their way to Brighton unrestricted by red flags or a 4 mph speed limit made a lasting impression on Henry Edmunds. *'It is almost impossible to describe that scene, or to recall the feelings of those of us who saw it'*, he wrote afterwards. During the next 18 months his interest in motoring gradually increased and in May 1898 he went to Paris to buy his first motor vehicle. This was not a true motor car but a De Dion motor tricycle and trailer, built by the company formed by the Comte Albert De Dion and Georges Bouton. Their partnership bears a resemblance to the one that Henry Edmunds helped to form several years later: De Dion and Rolls were both wealthy aristocrats and motoring enthusiasts, who were fortunate enough to meet and collaborate with two of the most talented engineers of their day. The tricycle that Henry Edmunds bought from De Dion

Chauffeur-driven transport in 1898.
William Goody and Henry on the De Dion motor tricycle and trailer, probably photographed at 71 Upper Tulse Hill, Streatham.

and Bouton was driven by Bouton's air-cooled single cylinder engine, which ran at up to 1500 rpm. A precursor of the high-speed internal combustion engine, it later powered the well-known De Dion-Bouton *Vis-à-Vis* voiturette. Henry was particularly impressed by the engine's electric ignition, a feature he quickly mastered while learning to drive the machine in the Champs Elysées. It was then taken by rail from the Gare du Nord to Boulogne, and thence by ferry to Folkestone. Henry was accompanied by Ellen Edmunds, and between them they somehow managed to smuggle a gallon of petrol into England, as fuel for their first rides.

From Folkestone, Henry, Ellen and their tricycle travelled by train to Herne Hill, in south London. Few people had seen a motor vehicle before and a crowd soon gathered as they prepared to drive the few miles from the station to their home. Eventually a policeman arrived to hold back the throng and Henry inched his way out of the station yard and set off for Streatham on his first motor journey in London. In the months that followed he became something of a local celebrity:

> *'The De Dion caused much interest among my friends, who now had their first experience of riding in a horseless vehicle. My gardener, William Goody, forsook his ancient trade and applied himself to the most recent, that is, motor driving; and he speedily became expert, as far as the mechanism of that time would allow. There were occasional contretemps. On one occasion Goody was sent to Wimbledon, to bring a lady and gentleman to dinner. All went well until they came to a long, steep hill. Then the machine slowed down, and threatened to stop altogether. To relieve the weight temporarily the husband stepped off the trailer. The car [sic] immediately responded and went off in fine style, to the delight of the driver, who did not guess the real cause of the improvement. The lady screamed, but the noise of the engine drowned her voice and it was not until the driver brought the car in triumph to my house that he discovered that he had lost one of his passengers. Needless to say, there was great consternation. The chauffeur went back to look for the husband, and he met a very annoyed man who had walked uphill for a very long way and was not at all favourably impressed with the new mode of travelling.'*

In 1899 Henry decided to buy a proper car and went to the Paris Motor Show, where he was attracted by a *'charming looking, four-wheeled vehicle, with leather hood and silver-plated lamps, tiller steering, and a horizontal engine carefully hidden away under the back seat. It looked like a phaeton that had lost its horse. There was nothing about it to suggest that it was mechanically propelled'*. Henry bought the car there and then, and sent William Goody to Paris to learn how to drive and maintain it. Meanwhile, Henry went to visit W P J Fawcus at his home at Derwentwater, in the English Lake District. Henry proudly told Fawcus that he was expecting delivery of a fine French car, which would be driven from Paris to Le Havre, shipped to Southampton, and brought by train to Keswick. Henry was there when it arrived, hoping to drive back to Derwentwater, but the car stalled every few hundred yards. Henry sent it by train to London where for several months a mechanic tried, without success, to diagnose its defects.

Like many of his contemporaries, Henry eventually joined the ranks of Britain's motor car pioneers at the wheel of a Daimler. By now The Prince of Wales had given the marque a unique distinction by making it the first petrol car to convey British Royalty. Although the one that had been demonstrated to him had been built in Germany, Daimlers were being assembled at the company's new factory in Coventry by the time they came to Henry Edmunds' attention. In the autumn of 1899 he met Campbell Muir, who owned a Coventry-built two-cylinder 4 hp model, which had solid rubber tyres, tube ignition, a chain drive and tiller steering. Muir told Henry that he had made a number of long journeys, including one from Oban in Scotland to London, at speeds of up to 18 mph (illegal, but frequently achieved outside police 'speed traps') without mishap or difficulty. This was a good enough recommendation for Henry, who promptly purchased an identical model. No registration numbers had to be carried in those days, so in common with other motorists of the day Henry and Ellen decided to give their car a name. Like their first home, their first car evoked memories of Rhode Island. They called it *Rhoda,* and in it they took part in the first great motoring adventure of the twentieth century, the One Thousand Miles Trial.

Henry's 1899 Daimler, named Rhoda, with Goody (wearing his chauffeur's uniform). Henry and three young passengers on board – two of them are probably his sons Howard (on Henry's left) and Claud (behind Henry's right shoulder)

THE 1000 MILES TRIAL of 1900.

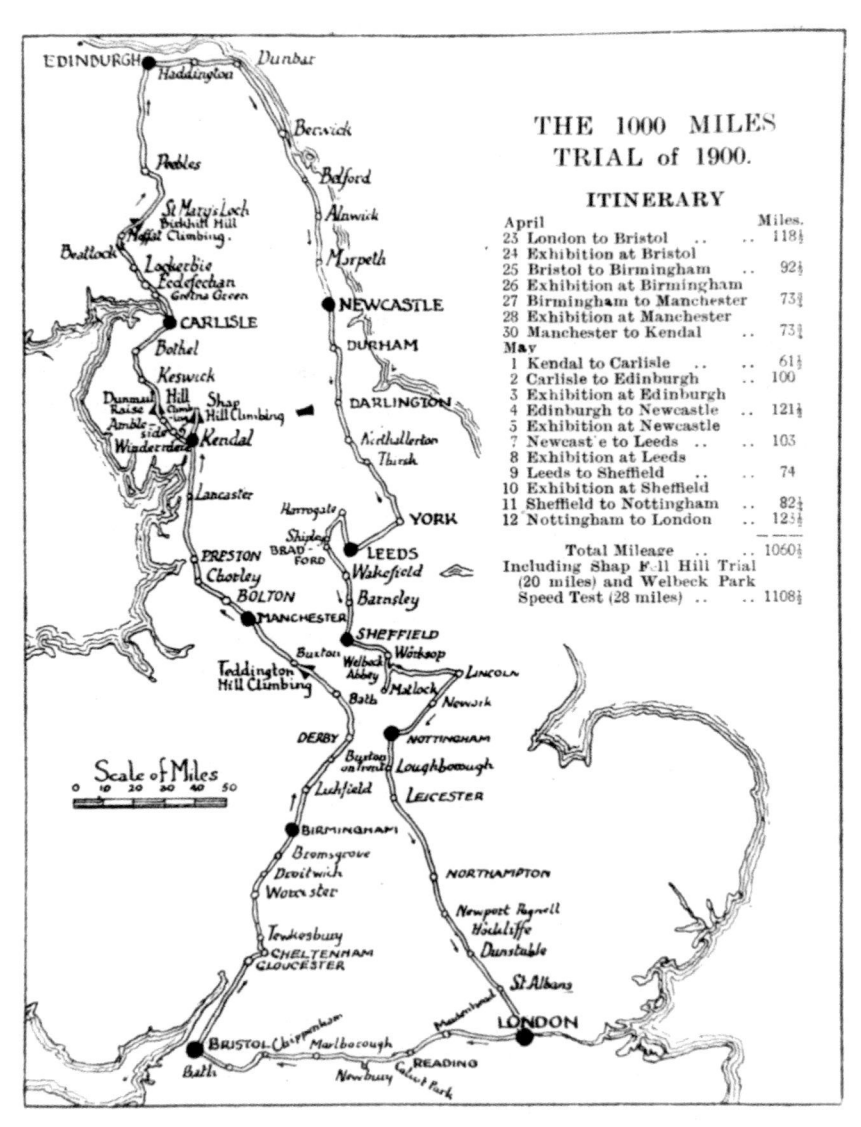

ITINERARY

April		Miles.
23 London to Bristol	..	118½
24 Exhibition at Bristol		
25 Bristol to Birmingham	..	92½
26 Exhibition at Birmingham		
27 Birmingham to Manchester		73¾
28 Exhibition at Manchester		
30 Manchester to Kendal	..	73¼
May		
1 Kendal to Carlisle	..	61½
2 Carlisle to Edinburgh	..	100
3 Exhibition at Edinburgh		
4 Edinburgh to Newcastle	..	121½
5 Exhibition at Newcastle		
7 Newcastle to Leeds	..	103
8 Exhibition at Leeds		
9 Leeds to Sheffield	..	74
10 Exhibition at Sheffield		
11 Sheffield to Nottingham		82½
12 Nottingham to London		125½

Total Mileage 1060½
Including Shap Fell Hill Trial (20 miles) and Welbeck Park Speed Test (28 miles) 1108½

A contemporary map of the route of the One Thousand Miles Trial

CHAPTER TEN

'My association with Mr Rolls'

The Automobile Club of Great Britain and Ireland was formed by C Harrington Moore and Frederick R Simms and held its inaugural meeting at 4 Whitehall Court, London SW1, on 10 August 1897. Moore and Simms had been secretary and vice-president respectively of the Motor Car Club but had resigned when it began to be exploited for business and company-promoting purposes. They based the constitution of the ACGBI on that of the Automobile Club de France, insisting that it should be essentially a members' club. Only 30 people attended the first meeting but four times that number were present at a general meeting and luncheon on 8 December, at which the club was formally launched. Charles Rolls was one of the founder members, and Claude Johnson was appointed full-time secretary, at a salary of £5 a week plus a commission of ten shillings for every member enrolled.[20] Henry Edmunds was not one of the founder members (in December 1897 he had yet to buy his first motor vehicle) but joined in 1899; he soon became an enthusiastic supporter of the club's events and was chairman of its touring section for a year. One of the first references to Henry in reports of the Automobile Club's affairs shows that on 14 February 1900, he attended a lecture given by John Montagu on *General aspects of British Automobile Manufacture*.[21] On that occasion Henry enjoyed the company of Charles Cordingley, T W Staplee Firth, Hiram Maxim, H Mulliner, Percy Northey, J D Siddeley, Frank Wellington and many others whose names occur again and again in the history of motoring.

In 1900 Henry was still busy with electrical inventions; he filed eight patent applications, including one for a self-propelled vehicle. Although he subsequently abandoned this application, it was significant because from now on Henry devoted more and more of his time to the engineering problems of mechanical transport and less time to those of electrical generation and distribution.

The practical problems of designing, driving and maintaining motor cars were impressed upon Henry and 64 fellow 'automobilists' in the spring of 1900, when they took part in the One Thousand Miles Trial, the route of which ran from Hyde Park Corner in London to Edinburgh, and back again. For Henry and most of the other contestants it was their first attempt to drive long distances, day after day. The event was

---

[20] *RAC Jubilee Book 1897-1947*, p25.
[21] *The Autocar*, 17 February 1900, p 171.

organised, almost single-handed, by Claude Johnson and sponsored by a wealthy newspaper tycoon, Alfred Harmsworth (the future Lord Northcliffe) and was intended to pull the Automobile Club out of the morass of financial problems and apathy into which it had fallen following its promising inauguration. Johnson was a brilliant organiser and publicist, and few were more enthusiastic about the future of motoring than young Harmsworth; together, they ensured that the trial was a success, both as a test of driving skill and as an exercise in public relations for the nascent motoring movement. Henry Edmunds entered Section II, Class 2, of the trial. Section II was for privately-owned motor vehicles *'driven by the owners or their substitutes or servants'*, Class 2 was for vehicles selling at more than £300 but less than £500. Henry's car, *Rhoda,* was one of 12 Daimlers among the 30 vehicles in Section II and according to his entry details it was of 6 hp, cost £410, had a seating capacity of four, weighed 18 hundredweight (2016 pounds) and carried a minimum of two passengers (including the driver) during the trial. Henry and William Goody shared the driving duties; we do not know who accompanied them but it seems likely that on some stages of the trial Ellen and Howard Edmunds and the twins, Claud and Dorothy, rendezvoused with *Rhoda* and took turns to be passengers. Goody wore his new chauffeur's uniform and, according to Henry, this was the first appearance of a uniformed chauffeur in Britain. For the trial, all the vehicles were given a number; *Rhoda's* was A12 and, numerically if not physically, followed A11, the 12 hp Daimler driven by John Montagu, who three years later would promote the legislation that became the Motor Car Act. Among other things, this required motorists to register their cars and fit number plates. Henry wrote a brief account of the trial:

> *'Up till that period, motoring was looked upon by the general public as an eccentricity. The Automobile Club speedily dispelled that idea and the energetic management of its first secretary, Mr Claude Johnson, established the motor car as a practical means of conveyance, and thus laid the foundation of one of our largest industries... the Thousand Miles Trial can, without exaggeration, be styled as 'epoch making' for it brought the new vehicle into a prominence that it could hardly have otherwise attained. The trial extended over three weeks, Sundays being carefully reserved as rest days. There were no less than 83 entries, comprising all sorts of vehicles, including motor tricycles, quadricycles and bicyclettes. We started at eight o'clock in the morning, in the presence of immense crowds, and all along the*

route mobs of people turned out to witness the unaccustomed sight. We who took part in the run had a most exciting time, although the enjoyment was considerably blurred by the flies and the dust, because at that time there were no windscreens and no tarred roads. An unkind critic said, "After the start the face of the motorist becomes a grimy one, in whose wrinkles the dust finds lodging, and the general appearance is akin to that of an employee at the Corporation dust destroyer". Nevertheless, we all felt that we were suffering in a glorious cause and we can now look back with pride at what we did for the world. The Thousand Miles run showed what could be accomplished by careful preparation and organisation. It was still a novelty for the ordinary individual tourist to make his journeys in speed and comfort, but the enthusiasm and experience of motorists soon rendered this possible.'

The event was not a race but a long distance rally. Drivers were judged on such matters as their average speed, the mechanical reliability of their cars and their performance in hill climbs and speed trials (the latter taking place on private tracks, because of the 12 mph speed limit on public roads in England and the 10 mph limit in Scotland). The ultimate prize was a Gold medal for *'the most meritorious vehicle to be accompanied throughout by its owner and driven or steered by him for at least half the distance of the trial'*. Silver medals went to vehicles which successfully completed the trial with their owners on board all the time and at the wheel at least half the time. Finally, there were Bronze medals for vehicles which successfully completed the trial, without qualifying for a Silver. As all the *aficionados* had forecast at the outset, Charles Rolls won the Gold.

Although Henry did not leave a detailed account of his experiences, his progress (or lack of it) was mentioned from time to time in official reports and articles in the press. On Monday 23 April, the first day of the trial, Henry arrived at Bristol, the first overnight stop, at about 9.00 pm, having taken more than 12 hours to cover the 118½ miles from London; Rolls, Montagu and S F Edge had been among the first to arrive, from 6.30 pm onwards, and about 40 others turned up during the next two hours, so Henry was truly one of the stragglers. However, *Rhoda* managed to keep pace with the rest of the field on the second stage to Birmingham, arriving there before 9.45 pm on Wednesday 25 April. On the previous day, the contestants' cars had been on display in the Drill Hall at Bristol at one of several motor exhibitions organised by the Automobile Club at major towns along the route. Like most of the contestants, Henry seems to have completed the early stages without major incident, but greater demands were placed on the cars and their drivers as they ventured further north, where the scenery became more spectacular, the hills steeper, and the bends sharper. More and more contestants began to drop out because of mechanical trouble and on Friday 27 April, between Birmingham and Manchester, the survivors tackled the first of the three obligatory hill climbing trials that had been arranged for them. This took place on Taddington Hill, a long but not especially steep ascent of two and a half miles en route to Buxton, which is just over a thousand feet above sea level and the highest town in England. Charles Rolls swept to the summit in his 12 hp Panhard at 17.7 mph and was the first car driver to reach the top. A J Wilson on an Ariel tricycle was first overall at 18.9 mph. *Rhoda* could manage only 6.43 mph and came 31st out of 44 competitors.

From Buxton, Henry and his companions took the road to Manchester and on the way enjoyed one of England's finest scenic drives, the four-mile climb to the Cat & Fiddle Inn. Some years later this hill would become one of Henry Royce's favourite places for testing his cars and the inn would form the background to a photograph of early Rolls-Royce cars that is familiar to all admirers of the marque. In 1900, though, the road to the Cat & Fiddle earned a place in the history of Rolls-Royce not only because it tested the driving skills of Rolls and Henry Edmunds (or chauffeur Goody) but also because Rolls took one of its bends too quickly, flinging Poole, his mechanic, into the road. Characteristically, Rolls was furious rather than sympathetic and told Poole that if he fell out again he would not stop to pick him up.[22] By now nothing could hold Rolls back and he was the first to arrive in Manchester; *Rhoda,* though, had suffered a broken accelerator cable somewhere along the way and was delayed for half an hour while repairs were made. The next day, Saturday, was reserved for the trial's third motor car exhibition, in the conservatories of the Manchester Botanical Gardens. *The Autocar* reported that for some, including the journal's own reporter, the day closed with *'a very recherché little dinner given by Mr Edmunds at the Conservative Club at which, of course, petrol talk was a feature of the hour'.*

The fourth stage, from Manchester to Kendal on Monday 30 April, was accomplished without incident. In the evening there was an optional ten-mile hill climbing trial up notorious Shap Fell, but *Rhoda* did not take part; Henry does not seem to have been imbued with a very competitive spirit and his own accounts of his motoring experiences leave the

---

[22] *Rolls of Rolls-Royce*, Lord Montagu of Beaulieu, p46.

impression that his main delights were touring and taking his friends and family for a spin, rather than striving for medals and trophies. The next hill trial was obligatory and was held on Dunmail Raise, a long straight road going north out of Grassmere, during the 61½ mile fifth stage from Kendal to Carlisle, via Keswick. This time, *Rhoda* finished about half way down the results table (26th out of 49), having climbed the 3,013½ yard course in 14 minutes 38 seconds, at an average speed of 7.08 mph. We do not know whether it was Henry or Goody who drove on this occasion, but whoever it was had the satisfaction of narrowly beating S F Edge's 8 hp Napier (6.84 mph) and John Montagu's Daimler (5.26 mph). Rolls took only five minutes to complete the climb, at 20.54 mph, and by now only the boldest gambler would have backed anyone but Rolls to win the trial. With Dunmail Raise conquered, everyone was looking forward to a troublefree journey to Keswick for lunch but, as *The Autocar* reported, that was not to be the case:

> *'Up to now the run had been devoid of incident, save that Mr Edge had suddenly found his clutch fail ... and not being ready with the sprag, his Napier had made a record trip backwards for one hundred yards or so, happily without mishap. Now, however, the incidents became numerous ... we had scarce got well to the level of Thirlmere, and were skirting its beautiful waters along an excellent road, when we came across Mr Edmunds' car with a broken spring and a hole in the adjacent wall.'*

What had happened was that the car's offside forward spring had broken, causing the car to swerve and collide with the wall. A photograph of the unfortunate *Rhoda* was published with the report, with a helpful caption drawing attention to the displaced spring and the hole the car had made. This accident put *Rhoda* out of the trial temporarily; the car had to return to Kendal for repairs.

Meanwhile, the other contestants embarked on the final outward stage, from Carlisle to Edinburgh; took part in an exhibition in the city's Waverley Market, and on Friday 4 May, began their homeward run by driving to Newcastle-upon-Tyne, via Berwick-upon-Tweed. One report says that *Rhoda* rejoined the rally at Edinburgh; another says Newcastle, in which case Henry would have bypassed the Scottish sections of the route. On Monday 7 May, *Rhoda* completed the run of 103 miles from Newcastle to Leeds in good time, arriving before 8.00 pm, and on 9 May drove without incident to Sheffield. *Rhoda* is not mentioned in reports of the speed trial held on the Duke of Portland's estate at Welbeck Park on Friday 11 May, but does make an ignominious appearance in an account of the final run, from Nottingham to London, that took place next day. This last stage, of 123 miles, was the trial's longest, and before much distance had been covered the drivers met an unadvertised challenge. Near Rempstone loomed Bunny Hill, which rises 110 feet in 1490 yards and has a final gradient of 1 in 7. This was as steep as any of the hills that had been climbed in the timed trials and *Rhoda,* which was carrying three passengers at the time, became well and truly stuck; nevertheless she was extricated and soon made up for lost time, completing the entire stage at an average speed of 12 mph. Of the 65 motor cars that had set off on 23 April, 35 completed the 1060-mile course under their own power. *Rhoda* won a bronze medal, despite the mishap at Thirlmere that may or may not have caused Henry to miss the trial's most northerly stages; according to the Automobile Club's official report, Henry's car maintained an average speed 'up to the legal limit' on four of the 11 stages of the trial.

Rhoda after colliding with a wall at Thirlmere during the One Thousand Miles Trial. Chauffeur Goody is at the controls. (National Motor Museum, Beaulieu).

Many friendships were formed or strengthened during the One Thousand Miles Trial, including that of Henry Edmunds and Charles Rolls. Henry saw very little of Charles during the event's motoring activities - an occasional glimpse, perhaps, of the leader's Panhard disappearing over the brow of a distant hill but in the evenings, at the informal dinners and official functions that provided relaxation after a demanding day on the road, the two men would have had many opportunities to talk about the exciting new movement they were pioneering. Claude Johnson would have been drawn into their discussions and perhaps it was during those April and May evenings in 1900 that they found common ground and developed the mutual ideas about the future development of the motor car that eventually drew the three of them and Frederick Henry Royce together. We can only speculate whether the presence of so many motor cars and motoring pioneers in Manchester from the evening of Friday 27 April until the following Monday morning was known to Royce. He would surely have been aware of the arrival of the 'automobilists' and their exhibition at the Botanical Gardens. There is no evidence that he took any interest in these events: he was probably too engrossed in his work at his factory in Cooke Street on the morning of the exhibition, and in the afternoon may have been working in his two acre garden at Brae Cottage, Knutsford, 15 miles from Manchester, where he and his wife Minnie had lived since 1898. But is it possible that, instead, he went to the motor show in Manchester? In Royce's biography, G R N Minchin related how Royce made an electric motor for an electrically propelled car built by Pritchett and Gold in 1900.[23] Royce now had a professional interest in motor cars; this, plus his insatiable curiosity in matters mechanical, may well have drawn him to the Botanical Gardens on Saturday 28 April 1900, to see the various types of engines and motors offered by other manufacturers. If so, he may even have exchanged a few words with Charles Rolls and Claude Johnson, four years before their first formal discussions.

A week after the One Thousand Miles Trial, Henry Edmunds was one of several motoring pioneers who dined with Rolls' father, Lord Llangattock, at South Lodge, Kensington, the family's London home. This is how he remembered the occasion:

> 'Much enthusiastic and informing conversation was exchanged. After dinner the guests retired to another room where cigars and cigarettes were in evidence. I recollect that the butler

---

[23] *The Life of Sir Henry Royce*, Sir Max Pemberton, p 172.

came in and said to Lord Llangattock that he had an important communication to make to him. His Lordship retired for a moment and then returned to inform us that Mafeking had been relieved. All the interest that had been exhibited in motoring and other matters was forgotten in view of this important news and that night I had great difficulty in getting to my home in Streatham through the crowded streets. That was one of the most vivid recollections left to me by my association with Mr Rolls in those early days.'

Later that summer Charles Rolls' Panhard and other cars earned £30 for Lady Georgiana Curzon's Mafeking Fund by giving rides at a fete at Crystal Palace. Henry bought £10 worth of tickets and spent them all on rides with Rolls.[24]

In August, not content with having only recently completed an official One Thousand Miles Trial, Henry decided to take his family off on another long journey but this time employing two cars, one for passengers, the other for luggage. He wanted to enjoy a holiday independent of railways and timetables and *'to feel the freedom of being able to go as you please and stop as you like'*. Their destination was Scotland and they decided to depart on Friday 3 August, the day when their second car, a new 10 hp Parisian Daimler was due to be delivered to their home at Streatham. The car had 'all the most recent devices', including Mossberg roller bearings, an Estcourt engine cooler, electric ignition, Falconnet compound tyres - and a steering wheel, instead of a clumsy tiller! Henry called this car *Antrona* (an allusion, maybe, to the curious second name 'Antron' he seems to have given himself some years earlier). Alas, like many holidaymakers, Henry and his entourage experienced an unexpected hitch in their plans; delivery of *Antrona* was delayed by a week but it was August Bank Holiday weekend and the family was anxious to set off. Henry decided to take delivery of the car en route, at Leamington Spa, so he sent Goody ahead by train with the luggage so that he, Ellen, Claud and Dorothy (now 19 years old) and Howard (now 17) could cram themselves aboard *Rhoda* for the first stages of their journey. Dorothy Edmunds wrote a long account of the holiday, entitled *A Cruise on Land; or the Log of a Motor-Car*, which was published in *The Motor-Car Journal* and reprinted as a booklet, which members of the Edmunds family distributed to their friends and relations the following Christmas. Her article provides the quotations

---

[24] *Rolls of Rolls-Royce*, id, p47.

that appear in the following story of what was, in 1900, an ambitious motoring accomplishment.

> *'July had been warm and sunny - ideal weather for touring in open cars - but during the morning of August 3rd the barometer fell precipitately and a sudden change in the weather seemed imminent. The family considered postponing their departure but friends at Banbury, seventy-eight miles away in Oxfordshire, were expecting them for dinner at seven o'clock, so at noon Rhoda left Streatham and headed through Putney and across London to Uxbridge and Amersham and on to Aylesbury, for a four o'clock tea: the roads we had traversed were fairly good, though many of them were wet through after recent showers; but we did not experience any rain to speak of.'*

At Aylesbury the car was refuelled; its petrol cost Henry 1s 3d a gallon (6p). On the road to Bicester the long-awaited storm broke in full fury, drenching Henry's party within a few minutes; Henry pressed on into the teeth of the gale while *'the engine behaved admirably, the burners keeping alight and the car making her average twelve miles an hour'*. A common hazard to early motorists was the presence on the roads of unharnessed horses and the horse-drawn caravans of gipsies (in fairness, perhaps it should be said that it was the motorists who were the hazard). Near Bicester and Aynho about 20 horses, free of halters and bridles, showed no fear as *Rhoda* passed them, but it was with some difficulty that Henry negotiated his way through the caravans of a country fair, whose drivers were almost deafened by the howling wind and could not hear the car approaching. The storm became fiercer as Henry drove towards Banbury along a road littered with leaves, branches and occasional large trees. The Edmundses arrived only 15 minutes late, although their friends had long since assumed that they would not attempt the journey in such weather.

A week later, Henry and his family drove the 21 miles to Leamington Spa (at an average speed of 10 mph) and stayed at the Regent Hotel for a few days until *Antrona,* her paintwork incomplete, was delivered. The first run by the two cars, to Shrewsbury via Stratford-upon-Avon and Wellington, was accomplished on Tuesday 14 August. *Antrona,* driven by Henry, lead the way:

> *'The cars were weighed, the old one, with luggage and driver, about 26 hundredweight, empty, 22 hundredweight; the new one, with five passengers on board, turned the scale at 31½*

> hundredweight, empty 24 hundredweight. The dimensions of the engine [were] practically the same and therefore we were looking forward with great interest to the relative performances. The new one was of the Iveagh phaeton design, carrying a hood and good leather aprons ... This being the first journey of the new car we ran cautiously and not much on top speed and arrived [at Stratford] ahead of the old car by about 10 minutes. She was running entirely on electric ignition and not using the burners at all.'

Antrona coped 'fairly well' with the steep hills and rough roads beyond Stratford and proved to be about 20 per cent faster than *Rhoda*. At Shrewsbury the family stayed at the Raven Hotel. While the cars were being overhauled next morning (15 August) Henry noticed that several bolts were missing from the flanges of the tyres. Replacements were made by a local cyclesmith and at 12.25 pm the cars set off for Liverpool via Wem, Whitchurch, Chester and Birkenhead. At Chester tea was taken at the Grosvenor Hotel but *Antrona* was now many miles ahead of *Rhoda;* Henry waited at Chester for an hour and three-quarters but as there was no sign of *Rhoda* he decided to press on as they wanted to get to Liverpool in time for dinner. At Birkenhead they endured a long and tedious wait for the Mersey ferry.

> 'The surroundings leading to the boat were not pleasing and the behaviour of the horses, the drivers of which were unaccustomed to motor-cars, was very trying to the nerves of some of us. Through the kindly offices of a man waiting to cross the ferry the car was enabled to get an exceptionally good position on the boat, so that it was the first vehicle to leave on reaching the other side, greatly to our own relief and to some of our fellow passengers. Our new friend volunteered to act as a pilot to take the most direct route to the Adelphi, where we arrived among a gaping crowd at 7.15. Meanwhile nothing had been seen of the second car with the luggage and as this was a somewhat necessary accompaniment to our night's enjoyment at the hotel our pilot was sent down to the ferry to make enquiries. However, it arrived at about 8.30. Though the Adelphi was a very comfortable hotel we were very pleased to leave at 11.30 in the morning. I overheard my father say something about the charge for storing motor cars in the livery stables of the hotel being outrageously high.'

The destination that day was Windermere, in the English Lake District, via Ormskirk, Preston, Lancaster, Carnforth and Kendal. Dorothy was highly critical of the state of the road between Liverpool and Ormskirk:

> 'Fortunately the tires [sic] of the car were new and thick, and we didn't go at any speed at all; the feeling was something like tobogganing in a bath chair down a flight of stone steps. Suddenly, a few miles from Ormskirk, the machine stopped altogether. I overheard some remarks about valves, electric ignition and burners, and apparently some sort of game of hide and seek was going on which occupied over an hour, during which all sorts of spanners and tools seemed to be used in all parts of the engine, but it still refused to go; meanwhile the other car had come up and a consultation was being held as to what should be done. Owing to the condition of the roads it could only just drag itself along and therefore could not think of taking us in tow. However, I heard something about the spindle on the camshaft being jerked out of place; a single touch and it was immediately right, and directly afterwards we were again on the way.'

Henry on *Antrona*, his new 10 hp Parisian Daimler, outside the Grosvenor Hotel, Chester, on 15 August 1900.

Henry and friends leaving Derwent Park for a drive round Bassenthwaite.

The road beyond Ormskirk was in better repair, allowing some of the lost time to be made up. Near Preston they were intercepted by two friends who were out for a cycle ride; they were taken aboard *Antrona,* their bicycles loaded on to *Rhoda,* and the party headed for the Preston Park Hotel, arriving at 1.30 for a 'capital lunch'. The Edmundses then set off again in the two cars, giving their friends a lift as far as Carnforth before proceeding to Kendal (stopping for tea from 6.10 pm until 6.35 pm) and Windermere, where they stayed overnight at the Belsfield Hotel, in the neighbouring town of Bowness.

Next day (Friday 17 August), as *Antrona* led the way along the 'low road' to Keswick from Windermere, there was more mechanical trouble:

> 'On climbing a hill the engine did not appear to be pulling very well and as the hill grew rapidly steeper it was deemed best we should all get out and walk, in order to lighten the car; except my younger brother, who thought he would take it up at its lowest speed with the sprag down. We had not gone far when it

> seemed as though the engine would stop, upon which he put on the hand-brake, which releasing the clutch, allowed the engine to get up its speed again, but in consequence of too rapidly releasing the brake and the clutch engaging, the car suddenly jumped forward, but for some unaccountable reason suddenly halted, and then began to run back, leaping the sprag, and the car, quickly gaining momentum, began rapidly to descend the hill backwards. My father called out to turn the car into the wall; this was done and, striking a small tree, it came to an abrupt stand, the engine however still running. Upon examination we found the concussion had bent one of the radial bolts and thrown off the near chain. It was at once apparent that the car would not proceed until the bolt and bent sprag had been straightened.'

As often happened in those transitional years of horse-drawn and horseless carriages, a local blacksmith was called upon to repair a mode of transport that would eventually bring about an abrupt decline in his trade. *Antrona* (for we presume that it was this car, not *Rhoda* the baggage car, that foundered on the hill) was restored to running order and the journey continued. Dunmail Raise was conquered by the motoring Edmunds family for the second time in four months and Keswick was reached without any more mishaps. The next few days were spent with friends and then, on Thursday 23 August, the party set off for Carlisle, running into a violent hailstorm at Kirkland Green, which obliged them to force their way through several inches of slush. The County Hotel, Carlisle, provided the high standard of overnight accommodation to which everyone had by now become accustomed, and in preparation for the hilly country that lay to the north, smaller sprocket wheels were fitted to both cars; thus equipped, they coped quite easily with the steeper gradients. On the Saturday they drove to Dumfries, the road through Gretna Green and Annan being of *'excellent quality'*. During their two nights at the Station Hotel the cars were housed at the nearby King's Arms stable yard whose proprietor, a Mr Irving, *'asked many questions as to the relative merits of motor cars versus horses for excursion purposes'*. The stables were vacated at noon on Monday 27 August, as *Antrona* and *Rhoda* headed for Cassillis, in Ayrshire, encountering a long, taxing rise of 17 miles soon after leaving Dumfries:

> 'Much... had to be done on the first and second speed. This tested very practically the relative merits of the Estcourt cooler attached to the new car, with the pump and ordinary radiator

of the old car, for circulating and cooling the water of the two engines. It was interesting to note that although it was a hot day the Estcourt cooler appeared to do all that was requisite, and although some steam was produced yet the engine ran well and continuously without any signs of overheating or trouble from this cause in any way.'

Henry's Daimlers on the road from Dumfries.
Antrona, with Henry at the wheel, leads, while Goody follows in Rhoda and gives a local postman his first ride in a motor car.

A halt was made at Dalry for lunch. Later, the cars overtook a postman, who gladly accepted a lift and thus experienced his first ride on a motorcar. At about this time *Antrona's* electric ignition developed a fault and on the long, tedious ascent to Dalmellington, via Carsphairn, the burners were lit and the platinum 'hot tube' ignition brought into use:

'We had not gone far before we slowed down. Evidently something had happened and we found that one of the tubes had been perforated. It took some time to replace this but the time waiting was not lost, as it enabled us to take several photographs and to admire the grandeur of the scenery.'

The family stayed with friends at Cassillis House for the rest of the week, making local excursions to Ayr, Girvan and Maybole. On one of these outings *Antrona* shed a tyre and in lieu of a pneumatic tube a solid rubber filling, obtained from Glasgow, was placed in the outer casing. This worked well enough for the time being but was to create its own problems 200 miles later.

Meanwhile, though, the tour continued; Peebles was supposed to be their next destination, but due to a late departure from Cassillis on Sunday 2 September, it was 6.00 pm before they arrived at the King's Arms Hotel, Douglas, for their scheduled halt for afternoon tea. They were given such a welcome that they decided to spend the night there instead of in Peebles. Douglas became the turning point for their holiday and next day they set off on the first stage of their journey home. Dorothy vividly captured the pioneering spirit of turn-of-the- century motoring:

> *'We started in good time en route for Carlisle, and made some of the best running over immense stretches of moorland and beautiful roads, going through Crawford and Beattock. For many miles we ran parallel with the railroad and had the advantage of a long down grade. The engines were pulling splendidly and there was an indescribable charm in the exhilaration of rapid motion through the fresh moorland air, startling every now and then in our run some grouse or rabbits, occasionally passing flocks of sheep but for the most part we had the road practically to ourselves. We exchanged salutes several times with the engine-drivers of the passing trains, they blowing their whistles and we tooting the horn, each recognising the peculiar advantages of horseless vehicles.'*

Near Beattock, another postman carrying a heavy mailbag enjoyed his first motor car ride. Lunch was taken at Lockerbie; a visit was made to the early home of Thomas Carlyle, the Scottish historian, at Ecclefechan; and an unsuccessful effort was made to find the legendary blacksmith's smithy at Gretna Green. After staying overnight at the County Hotel, Carlisle, Henry had further repairs carried out to *Antrona's* ignition:

> *'As we had on several occasions experienced some trouble through the burners blowing out, my father had a small alteration made to the chimney and several holes perforated in the door of the burner chamber, which we were glad to find completely cured this trouble.'*

Their route on Tuesday 4 September, took them to Barnard Castle via Penrith, Temple Sowerby, Appleby, Brough and Bowes, the road into the last of these places proving to be rougher than any they had previously encountered:

> 'We followed a mere track, with deep cart ruts in several places and covered with loose stones. It was very hard work for the car and certainly did the tires no good, but after leaving Bowes we again struck a good road. Then we discovered that the tire which we had repaired in Scotland had become loose and we had to crawl on very slowly in order to prevent slipping it altogether. We did not arrive at Barnard Castle till 6.30. The climb up the hill from the river to the hotel was about the steepest grade we had yet encountered ... the novelty of a motor car attracted a considerable crowd and we found it very necessary to get up without stopping or unloading. We were heavily laden and the tire was loose but we managed to negotiate the hill successfully.'

Next morning, Henry measured the gradient and found it to be 1 in 6. He also called on a local engineer and a cycle and clock repairer to repair the damaged tyre. They found that the solid rubber filling had been pulverised into a powder; the wheel had also been damaged, but somehow they repaired it and the tyre, and that afternoon the Edmunds family drove on to Leyburn. On the way, at Richmond, they weighed *Antrona,* fully laden, and found that it made 31¼ hundredweight. Commented Dorothy: *'It certainly spoke well for the Mossberg roller bearings when one considers the speed and load we could carry with only a 6 hp [sic] engine'.* Bad weather marred a day's stay with friends at Leyburn, to whom they said farewell on Saturday 8 September, and set off for York. Unfortunately, more mechanical problems dogged their journey:

> 'Again there were indications of coming trouble with the tire which had on previous occasions been several times repaired, so we ran slowly and cautiously, but just as we were within a quarter of a mile of York ascending a slight incline, the tire suddenly parted company with the wheel and came off altogether. This was most awkward and annoying but it was fortunate we were so near our destination. The tire having become badly cut it was impracticable to replace it, so we sought shelter for the car at

the hands of a friendly blacksmith and, unloading the luggage into a passing cab, proceeded to the Station Hotel.'

Henry had intended to have the car repaired and then continue on to London but while in York he heard that urgent business problems had cropped up while he had been away. *Antrona* was put on a train to Mulliner's, the coachbuilder, so that its paintwork could be completed; the wheel was sent to Paris to be mended. *Rhoda* was driven to Coventry (probably by Goody) to be overhauled, and earned fulsome praise from Dorothy:

> *'The record of its run, though not so quick as the new Parisian Daimler, was certainly most satisfactory. It practically never broke down or stopped for repairs and alterations during the whole run, and though by no means as swift as its new companion it proved that it is possible to get a good average speed Daimler motor car that can accomplish a run of this distance without fear of interruption or breakdown.'*

Antrona (right) and *Rhoda* at Leyburn in the North Riding of Yorkshire

It is interesting to note that Dorothy's meticulous account of their journey gives the time taken to complete the various stages of their journey, but no mileages. It was not until 1901 that the first motor car mileometer, the Bell Odometer, went into regular commercial production, at S H Davis's factory in Portland, Massachusetts. Henry's cars do not appear to have been equipped with any means of measuring distances. Had she wished to do so, Dorothy would have had to count the milestones erected at the roadside during the coaching era, 60 years earlier.

Antrona was soon back in service, and on an Automobile Club run to Portsmouth won a prize donated by Alfred Harmsworth for 'the smartest car on the road'. A photograph taken on that occasion shows the Mayor of Portsmouth climbing aboard *Antrona* while two lady passengers in the rear seats, presumably Ellen and Dorothy, snuggle into their fur coats on what appears to have been a rather chilly day in late summer. On 4 December 1900, Henry delivered a lecture on *Automobiles, their history and development* to the Streatham and Tulse Hill Literary Society, illustrating his talk with lantern slides of his own pioneering journeys. Soon he would embark on another, carrying three passengers in *Antrona* from London to Falmouth, no adjustments or repairs being required during the journey of 320 miles. On 29 September 1900, the Automobile Club Journal published a poem contributed by Henry and inspired by his trip to Scotland. This also appears in Dorothy Edmunds' account of their holiday and may have been a joint effort by father and daughter:

> 'You may ride on a horse or a mule or a moke,
> You may drive in a carriage or sail in a boat,
> You may swim in the water or fly in the air,
> Go just as you like, but only take care.
> You may skate, you may walk, take train, tram or 'bus,
> Go in great state, or without any fuss,
> You may bike on a wheel, a single or tandem,
> Go just as you please, at will or at random;
> You may stay at home near, or travel afar,
> But nothing can equal a mote on a car.'

The Mayor of Portsmouth boards *Antrona* during an Automobile Club rally. Henry is at the wheel and his passengers are probably his wife Ellen and daughter Dorothy. Goody and two passengers following in *Rhoda*.

Aerial view of the Glover and Royce factories in Trafford Park, Manchester, in the 1930s. A fine layer of snow highlights the outline of the buildings.

CHAPTER ELEVEN
The first Royce motor car

The urgent business problems that caused Henry to abandon, three hundred miles from home, what would have been his second One Thousand Miles Trial of 1900 were probably connected with construction of W T Glover & Co's new factory. Trade had expanded rapidly since the firm became a limited company in 1898, and it had become increasingly urgent to move from Salford to larger premises. The Trafford Park Estate Company was now developing a 1200-acre industrial estate on Trafford Park, an island between the old Bridgewater Canal and the Manchester Ship Canal. Henry and his co-directors were among the first businessmen to appreciate the benefits of moving to what was one of the world's first industrial estates; a lease on a large plot of land was signed in 1899 and by the beginning of 1900 work on a new factory for cable and wire manufacture, and associated activities, was well underway. Glover was one of the first companies to move to Trafford Park; another was an enterprise that eventually earned the reputation of being one of the 'universities' of engineering, the British Westinghouse Electrical and Manufacturing Co. Until Glover's power station (referred to in Chapter Nine) was built the company supplied electricity to Westinghouse and Trafford Park's other first occupants from a generator in its stores. In years to come the power station would serve such famous companies as Metropolitan-Vickers and Ford (which opened a factory for its famous Model T at Trafford Park in 1911).

As Glover's new buildings became ready for occupation, machinery was transferred from Salford on horse-drawn wagons that made their way through what was then wooded parkland. Output was not affected; indeed, several large contracts were taken on during this changeover period, including Britain's first main line railway electrification programme, on the Lancashire & Yorkshire Railway's line from Liverpool to Southport. Glover also became involved in lead mining, took over a 'Blue John' mine in Derbyshire and formed a company called the Ashover Fluo Spar Co. The project was eventually abandoned, although for a time the mine supplied a considerable quantity of lead for Glover's cables. Henry also took a personal interest in minerals at about this time and obtained the US rights to a number of German patents for making Portland cement from a mixture of blast furnace slag and limestone. Why Henry considered diversifying into cement production, apparently in America, is a mystery, but it may have been because the new construction projects, such as Trafford Park, that he saw all around him made him realise that there would soon be a huge demand for cement and concrete; he would also have been aware that Thomas Edison was building a vast cement works in eastern Pennsylvania. Henry said nothing about his own cement venture when writing his *Reminiscences;* by then he had probably forgotten all about it. The venture seems to have been short-lived and unsuccessful: William Ransome's process for producing Portland cement in rotary kilns was already well established in the USA and from 1903 onwards became a commercial success in Britain. Virtually the only documented references to Henry's cement patent rights that have survived the passage of some ninety years are to be found in patent literature, and in entries for payments for translations and other small items recorded in the cash book of the Henry Edmunds Trust Account, which survives in the archives of Claremont, Haynes & Co, a London firm of solicitors, where Albert William Claremont, brother of Henry Royce's partner Ernest Claremont, was Henry Edmunds' private solicitor from about 1900.

While Glover & Co was establishing itself at Trafford Park, the two men whom Henry Edmunds would soon introduce to one another were busy with new enterprises. Henry Royce's firm had found itself in a similar position to Glover, occupying a factory hemmed in by other buildings and unable to expand to meet the demand for its products. In 1899, barely a year after Glover had completed a somewhat similar exercise, Royce's firm (now called Royce Ltd) raised additional capital and looked for a site for a new factory. It was no coincidence that one opposite Glover's new works was chosen; by now the two businesses had very close ties. In 1901 Royce Ltd moved its iron foundry and electric crane manufacturing departments to Trafford Park. The Cooke Street works were retained for the manufacture of small electrical equipment and, as we shall soon see, for purposes that were to become of immense importance to the development of the motor car. Royce designed most of the new factory himself; this work, combined with the pressure to reduce costs to cope with a sudden and an unexpected recession, and competition from German exporters and new firms like British Westinghouse, affected Royce's health. He was by now a 'workaholic' and sometime in 1901 or 1902, to encourage him to get away from his work and out into the fresh air, Ernest Claremont persuaded him to buy a De Dion motorised quadricycle; this was Royce's first documented involvement with a petrol-engined vehicle, and marks the point at which he started to become more interested in internal combustion engines than in electric power and lighting. Meanwhile, in London, Charles Rolls was planning his future. Unlike Royce, he had no money problems; his allowance of £500 a year enabled him to live very comfortably in

London or at the Llangattock's family seat in Monmouthshire, but he needed additional income to cover his motoring expenses and his new interest, ballooning, and so in January 1902 he became an automobile agent at Lillie Hall, Fulham.[25] The business, C S Rolls & Co, was, of course, financed by his father.

The activities of Claude Goodman Johnson at this important period in the careers of Rolls and Royce are also of interest. By 1902 he too was looking for new horizons. For five years he had worked tremendously hard to establish the Automobile Club and steer it through a series of difficulties; it was now at a stage where it had two thousand members and needed larger premises, necessitating a move from Whitehall Court to 119 Piccadilly, a building which, as Cambridge House, had been the London home of King George III's brother, the Duke of Clarence and, more recently, the Naval and Military Club. A report that Johnson was to resign from the Automobile Club appeared in the Christmas 1902 issue of John Montagu's glossy motoring periodical *The Car Illustrated;* he remained in office until the summer of 1903, joined the City and Suburban Electric Carriage Company for a short time, and at the end of 1903 joined Charles Rolls' firm, C S Rolls & Co, which had recently opened a showroom in the West End of London, at 28 Brook Street, Mayfair. Between late 1900 and 1903, Henry Edmunds' name continued to appear in articles on the activities of the motoring pioneers. One of these reported that at a meeting of the Automobile Club committee, held shortly after Queen Victoria died on 22 January 1901, Henry proposed that the club should send a token of affection and respect to her funeral; this took the form of a wreath, 4ft 3in in diameter, composed of lilies-of-the-valley, orchids, violets and lilies. Two weeks later Henry suffered a personal bereavement when Thomas Wayman, father of his first wife Annie, died at South Bank, Banbury, Oxfordshire. He had lived there in retirement after an active life of public service in Halifax, where he had been a councillor, a governor of the Crossley and Porter Orphanage, a Congregationalist church deacon and the town's Liberal MP. His two younger daughters, Kate and Alice Mary, had both married men from Banbury (Albert Sutcliffe Edwards and Henry James Edwards). Henry often wrote of visiting Banbury, where he had several friends and relations, including Thomas Wayman and his wife Sarah (maternal grandparents to Henry's twins, Claud and Dorothy) and Albert and Kate, who lived at a house called Southlands.

Patent applications by Henry continued to proliferate in the years 1901-03, including some for automobile valves and clutches, and others for

---

[25] *Rolls of Rolls-Royce*, Lord Montagu of Beaulieu, p90.

machines for making and cleaning roads and paths. Several of these patents were soon abandoned, and none seems to have progressed beyond the design stage, but Henry did make a more tangible contribution towards improving the performance of motor cars by offering to donate a trophy to the Automobile Club for a hill climbing competition. Henry's offer was announced in the club's Journal of 31 July 1902. By this time the trophy had already been designed by Gustav Gurschner of Vienna, a well-known sculptor; the trophy is a representation in bronze of a motorist and his companion, wearing caps, goggles and oilskins, crouching in a car and determinedly heading for some distant summit. Henry asked the executive committee to work out the particulars of the competition, but suggested that it should be held annually and the trophy awarded to the car that was the fastest to ascend Dashwood Hill, or any other hill selected by the committee. The winner would receive a medal bearing an impression of the design of the trophy, or a miniature reproduction of the bronze; the trophy itself, with the winner's name engraved on its pedestal, would be kept permanently at the club. These proposals were accepted and in November, shortly before another committee meeting, Henry called at the club to offer to donate the dies for the medals that would be presented to the winners. The bronze, officially called the Automobile Club Hill Climbing Trophy but popularly known as the Henry Edmunds Hill Climbing Trophy, was delivered to 119 Piccadilly in December 1902 and displayed in the Smoking Room shortly before Christmas. It was put up for competition during the Irish Fortnight that followed the Gordon Bennett Cup motor races in July 1903, organised by the Automobile Club.

The obligation to stage the 1903 'Gordon Bennett' was a considerable embarrassment. The competition, for a trophy donated by James Gordon Bennett, a flamboyant American publisher, was held annually among national motor clubs and was a race over 550-650 kilometres of public roads. The rules required that the race should take place in the country that held the cup. In the years when the winners were from countries where there were no speed limits, finding a suitable course for the following year's race was no problem. Britain, though, had a 12 mph speed limit (one reason for her backwardness in motor car design and lack of success in international racing), so when Selwyn Francis Edge won the cup during the 1902 Paris to Innsbruck race (and thus gave Britain her first victory in international motor racing), the Automobile Club had barely twelve months to find a way round the legal and political problems that prevented the cup being defended in Britain. At first there was a chance that the Motor Vehicles Registration Bill, which proposed the abolition of the speed limit, would become law by 1903 but as the months passed and public opinion against the Bill hardened, it became obvious that any change in the law would come too late. Fortunately, at least from the point of view of those who supported motor racing, Ireland was still governed from Westminster and John Montagu MP introduced a special Bill to allow the race to take place on a course near Dublin. Held on 2 July, the race was won by Germany for the first time; there then followed two weeks of motoring tours and trials, including a speed trial in which the first prize was the Graphic Trophy. Touring cars valued at over £300 and under £1000, carrying a driver and three passengers, could enter, and the course was over five miles of hills and dales near Castlewellan, in County Down. One of the hills, on the road to Clough, had gradients as steep as 1 in 9 and it was here that the first trial for the Henry Edmunds Trophy was held, the competition being open to any gas-engined car carrying two people seated side-by-side.

The Henry Edmunds Hill Climbing Trophy
(Philip Hall, Sir Henry Royce Memorial Foundation)

The event was reported in *The Car Illustrated* on 15 July:

> 'The distance cannot have been more than 600 yards but it was never actually measured. Mr Sturmey's little three-wheeled Duryea Phaetonette was the first car to take the hill... and she was followed by three 22 hp light Daimler cars, Mr [John] Scott Montagu's, Mr Manville's and Mr Instone's. The close running of these cars in this and the race for the Graphic Trophy was remarkable and they beat every touring car with the exception

of Mr J W Cross's 20 hp Humber in both races on Friday. Mr J E Hutton's 60 hp Mercedes was the first racing car to take the hill, which she negotiated in 38 and one-fifth of a second. Mr Stocks, on Mr Edge's big Napier car, went up in 37 and three-fifths and Mr Higgenbotham on a 60 hp Mercedes in 46 and four-fifths. Then came Mr Campbell Muir on his 60 hp Mercedes. Mr Muir has been practising on the course for some time and has become well known to the inhabitants of Castlewellan, who greeted him with cheers whenever he made his appearance on the road.'

Campbell Muir was the winner, in thirty-two and two-fifths of a second; Charles Rolls came second, in thirty-three and four-fifths. Thus began a competition that remained a fixture in the British motor sport calendar until 1914 and has left a mystery, to be discussed later, which remains unsolved to this day: where is the Henry Edmunds Trophy?

E Campbell Muir winning the Edmunds Trophy in 1903 in his 60 hp Mercedes. (From *The Car Illustrated*, 15 July 1903, National Motor Museum, Beaulieu)

Henry's motoring activities led inexorably to his becoming intimately acquainted with the first car that Henry Royce built, but it was no casual acquaintance stemming simply from the fact that, as a shareholder and, it has been said, a director of Royce Ltd, Henry Edmunds was in a position to encourage and advise Royce when he started to show an interest in motor vehicles. What actually brought the two men together as motoring pioneers, and not just as electrical engineers with common business interests, was a succession of events which began, not at the Royce or Glover factories in Manchester, but in London.

As we have seen, in the middle of 1903 Claude Johnson joined the City and Suburban Electric Carriage Company, which was designing and building electric broughams. Silent, clean and easy to handle, these were, in Johnson's opinion, ideal town cars. The arguments in favour of electric cars have been repeated many times, prompted by public concern over pollution, traffic congestion and the price of petrol, but their limited power and range have prevented them becoming popular, although forecasts that these problems will soon be overcome are still announced almost annually. Johnson's venture into electric cars was short-lived but was interesting because the founder and owner of 'City and Suburban' was his friend Paris Eugene Singer, who appears in many stories of the lives and times of Edwardian London's playboys, artists and actresses, whose company Johnson also enjoyed. Singer, more than six feet tall, with copper-blond hair, was one of the youngest sons among the 23 children of Isaac Merritt Singer (1811-1875), the manufacturer of the sewing machine that bears his name. Paris (named after the city where he was born) was 36 years old at the time he and Johnson became business partners; thanks to his family's fortunes, Paris was a millionaire and could well afford to invest in electric cars or any other inventions that took his fancy. In six years' time he would become one of Isadora Duncan's lovers (a relationship that was marred by tragedy when their son Patrick, his half-sister Deidre and their nurse drowned when Singer's car rolled into the Seine), but in the story of Henry Edmunds and Rolls-Royce, the dramas of Paris Singer's colourful private life are irrelevant; what does matter is that in 1903 one of his employees was a young engineer named Harry Parsons, who lived at 67 Beechdale Road, Brixton Hill, only a short distance from Henry's home in Streatham. Harry was a member of the Polytechnic Racing Bicycle Club and while racing on wet grass tracks had become painfully aware of how bicycles were liable to 'side slip' and go out of control on slippery surfaces. He had probably taken many a tumble while cornering or overtaking. One day he had the idea of interlacing whipcord through the spokes of his wheels and across the tyres.[26] This led him to invent and patent the first non-skid chain for motor cars and form the Parsons Non-Skid Company Ltd, which held its first board meeting on 10 February 1903.

---

[26] *The Link*, Parsons Controls Holdings Ltd, June 1978.

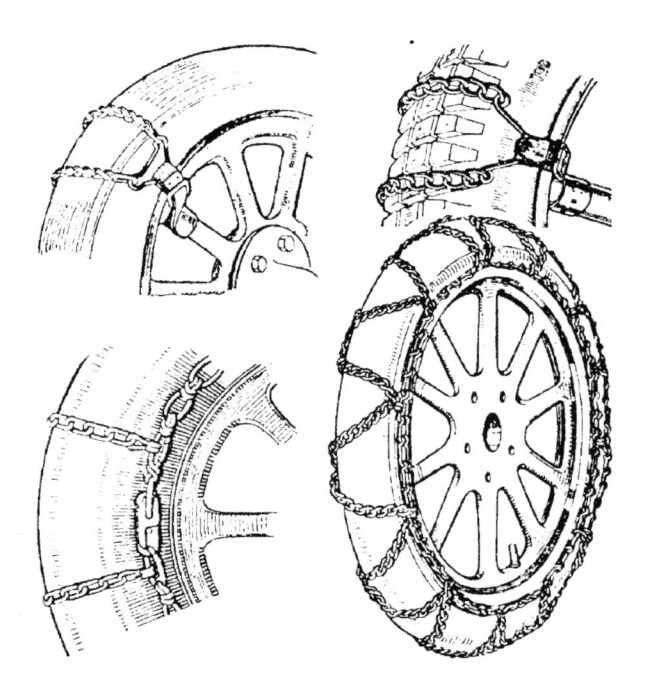

Non-skid devices of the early 1900s

Top left: Parsons' 'emergency' grip
Top right: Griff non-skid chain
Bottom left: 'Off-'n-On' non-skid chain with self-locking catch
Bottom right: Parsons' non-skid chain

Paris Singer, obviously impressed by his former employee's invention, was one of the new company's directors. Henry Edmunds became its chairman. We can only guess how he became involved in the Parsons venture; the most likely explanation is that, as an entrepreneur and motoring pioneer, he quickly recognised the potential for a 'non-slip' attachment and was eager to back the company. Its register of members and board minutes show that its registered office and the venue for its first board meeting was 2 Queen Anne's Gate, Westminster, where Glover had its London office and where Henry ran other ventures which seem to have had only tenuous connections, if any, with his activities at Glover. At the first board meetings of the Parsons company, appointments and shareholdings were minuted. Edward John Pilcher of Parliament Mansions, Westminster, described as secretary to a publishing company, was appointed company secretary; for the next 20 years he was one of Henry's closest and most trusted business associates. In May, 694 Ordinary shares were acquired by Harry Parsons, while Henry Edmunds, Edward Pilcher, Alice M Parsons, Arthur E Clarke, William John Crampton and Paris Singer all bought one share each. Preference shares (200 per two person) were sold to Henry, Crampton and Singer. Five months later Henry acquired another 134 Preference shares and Singer another 133.

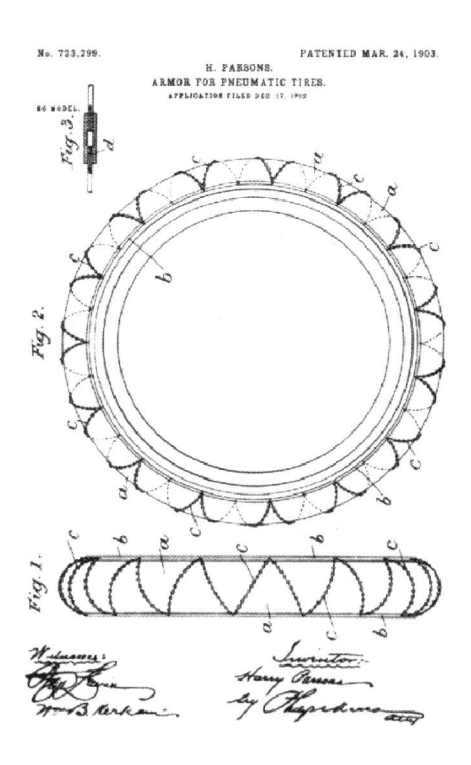

From Harry Parsons' patent application for his non-skid device or 'armor for pneumatic tires'

At Parsons' first board meeting Henry reported that the company had received orders for 66 pairs of non-skid attachments, 48 of which had been delivered. The device was fitted to cars' rear wheels, so we can deduce that in early 1903 there were 24 cars ready to cope with the slippery conditions imposed by that winter's ice and snow, and by the treacherous wood-block paving encountered on main thoroughfares in London and other major cities. Contemporary photographs show W J Crampton's 10 hp Decauville and Henry Edmunds' Daimler, *Antrona,* fitted with Parsons 'non-skidders'; these were certainly among the first, if not the first, cars to be thus equipped. Despite being able to record a healthy influx of orders at their first meeting, the directors already had problems; a notice to quit had been received from the owners of its workshops in Manor Street, Clapham, but fortunately suitable premises were soon found behind a terraced house further along the street. At around this time, Harry Parsons' business address was c/o the City and Suburban Electric Carriage Co, 157A Manor Street, so the two companies were obviously closely associated; Parsons was to remain in Manor Street until 1917, long after 'City and Suburban' ceased trading. On 10 January 1903, the first article on the Parsons non-skidder was published in *The Autocar:*

> 'The device consists in its approved form ... of two flexible wire hoops, one on each side of the wheel and of slightly larger diameter than the rim. The hoops are connected together by steel chains passing diagonally from one hoop to the other round the tyre. The hoop or ring on the inside of the wheel is endless but the outer hoop is supplied with a right and left-hand screw coupling, which affords a ready means for adjusting the non-skidder to the tyre. The diameter of the hoops is such that they cannot pass over the periphery of the tyre and we are assured they cannot come off even when it is deflated. The non-skidder is not fitted tightly enough to impress the tyre visibly and in running 'creeps' slightly, so that the chains never bear on the same point of the cover at any two consecutive revolutions. Any very slight loss in efficiency from this cause is probably more than made up by the superior adhesion of the wheel and non-skidder as one. That is to say, the loss is probably far less than it would be with a plain tyre on a greasy road; but not only so, there is the immunity from danger at good speeds and the entire freedom from nervous stress, which can only be obtained with plain tyres by driving at a very low speed indeed, and even then, in certain conditions of road surfaces, a little slipping may take place. We are informed that some dozens of wheels have been running on different cars over long distances and that none of the covers have [sic] shown any signs of wear from the non-skidder having been used.'

The article helpfully went on to explain the nature of side-slip', the phenomenon the non-skidder was designed to prevent:

'[It] is caused by failing to bite the road proper, the mud, when being in what is known as a greasy state, acting as a sort of lubricant and presenting a film between the tyre and the road surface, so that the car has little lateral stability; and any deviation from the line of progress, whether caused by steering or the disturbing effect of brake application, results in a side-slip more or less serious, according to the speed and general circumstances of the moment. The action of the non-skidders appears to be that they cut through the grease and get a bite upon the road itself.'

The Autocar went on to report that a set of non-skidders had been supplied to King Edward VII, though this is not mentioned in the company's minutes.

Crampton's 10 hp Decauville, with Parsons' non-skid chains fitted to its rear wheels (From *The Autocar*, 10 January 1903). Crampton is at the controls. His passenger is Harry Parsons.

Enquiries were received from France, Belgium, Germany and the USA, and Parsons applied for patents in Italy, Hungary and Switzerland. Henry Edmunds took on the responsibility for negotiating overseas contracts and patent rights - something in which he was well-experienced - and at the company's second board meeting, on 27 February, he reported that he had visited the German Patent Office in Berlin with Karl Piper, the company's patent agent. The officials there had told him that they would recommend acceptance of Parsons' patent. In Berlin Henry also met Karl Gossi, a director of Neue Automobil Gesellschaft, who asked to test the non-skidder, and in Brussels Henry agreed to give a Captain Macui a discount of fifty per cent for two months, while he attempted to sell the device to Belgian motorists.

Henry developed export markets for the non-skidder very quickly, for on 12 March he was able to advise that Mr Williams of the Collier Tyre Co had passed on an offer from Vital Bouhourf et Cie of 22 Rue des Arls, Le Vallois, Seine, to deposit 10,000 francs with Parsons and order 2000 non-skidders for resale under a royalty arrangement, the 10,000 francs to be considered as advance royalties. The offer was rejected but Henry also reported that Etienne Jacquemin of 16 Avenue d'Antin, Paris, had visited the company and after discussions with his business associates had offered a down payment of £500 for the French patent and thirty per cent of the shares of a company that he proposed to form in Paris to market the invention. The directors accepted the offer, subject to the share allocation being increased to thirty-five per cent. Further negotiations were held with M Jacquemin and on 7 April Henry presented a draft contract whereby Jacquemin would purchase the French rights in return for a cash payment of 12,500 francs, and 48 fully paid shares of 500 francs each in a company to be formed by Jacquemin with a total capital of 60,000 francs. Two months later Parsons was able to announce that the Societe Francaise de l'Antiderapant Parsons had been established at 9 Rue de Rocroy, Paris, to manufacture non-skidders for France and the French colonies. There was only one more board meeting during the next six months; this was held on 20 May, when the only matter that required approval was the purchase from Henry, W J Crampton and Paris Singer of various tools, instruments and models used by the company prior to the time when it took over Harry Parsons' patents. On 12 October, W J Crampton resigned from the board; his place was taken by another engineer, Edward Manville. Later, Manville would become chairman of the Daimler Company and of Car and General Insurance, BSA, the Royal Exchange Assurance Company and the Metropolitan Railway, and president of the Society of Motor Manufacturers and of the Association of British Motor and Allied Manufacturers. He would also serve as Unionist MP for Coventry from 1918 to 1923 and receive a knighthood. Henry and Edward Manville became lifelong friends, and Henry played an important part in Manville's early career in the motor car trade, by teaching him to drive.

The minutes for the meeting at which Manville became a director of Parsons contain a resolution asking *'Mr Claud [sic] Henry Edmunds'* to negotiate the sale, under licence, of the company's patents in the USA, in return for a commission of ten per cent on the net proceeds of the sale.

This is one of the few recorded instances of Claud becoming involved in his father's business affairs. Although Claud eventually became a clergyman, as a young man he studied engineering at Trinity College, Cambridge, and worked for Glovers. Despite what the Parsons' minutes tell us, it is difficult to believe that Henry totally entrusted the patent negotiations to his son. The cash book for Henry's personal account shows entries for *'Fare to America, £117'* (14 October), *'Balance of passage money to America, £107'* (26 October), *'United States consul's fees, £6.6s'* (25 November) and *'Expenses to New York, £75'* (30 November). Parsons' minutes reveal that Edward Manville took the chair at the four board meetings held in November and December; we also know from Henry's own *Reminiscences* that on 6 January, 1904, he was on board the White Star liner *Cedric* at Queenstown and received a telegram from George Sutton which read:

'Cable Makers' Association toasted its founder and regretted his absence from Annual Assembly.'

All this confirms that Henry was in the USA in October and November 1903. If Claud was negotiating for Parsons, he was doing so under his father's strict supervision. Henry was probably accompanied by his entire family - Ellen, Howard, Dorothy and Claud - who would have taken the opportunity to visit their relations in Rhode Island and spend Christmas there. When the next Parsons' board meeting was held, on 26 January 1904, Henry acquired another 198 Ordinary shares and other directors transferred part of their shareholdings to Edward Manville. Henry signed the minutes of the meetings held in his absence and reported on the outcome of his visit to America. It had in fact been something of an exploratory venture; nothing definite had been agreed with potential licensees although, as we shall see later, the company did eventually enjoy great success in America. The year 1904 was, however, to be the one in which Henry made his biggest contribution to motoring history, for the time was approaching when Henry Royce would assemble and build his first car and be persuaded to form a partnership with Charles Rolls.

What helps make the history of motoring so fascinating is the way in which unrelated events converge, with consequences that lead to major progress in the development of motor cars or the establishment of new business ventures. In the history of Rolls-Royce, two unrelated events spanning the period from the autumn of 1903 until the spring of 1904 had unforeseen but significant repercussions. They were the Automobile Club's Side Slip Trials and Henry Royce's decision to build three motor cars of his own design. Henry Edmunds' role in the trials is well documented but we cannot prove that he played any part in the development of the Royce car; we can only assume that, as the most experienced motorist among Royce's friends and colleagues, he readily offered advice and encouragement as Royce painstakingly turned his ideas into reality. Henry also had sound business reasons for helping Royce; as a shareholder in Royce Ltd he would have been concerned about the poor sales prospects for the company's electrical products at that time, and anxious to help it diversify into new and more profitable ventures. Henry Edmunds realised, though few industrialists would have agreed with him, that building motor cars was going to become big business.

As we have seen, the first petrol-engined vehicle that Royce owned was a De Dion Quad. His transition from driving this primitive form of conveyance in 1901 or 1902 to producing his first car in 1904 has not been chronicled in great detail - too little information has survived the passage of time to allow this to be done, but we do know that his first excursions and experiments with internal combustion engines were carried out at around the time he was developing an electric motor. In Chapter Ten we named G R N Minchin as the source of a story that Royce built a motor for Pritchett and Gold's electric car of 1900. Royce and Minchin first met in 1902 and were friends until Royce died in 1933. Royce often spoke and wrote to Minchin about his early life. Minchin's recollections of his talks with Royce, his knowledge of Rolls-Royce's formative years, and the letters he received from Royce were quoted at length in Pemberton's Life of Sir Henry Royce. However, later research suggests that Minchin may not have been entirely accurate (either because he was misinformed or because of a lapse of memory), and that the motor he referred to was built in 1902, not in 1900. In 1902 Pritchett and Gold had a factory at Feltham, Middlesex, and were well-known as manufacturers of accumulators. An associate company, Pritchett Brothers, had for about ten years been agents for Royce Ltd's products and had installed Royce dynamos and Pritchett batteries in electrical systems in country houses in the south of England. Sometime in 1902, Pritchett and Gold started building a range of motor cars, including a petrol-driven model with a 14 hp Blake engine and Panhard-type transmission, and a two-seater electric car. The latter was described in the 7 February 1903, issue of The Motor Car Journal:

> *'The vehicle ... has been designed to meet the demand of owners of country houses who have an electric lighting plant. It is exceedingly simple, and can be safely driven by a lady. The motor is specially designed for running for long periods*

without attention, it being self-lubricating. It is mounted at about the centre of the frame, driving the rear axle through the bevel gearing. The controller is arranged to give four speeds forward, ranging from five to 18 miles an hour, and two speeds backward. The battery consists of 40 cells in ebonite boxes having a capacity of 120 ampere-hours. It is divided, one portion being carried in front of the car under a bonnet, the other being under the seat. This arrangement gives equal distribution of weight over the chassis. With the battery fully charged the car will on good level roads run a distance of about 40 miles.'

The idea of building an electric car whose battery could be recharged from domestic lighting systems was most ingenious, and who better to build its motor than Royce Ltd, the firm that made the dynamos for these systems? Further evidence that the designer of the motor was Henry Royce was discovered in 1984 by Michael Evans, while writing a book on Rolls-Royce's origins.[27] On Michael's behalf, Ralph Smalley of Herbert Morris Ltd, the company that acquired Royce Ltd in 1932, searched through Royce Ltd's drawings registers and found an entry dated 18 November 1902, entitled *General arrangement of 6" x 4 ½" Auto Car Motor.* The customer for the motor was Pritchett and Gold. The drawing itself was also discovered. We cannot be certain that this was Henry Royce's first design for an electric car motor, or that this was the motor that powered the production model of Pritchett and Gold's electric car, but unless and until any earlier drawings are found it seems safe to assume that Henry Royce's career as a designer of car engines and motors began in 1902, not 1900. Michael Evans also relates how, in London in 1984, Lamar H Gilbert, a member of the Rolls-Royce Heritage Trust, bought an English translation of a French textbook entitled *The Automobile - its construction and management.* The flyleaf is signed *'F H Royce'* and dated September 1902. The book had been found in the south of France, where Royce died. We can imagine it being taken from his bookshelves at La Villa Mimosa, his home at Le Canadel, when his personal possessions were removed, and perhaps changing hands several times until being acquired by someone who recognised the importance of the inscription.

These facts and theories about Royce's early interest in motor cars have emerged comparatively recently, but they dovetail neatly with the oft-told stories of his purchase of his first 'proper' car. These tell us that despite the efforts of his colleagues to persuade him to take time off

---

[27] *In the Beginning: the Manchester origins of Rolls-Royce*, Michael Evans, Rolls-Royce Heritage Trust.

for leisure and recreation, Royce collapsed from overwork in 1902 and had to take a holiday; for ten weeks he and his wife Minnie were away visiting relations in Cape Town. When he returned in late 1902 he bought a secondhand 10 hp two-cylinder Decauville car, and seems to have spent half of 1903 testing, dismantling and reassembling the vehicle in order to learn its innermost secrets. It is often said that Royce's new interest was a sudden whim, far removed from the mainstream of his professional life and ambitions, but this theory is less convincing now that we know that the purchase of the car more or less coincided with the design of the motor for Pritchett and Gold. Royce was highly critical of his Decauville and considered it coarse, noisy and unreliable. He put his views on record in a newspaper article published in 1923; later, in his biography, Pemberton wrote:

> '[Royce's] purchase was unfortunate, a little French carriage whose promise was greater than performance and whose shortcomings were speedily to reduce its owner, if not to weeping, at least to war. The contrivance apparently went nowhere and returned by the same route. The clever but inefficient design, the overheating, the inadequate system of ignition, all these must surely have exasperated a man of Henry Royce's development. He may at last have said, 'Be d---d to it', but if he did not, that destiny must have been in his mind.'

Pemberton may have been unfair to the Decauville, which had many admirers. H Massac Buist, author of the first history of Rolls-Royce[28], recalled that Royce's car was *'a notably cleverly schemed machine of the period having, among other singular attractions, a direct drive and also a live axle'*. Thirty-eight years later, in their book *The Rolls-Royce Motor Car*[29], Anthony Bird and Ian Hallows argued that the criticisms of the Decauville had distorted the true perspective: *'... the stature of Royce, and the Rolls-Royce cars, does not need to be artificially enhanced by exaggerating the defects of contemporary cars ... Decauville was one of the better makes of small car.'*

Whatever conclusions are drawn from the various accounts of Royce's experiences with his first motor car, what is certain is that he was not taking a mere academic interest in the internal combustion engine. In 1903 he also repaired and tested various makes of cars owned by friends and acquaintances and announced, to the evident dismay of Ernest Claremont that he intended to build a car to his own design.

---

[28] *Rolls-Royce Memories*, Cambridge University Press, 1926
[29] B T Batsford Ltd (1st Edition, 1964)

Significantly, despite his involvement with Pritchett and Gold and his twenty years' experience in electrical engineering, his design was based around a 10 hp two-cylinder petrol engine and not batteries and an electric motor. The design of the car, and the way in which it was assembled and tested, are well described in the works of the authors mentioned above, and by the doyen of Rolls-Royce historians, the late C W (Bill) Morton.[30] What is closely relevant to our story of the life of Henry Edmunds is that the car was built in the last four or five months of 1903 and first three months of 1904, the period in which Henry became anxious to enter the Parsons Non-Skid Company in the Automobile Club's Side Slip Trials, which were to begin on Monday 18 April.

News of the trials had been published in *The Car Illustrated* on 26 November 1902, when it was announced that Alfred Harmsworth had subscribed £100 towards a prize fund. *'Side-slip is undoubtedly the greatest drawback in connection with modern motor-cars'*, said the report, *'and affects every automobilist ... the importance of the trial cannot be overestimated. In order to stimulate clever inventors to give close attention to the prevention of side-slip, it is necessary that there should be a handsome reward held out in connection with the trial'*. Every member of the Automobile Club was asked to subscribe at least one guinea to the prize fund, and from the list of the first subscribers we can see that Paris Singer, Edward Manville and Henry Edmunds were already taking an interest in the prevention of side-slip, even though they had not yet formed the Parsons Non-Skid Company. Singer donated £100, Manville ten guineas and Henry one guinea - a comparatively small contribution, admittedly, but he had already made a generous donation to the club in the form of the Henry Edmunds Hill Climbing Trophy. The committee that organised the Side Slip Trials was headed by Sir John Thornycroft and among its members was Charles Rolls, whose presence may be significant in view of events to be described later. More than a year passed before final arrangements for the trials were made; it was originally scheduled for November 1903, then March 1904, but on both occasions was postponed due to difficulties in finding a suitable test track. Meanwhile, in February 1904, the French Automobile Club held a series of anti-skidding trials at Versailles. The Parsons non-skidder was among the entrants but did not distinguish itself. Undaunted, Henry and his colleagues went ahead with their intention to take part in the British trials and Parsons was among the 16 companies and inventors on the entry list when it closed on 29 February. On 17 March the *Automobile Club Journal* published details of the event:

---

[30] *A History of Rolls-Royce Motor Cars*, Vol 1, Foulis, 1964

> *'The various devices entered will first be submitted to an endurance test of 1,000 miles, each car having an official observer on board to see that no repairs are made. Those devices that come through the test will then be subjected to side-slipping and brake tests to prove that efficiency is not impaired by actual service. These tests will be held on the excellent private track which is being constructed round the new works of Messrs Clement Talbot Ltd near Ladbroke Grove [London], which has kindly been placed at the disposal of the club by that company. The tests will consist of a right angle turn on a greasy wood surface, followed by a zigzag course to be completed at a speed of 15 - 20 mph. Then will follow a brake test at the same speed.'*

A similar report appeared in *The Autocar*, which commented that the decision to precede the trials with an endurance test was *'unquestionably the right thing, as there are a good many arrangements which act excellently as preventers of side-slip when new but which have a comparatively short life. They either wear out completely or else the wear to which they are subjected so affects their anti-skidding properties that they become mere tyre protectors and make little or no difference to side-slip'.*

On Tuesday 22 March, the directors of Parsons held their thirteenth board meeting. It was announced that Paris Singer had resigned and had sold his shares; this may not have been unexpected, and does not seem to have generated much discussion. William Crampton was elected to take his place. The directors also approved a few changes in the shareholding structure of the company: Crampton transferred some of his shares to Henry Edmunds, who at the same time purchased another 50 Ordinary shares and 166 Preference shares. The most urgent item on the agenda, however, was the provision of a car for the Side Slip Trials. One would have thought that a group of motoring pioneers would have been spoiled for choice. According to the previous year's *Motoring Annual and Motorists' Year Book,* Henry himself had by now covered more than 40,000 miles in his Daimlers and it is surprising that he did not put *Rhoda* or *Antrona* at the company's disposal; as we know, *Antrona* had already been used to test the non-skidder. Despite this, William Crampton was empowered to 'acquire or hire' a car for the trials.

If Parsons had held further board meetings before the trials took place, the company's minutes would probably have recorded exactly what happened next, but from subsequent events we do know that Crampton was unable to acquire a car and that Henry Edmunds had to find one at short notice. Exactly when this became his responsibility is not known, but it was probably during late March. He may have considered entering Antrona but by now Royce's '10' was in an advanced stage of construction and Henry was attempting to persuade Charles Rolls to meet Royce and inspect his car. Sometime during this period the Royce 10 became the car that Parsons entered in the Side Slip Trials. We can only guess how this arrangement came about: Henry may have asked Royce if he could borrow the car or perhaps Royce offered it, without being asked. This asking or offering could have occurred before or after the car made its first road test run, on Friday 1 April.[31] Early April would seem to be the most likely time for the arrangement to have been agreed, since by then the roadworthiness and reliability of the car had been established; Henry was also now waiting for a response to his first letters to Rolls and Royce suggesting that they should meet, and may have had an ulterior motive in bringing the Royce 10 to the Automobile Club. That motive would, of course, have been to give Rolls an opportunity to drive the car without having to go all the way to Manchester to do so.

---

[31] Harold Nockolds, C W Morton and other Rolls-Royce historians have given 1 April 1904 (Good Friday), as the date on which the first Royce 10 went out on its first road test. It is also said that, to avoid being called April Fools by anti-motorists, Royce and his team for some time afterwards maintained that the car went on its first test on 31 March. The car was evidently 'ran-tanned' as Royce drove it out of the factory. One wonders whether, in view of the strong views in those days against working on significant days in the Christian calendar, 1 April can be accepted without question as the day of the Royce 10's outing.

Monday 18 April 1904, soon after 9.38am. The first Royce car sets off along Piccadilly, London, on the first stage of the 1000 mile endurance test that preceded the Automobile Club's Side Slip Trials.
(National Motor Museum, Beaulieu)

A detail from the previous picture. Close scrutiny suggests that Henry is the driver and that the man sitting behind him is Goody, his chauffeur.

The first road test of the Royce 10, from Royce's factory to his home at Knutsford, passed without incident. About two weeks later the car was taken to London, either by train or under its own power, to join the ten other entrants in the Side Slip Trials. The other contenders included two Panhards, two Wolseleys and a Lanchester. They were all despatched from the Automobile Club's garage in Down Street, Piccadilly, on Monday 18 April, by the club's technical secretary, Basil H Joy. The Royce 10 was the third to leave, and could be seen setting off along Piccadilly shortly after 9.38 am. Fortunately, a photographer was there to capture the moment for posterity and his picture was published on page 349 of the 3 May issue of *The Motor*. The picture is fascinating for what it does show, and tantalising for what it does not. Two numbers are prominent: N-MR-6, on the car's registration plate, and 14, its entry number. The entry numbers bore no relation to the order in which the cars ran or the number of entries; five competitors withdrew before the start. The registration plate is itself a minor memento of motoring history. The 1904 Motor Car Act, the culmination of a long parliamentary campaign fought by John Montagu, a friend of Henry Edmunds and Charles Rolls, had been in force for 15 weeks. Car owners now had to licence their cars and display registration numbers but manufacturers and traders could carry trade plates. N-MR-6 was one of three trade plates used by Royce when he was embarking on his career as a motor car designer; the others were N-MR-7 and N-MR-8. [32]

The Motor's photograph also gives us a glimpse of Royce's 'pre-Parthenon' radiator, which preceded the famous grille and pediment that graced his later cars. With a little care, mechanical details can be picked out although not (unless a little imagination is applied!) the Parsons non-skidders on the rear wheels. But who are the blurred figures riding in the car? One would expect Royce to be at the wheel, but if he had driven the car during the trials that fact would surely have come out in the press reports of the competition. If by some chance it escaped attention then, it could hardly have failed to be mentioned in Royce's own accounts of his early motoring experiences, or in the reminiscences of those who knew him. We must, therefore, assume that he was too busy in Manchester - where he was now building a second Royce 10 - to be able to go to London for the Side Slip Trials. So who would he have allowed to drive N-MR-6? Royce had not yet met Rolls, so it is unlikely that he would have let a stranger - even someone of Rolls's reputation - drive his precious first car. In any case, Rolls had not yet been convinced that the Royce 10 was worth testing; it is also

---

[32] An account of the registration numbers allocated to Royce Ltd was published in *The Rolls-Royce Owner* Vol 1, No 7, 1964 (Ed. Jeremy Bacon).

likely that he would have been too busy working with Claude Johnson on other matters to have been able to spend several days trying to win a competition for a company in which he had no financial interest. Ernest Claremont had not yet been converted to motoring, so it is most unlikely that he would have volunteered to take any part in a journey of one thousand miles, let alone drive during a competition.

This surely leaves only one candidate: Henry Edmunds, for who else would Royce have trusted to drive the car? Unfortunately, the photograph in *The Motor* does not help us answer this question, for the driver of the car was looking to his left at the moment it was taken and we do not get a good view of his face. But when this photo is compared with others taken during Henry's motoring career the fellow in the offside rear seat looks suspiciously like Henry's chauffeur. There were few more experienced teams for a 1000-mile trial than Henry Edmunds and William Goody, and they more than anyone else are likely to have been the men who shared the driving chores. Two other passengers can be seen on the car: a burly, bearded and begoggled figure next to the driver and, behind him and almost concealed from view, another passenger who appears to be looking to his left and perhaps exchanging a few words with the occupant of a carriage on the edge of the picture. We know from contemporary accounts of the trials that the Royce 10 carried Massac Buist as an official Automobile Club observer and an unnamed reporter from the *Morning Post.* They must be the two passengers on the nearside of the car; the bearded man can only be Buist, since he would have sat next to the driver. He is holding what appears to be a map or itinerary and his duties probably included acting as navigator. In his *Rolls-Royce Memories* Buist had this to say:

> 'I consider myself peculiarly favoured to have ridden on it [the Royce car] on the 18th of that month [April] ... it did all its work with a splendid ease, and had no use for 'followers', whether hansom cabs or cars.'

Without naming Royce or Royce Ltd, the man from the *Morning Post* wrote:

> 'It is the first car to be built by the well-known Manchester firm of electrical engineers and as it comes newly from the workshop it is pleasant to be able to record its excellent running, whether on the level or in negotiating long and steep hills, with four passengers, on the second of the three forward speeds. The engine is at all times very flexible and it picks up splendidly

after ascending trying gradients and on encountering less stiff ones.'

To compound our frustration about the lack of vital facts about the driver of the car, Henry omitted to say anything about the Side Slip Trials in his *Reminiscences,* nor it seems have any Rolls-Royce historians attempted to find out how it was that the Royce 10 came to be entered in the Side Slip Trials. However, there is no doubt that Henry Edmunds and the Parsons company were involved.

Margate, on the north Kent coast, was the destination for this first outing for the Royce car and its rivals, and as they crossed Blackheath and climbed Shooters Hill the drivers saw before them the orchards and hop gardens that would line most of their route. The Royce 10 arrived at Gravesend, on the lower reaches of the Thames, at 11.14 and then headed for Rochester and Canterbury, down the long, straight highway (now the A2) called Watling Street that the Romans had built from Dover to London. By one o'clock the Royce 10's driver was negotiating the descent from Harbledown into Canterbury. The temptation to halt for lunch at one of the city's ancient inns must have been almost irresistible but this was a serious outing and only one stop (a brief one, to ask the way) was made during the entire outward run. The Royce car was the first to arrive at the turning point, the Clock Tower on Margate seafront, after a journey lasting four hours and sixteen minutes.

Shortly before 3.00pm on 18 April 1904. Competitors in the endurance test at Margate. The Royce car is the third from the left and partly obscured.
(National Motor Museum, Beaulieu)

The Royce 10 was in Margate for only 52 minutes, during which a photographer working for *Motoring Illustrated* took a picture of a group of the cars, among them the Royce, a 12 hp Parsifal fitted with special anti-skid tyres, and an Argyll equipped with Sainsbury Anti-Skidders, a kind of spring fork device carrying an arrangement of blades each side of the wheel. These were the only cars that had arrived when the picture was taken shortly before three o'clock, since several of the others had lost their way. Here again the photographer teases us, for the Royce car is partly obscured by one in front; two people are inspecting the Royce's rear offside wheel, but neither of them are recognisable.

The return journey, which retraced the outward route, began at 2.56 pm. The Royce car had been the third to leave London that morning and now, by coincidence, was the third one to return, arriving at 7.20 pm after a day in which it covered 145½ miles in 8 hours 50 minutes. The day had passed without incident for the Royce but not for some of its rivals; Samuel Butler's 15 hp Panhard suffered a 'severe puncture' at Crayford and had to retire. Those who organised and reported the trial were disappointed at the lack of excitement. Between central London and New Cross, on the outskirts, there were tramlines and paving sets, which could have set the cars skidding in all directions, in wet weather. *'What was wanted'*, complained *Motoring Illustrated, 'was pouring rain all day so that the many kinds of anti-skidders should have every opportunity of proving their worth or depositing the passengers or car in the hedge or ditch ... the road was perfectly dry for the whole of the distance ... so it is hoped that heavy showers will descend at least on two or three days of the total run'.*

This was the first of several days of long-distance motoring, and on the stages that involved an overnight halt in London the cars were kept at the Locomobile Garage in Sussex Place, Bayswater. Security was very strict; the premises were selected because they had separate facilities for storing the vehicles under lock and key, and an entrance by which they could enter and leave without mingling with the normal traffic using the garage. Evidently, such facilities were not available at the Automobile Club's garage in Down Street, which would have been busy with members coming and going to club functions.

The Locomobile Garage was a ten-minute drive from Piccadilly and a similar distance from South Lodge, the Llangattocks' London residence in South Kensington. We will discuss later the tantalising proximity in April 1904 of the Royce car and Charles Rolls, who by now had heard all about the car from Henry Edmunds but, according to accepted history, had not yet seen it.

Thursday 21 April 1904: competitors in the endurance test set off for the Midlands from the Locomobile Garage.
The Royce car is immediately behind the tree furthest from the camera and is identifiable by its entry number (14) and part of its registration plate.
(From *The Automotor Journal*, 7 May 1904. National Motor Museum, Beaulieu)

After the run to Margate the little car doggedly clocked up the road miles that would qualify it for the trials on the skid track a few weeks later. On the day after the Margate run the cars drove down to Marlborough in Wiltshire and back; and on Wednesday 20 April, they tackled a hundred miles of slippery tramlines by twice covering a route between London, Slough and Beaconsfield. Next day, the cars set off from the Locomobile Garage on a three-day run to the Midlands. A photographer was there to record the scene for *The Autocar* and *The Automotor Journal* as the convoy departed. The Royce 10 is again visible, partly obscured by a group of people but still identifiable by its registration plate.

On all the outings from London the car performed without attracting adverse comment but on the Friday, midway through the Midlands run, serious trouble with the car was experienced. A reporter from *Motoring Illustrated* who was due to board the Royce at 10.30 one morning and travel from Birmingham to Nottingham wrote an account which more than made up for the previous lack of incidents:

> 'We were appointed to car number 14, fitted with the Parsons non-skid, but on taking possession learned that the differential was damaged and needed repair before starting. The repairs would not, we were told, take long, so we contented ourselves with the idea of making up some lost time on the road. In the end these repairs were not finished until 8.30 pm, when a start was made for Nottingham by the direct route through Tamworth and Long Eaton, 53 miles. [The official route was a circuitous one of 116 miles.] At one point a wrong turning was taken and we found ourselves in the centre of a lawn heading straight for an ornamental lake. However, we regained the right road only

> to miss it again after passing through Long Eaton and found our progress barred by a gate across the road, collision being avoided by a sudden application of the brakes which brought us to a standstill within a couple of inches of the obstacle. Nottingham was reached just before 1 am and we were surprised to hear that there were still some of the morning starters to be accounted for. Next day we heard tales of woe, of rain, of lost roads and discomfort; it had rained throughout the day, cars had missed their way time and again, roads were heavy and all reached Nottingham weary and wet through.'

On the Saturday the cars were driven back to London. Sunday was a rest day and there was a further trial on Monday 25 April, over the Slough and Beaconsfield route that had been followed the previous week. A reporter from *The Motor-Car Journal* noticed 'the Parsons' parked by the roadside at 11.30 that morning but the car was not mentioned in any other reports and if it had a problem, it could only have been a temporary one. There were more road tests on the Tuesday and Wednesday and on the Thursday (28 April) the judges met to examine the surviving devices. One contemporary report reveals that competitors were allowed to change cars during the trials; such an incident occurred while the cars were returning to London from Nottingham, when Mark Vivian's Parsifal hit a dog and capsized. The Parsifal's anti-skid equipment, in the form of a set of tyres with non-slip treads of alternate strips of hard and soft rubber, was removed and fitted to a replacement car. Vivian then continued in the competition. In the absence of any reports and photographs to suggest that the Royce 10 was at any time replaced, we must assume that it was Parsons' entry throughout the 1000-mile endurance test and for the subsequent trials on the skid track. If that assumption is correct, the events of late April and those of Wednesday 4 May (accepted by most historians as the day on which Rolls and Royce first met) become more and more fascinating, as we attempt to unravel this tangled thread of time.

CHAPTER TWELVE

Rolls meets Royce

In his *Reminiscences* Henry Edmunds published what is now the only surviving first-hand account of the first meeting between Charles Rolls and Henry Royce, but unfortunately he left no record of the actual date of that meeting. His description of his patient and ultimately successful attempt to bring Rolls and Royce together has been quoted many times, and will be repeated here yet again in an effort to deduce precisely when the two men were introduced and the events of the days before and after their meeting.

Some time before the meeting Ernest Claremont, Royce's partner, had, according to Henry:

> '... decided to take up an interest in W T Glover & Co Ltd ... [and] I agreed to exchange a certain number of my shares [in Glover] for a block of shares in Royce Ltd ... Mr Claremont informed me that Royce Ltd was specialising in electric crane work but Mr F H Royce had been building a motor car according to his own ideas which he wished me to see.'

Soon after Claremont told him this, Henry had a discussion with Charles Rolls who said:

> 'I wish you would give me any information you may get hold of relating to improvements in the building of motor cars. I have some ideas of my own which I should like to follow out; and there may be opportunities of doing so.'

Henry recalled this conversation some twenty years after it took place and it is unlikely that he expected his readers to regard this as a verbatim quotation of what Rolls said; nevertheless, we can clearly see what was in Rolls' mind at this time. We know from other sources that Rolls was now looking for a replacement for the Panhards he had been selling from his garage at Lillie Hall, Fulham, and his showroom in Brook Street, in London's West End.[33] The ambitions of Rolls and Royce at this time form a fortunate confluence. When Henry told Rolls about Royce's car, Rolls said that he would like to see it and try it for himself. Henry now started to make a determined effort to arrange this

---

[33] *Rolls of Rolls-Royce*, id.

and on Saturday 26 March 1904, he wrote to Royce Ltd, saying (among other things):

> 'I saw Mr Rolls yesterday, after telephoning to you: and he said it would be much more convenient if you could see him in London, as he is so very much occupied; and, further, that several other houses are now in negotiation with him, wishing to do the whole or part of his work. What he is looking for is a good high-class quality of car to replace the Panhard; preferably of three or four cylinders. He has some personal dislike to two-cylinder cars. I will do all I can to bring about this arrangement with Mr Rolls; for I think your car deserves well; and ought to take its place when it is once recognised by the public on its merits.'

On that same day, Henry wrote to Rolls:

> 'I have pleasure in enclosing you photographs and specification of the Royce car, which I think you will agree with me looks very promising. I have written them asking if they can make an early appointment to meet you in London; and also whether they can arrange to send up a car for your inspection and trial. The point that impressed me most, however, is this. The people have worked out their designs in their own office, and knowing as I do the skill of Mr Royce as a practical mechanical engineer, I feel one is very safe in taking up any work his firm may produce. Trusting this matter may lead to business to our mutual interest in the future.'

These two important letters were written four days after the Parsons' board meeting at which the provision of a car for the Side Slip Trials was discussed. Unfortunately, the letter books (which we would now call correspondence files) that Henry referred to while writing his *Reminiscences* disappeared without trace long ago and we have no means of knowing whether Henry wrote any more letters to Rolls and Royce in the spring of 1904, or received a reply from Royce. On Friday 1 April, six days after Henry wrote his letters, the first Royce 10 made its first run. Seventeen days after this, the first qualifying run for the Side Slip Trials took place; we can only speculate as to whether there was any connection between the Royce 10's appearance in this event and Henry's comment to Rolls that he had asked Royce Ltd *'whether they can arrange to send up a car for your inspection and trial'*. There is no record of any communication between the three men for several weeks after 26 March, probably because Henry was too involved with the Side Slip Trials and other business, Royce was concentrating on testing his first car and building the second, and Rolls was otherwise occupied at Lillie Hall.

One of the photographs of the Royce car that Henry sent to Charles Rolls on 26 March 1904 (Rolls-Royce Heritage Trust)

Another photograph from the same series (Rolls-Royce Heritage Trust)

Henry's motor car, *Tulsilla* (registration number A 875), a 1904 Daimler, at 71 Upper Tulse Hill in 1904. Henry is in the rear nearside seat with, presumably, Ellen Edmunds.

Tulsilla at Swanage, Dorset, in April 1904. Henry is in the front passenger seat. The other passengers are probably Ellen and Dorothy Edmunds.

All that is known for certain about Henry's whereabouts in April is that sometime during that month - at a guess, over Easter weekend (Easter Day was 3 April) - he was enjoying some day trips or short tours with his family in the south of England in a new motor car, *Tulsilla* (named after Tulse Hill, and registered A 875) which, from the few photographs of it that have survived, appears to have been a 1904 Daimler. This was one of two cars that he owned in 1904/5, the other being a 15hp or 24hp 1905 De Dion Bouton (named *Antronette* and registered A3558). This was a curious purchase, since by 1905 Rolls-Royce motor cars were in production and as a shareholder in Royce Ltd Henry could surely have bought one at preferential terms, had he wished to do so. Indeed, why, in view of his financial interest in Royce Ltd, did he buy a car built by a competitor?

While the first Rolls-Royce motor cars were being built and sold, Henry purchased a new car, which he named *Antronette*.

Above: Roadside repairs to *Antronette* on the road between Banbury and Oxford, July 1905. (Michael Pritchard Collection)

Antronette, outside Greystones, a house in Banbury.
(Michael Pritchard Collection)

On Friday 29 April, the entrants in the Side Slip Trials assembled at Stag Hill, Potters Bar, north of London, for the last of the 'preliminaries' to the tests on the skid track; this event was a power absorption trial, to determine the extent to which the cars' non-skid devices retarded their normal performance. Each car had to coast down the hill while the distances it covered while fitted with and without its skid preventer were measured. The results show that Parsons' car freewheeled for 380 feet without its non-skidder and for 364 feet with it. We must presume that the Parsons car was still the Royce 10; according to *The Autocar* of 7 May it was certainly a 10 hp car weighing 22 hundredweight, which fits the description of the Royce car given in the list of entries for the trial, published three weeks previously.[34] On the day of the power absorption trial, Rolls wrote an important note: *'Dear Edmunds. Can you come to Manchester any time next week?'*

---

[34] A photograph in *The Automotor Journal* of 7 May 1904 shows the cars assembled at Potters Bar for the power absorption trial almost reveals whether the Royce 10 was present! Parsons' car, bearing entry number 14, is the fourth car in the convoy (in front of the two trees) but is too far from the camera, and too indistinct to be identified with 100 per cent certainty as the Royce 10.

Entrants in the Side Slip Trials at Potters Bar, Friday 29 April 1904. Parsons' car is the fourth one from the front of the convoy. (From *The Automotor Journal*, 7 May 1904. National Motor Museum, Beaulieu)

On 26 March Henry had told Rolls that he was trying to arrange a meeting in London; Rolls' note of 29 April suggests that Henry had subsequently convinced Rolls that even though he was *'so very much occupied'* he would have to go to Manchester, if a meeting with Royce was ever to come about. Provided that Henry received Rolls' note on the day it was written or on the following day, he would just about have had time to arrange to take Rolls to meet Royce 'next week' as requested; that is to say during the week ending 7 May. As nothing in Henry's *Reminiscences* suggests that the trip was subsequently delayed, we must assume that it did take place 'next week'. But on which day of that week? The Saturday 7 May can be ruled out: on that day, according to a report in the *Daily Graphic*, Rolls, who had been an enthusiastic aeronaut since 1901, went flying in his gas-filled balloon at a temperance festival at Crystal Palace. The Monday - 2 May - can perhaps be discounted on the grounds that there may not have been time, during the preceding Friday and Saturday (29 and 30 April), for Henry and Royce to cancel previous commitments and prepare to entertain Charles Rolls. The Friday, 6 May, is perhaps also an unlikely date, on the admittedly less convincing assumption that Rolls would have wanted to be in London that day to prepare for his balloon flight. This leaves only three days – 3, 4 and 5 May - open to consideration. Most historians accept (or at least do not question) that the meeting took place on the Wednesday, 4 May, and as Rolls, Royce and Henry Edmunds did not leave any documented evidence to support this, the reason why it has become part of Rolls-Royce lore and legend needs to be examined. The source, we find, is once again Royce's friend, G R N Minchin, who quite by chance found himself in a privileged position to research Rolls' career. After taking over the lease of a house in Knightsbridge, London, Minchin discovered that the property was owned by Rolls' sister, Lady Shelley-Rolls, who lived nearby at South Lodge. She had many conversations with Minchin about her late brother's motoring exploits and showed him his personal papers. In his memoirs,[35] Minchin published what purported to be verbatim transcriptions of remarks made by Henry Edmunds to Rolls:

> "'You must see this car, Charlie ... and then you might change your views!" Some time later, finding that Rolls had done nothing about it, Edmunds took the law into his own hands. Two days later he went to Rolls and said, "Charlie! You and I are going to Manchester on Wednesday to see Mr Royce and his car. All is arranged and accommodation is reserved". Rolls bowed before so much insistence and the two went to Manchester to see Royce.

The quotation did not come from any documents that can be traced today. Minchin was probably repeating something that Lady Shelley-Rolls had been told, perhaps by Rolls himself. Whatever the origin of the story, 4 May is as good a day as any on which to commemorate the meeting of the men who formed the most famous partnership in the history of the motor car; and if one day that date, in the light of information yet to be discovered, proves to be correct, then the Prologue to this book and what follows in this chapter will not be regarded entirely as fiction. What would finally establish the missing date would be the discovery of Rolls', Royce's or Henry Edmunds' appointments diary for 1904. A potentially exciting discovery was made a few years ago, when some pages from Henry's personal and business cash books for the years 1902 to 1906 were found in the archives of Claremont, Haynes & Co, Henry's solicitors. These contain entries for telegrams, fares and other minor expenses but unfortunately the pages covering the period from May to December 1904 are missing. Let us, therefore, proceed on the understanding that 4 May was the date for the historic meeting, and accompany Henry and Rolls on their journey to Manchester. Henry's own words will send us on our way:

> 'Mr Rolls accompanied me to Manchester, to which I was then a frequent visitor, as I had to look after several business concerns there and held a trader's ticket between London and Manchester. I well remember the conversation I had in the dining-car of the train with Mr Rolls, who said it was his ambition

---

[35] *Under My Bonnet*, id.

to have a motor car connected with his name so that in the future it might be a household word, just as much as 'Broadwood' or 'Steinway' in connection with pianos; or 'Chubbs' in connection with safes. I am sure neither of us at that time could foresee the wonderful development of the car, which resulted from my introduction of these two gentlemen to each other. I remember we went to the Great Central Hotel at Manchester and lunched together. I think both men took to each other at first sight and they eagerly discussed the prospects and requirements of the automobile industry, which was still in its early infancy. Mr Rolls then went to see for himself the Royce car; and after considerable discussions and negotiations on both sides it was decided to form a separate concern in which the name of Rolls was conjoined with that of Royce, forming the compound which is held in the highest regard today. Eventually they opened their works at Derby. I recollect the gathering of people there and the lunch which was given, where there were many complimentary and prophetic speeches and all expressed their hopes and good wishes for the new organisation: and I had the flattering experience of being alluded to as 'the Godfather of the Rolls-Royce Company'. My interest, however, did not extend any further beyond the fact that as a shareholder of Royce Ltd I received some slight benefit from the formation of the new concern.'[36]

---

[36] No documents giving details of Henry's shareholding in Royce Ltd have yet come to light. At present the only known sources stating that he was a shareholder are his *Reminiscences* and two letters written by his son Claud after Henry died. One of these is to Claud's twin sister, Dorothy, and is dated 4 July 1929. The other is to Claud's half-brother, Howard, and is dated 14 October 1929. Both letters refer to 1000 Royce shares in Henry's estate that were divided between Claud, Dorothy and Howard. Perhaps these constituted Henry's original and total shareholding in Royce Ltd. (For later information see the Postscript to the Second Edition).

The Hon Charles Rolls – usually photographed at the wheel of a car, but seen here against the less familiar background of his office.
(Rolls-Royce Heritage Trust)

Henry Royce in 1907
(Rolls-Royce Heritage Trust)

From this extract from Henry's *Reminiscences,* and circumstantial evidence gleaned from other sources, we can recreate the meeting in Manchester with reasonable accuracy. His reference to his trader's ticket clearly establishes that he and Rolls began their journey in London; but which route did they travel on, and which train did they catch?

In 1904 four rival railway companies ran services to Manchester: the 'Great Central', the 'Midland', the 'Great Northern' and the 'London & North Western'. They all operated express trains, some of which completed the journey in less than four hours, so without having to make an inconveniently early start from their London residences, Henry and Rolls could comfortably have arrived in Manchester in time for lunch, and returned to London the same day. The comment *'accommodation is reserved'* that Henry is reported to have made to Rolls cannot be relied on. Minchin may have been using his imagination, or merely repeating something that Lady Shelley-Rolls had told him. Whatever the origin of the comment, having expressed reluctance in March to the idea of travelling to Manchester, Rolls was probably unwilling by May to make a trip, which would require him to stay there overnight. The reserved accommodation may have been hotel accommodation - but it may instead have been reserved seats on a train. Support to the theory that the visit to Manchester was a day trip is provided by a careful study of the text of Henry's account of the visit and the order in which he unfolds the day's events. He begins by describing his conversation with Rolls in the train, and Rolls' and Royce's conversation over lunch, and continues by saying *'Mr Rolls then went to see ... the Royce car'.* The word 'then' is significant, establishing that the car was inspected after lunch. If Henry and Rolls had travelled to Manchester the previous day, surely they would have seen the car before they had lunch with Royce? What else could they have done before lunch? Neither Henry nor Rolls would have wanted to kill time for an entire morning. So, assuming that the outing was a day trip, which trains could they have considered catching? To seek the answer we must consult the Edwardian travellers' 'bible', *Bradshaw's Railway Guide.*

The Great Central Railway had set new standards of speed and comfort on its Manchester service, with express trains composed of electrically-lit corridor coaches and buffet or restaurant cars on all except the first and last trains of the day.[37] The company's services from its London terminus at Marylebone had previously been somewhat slow and infrequent, but by 1904 improvements had been made and there were seven expresses a day to Manchester, the fastest completing the

---

[37] *London's Termini*, Alan A Jackson, David & Charles, 1969

206 miles in 3 hours 50 minutes. The only one that could have delivered Henry and Rolls to Manchester in time for lunch was the 8.45 am, a 'first and third class breakfast and luncheon car express', but it did not arrive at Manchester London Road Station (renamed 'Manchester Piccadilly' in 1960) until 1.32 pm and Manchester Central Station until 2.00 pm, a journey time of 4 hours 47 minutes and 5¼ hours respectively. Henry would have wanted Rolls and Royce to start lunch long before 2.00 pm and would have checked the timetable for a faster service - or, as a regular traveller, already have known of one.

From the Midland Railway's St Pancras Station there were two morning departures: the 8.30 am Manchester, Liverpool and Leeds Express (arriving at Manchester Central at 12.50 pm and Manchester Victoria at 1.00 pm) and the 10 o'clock to Manchester Central, arriving at 1.50 pm. The former was not advertised as having a dining-car, whereas Henry distinctly remembered discussing cars and grand pianos with Rolls 'in the dining-car of the train'. The 10 o'clock train was advertised as having a luncheon-car but here again it was scheduled to arrive at 1.50 pm, rather late to be entirely convenient for its passengers to have lunch in Manchester (which is why, of course, it contained a luncheon-car). At King's Cross Station the Great Northern Railway was not a serious contender for Manchester-bound passengers; it had a 7.15 am departure for Manchester Central, arriving at 12.13 pm, but few travellers would have endured such an early start and a journey of nearly five hours, when the station next door offered a train that departed two and three quarter hours later but arrived only 37 minutes later. Furthermore, no dining car was advertised, so this train certainly played no part in the future of Rolls-Royce.

We can be certain that it was to the London and North Western Railway's station at Euston that Henry and Charles Rolls made their way, on that May morning in 1904. During that month the company had introduced faster services to Manchester; some of its expresses were now clipping 20 minutes off their previous schedules and covered the 189 miles to Manchester London Road in three and a half hours. No other company could match this, although the fastest express operated by the 'Midland' was a close rival, with a journey time of three hours, thirty-five minutes to Manchester Central. The L&NWR's earliest departure for Manchester London Road was a slow train that left at 7.10 am, arrived at 12.05 pm and did not have a dining car. So this one must be discounted. The next train, the 8.30 am, was not one of the company's fastest services but it could not have been more convenient for Henry and Charles Rolls. It was in fact a semi-fast service to Liverpool, probably hauled by a class 3 4-4-0 locomotive or (less likely, as there were only five in service) a class 4 compound 4-4-0. The train called at Northampton (9.06 am), Rugby (10.12 am), Stafford (10.58 am) and Crewe (11.39 am), where one of its carriages was detached and taken on to Manchester, arriving at 12.30 pm. There was a dining car in which breakfast was served as the train left London. No other train fits so neatly into Henry's description of his day out with Charles Rolls, and we can imagine them speeding through the English Midlands on the 8.30 am from Euston as Rolls enthusiastically described his hopes and ambitions.

After alighting at London Road Station the two men headed for the hotel for their appointment with Royce. Henry Edmunds, we presume, was the host on this occasion and he confused later generations by saying that they met at the Great Central Hotel. There was no hotel of this name in Manchester, but even though the true venue was identified by Max Pemberton in his biography of Royce, published little more than ten years after Henry wrote his *Reminiscences,* the 'Great Central Hotel' survives in Rolls-Royce mythology. Henry made a natural mistake; the place to which he and Rolls hurried to meet Royce was the Midland Hotel but because it was a brand new building (formally opened on 5 September 1903) and adjacent to Manchester Central Station, Henry remembered it as the 'Great Central Hotel'. While writing about his railway journey with Rolls he probably had vague memories of the Great Central Railway's prominent presence in Manchester; the company's headquarters were at London Road and occupied one wing of the station, on which there was a prominent sign reading 'Great Central Railway'.

Lunch would have been taken in the Midland Hotel's Grill Room, then *the* midday rendezvous for Manchester's business community; the hotel also had exclusive French and German restaurants, but these were open only in the evening. When the moment came for Rolls to see the Royce car it was probably driven into the hotel's vaulted Carriage Court, where guests could alight from or board their carriages under cover, close to a twin-arched entrance to the hotel. The Carriage Court was demolished in 1936, when one of the arches became a canopied doorway and the court was converted into a new reception area. The entrance was extensively remodelled again in 1966; more recently the hotel underwent major refurbishments, re-opening as the Holiday Inn Crowne Plaza. It is now difficult to form a mental picture of exactly where Rolls met Royce and where Rolls would have boarded the Royce car, but plaques placed at the hotel by the Institution of Mechanical Engineers (which Royce joined in 1897) and by Rolls-Royce Ltd commemorate the meeting. Originally on display near the foyer, Rolls-Royce's plaque was moved to the new 'Rolls' and 'Royce' function rooms. Unfortunately the plaque is now missing. Despite all the changes, the building will always be 'the Midland Hotel' in the minds of admirers of Rolls and Royce.

The Midland Hotel (Holiday Inn Crowne Plaza/Peter McCormack Photography). The Carriage Court stood where the double arch can be seen.

The plaque (now lost) erected at the Midland Hotel by Rolls-Royce Ltd to commemorate the first meeting between Rolls and Royce.
(Rolls-Royce Motor Cars Ltd)

The events of early May 1904 have been described in many books on Rolls-Royce and it is entertaining to review some of the more imaginative accounts of what happened, since they illustrate the fascination that the formation of the Rolls-Royce partnership holds for successive generations of authors and readers. For example, in *Under My Bonnet,* G R N Minchin quoted this conversation:

> *"But where did you get such well-made and such well-designed electrical ignition apparatus, Mr Royce?", enquired Rolls. "I designed it and made it myself", was the reply. "It is in advance of anything similar", said Rolls.*

In 1961 Minchin published a second book[38] in which he elaborated on his earlier account:

> *'The two men quickly took to each other and Rolls asked if he might try the car. Hearing from Edmunds of Rolls's ability as a racing driver, Royce insisted that Rolls should drive through the Manchester traffic. Rolls found the car was easier to control than any he had previously driven and without the need of skill or caution they soon found themselves in the Cheshire country. When Rolls, who ignored the speed limit and showed no signs of stopping, gave several grunts. Royce interpreted these as denoting satisfaction. As they passed through Crewe, neither dreamt that ultimately in this very town the 'World's Best Car' would be made.'*

Minchin went on to describe how Rolls stopped to help a local doctor whose car had broken down; an incident in which he had to brake suddenly to avoid running over a dog is also related.

Despite Minchin's opportunities to discuss Rolls' career with Lady Shelley-Rolls and see his papers, we must suspect that fact has been embellished with imagination in his description of Rolls' first car ride with Royce. Another imaginative account was written by Laurence Meynell and published in 1953.[39] Meynell purported to quote verbatim conversations between Henry and Rolls, Rolls and Royce, and Rolls and Claude Johnson. Like Minchin, Meynell knew Lady Shelley-Rolls and had access to Rolls' private papers. Attempts to locate them, and to find out whether Minchin and Meynell were quoting from documented

---

[38] *The Silver Lady*, G T Foulis & Co Ltd
[39] *Rolls: Man of Speed*, Bodley Head, 1953

sources or from Lady Shelley-Rolls' memory, have not been successful. The only surviving Rolls papers appear to be those kept at Gwent County Record Office, Cwmbran. These, however, concern his business affairs and his father's investments in C S Rolls & Co. Very little of the material covers the year 1904 and none of it contains any references to Henry Edmunds or to the formation of Rolls' and Royce's partnership. The diaries of Rolls' eldest brother, John, and their father, Lord Llangattock, have survived. Lord Llangattock's diary has an entry dated 20 May 1904, saying *'Charlie and friend came'*, which is confirmed in John Rolls' diary; this at least rules out that day (a Friday) as one during which Charles Rolls was busy meeting Royce or testing the Royce car.

Yet another verbatim report of what was said and by whom during May 1904 was published in 1953, by W.J. Bentley:[40]

> *"My dear chap, if this car of your man Royce is all that you say it is, why doesn't he drive it down to London to show us?",* complained Rolls, whose diary of social, sporting and business engagements was always overfull.
>
> *"Yes Edmunds",* said Royce when the tactful negotiator returned north, *"I have a great respect for Llangattock's son as a sporting driver; but really I am much too busy to take the car to London at this stage. If he is so anxious to see it, why doesn't he come up here?"*

As C W Morton has commented,[41] no reliable evidence has ever come to light as to precisely what was said by Rolls and Royce at their first meeting, or what business arrangements they made then. It is a great pity that Edmunds devoted only a few sentences of his *Reminiscences* to the occasion, and that Pemberton did not obtain a first-hand account of it from Royce. Rolls' only words on the subject were uttered when he spoke at a dinner given by Rolls-Royce to mark the achievement of Percy Northey, the driver of one of the company's first 'Light 20 hp' cars, in coming second in the 1905 Tourist Trophy Race on the Isle of Man:

> *'You may ask yourselves how it was that I came to be associated with Mr Royce and Mr Royce with me. Well, for a considerable number of years I had been actively engaged in the sale of foreign cars, and the reason for this was that I wanted to be able to recommend and sell the best cars in the world, irrespective*

---

[40] *Motoring Cavalcade*, Odhams Press Ltd, 1953
[41] *A History of Rolls-Royce Motor Cars*, Vol 1, id

of origin ... the cars I sold were, I believe, the best that could be got at that time, but somehow I always had a sort of feeling that I should prefer to be selling English instead of foreign goods. In addition I could distinctly notice a growing desire on the part of my clients to purchase English-made cars; yet I was disinclined to embark in a factory and manufacture myself, firstly on account of my own incompetence and inexperience in such matters, and secondly on account of the enormous risks involved, and at the same time I could not come across any English-made car that I really liked ... eventually, however, I was fortunate enough to make the acquaintance of Mr Royce and in him I found the man I had been looking for for years.'

Not only are the details of what happened during Rolls' and Royce's first meeting difficult to reconstruct; we are also unsure what happened immediately afterwards, although we do know that Rolls soon told Claude Johnson that he was convinced that the Royce car was the one that they needed to secure the success of their automobile agency. According to Pemberton, Johnson accompanied Henry and Rolls when they went to Manchester to meet Royce, but this seems unlikely; had Johnson been there, Henry would surely have said so in his *Reminiscences*. Wilton J Oldham, Johnson's biographer, confined himself to a brief and unembellished account of Rolls' return to London:

'[Rolls] returned to London full of enthusiasm and went straight to CJ's flat to tell him about his trip to Manchester, saying, "I have found the greatest engineer in the world" ... Claude Johnson was as enthusiastic as his partner when he, too, had inspected the 10 hp Royce car and met its designer; so it was quickly arranged that the firm of C S Rolls & Co would have the sole selling rights of the marque, one of the conditions being that the car would be sold under the name Rolls-Royce.'[42]

---

[42] *The Hyphen in Rolls-Royce,* G T Foulis & Co Ltd, 1967

In another book,[43] published a few years later, Oldham added another nugget or two to his previous account of what happened after Rolls met Royce:

> '[Rolls] persuaded Royce to let him make arrangements for the car to be sent down to London by rail. He accompanied the car himself and arriving at midnight he triumphantly drove round to Claude Johnson's flat and knocked him up, declaring excitedly, "I have found the greatest engineer in the world". He insisted on Claude Johnson dressing and then drove him round the deserted streets of London in the car.'

One of the classic histories of Rolls-Royce is *The Magic of a Name*.[44] Its author, Harold Nockolds, acknowledged that while researching the early life of Sir Henry Royce he was much helped by Sir Max Pemberton, and that his knowledge of the beginnings of Rolls-Royce was greatly expanded by Massac Buist's *Rolls-Royce Memories* and conversations with T S Haldenby, one of Royce Ltd's apprentices at the time the first Royce car was built. Unfortunately, Nockolds dealt only briefly with Rolls' and Royce's first meeting:

> 'Rolls at this time had a prejudice against two-cylinder engines and he climbed into the high passenger seat of the little Royce prepared for all the vibration and roughness that were usually associated with the type. To his amazement he found that the car had the smoothness and even pull of the average 'four', allied to a quite phenomenal degree of silence. He came, he rode, and was conquered. As for Claude Johnson, he was raked out of bed one midnight to have the remarkable qualities of the car demonstrated to him by his excited partner, and after a drive round the West End he, too, fell under the spell of the little Royce. Arrangements were immediately made for the drafting of an agreement between the two concerns whereby C S Rolls and Company should take the entire motor-car output of Royce Ltd.'

John Rowland also wrote an account of the Royce 10's midnight road test[45]:

---

[43] *The Rolls-Royce 40/ 50 HP*, G T Foulis & Co Ltd, 1974
[44] GT Foulis & Co Ltd, 1938
[45] *The Rolls-Royce Men*, Lutterworth Press, 1969

> *'... as the ride went on ... Johnson gradually became more fully awake.*
> *"This is Royce's car?", Johnson asked. "The one that Edmunds has been writing about?"*
> *"Yes. Don't you think it is a marvellous job, for a two-cylinder model?", Rolls said.*
> *"Pretty good", Johnson agreed.*
> *"I think we should take this up in a big way. These cars will sell like hot cakes", Rolls said.*

These stories have plenty of entertainment value - particularly those purporting to give verbatim transcripts of conversations - but are not taken literally by Rolls-Royce scholars!

One question that does arise from the assumption that the history of Rolls-Royce began on Wednesday 4 May is this: if that assumption is correct, then which of the Royce 10s did Rolls inspect that day? If, as seems likely, No 1 was used throughout the Side Slip Trials, it was garaged in London until the power trials on Stag Hill on Friday 29 April and would have been required again for the tests on the skid track at the Locomobile Garage Riding School (not at the Talbot Works, as originally planned) on Saturday 7 May. Unless a rule of the trials required the competing cars to be kept 'in quarantine' from 29 April until 7 May - and there is no evidence that there was such a rule - the Royce car could have been taken back to Manchester during this period, perhaps for precautionary servicing prior to the skid track tests. If so, it would have been at Cooke Street during Rolls' visit on 4 May. But would not a 400-mile drive to Manchester and back have been regarded as an unnecessary expense and complication, during which an accident or mechanical problem could prevent the car from returning to London - a risk that could have been obviated by servicing the car at the Locomobile Garage?

By 4 May, the second Royce 10, which was allocated to Ernest Claremont, would have been roadworthy and keeping Royce fully occupied; its engine had completed its tests on 7 April. Either (or both) of the Royce cars could have been prepared for Rolls' visit. But if No 1 was still in London at the time Henry was trying to persuade Rolls to consider selling Royce cars, then despite the lack of proof in Henry's *Reminiscences,* surely Rolls would have been offered an opportunity to drive, ride on or at least inspect the car before he went to Manchester? And surely he would eagerly have accepted that opportunity, if only to prove to his own satisfaction that Henry's persistent advocacy for Royce's design was justified and that a visit to Manchester would not be a waste of time? Because of his dislike of two-cylinder cars, Rolls had to be convinced that Royce had something worthwhile to offer, and although he may not have had the time or inclination to test the Royce 10 during the first week of the Side Slip Trials (or been offered the chance to do so), the programme for the second week was confined to London and the Home Counties and was less hectic; by now, Henry's persuasiveness would have started to take effect, and Rolls could easily have found time for a test run. If that was the way it happened, then Rolls' midnight drive around the West End with Claude Johnson could have preceded his trip to Manchester; as suggested in the previous chapter, when borrowing the Royce 10 for the Side Slip Trials. Henry may have seen this as an opportunity to bring the car to London so that Rolls – whose appetite had by now been whetted by the photographs and specification that Henry had sent him on 26 March - could hardly avoid inspecting it! It would subsequently have been necessary, of course, for Rolls and Royce to get together and discuss their future plans, so although their meeting in Manchester on 4 May (or whenever) was undoubtedly their first, it may not have been the first occasion on which Rolls saw Royce's car.

But how does Oldham's story that Rolls arranged for the Royce car to be sent down to London by rail fit into all this? Perhaps what really happened was that the car was delivered to London by rail for the Side Slip Trials, and not for inspection by CJ; and that it was Henry Edmunds who arranged for the car to be sent down, not Rolls. The story that Oldham published (in 1974) could easily have become rather muddled during the years that had elapsed since the events in question took place, but the idea that Royce's new and precious first car made its first long distance journey on a railway wagon is entirely credible.

While Charles Rolls soared above Crystal Palace in his balloon on 7 May, the 11 cars that had qualified for the tests on the slippery track were marshalled at the Locomobile Garage. *The Car Illustrated* described the scene:

> *'A section of the cement floor had been coated with Thames mud, which was then muddied, while soft soap was laid over the top to keep the surface moist. The result was to form a surface that was villainous in its excess of sliminess, and seldom would anything so vile be encountered on the road. On the other hand there was no camber to be coped with, nor were the cars with a short take off of 88 feet able to approach the slippery area at the same pace at which the driver would usually be proceeding, especially if not driving on a uniformly wet road but one on*

which a patch of grease might be unexpectedly encountered. In the first instance, all the cars were required to drive on to the greasy section and steer off it with as short a turn as possible. So effectual, however, was the preparation that the front wheels invariably failed to obtain any hold, and scarcely a single car was driven off the course before the front wheels at least had passed over the patch and reached the dry gravel, which had been spread beyond. In some cases the turn was not effected until all four wheels had left the coated area.'

The results of the Side Slip Trials were not announced until two weeks later. On Monday 16 May, Henry chaired a meeting of the Parsons board at which Harry Parsons reported that the behaviour of the non-skidder had been *'highly satisfactory'*. The board decided that if it won a prize, Harry would receive *'extra remuneration'*. The winner was, in fact, the Empereur non-skidder but Parsons won the second prize - £100 and a Silver medal. Another board meeting was held on 3 June, at which Edward Manville took the chair. This may have been the last meeting to be held at 2 Queen Anne's Gate, since some time in the first half of 1904 the Parsons company, and Henry Edmunds, moved to offices at Parliament Mansions, Victoria Street, Westminster. On 3 June it was resolved that Harry Parsons' *'extra remuneration'* would be £25 - equivalent to more than £1000 today.

The minutes of the May and June meetings were not signed by Henry until 9 August. This was because soon after 16 May he was absent for nearly two months. Having brought Rolls and Royce together and ensured a creditable performance by Parsons in the Side Slip Trials, Henry had other business to attend to, but he would return in time to see the culmination of the famous introduction he had arranged in May.

CHAPTER THIRTEEN

Side-slips and hill climbs

After spending much of April and early May 1904 organising Parsons' entry in the Side Slip Trials and bringing Rolls and Royce together, Henry Edmunds became fully committed to promoting the Parsons non-skidder and patenting some more of his own inventions. During 1904 he registered eight patent applications, including three for internal combustion engines and one (subsequently abandoned) for a side-slip controller. Another of his inventions was meant to eliminate an anti-social habit that was a cause of considerable controversy in the days before roads were surfaced with tarmacadam - the tendency of motor cars to throw up swirling clouds of dust. Henry designed a device, which fitted behind the rear wheels and was supposed to collect dust on an absorbent sheet moistened by water drawn from an internal tank. Sadly, success as an inventor continued to elude him but his efforts for Parsons proved to be more promising. His absence from the company's board meetings in May and June is accounted for by a long visit that he made to the USA. In July he was in New York City, negotiating a licence with the Pope Manufacturing Company. When he next attended a Parsons meeting, on 9 August, he reported that on 20 July Pope had offered to make and sell the non-skidder in America with effect from January 1st, 1905, and pay a minimum royalty of $1000 in the first year, rising to $5000 in the fifth and subsequent years. Parsons would be responsible for taking proceedings against anyone who infringed the company's patents in the USA.

The directors accepted the proposal but invited Pope, as exclusive proprietors of the invention in the USA, to defend the patents with the assistance of the Parsons company. The negotiations came to nothing, but this first foray by Henry into the American non-skidder market was the precursor of a highly profitable project, which will be described later. At the August board meeting, Henry also reported that following the success of the Empereur anti-skid device in the Side Slip Trials he had intended to open negotiations with his acquaintance the Marquis d'Audiffret Pasquier, a director of L'Empereur company, with a view to agreeing on a 'working arrangement'. However, in the interim the Marquis had died. Henry was, therefore, authorised to negotiate with L'Empereur's English agents, Mann and Overton. Shortly before this meeting, Henry caught up with the progress that Charles Rolls and Henry Royce had made since he last saw them in May. This period is undocumented, but clearly there had been discussions and negotiations, for as Henry recalled in his *Reminiscences,* Royce wrote to him on 8 August, saying:

> *'With reference to Mr Rolls taking our manufactures, he has at present in his possession an agreement we have got out on these lines, and with reference to his suggestion that you should be named as umpire, I should be most happy to agree to this as I know your anxiety would be for everything to be quite fair on each side. I must thank you for your introduction, which is promising well, and I think we ought to be of great service to each other.'*

It is obvious from this that Rolls and Royce had a high regard for Henry. As their 'umpire' he was, from August onwards, closely involved in the negotiations leading to the completion of the agreement they had drawn up in his absence; however, any business meetings he had been due to attend on 4 September with Rolls or Royce would have been cancelled since on that day he went to Halifax for the funeral of his father, who had died at Cheadle, Cheshire, at the age of 81. By early December the negotiations had made such progress that, thanks to an all-out effort by Royce and his team, Rolls was able to exhibit, at the Paris Salon motor show, a roadworthy 10 hp demonstration car, a 10 hp 'show' car, and a 15 hp chassis, a 20 hp car and a 30 hp six cylinder engine. The demonstration car was in fact the first Royce 10 with a new body. *The Car Illustrated's* report on the Paris Salon contained the following significant statement:

> *'Mr C S Rolls is perfecting the design and details of the new all-British car which his firm, C S Rolls & Co, have put on the market under the name of the 'Rolls-Royce' car.'*

The exhibition of the first Rolls-Royces was in fact held before Rolls and Royce concluded their agreement. This is dated 23 December 1904 and is between Charles Rolls and Royce Ltd (not Henry Royce personally). In the agreement, Rolls contracted to take all the cars built by Royce Ltd, who agreed to deliver a range of two-, three-, four- and six-cylinder chassis rated between 10 and 30 hp.

After December 1904 Henry Edmunds became preoccupied with other interests and his links with Rolls-Royce became tenuous - in his own words, his interest in the new enterprise *'did not extend any further beyond the fact that as a shareholder of Royce Ltd I received some slight benefit from the formation of the new concern'.* Nearly four years were

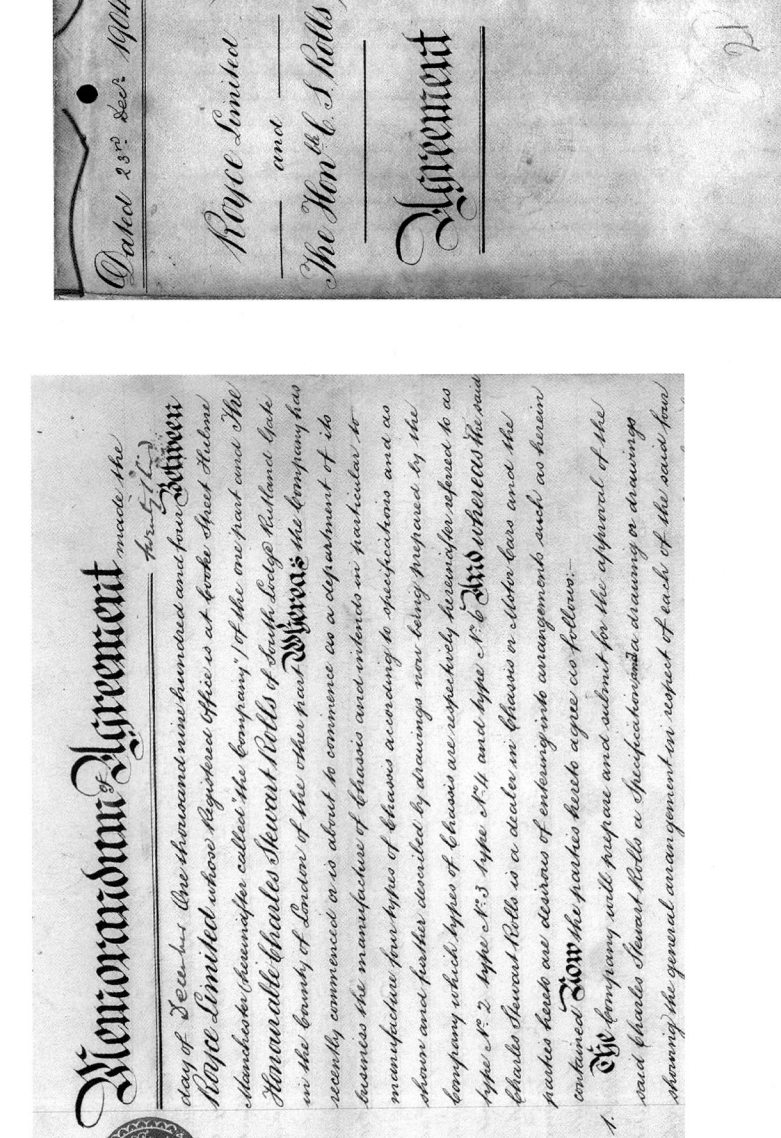

The culmination of Henry's efforts to bring Rolls and Royce together: the historic agreement of 23 December 1904 between Royce Limited and Charles Rolls. (Rolls-Royce Heritage Trust)

to elapse until the official opening of Rolls-Royce's factory at Derby on 9 July 1908 - the function at which Henry had the *'flattering experience'* of being called *'the Godfather of Rolls-Royce'*. All that remains to be discussed here about his connections with the company is the question of whether he owned one of the Royce cars. The general belief that he did seems to have originated in a passage in The Magic of a Name in which Harold Nockolds wrote:

> *'... it was Mr Henry Edmunds who, as a newcomer to the directorate of Royce Ltd, became the owner of the third of the experimental 10 hp cars.'*

Other authors subsequently made similar statements. Nockolds acknowledged Buist's *Rolls-Royce Memories* (published in 1926) as a source of his knowledge of the beginnings of Rolls-Royce,[46] although all that Buist had to say about the ownership of the Royce cars was this:

> *'By the Spring of 1904 those three cars were built. The late Mr A E [sic] Claremont, then chairman of Royce Ltd ... had one; Mr Royce another; and the third was brought to the notice of the late Mr C S Rolls by Mr Henry Edmunds ...'*

Recent research by Tom Clarke of the Rolls-Royce Enthusiasts' Club casts doubts on previously published accounts of the history and ownership of the first Royce cars. Publication of Mr Clarke's findings in John Fasal's book *The Edwardian Rolls-Royce* is eagerly awaited and will not be pre-empted here. All that needs to be mulled over in this biography of Henry Edmunds is how he came to be acknowledged as a Royce owner - despite lack of documentary proof, or anything in Henry's own *Reminiscences* to support the idea. Despite omitting many details of the events of the early 1900s that would today fill many gaps in our knowledge of Royce's activities, it is unlikely that Henry would have failed to mention becoming the owner of one of Royce's first cars!

Although Buist had confined himself to talking of a Royce car being brought to Henry's notice, Max Pemberton went further in his biography of Royce (published in 1933) and said Henry Edmunds was *'temporarily the possessor of the third of the famous Tens'*. Harold Nockolds was the first author to go so far as to call Henry an *'owner'* and it is his book - written in 1938 - that seems to be the source of the story. It is easy

---

[46] Harold Nockolds was mistaken. Henry Edmunds was not at any time a director of Royce Ltd.

to see how the mistake - for that is what it almost certainly is - arose. In the 1920s and 1930s, when Buist, Pemberton and Nockolds were researching Rolls-Royce's history, memories and handed-down stories of the first Royce cars and those who owned and drove them were still fairly fresh in the minds of those who had known the company since its early days. Henry Edmunds was indeed a 'temporary possessor' of a Royce 10 - the first one, not the third - for the Side Slip Trials in 1904 and because of this could easily have been remembered as an actual owner by those unaware of the circumstances in which Henry was allowed to use the car.

None of the Royce 10 hp cars has survived, so motoring historians and enthusiasts are unable to obtain a first hand appreciation of the features that so impressed Henry Edmunds, and inspired Charles Rolls to tell Claude Johnson: 'have found the greatest engineer in the world'. However, the engine and gearbox from the second Royce 10 are preserved at the North Western Museum of Science and Industry in Manchester. The Museum also has a photographic collection which includes the above photograph of the first Royce 10 apparently taken on 1 April 1904 - the day on which it is said to have made its first run. The driver is A J Adams, head of Royce's drawing office. His passenger is John DeLooze, Royce Ltd's (and later Rolls-Royce Ltd's) first company secretary. Happily, three Rolls-Royce 10s derived from the Royce 10 are still in existence. These cars - from a production run of 17 - are our closest link with those that Henry would have seen being built and tested by Royce Ltd at the time he was acting as 'umpire' during Rolls' and Royce's negotiations. The most significant difference in the appearance of the Rolls-Royce 10 compared with the Royce 10 is that Rolls-Royces were soon equipped with the famous 'Grecian' radiator.

The ownership records of the second Royce 10 are another possible source of the belief that Henry owned a Royce 10. This car was originally allocated to Claremont but on 6 August 1909, its registered owner became W T Glover & Co Ltd - where, as we have seen, both Henry and Ernest Claremont were directors. The car was used by Glover's contracts department - in the company's centenary brochure there is a splendid photo of it, parked on a country lane alongside a gang of men digging a trench for, presumably, an electricity conduit. Perhaps some of those whom Nockolds interviewed dimly remembered a Royce 10 going to Glovers and assumed that it belonged to Henry?

The second Royce 10, in service with Glover in 1910.
[From *Glover's Centenary, 1868-1968* (BICC Cables Ltd)]

Royce owner or not, Henry became heavily committed to the development of safe and comfortable motoring in the years after the creation of the Rolls-Royce partnership. It is somewhat curious that he was not given any further responsibilities in the new venture after he had played his part as 'umpire', but the reason for this could be that he did not aspire to a position in the Rolls-Royce hierarchy or because - in Rolls, Claude Johnson, Royce and Claremont - the new enterprise had all the managers it needed. In the event, Henry went on to lead the Parsons company to considerable success. The next board meeting, following the one at which the Pope Manufacturing Company's proposition was discussed, was held on 9 December and the one after that took place on 14 February 1905, on the stand of the Collier tyre company at the Automobile Show at Olympia, London. Henry would have noted with satisfaction the presence of four Rolls-Royce cars - a 20 hp four cylinder model on demonstration outside the exhibition hall and, on C S Rolls & Co's stand inside, a 30 hp six-cylinder (forerunner of the Silver Ghost) offered at £890, the 'Paris Salon' 10hp, and a 15 hp three-cylinder.

The oldest surviving Rolls-Royce 10, registration number U 44 (chassis number 20154), built in 1904 and exhibited at the Paris Salon motor show in December 1904 and at the Automobile Show at Olympia, London, in February 1905. Restored by Oliver Langton of Leeds, it is now in Perth, Scotland.
(Michael Evans)

The second oldest surviving Rolls-Royce 10
(engine tested 19 September 1905),
registration number AX 148 (chassis number 20162).
The car's first and last private owners were Paris Singer
(1906) and Sir John Prestige (1930-35).
It was purchased by Rolls-Royce Ltd in February 1935
and presented to the Science Museum, London, where it is now exhibited.
(Rolls-Royce Motor Cars Ltd)

The third, and only other, surviving Rolls-Royce 10, registration number
SU 13 (chassis number 20165), completed in early 1907 and now owned
by Bentley Motors. (Rolls-Royce Motor Cars Ltd)

The Parsons board next met on 3 March, when Henry was appointed managing director. He remained chairman of the company. The Westminster branch of the London Joint Stock Bank was instructed to honour all cheques signed by Henry alone and countersigned by the company secretary. Then, for nearly a year, there is an almost complete lack of documented information about Henry's career, although we do know that on 25 July 1905, a US patent for manufacturing Portland cement from slag was assigned to him by C von Forell of Hamburg[47] and that during that year he registered nine patent applications of his own, for tyres, car wheels and electrical inventions. There were only two Parsons board meetings during this period, one chaired by Edward Manville, the other by Harry Parsons. Henry, obviously, was occupied elsewhere. He next took the chair at a board meeting on 23 February 1906. From the minutes it is clear that he had spent some time (how much time, we do not know) in the USA. He was probably engaged on electrical work for Glover and trying to make progress in other fields, such as cement manufacture; he was almost certainly also enjoying another visit with his wife and family to the Howards in Rhode Island. We do know that he spent some of his time negotiating a licensing agreement with Harry Weed, whose Weed Chain Tire Grip Company had premises at 28 Moore Street in New York City. Weed was the inventor of the first tyre chain in America, but unfortunately for him, his design infringed the American patent for the Parsons non-skidder. Henry negotiated an amicable solution to the problem; Weed was licensed to work under the Parsons patents on payment of a royalty of five cents per non-skidder. This was undoubtedly one of Henry's most profitable business deals, for the American motor car industry was now moving into the position from which it would later dominate the world; Henry Ford's Model T would be launched just over two years later.

The year 1906 was one in which the Parsons company began to consider diversifying into all kinds of new car tyre and wheel accessories - a logical policy, in view of the fact that, two years after the introduction of the Motor Car Act, there were now nearly 30,000 private motor cars on Britain's roads, compared with less than 9000 in March 1904. Like it or not, the motor car was here to stay. Lord Montagu of Beaulieu, who

---

[47] *Journal of the Society of Chemical Industry*, 31 August 1905, Henry's interest in cement production processes never developed into a trading venture. Various US patents were assigned to him by Dr Hermann Passow of Hamburg and others between 1903 and 1907. Henry was the chairman of the General Cement Company and evidently intended to exploit a 'revolutionary' process that was expected to threaten conventional cement making processes, but failed to become commercially viable.

as John Montagu MP, had been largely responsible for liberalising the motoring laws, had said:

> '[The motor car] will to a great extent replace nearly every other kind of traction upon the face of the earth ... travelling will increase enormously ... dustless motorways will be constructed to carry ceaseless traffic ... Europe in a few years' time will become for the motorist one vast holiday area.'[48]

Henry Edmunds was equally enthusiastic, but his attitude was that of a businessman rather than that of a romantic visionary. He registered seven patent applications for motor car equipment in 1906 and under his guidance Parsons examined a host of new products, including the Hamilton non-skidder for motor omnibuses, the 'ER' detachable wheel rim, the 'Cinch' repair kit, sheathed tubes, the Marshall tyre jacket, Duval laminated springs, spare wheel carriers, and a carbon dioxide tyre inflater. The 'ER' rim, probably co-invented by Henry and M D Rucker, was described thus in their patent application:

> 'In wheels having detachable rims the rim and body of the wheel fit together for a portion of their circumference, leaving a space at the other portion for the accommodation of wedging pieces by which the rim is tightened and secured. The contacting parts of the rim and wheel body may consist of two projections, continuous or segmental and integral with or detachable from the rim or felloe.'

Parsons' interest in tyre inflaters reminds us of the lack of roadside facilities, such as petrol pumps and compressed air lines, in the days of the motoring pioneers. On 6 July 1906, Henry chaired a meeting at which an offer of a sole licence for tyre inflaters made by Aerators Ltd was discussed. A J Campbell of Aerators and Julian Orde (who in 1903 had succeeded Claude Johnson as secretary of the Automobile Club) attended the meeting and discussed various aspects of the offer. The directors considered that the agreement proposed by Aerators was not sufficiently favourable, considering the risks involved in putting a new product on the market. Henry was given full powers to renegotiate with Aerators and accept or reject their revised proposals as he saw fit. No further references to the agreement appear in the Parsons' minutes, although on 9 November Henry was still sufficiently interested

---

[48] *John Montagu of Beaulieu*, Paul Tritton, Golden Eagle/George Hart, 1985

in the subject of inflaters to apply for a patent for a device described in his specification as *'a box for containing an equipment for inflating pneumatic tyres'*. This had *'a body part provided with two parallel recesses for cylinders of compressed gas and a recess for connecting tubes and attachments'*.

The next board meeting was on 1 March 1907. By now, the company was considering marketing the American Dow patented inner tube and this gave Henry another opportunity to visit the USA. Ellen probably went with him again, for she would have taken every opportunity to see her relatives in Rhode Island. Henry and Ellen returned on the Royal Mail steamer *Caronia,* which left New York on 2 July and arrived at Liverpool on 10 July. Fortunately, the original typescript of an article by Henry entitled *Chronicles of a voyage,* in which he described a typical Atlantic crossing during an Edwardian summer, has survived the passage of more than 80 years. The *Caronia* sailed on a hot, sultry morning and 'all the passengers looked happy and glad to escape the heat of the city for the cool of the sea'. Soon, life at sea settled into a familiar pattern:

> *'First we had Sports. Then the College youth was seen to adventure; men from Yale, Harvard, Chicago and other seats of learning now struggled in friendly rivalry with each other, or the ladies, or with the 'Old Brigade' from England. The English were but a small percentage among the many holiday passengers but they held their end at the tug of war, American v English, which was held on the Fourth of July. In the evening there was a concert in aid of the Liverpool and New York seamen's charities. Senator Clark presided ... and the good round sum of £70 was collected by a bevy of pretty American lasses.*
>
> *Thanks to the excellent management and organisation of Mr Martin Rucker, an old traveller, well remembered by many who have had the good fortune to meet him ... there was soon formed a group of minstrels whose programme of fun, frolic and foolery was carried out with a perfection that was truly astonishing. It was in the Grand Saloon, everyone was there, no one left, even in the Smoking Room, and such a row of bright, charming, happy faces has seldom been seen as when the extemporised curtain was lifted. And how the audience shouted with glee and amusement when they saw the performers all with blackened faces. The two end men in pyjamas, the middle men in strict evening dress, and the rest [in] dark trousers, white shirts and white shoes, making a motley crew indeed. There were choruses, solos and jokes galore... When the curtain fell the*

audience cheered to the echo and the oldest inhabitants on board were heard to say that this was a record performance in every way. Even at the barber's shop, where one generally learns the truth, this was confirmed.'

Henry reported on his trip at a board meeting held on 24 July at the Royal Automobile Club (it owed its new 'Royal' status to the patronage of King Edward VII). Henry had had a meeting with members of the Dow Patent Tube Syndicate at which he, Edward Manville and W J Crampton had been allocated a two-fifths interest; clearly, the three men had indulged in a little private entrepreneurial activity, perhaps to prevent any competitors from gaining an advantage over them. The question the Parsons directors now had to consider was whether the Parsons Non-Skid Company should buy this interest, the price required by the syndicate being £750. The directors agreed to buy. The question of the distribution of Parsons' profits was also discussed. To avoid having to debate the subject every time the annual accounts had to be approved, it was decided that £1000 would be set apart every year and distributed equally among the directors as fees. In the event of the net profits exceeding £6000, the sum to be divided would be open to discussion. If the profits were less than £3000, one-third of the profits would be divided. In all cases, the directors' fees would be exclusive of the managing directors' special remuneration.

The board did not meet again until 14 May 1908. Changes in commercial law had recently come into force and the directors decided to alter the status of the firm to that of a 'private company'. The Parsons Non-Skid Company Ltd, as originally established, was therefore put into voluntary liquidation and at the same time a new company of the same name but with a different constitution was formed. Business continued as usual, although Henry reported that during the ten months that had elapsed since the decision was made to acquire an interest in the Dow Patent Tube Syndicate, the device had been examined and tested and found to be too unsatisfactory to justify its introduction into Britain. The company had therefore withdrawn from the syndicate. If, by then, it had paid the £750 called for by the syndicate, Henry had steered the company into a very unprofitable venture but the minutes of the May board meeting give no hint of any dismay or dissatisfaction at the way the business was being run; the directors immediately went on to discuss the 'ER' wheel rim, which had been well received by the public and the motor trade. One of Parsons' employees, a Mr Green, reported that he was negotiating with a large taxi cab company with which he expected to make *'a satisfactory and profitable arrangement'*.

We know of only one other engagement in Henry's schedule during the summer of 1908. This was to attend the official opening of Rolls-Royce Ltd's factory at Derby. By now the old factory in Cooke Street, Manchester, was far too small to cope with any significant expansion in demand for Rolls-Royce cars and the company had made its momentous decision to build only one class, the Silver Ghost. This was named after the extraordinary 40/50 hp tourer, which had been given a finish of aluminium paint and adorned with silver-plated fittings for an epoch-making series of trials and demonstrations by a team of drivers headed by Charles Rolls and Claude Johnson. The Derby works were opened by Lord Montagu of Beaulieu. Henry was one of several motoring pioneers who attended.

Back at Parsons, Henry had to initiate several court actions against infringers of the company's patents. The Weed Chain Tire Grip Company was especially vulnerable and on 27 November 1908, Henry told his board that he had instructed Duncan & Duncan, a New York firm of lawyers, to help protect Parsons' patents in the USA, provided that the cost of doing so did not exceed $1000. All Parsons' court actions were successful, greatly strengthening the company's position.

Board meetings became a rare occurrence at Parsons after its formative years. By 1908 Henry held the majority of the company's Preference shares, Harry Parsons owned most of the Ordinary shares, and Edward Manville and W J Crampton were the main minority shareholders. Day-to-day management was in the hands of Henry and Harry, and any major problems that needed to be discussed with the other directors would have been handled without requiring Henry to call a formal board meeting. In 1909, for example, there was only one such meeting, held on 23 February to approve the sale, to the Pfleumatic [sic] Company of Parsons' interest in the 'ER' rim, in return for a cash payment and shares in a new company that was being formed.

The next meeting was held nearly a year later, soon after Henry returned from Albany, New York, where he had given evidence at a public inquiry to determine what official action the State of New York should take regarding motor car anti-skid attachments. Henry's minutes cryptically refer to the result of the inquiry proving 'perfectly satisfactory' to the Weed Company but they also reveal that due to the success of the Parsons non-skidder in the USA, Weed's president, Walter B Lashar, was interested in acquiring the company's European interests. This is the first hint of Parsons' eventual destiny. Henry reported that no conclusion was reached during his talks with Mr Lashar, but he reminded the board that he had taken out additional patents *'with a view to prolonging the company's property, but these had not yet been assigned to the company'*. Henry was obviously referring to some of the patents he had registered during the years he had been associated with Parsons; in the years 1907-10 he registered another 12 patents, including several for non-skidders and other wheel accessories. In those days, patents on inventions expired after 14 years. By 1910 Henry and his colleagues would have started planning for the time when the original non-skidder patents expired. The board decided that Henry should receive 50 fully paid up shares in return for assigning two of his recent patents to the company; these were for an improved non-skid tyre chain for pneumatic tyres (which was also said to prevent punctures by removing 'foreign bodies' from treads) and for a special chain fastener.

The directors then moved on to the most important item on their agenda - the future expansion of the business. They decided to wind-up the company and form a new one, called the Parsons Non-Skid (1910) Co Ltd, with a nominal capital of £25,000 in 25,000 £1 shares, of which 20,000 would be issued as fully paid up shares for the purchase of the previous company, which would be put into voluntary liquidation. Instructions for the immediate registration of the new company were given to Claremont, Haynes & Co.

Henry then reported that Weed had become involved in a considerable amount of litigation while defending Parsons' patents in the USA. The Parsons company had helped Weed by collecting information in Britain and on the Continent, and preparing affidavits and other evidence for submission to the courts. Henry had been helped by his friend Col R E Crompton, who was not only a respected electrical engineer but also someone with many years' experience of wheel and tyre design. In Germany, sales of Parsons non-skidders had increased to such an extent that, under that country's laws, the devices would now have to be manufactured in Germany or lose their patent protection. Henry and his colleagues decided that, in the circumstances, they would grant a sole manufacturing licence to their agent in Germany, Romain Talbot.

The first board meeting of the new Parsons company was held on 18 March 1910 but it was not until three months after this that the first steps were made in what was to develop into the sale of the business. Mr Lashar had written to the company, asking them to name a price for the purchase of Parsons' British, American and European patents. Henry was authorised to proceed to New York 'with the least possible delay' and given powers to negotiate and conclude a sale at whatever terms he considered acceptable. He was also paid a fee of 300 guineas for his services and expenses. Henry wasted no time in setting off for the country that was now his second home, and while there he heard tragic news:

> 'While walking near Central Park I heard a newsboy shouting 'Fatal accident to a well-known English aviator' and ... I read with deep regret that at Bournemouth Rolls' 'plane had crashed. Later on I learned from my friend Mr W J Crampton that he was probably the last person to speak to Rolls on the day of that fatal ascent.'

In 1910 Charles Rolls had become the second aviator to obtain a Royal Aero Club pilot's certificate and during that year he owned three aeroplanes. One of these was a French-built Wright Type A biplane, to which Rolls fitted an auxiliary elevator designed to improve the machine's horizontal stability. On 12 July Rolls flew the Type A in an alighting competition during Bournemouth Aviation Week and crashed while attempting his second landing; he was the first person to be killed in Britain in a powered flight accident.

On Friday 22 April, about two months before he departed for New York, Henry had taken part in celebrations to mark the tenth anniversary of one of the events at which Rolls had gained fame as a motoring pioneer, the One Thousand Miles Trial. Many of the original competitors took part in a commemorative run from London to Northampton, driving cars that were of considerably advanced design compared with those of 1900. Writing in the 27 April issue of *The Car Illustrated,* C L Freeston commented:

> 'Mr Henry Edmunds' solid tyred 6 hp Daimler 'Antrona' would ... offer a quaint comparison with his present Standard limousine. Mr T B Browne and Mr Edmunds were able to bring forward the original number plates which they carried on their competing cars in 1900 ... Mr Edmunds expressed his delight at seeing so many old friends present and said that motorists must have discovered the secret of perpetual youth.'

Maybe, but Henry was now 57 and may have thought the time had come to slip into a lower gear. In 1911 he retired from W T Glover & Co and, perhaps because he now had a little time to spare for non-commercial ventures, he successfully stood for membership of the Royal Institution's Committee of Visitors; he had been a member of the RI since 1897. At about this time he also became Master of the Glaziers' Company. In 1912 he accompanied Professor William A Bone, an authority on gas combustion, to St Louis, for a meeting of the Gas Association of America. Henry's apparent sudden interest in gas-fired heating seems to have led nowhere but is perhaps a further illustration

Henry at the wheel of his limousine at Queen Eleanor's Cross Northampton in 1910, during the RAC's run commemorating the tenth anniversary of the One Thousand Miles Trial. Henry is displaying the entry number he carried during the Trial.

of his fascination for new forms of technology. After the meeting, at which Professor Bone read a paper and gave demonstrations of a new diaphragm for surface combustion, Henry reverted to his previous interests. He was, however, less prolific in the field of invention than before. Between 1911 and 1914 he registered only five patents, including one for a tyre pressure indicator.[49] He was almost certainly now looking ahead to some form of semi-retirement and probably anxious to do as well as he could out of the proposed sale of Parsons' patents to W B Lashar, and any other deals from which he could obtain a capital sum. The sale of Parsons took longer to complete than he must have expected. At a meeting of Parsons' board on 3 January 1913, Henry reported on a meeting he had had in New York with W B Lashar (probably shortly before Christmas) at which Lashar had proposed combining Parsons' American and European businesses. At the same board meeting, Henry was authorised to release Harry Weed from all his obligations under his licence contract with Parsons, subject to the completion of an agreement under which Weed would assign, to Lashar or the Weed Chain Tire Grip Company, all his rights and interests in the licence.

Discussion on Lashar's proposals for a merger was adjourned, and it was not until 15 November 1915 that any more progress was reported. On that day the board gave Henry and Edward Manville permission to sell Parsons' assets. An agreement with Lashar was concluded on 13 December and approved by the board on 31 December. By now, due to the huge wartime demand for non-skidders for military vehicles, Parsons was Britain's largest producer of tyre chains. On 18 May 1916, at the last board meeting of the company under British ownership, it was agreed to transfer all its shares to W B Lashar. No record exists of how much money Henry made from this deal, but it would not be enough to prevent him from experiencing serious money problems in the last years of his life.

Thoughout his business career Henry remained closely associated with the Royal Automobile Club, whose sporting calendar continued to include contests for the Henry Edmunds Hill Climbing Trophy. The event was supposed to be an annual one but it lapsed after E Campbell Muir's victory in 1903, and was not held again until 1905, when it was won by the Rev F A Potts - or, to be more accurate, won *for* Mr Potts by C Grinham, the driver of his 38 hp Daimler. In 1906 George S Barwick won the trophy, driving his own 38 hp Daimler. These two competitions were held at Blackdown House but in 1907 the venue was moved to Carter's Hill at Underriver, on the North Downs near Sevenoaks in Kent. Here, on Saturday 8 June, on a fine and warm afternoon, the competition was held on a 1000-yard course with a gradient of 1 in 6.25 on its steepest stretch and an average gradient of 1 in 11.225; then, as now, the RAC was most precise in its measurements. The course was described in

---

[49] Henry's last patent application while with the Parsons company was for a car headlight: this application was filed in 1915.

The Car Illustrated as *'severe, narrow and in places ... dangerous, the first corner after the easiest portion being one to tax the skill of even the most intrepid driver'*. Entry was restricted to cars whose cylinder diameter in inches squared, multiplied by the number of cylinders, did not exceed 100. Later in the day there was another competition for the Carter's Hill Cup, for less powerful cars whose engine formula, measured in the same way, did not exceed 65.

The contenders for Henry's trophy are worth listing in full, because they give us a fascinating 'snapshot' of the cars and drivers of the early days of motoring:

1	George S Barwick	30 hp Daimler
2	J E Hutton	40 hp Berliet
3	W Hillman	20-25 hp Hillman-Coatalen
4	John S Napier	40 hp Arrol-Johnston
5	Paul Brodtmann	30-40 hp Daimler
6	Frederic Coleman	30 hp White steamer
7	W T Clifford Earp	26-30 hp Nordenfelt
8	Montague S Napier	40 hp Napier
9	K O Kura	24 hp Fiat
10	Arthur E Perman	35 hp Iris
11	Captain G Hinds Howell	40 hp Iris
12	L Carle	45 hp Mors
13	E Herington	28 hp Ariel-Simplex
14	G Stanley Monck	35 hp Horch
15	A C Hills	24 hp Martini

The drivers had to climb the hill twice - first non-stop, and then after halting on a steep 15-yard length on the approach to the summit. *The Car Illustrated* made a careful note of some of the performances:

'Picking up finely at the top of the first rise [Mr Barwick] took the first corner at a fine speed. The next car was the Berliet, which to the looker on seemed to come up faster than No 1. It was beautifully driven at the bad turn and a bad skid was well corrected. The Hillman-Coatalen took the corner easily; Mr Coleman's White steamer shrieked on its way up the first rise and then, much to everyone's surprise, slowed down and made bad time, perhaps having run short of steam. No 8 Napier furnished some excitement at the corner as it came up at great speed and just missed the bank at the turn. Had its course been six inches further up the bank, disaster must have occurred. Mr Kura's Fiat was misfiring all the way up. The two Iris cars with

their smoothly running engines seemed to come up particularly easily and well. No 12 Mors had probably sprockets of too large a size for a hill of such calibre but nevertheless did the turn at a fine speed, showing that the Mors cars of 1907 are worthy of their predecessors.

The stopping and starting test was, perhaps, the most interesting event to the general public - at any rate, it brought a goodly crowd of people climbing up the steep hill, for it was most amusing and interesting to see how different drivers conquered the difficulty of restarting. It is not easy to stop a heavy and powerful car on a 1 in 8 gradient, and without the aid of a sprag to get her going again. The test was a very severe one, and No 1 Daimler hardly seemed to stop at all, so well did her driver understand his business. The car picked up wonderfully and sped to the top. The Berliet almost equalled the performance of the Daimler. No 3 [the Hillman-Coatalen] was a long time over it, but No 6 White steamer had recovered itself and came up to the stopping place at great speed and got away well again, pouring forth its hissing melody. The Fiat unfortunately was still misfiring and spent a long time between the marked lines before restarting again. No 11 Iris lost several seconds by running back, while the Mors did not get away quickly. The Ariel and Horch both did well.'

George Barwick understood his business so well that he won the trophy, by a margin of two seconds over J E Hutton. Carle, the driver of the Mors, was not at all happy with the rules of the competition and dashed off a letter to Lord Montagu, the editor of *The Car Illustrated:*

'I was astounded to find on my arrival at the hill that the entry of a certain steam car had been accepted to compete against the petrol cars, although the size of the petrol cars was restricted ... To my astonishment, on raising the matter with the officials of the club I was informed that the entry of the steam car was in order. The idea of putting steam and petrol cars together, merely on cylinder dimensions, seems to me to be so absurd that if it is persisted in it will mean that these club competitions will be looked on with ridicule. Everybody knows that a steam car, with the aid of a specially large boiler ... can obtain a very big head of steam which will enable a car to rush up a short hill at a very high speed.'

Perhaps as a result of Carle's protest, there were no steam cars in the next competition for the trophy, held on 17 July 1909 on the Midland Automobile Club's course on M C H Taylor's Court House estate at Shelsley Walsh, in Worcestershire. The competition was uneventful and uncontroversial, and won by A J Hancock driving a Vauxhall. On 2 July 1910, at the same venue, the event was part of the MAC's annual meeting and was one of three hill climbs arranged that day. This time entries for Henry's trophy were restricted to vehicles with single-piston four-cycle internal combustion engines not exceeding 16 hp and strokes of not more than 121 millimetres. The cars had to be of a recognised tourist type, equipped with mudguards, an efficient silencer and a 'properly upholstered' body, and have a projected wind area of not less than 16 square feet. Clearly, the organisers intended to make the competition test the performance of the kind of cars that were in everyday use, rather than 'specials' and sports cars. Rain had made the 3400 ft course heavy going and conditions must have been rather treacherous by the time the drivers lined up to compete for the Edmunds' hill climb, the final item on the programme. It was not one that generated a great deal of excitement. Because of the unsettled weather there were fewer spectators than had been expected, and the day was about to end with a violent thunderstorm. Twenty-one drivers had taken part in the preceding events but only five responded to the Edmunds challenge; R Lisle, driving his 15.9 hp Star, was the winner, with a time of 1 minute 30.6 seconds, but only ten seconds separated him from the man who came last, G Hubert Woods, driving a 15.6 hp Crossley. The three other competitors, in finishing order, were A J Hancocks, driving Percy C Kidner's 15.6 hp Vauxhall, L Coatalen driving a 15.9 hp Sunbeam, and H C Day driving the Earl of Shrewsbury's 15.8 hp Clement-Talbot.

That forgotten hill climb at Shelsley Walsh took place at the very end of the Edwardian motoring era; to be pedantic, it was held after the era ended. Only six weeks earlier, the funeral of the colourful and controversial monarch who had himself been one of motoring's pioneers, and the patron of their club, had taken place at St George's Chapel, Windsor. The 1910 'Henry Edmunds' hill climb should, to comply with folk memories of Edward VII's monarchy, have been enacted on a warm and sunny summer's day, not under a rain-laden sky.

Ironically, the weather for the Midland Automobile Club's annual meeting at Shelsley Walsh on Saturday 10 June 1911 was glorious but it was to be the day that heralded the demise of the Henry Edmunds Trophy. The qualifications for entry (concerning engine rating, equipment and so forth) were the same as before, but mindful of the poor support the competition had received in 1910, the RAC reserved the right to abandon it if the number of entries was less than ten. That is indeed what happened. There were 19 entries for the first event of the day, an 'open' hill climb and 16 (but only 14 actual starters) for the 'closed' climb, for MAC members only. Several records were broken but there were too few entries for the Edmunds hill climb. If the entry lists for the two other races are any indication of the total number of cars of competition standard at Shelsley Walsh that day, we can see that the field for the Edmunds trophy would have amounted to about six. The event was abandoned, though the RAC's decision caused 'much disappointment and considerable criticism', according to H C Lafone, who covered the meeting for *The Car Illustrated.*

That, almost, was last that was heard of the Henry Edmunds Hill Climbing Trophy, which presumably was at this time still on display at the RAC. Originally it had been kept at 119 Piccadilly, the club's headquarters at the time it was despatched from Gustav Gurschner's foundry in Vienna; presumably it was safely removed to the new headquarters in Pall Mall which was opened to members on 23 March 1911. Among the first announcements to issue from Pall Mall was one from the competitions committee, giving the date and rules for the next contest for the Edmunds trophy, and we must presume that, to obviate being placed in an embarrassing situation, someone took the trouble to check that the trophy that they expected to be the focus of public attention three months later was still in safe keeping. The committee would have been looking ahead to the time when the winner's name would have to be engraved on the trophy's plinth. The non-event of 10 June made this unnecessary. No effort was made to revive the competition in 1912 or 1913 but on 9 October 1913 the competitions committee proposed that the trophy should become one of the prizes in the next Tourist Trophy races, to be held on the Isle of Man on 10 and 11 June 1914. The idea was that Henry's trophy should be awarded to the driver making the best performance on the six and a half mile climb up from Ramsey to 'the Bungalow', on Snaefell. A letter from Henry agreeing to the proposal was read at the next meeting of the committee, on 16 October, when it was decided that the trophy would be won by the driver making the best aggregate time on the hill during his 16 laps of the race's 37½ mile course.

It was an ignominious fate for Henry's trophy, which inevitably received little or no attention in the general excitement surrounding the Tourist Trophy. Kenelm Lee (Bill) Guinness won the race in his Sunbeam 1, in a time of 10 hours 37 minutes 49 seconds, at an average speed of 56.44 mph. He was also the fastest driver on the hill climb course, much of which was over a gradient of 1 in 10. 'KLG' thus became the last winner of Henry's trophy, but it is unlikely that his name was ever engraved upon it. The 1914 Tourist Trophy races were to be the last for many years; 17 days after Guinness's victory, Archduke Franz Ferdinand of Austria and his wife were assassinated at Sarajevo. Six weeks later, Britain was at war with Germany. Motor racing and its heroes were soon forgotten. When the sport, and the Tourist Trophy were revived after the war, no one seems to have asked what had become of Henry's trophy. Sometime during or after the war it evidently disappeared; it is not in the private collection of KLG's trophies and attempts to discover what became of it have so far been unsuccessful. This is sad, because although it was never one of motoring's most coveted prizes, it has a place in the history of motor sport if only because of the importance of the man who donated it.[50]

---

[50] Since the publication of the first edition of this book, the Henry Edmunds Hill Climbing Trophy has been found and is now awarded by the Sir Henry Royce Memorial Foundation annually. The first to receive the trophy was Damon Hill, Formula One World Champion; second was Squadron Leader Andy Green as the fastest man on earth.

CHAPTER FOURTEEN

Soirées and crises in Sussex

Moulsecoomb (sometimes spelled Moulsecombe) Place is one of the oldest estates in Brighton. Its earliest deeds date back to 1597 and refer to a 'messuage' (a dwelling house, with outbuildings and land) and two tithe barns. The present house was probably built in the late 18th century and in a land tax redemption document dated 1 March 1799, is referred to as a *'mansion house with houses, barns and buildings'*. The mansion was then, superficially, a fairly new building but the rear part of the structure dates from the reign of Queen Anne (1702 -1714) and is attached to an even older building, a late 14th century cottage. The property's romantic and rambling character is enhanced by a Tudor tithe barn, said to have been constructed with timbers recovered from one of the shipwrecks of the Spanish Armada. The barn is linked to the mansion and at some time during the early years of the 20th century was converted to provide a library or billiard room on its first floor and, on the ground floor, workshops and a garage for two cars.

Moulsecoomb Place, Brighton

During the final 25 years of the reign of George III, Moulsecoomb belonged to Benjamin Tillstone, a brandy merchant and ship builder, who was a close friend of the king's eldest son, George. As Prince Regent from 1811, George was king in all but name. For his benefit, Tillstone converted a dovecot in the grounds into a summer house which the prince used as a retreat, not only for the kind of activities that sullied his reputation but also for the less scandalous one of playing his silver lute. The summerhouse became known as 'the Prince's Bower'. When in residence at Moulsecoomb the prince slept in a room above the drawing room, while his guard stood on duty in a sentry box built into a niche in the south wall of the house. Other architectural oddities included a secret hiding place behind a panel in the entrance hall, and three massive mahogany doors. These were given to Tillstone by Prince George and were probably salvaged from Marlborough House (formerly Grove House) when it was demolished to make way for Brighton's famous Royal Pavilion.

Benjamin Tillstone died in 1829 and bequeathed Moulsecoomb to his friends the Rogers family, on condition that whichever member of the family lived there should assume a new surname, 'Rogers- Tillstone'. Thus, John Jefferies Rogers, who had married Benjamin's niece, Jane Monkhouse, became John Jefferies Rogers - Tillstone. When John died, Moulsecoomb was inherited by one of his relatives, Catherine Sedley, who duly took the surname Tillstone although not, apparently, Rogers-Tillstone. Catherine died soon after claiming her inheritance and the estate passed to John and Jane's son. It remained in the possession of the Rogers-Tillstone family for the next 100 years.

The colourful history of Moulsecoomb also encompasses a ghost, an old lady with grey hair piled high on her head. Family legend maintained that she had been murdered and thrown down one of Moulsecoomb's three wells, but that is how many ghost stories begin. The last of the 'Rogers-Tillstones' to live there knew the ghost as Lady Catherine Sedley, believing the apparition to be that of the lady of that name who had been James II's mistress. There seems, though, to have been some confusion over the identities of the two Catherine Sedleys; King James' Catherine, who married Sir David Colyer (the future Lord Portmore) in 1696, had no connection with Moulsecoomb, or indeed with Sussex, and 'Lady Catherine's ghost' is most likely that of Catherine Sedley-Tillstone.

Whether all these tales of ancient history, the Prince's Bower and the ghost of the grey-haired lady attracted Henry Edmunds to Moulsecoomb Place will never be known. What is certain is that in 1913 Henry, now 60 years old, and Ellen decided to move out of London to the coast or countryside. While house-hunting they heard that a 21-year lease was being offered on Moulsecoomb, so they motored down to inspect the property and decided that it was entirely suitable for their retirement years. The annual rental was £170.10s and the lease included an option to purchase the freehold of the whole of the property, excluding two paddocks, for £6,525. So after 30 years in Streatham, once semi-rural but now rapidly developing into a suburban dormitory for London's commuters, Henry and Ellen moved to within two miles of the Sussex seaside. Dorothy, who never married, went with them, as did her half-brother Howard, who would pursue his own career as an electrical and mechanical engineer. Claud, however, saw Moulsecoomb less frequently; he had become an Anglican priest and worked as a missionary in India before becoming vicar of St Augustine's, Leicester, in 1923. Howard too would soon become only a visitor to his parents' new home, for his career was interrupted when he was called up for military service during the First World War, which began only 18 months after the family moved to Brighton.

Britain's declaration of war with Germany on 4 August 1914 must have caused great concern among Henry and Ellen's relatives in the USA. Alice and Arthur Claflin (Henry's sister-in-law and brother-in-law) wrote from Rhode Island suggesting that Henry and Ellen (and presumably Dorothy too) should live with them in Providence until the war was over, but Henry declined:

> 'It is in times like these that one realises the force of the old proverb that blood is thicker than water, because in conditions of stress and strain we are all drawn much closer to each other. I hope and trust that there may be no necessity for anyone to leave England on account of shortage of supplies, or actual personal danger to those residing in this country. Thanks to a merciful providence, and our strong navy, we still feel quite secure in our island home. The seas have been cleared and the powerful German fleet, which was evidently constructed with a view to attacking this country, has been so far bottled up at Wilhelmshafen. You will get a lot of information from the papers, perhaps more than we do; some of it true, some of it otherwise. Owing to the strict censorship of the press, it is very difficult for us to know exactly what is going on, and after all the prognostications in the past, that the Germans were contemplating an attack of this kind, it has yet come as a shock to us to find ourselves involved in this terrible war. It is difficult for a stranger to realise what is going on here. London looks

very different to what it was when you last saw it. There is less traffic in the streets. There are practically no horses. People all go about serious and thoughtful. The walls and vehicles display large placards appealing for the enlistment of men to serve their country; and the response to this call has been very gratifying. There is intense interest in all the news that filters through, though it is very meagre, and this is probably just as well, for we have no wish to disclose the dispositions of our troops and navy or the position of our allies to those who might communicate with the enemy.

Howard is at Plymouth. His letters are very interesting. He is at Breakwater Fort, in the harbour, with a small company of men, about thirty, in charge of the signalling and search-light department; a very important matter, and one that requires constant attention all through the night.

I overheard a small incident yesterday, which shows the close watch that is kept. A few nights ago, the whole of the search-lights (and there are many) were concentrated upon one small moving object entering Plymouth Harbour. It was a sailing boat, a yacht, that had been away on the ocean, out of touch with all that was going on, and had no idea that England was in a state of war; and the surprise of the crew, on finding themselves the focus of such a blaze of light, may be better imagined than described.

We have frequent letters from Claud. The little grand-child appears to be a healthy, well-developed babe. Its suggested name is Dorothy Barbara, so there will be another D B in the family. Dorothy is staying with Claud and, I am glad to say, appears to be very much better. I think regular and constant employment in the quiet village of Wymeswold has been the best possible thing that could have happened to her. Please give my love and kind remembrances to the various relations and friends you may meet in Providence; and, again thanking you and Alice for your proffered hospitality, with best regards to all, I remain,

*Your affectionate brother-in-law,
Henry Edmunds'*

Visitors to Moulsecoomb would have been most impressed when they turned off the Lewes road into Henry's driveway, and stepped down from the private cars in which they had motored down to Brighton, or from

Henry's car, which would have been waiting for them at Brighton railway station. Leonard Simmons, Henry's chauffeur at this time, still had vivid memories in 1980 of life with the Edmunds family at Moulsecoomb during and after the First World War, and recalled that Henry owned two cars at this time: a second hand Cadillac V8 and a new Essex, registration number CT (or CD) 5412. The V8, first manufactured in 1915, was probably acquired with the assistance of some of Henry's American friends. The Essex, also an American car, was introduced in January 1919 and here again Henry's contacts there may have encouraged or helped him to purchase it.

Leonard Simmons remembered Henry and Ellen as a gregarious couple, who enjoyed entertaining their many friends and relations, especially those from Rhode Island. On arrival, they would be ushered through the entrance hall and corridor - pausing, perhaps, to be told about the secret hiding place behind the panel, or to admire the French tapestries hanging close by. As they did so, one of Henry and Ellen's seven servants would place their hats and coats on the pegs and brass rail on the oak rack in the hall, and put their gloves in one of the lockers beneath the four foot wide bevelled mirror in the centre of the rack. Too many people milling about in the hall could create a problem, where stood a pair of richly decorated Japanese Kobe vases perched rather precariously on their ebony plinths and a tall Persian brass baluster-shaped vase, chased and pierced in floral ornament and figures.

Moulsecoomb was a treasure trove of sculptures, porcelain, prints, books, china, glass and Oriental carpets and rugs. This was soon apparent to the guests as they wandered into the drawing room to enjoy a cup of tea or a glass of sherry *('Or would you prefer something stronger?')* and chat about their journey (*'Walter took the wrong turning in Lewes and got completely lost'; 'We caught the Southern Belle from Victoria; it took only sixty minutes'*). Seated on a carved mahogany framed settee with striped floral upholstery, a scroll-frame armchair in the Chinese style, or one of the carved mahogany Hepplewhite chairs, the visitors would place their cups and glasses on one of the Japanese lacquer tea tables or the Italian tarsia pedestal table, while Henry and Ellen fussed around, opening the windows in case anyone found the room 'fuggy' (especially if someone had lit up a pipe or cigar) or stoking up the fire from the oak panelled log chest. Some of the visitors would make a mental note to come back to the drawing room later on, when things were quieter, and browse through Henry's bound copies of *Punch*, dating back to 1841, or his collection of novels and scientific books.

While the guests were refreshing themselves after their journey, and catching up on the latest gossip, their luggage was carried upstairs and unpacked, perhaps by Violet, who first worked at Moulsecoomb as an under-housemaid and later as an under-parlourmaid, eventually she and Leonard Simmons were married, and went to live in the old cottage behind the house. With four spare bedrooms at their disposal, Henry and Ellen had room for several houseguests at weekends and holidays. One frequent visitor was Edward Manville, during the time he was at the height of his political and business career. A photograph taken on 2 June 1919 (four years before he was knighted) shows him and Henry on the terrace at Moulsecoomb.

Henry (left) and Sir Edward Manville at Moulsecoomb, 2 June 1919

Another visitor was Captain P J Dawson, whose father Sir Philip Dawson was electrical consultant to the London, Brighton and South Coast Railway, the electrification of which by the 'third rail' direct current system was completed in 1933, following the electrification of part of the line by a 6,600V single phase alternating current overhead system in 1909. In 1980, at the age of 81, P J Dawson recalled his friendship with the Edmunds family more than 70 years earlier.[51]

> 'I suppose my father first met Henry Edmunds ... at the end of the last century or perhaps [earlier] through Robert Blackwell, an American, for whom my father was working on the design

---

[51] P J Dawson to author, March 1980.

and construction of electric tramways in England. Before the 1914-18 war Howard Edmunds worked with my father for a time to gain knowledge of electric traction ... My first recollection is of motoring over from Sydenham, where we lived, to Tulse Hill, where the Edmunds lived. This was in about 1906 when I was seven ... My godfathers were Conrad W Cooke and Robert Blackwell.'

Although Capt Dawson's recollections of Henry Edmunds and his family are mainly of interest for what they tell us about their domestic life, his reference to his godfathers helps us learn a little more about Henry's connections with other electrical pioneers. We know that he had met Robert Blackwell in 1877 and again in 1883, when Henry went to America to try and interest him in Michael Holroyd Smith's electric tramway system. As we have seen, Blackwell preferred the 'Bently - Knight' system, but Henry did introduce him to the proprietors of the Rhode Island Locomotive Company. Perhaps at this time there was a short-lived, unchronicled business relationship in which Henry, Philip Dawson and Blackwell collaborated in some way on tramway development? Conrad Cooke was another of Henry's early associates.

To continue Capt Dawson's reminiscences:

'Howard Edmunds was a Territorial and went to France as an officer in the Royal Engineers. I became a regular officer of the Artillery towards the end of the 1914-18 War. After the war I was posted to Brighton on the reformation of the Regular Army and ... had a close association with the Edmunds family in 1919/20. I was brigaded at Preston Barracks, which was next door to Molescombe [sic] Place. As there were no officers' quarters available the Edmundses kindly offered to put me up. Howard had just been demobilised and he and I became close friends. I remember what their home looked like and in particular their drawing room, and the laboratory which adjoined one end of it. In the drawing room Henry had designed a most elaborate electrically operated pianola-organ, with most of its guts in the laboratory next door, where he continued to devise new stops and other improvements. Neither he nor I could play the piano and this pianola-organ gave us great pleasure. He taught me how to use it. There was a means whereby the sound could be made to come from any quarter of the room.'

Henry, photographed during the last few years of his life

Ellen Edmunds

Dawson's memory of Henry and Ellen's *soirées musicales* failed him in only small details. The pianola-organ, a combination by Smith & Morgan of a standard Orchestrelle, a reed organ and a pipe organ, was not in the drawing room but in the music room, at the southern end of the house. Built into a mahogany case with an oak panelled surround, the instrument was powered by wind from an electrically-driven fan and had two cabinets containing more than fifty rolls of music by Chopin, Gounod, Greig and Mozart. Today a motif in coloured glass can still be seen above the door that leads from the music room to the garden. It bears the initials and date 'HE 1913', suggesting that this was Henry's favourite part of the house and the one where he chose to leave evidence of his tenancy.

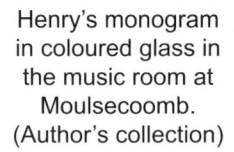

Henry's monogram in coloured glass in the music room at Moulsecoomb. (Author's collection)

After moving to Brighton, Henry continued to travel up to his office in London, mainly for meetings of the Parsons' board of directors (he had retired as a director of W T Glover & Co in 1911). In the autumn of 1915 he and Edward Manville completed the sale of the company to Walter B Lashar and at the end of the year Henry attended his last meeting as chairman. This was more or less the end of Henry's career as a full-time businessman, although he continued to file patent applications for, among other things, a headlight (November 1915) and another non-skid attachment (1917). On 23 May 1919, H Edmunds of Moulsecoomb Place, Brighton and the Patent File and Tool Company of 165 Queen Victoria Street, London, registered applications for a hacksaw blade 'with teeth curved to the arcs of circles' and a machine for cutting the blades. 'H Edmunds' may in this case have been Howard, now attempting to embark on an engineering career. Howard may also have been the 'H Edmunds' who on 31 January 1920, in partnership with B M R Co Ltd of Prudential Buildings, North Street, Brighton and A M Banister, F A Grimes, P J MacCarty and R D H Thompson (all of 55 Dyke Road, Brighton) filed a patent application for variable speed gearing, evidently for a machine tool of some kind. Howard's efforts to succeed as an engineer will be described later; before then, we must follow Henry into the early years of his retirement, or at least semi-retirement, from the time he ceased to have any responsibility for the Parsons company.

As if to create a clear break from his previous routine, yet remind himself of times past, Henry took Ellen to America for a holiday, departing soon after he attended the Parsons' board meeting on 15 November 1915. In December he made what was to be his last visit to Niagara Falls, where as a young man he had been awed by the potential of water power as a force for generating electricity. He saw that his dreams and those of his contemporaries had come true. Afterwards, he wrote:

> *'Within forty years two vast cities have arisen, one on the Canadian side, the other on the United States side. A vast source of energy has been exploited for the service of man. Not by exhausting the stores of the earth, as in the case of gas and oil, but by utilising the eternal force of gravity, which will remain undiminished as long as man exists in the cosmos. It is the utilisation of these natural forces and natural laws that has transformed human life during the last hundred years.'*

During December he also went to New York, where at the home of his friend Dr Byron E Eldred he heard the latest type of Edison phonograph and pronounced it to be *'a great advance over all other recording devices'*; perhaps the machine he heard was one that Edison had introduced in 1913, which played wax discs. Although they must have been tempted to spend Christmas with their friends and relations in Providence, RI, Henry and Ellen returned to England and on 31 December he was in London for his last Parsons' meeting. He had, it must be said, chosen a dangerous time to cross the Atlantic. In May the *Lusitania* had been torpedoed by a U-boat off the coast of Ireland. Admittedly, Germany abandoned its submarine blockade of Britain a few months later, but no one could be certain that the high seas were now safe. Few civilians ventured on a voyage unless their journey was essential; Henry was reminded of the dangers of war only a few days after he returned to England, when he heard that his fellow motoring pioneer, Lord Montagu of Beaulieu was on the P&O liner *Persia* that had been sunk in the Mediterranean. Lord Montagu was travelling to India when a German submarine torpedoed the *Persia*. Although the ship sank in a matter of five minutes he managed to survive in a damaged lifeboat until he and other passengers were rescued the following day. However, Eleanor Thornton, who was travelling with him, was drowned.

Henry was 65 when the war ended. He and Ellen had been fortunate; Howard had returned home safely, and they had been spared the sorrow and anguish that so many other parents had experienced. Family life continued to absorb much of their time at Moulsecoomb and on Wednesday 11 May 1921 their home was crowded with guests attending the wedding of Ellen Edmunds' niece, Ellen Margaret Howard, to a lawyer, L H Strain. The bride was the only daughter of Ellen Edmunds' brother, the late Albert Harris Howard, and his wife Jenny, who was living in London. The wedding took place at the parish church of Falmer, and as the *Sussex Daily News* reported next day, the journey from Moulsecoomb to the church was *'made in motor cars, and it need hardly be said that the event made a considerable stir in the village'*. Howard Edmunds was best man, Claud Edmunds conducted the service, Claud's daughter Cicely was a bridesmaid, and the bride was given away by her brother, Henry Bernon Howard. In its report, the *Sussex Daily News* included some more comments, which complement our impression of life at Moulsecoomb:

> *'Mr and Mrs Edmunds are well known in social circles in Brighton and in the county. The reception was held in the finely proportioned music room, with its handsome mantelpiece and organ, and refreshments were served in the adjoining dining room. The wisdom of arranging for an indoor reception was shown by an unfortunate break in the weather at midday. In the morning the gardens lay smiling in the summer sunshine but afterwards there were one or two sharp showers. Fortunately the rain did little more than freshen the foliage and the weather was fine at the time fixed for the ceremony.'*

Seven months before the wedding, Henry made out his Will. We do not know whether he had any particular reason for doing so at this time, or had simply decided to attend to a formality that he had put out of his mind during the busy years of his business career. The Will is significant because it shows that in 1920, Henry was a man of some substance. To Ellen he bequeathed all his *'carriages, horses, stable furniture ... motor cars and motor accessories'*, and all his plate, pictures and other valuables. Edward John Pilcher, his confidential clerk, was to receive an annuity of £100. To Howard he bequeathed *'the business carried on by me at Parliament Mansions ... any interest I may have in any invention ... and all shares held by me ... in any company of which ... I may be a director'.* He also instructed his trustees (Howard, Claud, Ellen and E J Pilcher) to retain Moulsecoomb as a residence for Ellen for the rest of her life.

Having attended to the future, Henry devoted some time to recalling his past. At one time he had been a director of Mavor & Coulson Ltd of Glasgow, a firm that began installing electric lighting and power systems in 1882. In July 1919 Henry's friend Sam Mavor realised that Henry's memories of the early days of electric lighting would be lost unless he committed them to paper. Sam invited Henry to write a series of autobiographical articles for *The M&C Apprentices' Magazine.* Motoring historians and those who are fascinated by engineering history are forever indebted to Sam Mavor; but for his initiative, little would be known of Henry's key role in several historic events. By the early 1920s Henry was making good progress with his *Reminiscences of a Pioneer,* a series of 20 articles published over a period of five years. The thread of history is indeed fragile, for although Sam Mavor's invitation encouraged Henry to gather together his collection of photographs of his contemporaries, and consult copies of his letters to Charles Rolls, Henry Royce, Thomas Edison and others. Few of these letters have survived in their original form: nor, sadly, have the originals of Rolls' and Royce's letters to Henry. We rely entirely on what was published in *The M&C Apprentices Magazine* for nearly everything we know about Henry Edmunds' meetings with some of the greatest inventors and engineers of the Victorian and Edwardian eras.

As successive chapters of his *Reminiscences* appeared, Henry sent copies to the people mentioned in them. Howard Edmunds went to America and met Edison in Orange, New Jersey, presenting him with a copy of the chapter in which Henry described visiting Menlo Park in 1877. The grand old man of science was highly delighted, telling Howard all about those exciting days and remarking that he and Henry had lived to see enormous developments in the electrical industry 'at whose birth we assisted'. Conrad Cooke (who was, incidentally, godfather to Howard Edmunds as well as to P J Dawson) received several chapters and responded by recalling how in 1873 he and Richard Werdermann had built what they called a 'dynamo electric' machine, based on Z T Gramme's ring armature. Cooke remembered that the machine had electro-magnet field coils and created intense excitement because it appeared to generate electricity out of nothing! As we saw in an earlier chapter, it was Werdermann who in 1877 sent Henry to America and was thus indirectly responsible for his subsequent career and the extraordinary events that were part of it, including the formation of the Rolls-Royce partnership. Admiral Lord Fisher wrote to Henry, saying that he was 'exceedingly obliged' to him for sending him the chapter describing the demonstration of Swan lamps at Portsmouth in 1881.

From *Reminiscences of a Pioneer* we can also glean details of the last invention with which Henry was associated. This was the Cameograph, the brainchild of Howard Edmunds and perhaps the cause of much disappointment and hardship in the last years of Henry's life.

The impression among Henry's descendants is that Howard was his favourite child. This view is supported by the fact that there are many more references to Howard than to Claud and Dorothy in *Reminiscences of a Pioneer*. When Claud took religious vows, this may have been a disappointment to his father, who had found him a job at W T Glover & Co and may have hoped that this would encourage him to take up engineering. Henry, though, was not disinterested in religion; some idea of his beliefs, and those held by Claud during a period of self-doubt, can be gleaned from letters they exchanged while Claud was serving in Cawnpore. Claud wrote:

> '*I really do think that if we had no High Church party in the Church of England I should probably become a Roman Catholic ... I think their position is infinitely sounder from both a scriptural and historical point of view ... the more one examines the Protestant position, the less one likes it. But at the same time there are lots of things in the Roman position which I don't like and I find I can for the present at least rest comfortably in our Anglican Church.*'

In his reply, which ran to three pages, Henry said:

> '*I have lived long enough not to be surprised at anything. I find people nowadays are looking into all kinds of questions as to their faith and beliefs and I can quite understand an attitude of mind which feels that the Romish Church with its long line of unbroken succession ought to be among the first as far as authority is concerned but ... there have crept into the Church many errors which have to a large extent sapped its vitality and interfered with those nations which have been guided alone by their Roman teachers ... I think we have a good example of this in the British Isles. Take the difference between Ireland, north and south ... you cannot but be impressed with the feeling that the lamentable condition in Ireland today is principally due to*

the influence of its Romish teachers and the deliberate attempt on their part to keep the lower people in ignorance ... personally I think that the good God made Heaven large enough to contain all the people who want to get there ... as your father, I should greatly regret that my eldest son should leave the Church of England for the Church of Rome... the Roman Church did all that it could to stifle freedom of thought ... had you been brought up as a child in an atmosphere distinctly Roman I should not have expected you to have departed from your environment but it was all to the contrary. You were brought up with as broad and liberal principles surrounding you as was possible. You went to Cambridge rather than Oxford, you went into business, you joined the Volunteers, you became a Free Mason and you travelled. Then your proper desire to inquire into the conditions of life and thought in other countries caused you to leave home and your friends and go to the East to study the life and conditions of India, all of which is highly commendable. Of course you are of age and a man and can please yourself but I almost feel like saying that if you elect to become a Romanist I shall as a set-off join the Society of Friends and become a Quaker. I mean by that I should then choose deliberately the most opposite of sects who are Christians that we know of and do it in order to show how father and son might each be aiming at the same goal through diversely opposite channels ...

I think there will always be two or more camps and that it is a good thing that this is so. In business matters where there is no competition there is apt to be either an overpowering domineering monopoly or stagnation and if we take the teachings of Christ we find that he said that he had other sheep not of this fold ... I am as you know much attached to the Church of England because we have a long line of ancestors who were connected with that church and I should therefore regret if you were to change, but if you must change I would rather you became a Dissenter or Congregationalist than a Romanist.'

Claud remained in the Church of England and it seems that Henry had a closer and more affectionate relationship with Howard than with Claud, perhaps because Howard had an aptitude for engineering and showed promise as an inventor. By arranging for Howard to meet Thomas Edison in January 1920, Henry was sending his son to one of the sources that had inspired him at the beginning of his own career.

On 12 May 1921, Howard accompanied Henry to a banquet held at the Royal Automobile Club in London to commemorate the 21st anniversary of the One Thousand Miles Trial. Henry proposed the toast to *'the organisers of the anniversary'* and introduced Howard to personalities whose names occur again and again in the history of motoring, including Lord Montagu of Beaulieu, Sir Herbert Austin, C Harrington Moore and Frederick Simms (the RAC's founders), and Roger Wallace (the club's first chairman). Their signatures and those of Henry, Howard and 61 other guests can be seen on a menu they autographed for Lord Montagu and which is now on display at Palace House, the Montagu's family seat

A menu autographed for Lord Montagu of Beaulieu by motoring pioneers and their guests who attended the banquet held at the RAC in 1921 to commemorate the 21st anniversary of the One Thousand Miles Trial.

at Beaulieu, Hampshire. Later that summer, Henry and Ellen visited the First World War battlefields in Flanders; Howard, almost certainly, was their guide and was probably the person who took a photograph of them standing in front of an abandoned tank. On the back of the picture there is a date (28 September 1921), Ellen's initials and a caption that reads: *'Taken near Ypres on the Menin Road, where Howard was in 1917. The tank is as it was left after the war'.* Howard had served with the 2nd Scots Guards, attaining the rank of captain and winning the Military Cross.

Henry and Ellen on the Menin Road near Ypres on 28 September 1921 while visiting First World War battlefields with Howard Edmunds.

When Howard was born in 1883, Henry was confined to his home while recovering from the road accident he suffered as he hurried to the Fisheries Exhibition in South Kensington, where he had arranged a display of Hochhausen lamps. In his *Reminiscences,* Henry recalled Howard's childhood:

> 'He was an observant little chap. When his godfather Conrad Cooke brought some books as presents ... Howard was silent. He was carefully turning over the 'untearable' pages of a coloured picture book which, being new, had stuck together, so that only blank leaves showed. His mother said, "Why don't you thank Mr Cooke?" He replied, looking at the book, "There's nuffin' in it". He was always fond of drawing, and making little sketches ... when [he was] about five years old I noticed a ship, barque-rigged, carefully drawn showing good perspective. I teasingly remarked, "The sails are not square". He replied, "You must not draw what you know, you must draw what you see". A little later, when the children were at Sandgate, their nurse took them for a treat to Shorncliffe Camp one Sunday afternoon, to the military service. The padre was holding forth, his text being 'One is our father: even God'. In the course of the sermon he

repeated this several times. It was too much for Howard. The piping voice of the child called out "My father is Mr Edmunds". Amidst some confusion he was promptly removed.'

From sketching, Howard progressed to photography, a subject to which he devoted time and thought while stationed in Cologne after the Armistice. He was demobilised in April 1919 and when he returned home he told his father about some ideas he had conceived for creating bas-relief portraits from photographs. It was clear that Howard's confidence in his concept was as great as Henry's enthusiasm for electric light and sound recording had been 40 years earlier, and together they set up a laboratory on the upper floor of the tithe barn at Moulsecoomb, intending to develop a process which they hoped would establish Howard as a successful inventor. At this time Howard relied almost entirely on his parents for an income and is unlikely to have had sufficient capital to finance what was to become an increasingly expensive venture. In his *Reminiscences* Henry described what happened when Howard's laboratory was ready:

A cameograph of Henry,
produced with Howard Edmunds' photo sculpture process

> 'Then began a series of weird experiments, in which I was a passive subject, wondering what was going to happen next, for I had no idea of the quest he was pursuing. I remember having my face smeared with streaks of dark paint which reminded me of the mummified face of a tattooed Maori chief I had once seen in a museum when a child. A photograph was taken, and the results noted. Later, a projecting lantern was used: a beam of light passing through a screen of glass, on which some straight parallel lines had been drawn. When these fell on a plain sheet, they were straight: when they fell on my face, they were curved. The photograph from the camera confirmed this. That was the birth, the beginning, of Photo Sculpture.'

Before the First World War, Howard had graduated at the Institute of Technology in Boston, Massachusetts. In 1920 he returned to America where, with the help of some friends, he built a machine which, when guided by the curved lines created by the optical process he had developed in his laboratory, could carve, in relief or intaglio, a three-dimensional portrait in ivory, bronze, alabaster and other malleable materials. Howard also discussed his idea with Henry's friend Dr Byron E Eldred, who offered much encouragement and, we imagine, practical help. Some time in 1921 Howard's machine, which weighed about a ton, was shipped to England and hauled, with some difficulty, into the tithe barn, where Howard embarked on further development work. Henry gave him engineering advice and a small workshop was set up in the laboratory, providing employment for one or two young mechanics. The London *Times* newspaper sent a correspondent to Moulsecoomb to report on progress and his article, published on 13 September 1921, was the first to describe Howard's invention in any detail, predating even Henry's own account in his *Reminiscences*. With some difficulty, one feels, the *Times* reporter told his readers how Howard's process worked:

> 'It is a little difficult for the ordinary layman to grasp how these carvings can be produced, and to understand the theory of their production calls for a knowledge of mathematics ... It was necessary to imagine an optical projector (magic lantern) constructed for use with a very long focus and well corrected lens, and a powerful source of illumination. The inventor has used with success a gas-filled incandescent lamp of about 1300 candle power. In place of the ordinary lantern slide an accurately drawn spiral photograph on a sheet of plate glass is used. This

> spiral has a form like that of the groove of a gramophone record. The spiral is projected and focused upon a plane surface at a distance of about 10ft from the projector lens. A camera is fixed to the side of the projector with the nodal points of its lens lying in the nodal plane of the projector lens. For all practical purposes it can be said that the optical axes of the camera and projector lens are parallel, and that a line joining the centres of the two lenses is at right angles to these lenses. A photographic plate put in the camera at right angles to the axis of the lens will photograph the spiral projected on the plane surface, and will do so without any distortion, provided both lenses are well corrected.
>
> The broad principle by which the carving is effected is that by substituting any solid object of an irregular form for the plane surface, the distortions produced in the projected spiral give a record of the object, and so provide means by which the carving can be effected. The photographic negative obtained is carefully enlarged on to an opal glass, which is necessary as the exact dimensions of the enlargement must not be altered by development, as would be the case if ordinary bromide paper were used.'

The reporter then went on to describe the carving machine that produced, from the photograph, a bas-relief of the sitter:

> '... in its elements the machine consists of three parts: (1) a face plate, which holds the material to be carved; (2) a moving carrier, which holds the photographic record; and (3) a high-speed drill and microscope mounted up together, which can be moved in and out by a controlling lever. The operator of the machine merely has to follow the lines indicated on the photograph with the cross-hairs of the microscope, moving the microscope to do this with the controlling arm already mentioned. In moving this microscope he also moves the drill, so that it cuts the material at varying depths according to the form of the original subject. Up to the present Mr Edmunds has worked with 20 and 40 lines per inch; and he finds that the latter gives a more delicate and faithful rendering of the original. Whether an increase beyond 40 would be better he cannot say, but he fancies that 40 represents the detail quite closely enough when looked at from the ordinary distance of two to three feet. The movement of the carrier of the enlargement is made to correspond exactly to that

> *of the movement of the carrier of the material to be carved, both movements being mechanically locked together for this purpose. Mr Edmunds has had good results in boxwood, mahogany and ivory but has found the greatest ease of working in alabaster. With regard to degree of relief, this is a question which requires a good deal of attention, as certain subjects show up better with a relatively deep relief. The inventor has found that portraiture about a third to a half of the full relief of nature gives the best results.'*

In 1878 *The Times* had, with Henry Edmunds' help, announced that Thomas Edison had invented sound recording. Now, 43 years later, the same newspaper had been the first to tell the public about Howard Edmunds' Photo Sculpture. It would be stretching imagination to compare the two inventions but they did have something in common. Edison's reproductions of the sound of the human voice were created by a stylus that was guided by incisions made in spiral grooves on a tinfoil cylinder; Howard's reproductions of the shape of the human face were created by a drill that was guided by spiral lines on a photograph. And, as in 1878, coverage in *The Times* was swiftly followed by a surge of interest among the public and the scientific community. Prototype Photo Sculptures were exhibited at the Royal Photographic Society, to whom Howard delivered a lecture in December 1921. On 25 January 1922, he read a paper to the Royal Society of Arts; the paper won him an RSA silver medal and brought enquiries from all over the world. From India, a Pharsee wrote to ask whether a photograph of his father could be used as a pattern for a Photo Sculpture. From California, someone enquired whether a 'much desired carving' could be made from a photograph of a lady. Henry helped Howard answer these enquiries; they had to point out that only specially-taken photographs were suitable for Howard's process, but in an instalment of his *Reminiscences* published in July 1922, Henry gave news of a further development:

> *'From now on, any person can have what we call a 'Cameograph Record'. Special cameras with suitable lenses, and a projecting lantern, are being made for this purpose. A sitting in a dark room (the face of the subject being illuminated for a few seconds only) is sufficient to give the necessary record, which can be filed away for future use. These records can be sent to the new carving machines for reproduction in the solid. In delicate ivory, a dainty miniature, or in enduring bronze, in any size or proportion, up to the large bas-relief in marble or stone, truly*

confirming the statement that 'A thing of beauty is a joy for ever', for these Cameographs can be very beautiful, both as works of art and as faithful records of those in whom we are interested ... If the Art of Photo Sculpture had been known two years before the war, instead of two years after, it is safe to say that fifty per cent of the war photos would have been taken by this new method, so that sculpture records would have been available for reproduction in the solid when wanted.'

In a letter to the RSA *Journal,* Henry said: *'When I was last in Genoa and visited the famous and beautiful Campo Santo I saw hundreds of memorials in marble which had ordinary photos let into the stone, and although protected by glass many of these were faded and useless'.* Cameographs, he believed, would have been a far more popular likeness of the deceased, and more enduring.

On 23 November 1921, the Edmunds Cameograph Co Ltd was incorporated, with a share capital of £25,000. Its address was Parliament Mansions, London SW1 – Henry's business address - and its directors were James S Gibson (chairman), Henry Edmunds, Howard Edmunds and J Dudley Forsyth. Howard and Henry kept their American friends informed of their progress with what was now generally known as the Cameograph machine, and in September 1922 Byron Eldred wrote to say that he proposed to come to England to study the latest developments. For some reason, Henry deterred him, preferring instead to take a collection of Photo Sculptures to show to Eldred and his other friends and business associates on the American east coast. He also took along a cinematograph film of the entire process. Henry liked to travel, to witness the latest developments in all branches of science, and to meet scientists and engineers, so it is not surprising that among his memoirs of his efforts to promote Photo Sculpture there is an account of what was probably his last visit to America. Accompanied by Ellen, he sailed on the world's fastest liner, the *Mauretania,* which left Southampton at midday on Saturday 28 October and arrived in New York on Thursday 2 November after a passage lasting five days, seven hours and thirty-three minutes, covered at an average speed of 24.11 knots. It was, he noted, the fastest post-war crossing of the Atlantic, accomplished by the ship that in 1910 had set up a record for the crossing by sailing from Queenstown to New York in less than four and a half days. Henry inspected the oil-fired boilers and engine room of the *Mauretania,* where he marvelled at the quietness of the engines and absence of dust and dirt, and recalled his first voyage to America in 1877 on the *Abyssinia,* a coal-fired ship that took 11 days to make the voyage. He also commented that the *Mauretania* and indeed all the transatlantic liners had electric lighting, *'a wonderful change since I myself superintended the lighting of the City of Richmond, the first ship to cross the Atlantic with the then new light. One naturally wonders what will be the end of all these improvements'.*

Henry's account of his visit to America in 1922 was written while he was actually making and keeping various appointments in and around New York City. It formed the 15th chapter of his *Reminiscences* and the typescript, complete with what the editor of the *M&C Apprentices' Magazine* called 'Americanisms in spelling', was posted to Sam Mavor before Henry returned home. As before, Henry was impressed by the skyline of New York as his ship approached its berth:

> *'It is almost impossible to describe the difference of impression of that period only 45 years ago, and now. Then there were no bridges connecting Manhattan Island to the mainland or to Long Island. The comparatively ancient Brooklyn Bridge was then in course of construction ... there are now three others, the Manhattan and Queensborough and Williamsburgh, as well as tunnels beneath the river.'*

The motoring pioneer was quick to note the huge growth in road traffic that had occurred since the bridges and tunnels were built, for he could see that they were 'quite inadequate to deal with the enormous traffic'. Soon after they arrived, Henry and Ellen were invited to Eldred's home at Great Neck, Long Island. They were staying at the Biltmore Hotel in Manhattan and Eldred drove in to collect them. The journey back to Great Neck took only an hour, but returning to Manhattan was an altogether different experience. They left at five o'clock one Sunday afternoon. Later, Henry described what happened:

> *'We had only proceeded a few miles when we got into an interminable jam of auto-cars. In the whole of my experience I have never seen roads so completely choked with traffic in both directions. The pace was that of the slowest vehicle and there were several horse-drawn vehicles, so you can imagine the congestion that ensued. We had spent nearly two hours and had gotten half-way to our destination. Our host was very much concerned and advised that at Flushing we should take to the overhead railroad ... it was therefore no wonder that we were very late in reaching our hotel ... In England we have no conception of the number of motor cars which are in daily use*

in the United States ... in New York the density has increased during the last twelve months to a point of almost complete congestion, there being one-third more cars added during this period. In New York ... there is a complete unified system of control, which all conveyances must obey. Every few minutes the vehicles up and down come to rest so that cross road traffic may pass, the result being that New York today is one of the most difficult cities in the world for a passenger to get from point to point with any certainty as to the length of time to reach his destination.'

Henry had, in fact, arrived in America when electric traffic lights designed to control conflicting streams of traffic were in their infancy. In 1914 the first signals of this kind, with red and green lights, were installed in Cleveland, Ohio, to be followed four years later in New York by the first signals with red, green and amber lights.

Henry remained in America with Ellen for Christmas and the first few weeks of 1923, travelling to Orange, New Jersey, on 16 January to meet Thomas Edison for the first time for 44 years. Writing after he returned to England, Henry described their reunion:

A photograph of Thomas Edison, a souvenir of Henry's meeting with the inventor in January 1923 – their first for 44 years

'We looked at each other, both realising that time had dealt kindly with us. I found Mr Edison had become very deaf but he was most pleasant and said he thought he remembered that I had married a niece of Governor Howard of Rhode Island; and he understood that our son was here in America and he enquired what he was doing. I replied, "He has just made a most interesting discovery which he has applied to a remarkable invention", and I showed him a block of ivory carved with the

features of a lady, who had been photographed. Mr Edison was greatly charmed when I explained the process and he expressed the desire to be one of the first to have his portrait executed by this new method. We then recalled the many mutual friends we had had in the past, each of whom had passed to his long rest, with the exception of Dr Chandler who was now in his ninetieth year.'

Shortly before visiting Edison, Henry received a letter from W J Crampton, asking him to broadcast from New York to Britain's amateur wireless enthusiasts. Radio was at this time in an even earlier stage of its development than the motor car; domestic 'wireless sets' for receiving broadcast programmes had been on sale for only three years, and sending and receiving transmissions across the Atlantic was something practised only by scientific experimenters and radio 'hams'. However, Henry had a friend, A L Doremus, vice-president of the Crocker Wheeler Company, who knew the manager of Western Electric's radio station on Broadway, whose call letters were WEAF. It was arranged that Henry would broadcast to Britain at 9.00 pm local time (2.00 am Greenwich Mean Time) on Saturday 20 January. This is how Henry described the experience:

'I was seated in a chair, in front of which stood a transmitting apparatus on a small tripod. When I explained to the manager that I wished to address the wireless amateurs of England he intimated that there might be some difficulty about this, in consequence of their commercial agreements with the British Marconi Company, and it would be preferable for me to address the American audience and at the same time I might be heard in England. I ...therefore slightly modified the remarks I had prepared and addressed myself more particularly to the wireless amateurs of America. It was an eerie feeling to realise that I was addressing over a million people, not one of whom I could see. I began by telling them about my first visit to America in 1877, my interview with Thomas A Edison and my meeting with him again two years later ... when he presented me with one of his earliest examples of the then new invention of the Phonograph. I went on to tell them that I had again had the pleasure of meeting that distinguished American a few days before.'

Henry's broadcast was followed by one by a choir from Pittsburgh. While this was on the air Henry received a message saying that a listener in Brooklyn had telephoned, asking Henry for some information about the early work of Lord Kelvin. Back at the Biltmore Hotel, Henry received a telegram from friends in Rhode Island, 200 miles away, saying that they had heard his broadcast very distinctly but asking why it had been immediately followed by the British national anthem! The Pittsburgh choir had not sung *God Save the King* and the mystery was compounded next day, when a friend in England cabled to say that the broadcast had been heard in Leicestershire and Lincolnshire; here too, Henry's words had been followed by the national anthem. Later, Henry discovered what had happened. While he was broadcasting from New York the British politician and businessman Sir Eric Campbell Geddes was making a speech to an audience in Montreal, and this was being broadcast by a local radio station on a wavelength close to that used by WEAF. When Sir Eric had finished speaking the Montreal station played *God Save the King* as a patriotic gesture. By coincidence, Henry and Sir Eric finished speaking at the same time, and when the national anthem from Montreal was played it cut into WEAFs wavelength.

However, what makes Henry's broadcast more remarkable than an accidental merging of adjacent wavelengths is that it preceded, by almost a year, one that Dr Henry Davis made from Pittsburgh to Station 2AZ in Manchester on 31 December 1923. This is recognised as the first transatlantic broadcast to England.[52] Henry's, perhaps, has not been accorded that distinction because, officially, it was for an American audience even though originally intended for (and, in the event, also heard by) British listeners.

While in America, Henry found an opportunity to learn about the latest developments in gas heating, a subject he had last studied in detail in 1912, when he accompanied Professor William A Bone to a meeting of the Gas Association of America in St Louis. Bone had demonstrated how a porous diaphragm of refractory material could become incandescent when a mixture of burning gas and air was passed through it. Controlling the heat radiated by this device at first proved difficult - it tended to explode when shielded - but by 1923 progress had been made and Henry went to the New York factory of American Surface Combustion Inc, which had taken up some of Bone's inventions, but not the diaphragm. Henry took with him an improved diaphragm, called the Radiophragm, that had been developed by his friend Frederick J Cox of 180 Arlington Road, Camden Town, London. The Radiophragm was successfully put through a variety of tests in New York and on 9 May, at a lecture at the Royal Society of Arts in London, Professor Bone was able to announce that the Radiophragm *'bids fair to put diaphragm heating into an unassailable position and*

---

[52] *The Shell Book of Firsts*, Patrick Robertson, Ebury Press, 1975.

greatly extend its scope and usefulness'. Soon, Radiophragm cookers for grilling, toasting and roasting were installed in J Lyons' restaurants in London. Henry noted with some awe that in an hour they could grill 1500 steaks or toast 1200 slices of bread. In his *Reminiscences* he also described how Cox's Radiophragm was being used *'for all kinds of industrial purposes ... such as biscuit, chocolate and confectionery manufacturing; also hotels, restaurants, jam boiling, lead and type melting, tin box soldering machines, enamelling ovens, foundry work and drying of moulds'*. Henry's very first patent application, filed in 1873, had been for a gas burner. And although he had devoted his life to electrical engineering his last patent, a joint invention with F J Cox, T G Tulloch and G E Millner and dated 29 June 1925, was for another gas-burning device, for heating calendering rollers.

Gas combustion, though, was only of secondary interest to Henry during this visit to New York; he spent most of his time promoting Photo Sculpture and soon found himself 'besieged' with friends of Byron Eldred who wanted to see the process. Henry showed some examples to the sculptor Daniel Chester French, commenting *"Possibly you consider this is a rival to your craft?"* French replied, *"Indeed not. This is a handmaiden to our craft and should prove of the greatest value, for we experience considerable difficulties, especially with living subjects, in faithfully recording the expression as well as the form of the features. An ordinary photograph only gives the suggestion of this in light and shade, whereas here you have got the most accurate delineation of the form, and have caught the expression. I understand that, as far as the subject is concerned, it is only a matter of a few seconds in taking the photograph and, after that, you can produce the image by mechanical means, giving the wonderful results that you have shown me"*.

A few days later French asked Henry whether he would show the Photo Sculptures to 'a few artistic friends and sculptors'. The 'few' turned out to be 70 or 80, who gathered at the Biltmore Hotel, where Henry hired a suite of rooms in which he set up a screen and projector for his cinematograph film. French made some introductory remarks and commented that it would have taken him more than one hundred hours of patient work to carve an alabaster likeness of one of the subjects who had had to pose for Howard Edmunds for only a few minutes. Henry's presentation created so much interest that a number of Eldred's friends asked him to invite Howard to bring to New York a complete set of optical apparatus and some carving machines for another demonstration. This was so successful that within a few months, probably during the summer of 1923, Howard opened what he called the Cameograph Studio at 80 West 40th Street, Manhattan. In London, Howard had a workshop at 15 Rochester Row, Victoria, and a studio at 45 Pall Mall (not far from the Royal Automobile Club). The studio was conveniently close to Whitehall, Westminster and the West End, from where it attracted some distinguished patrons, including the Prince of Wales, the Duke and Duchess of York, Prince Henry, Prince George, Stanley Baldwin (who became prime minister at about the time the studio opened), Lord Balfour, Robert Baden-Powell, George Bernard Shaw, George Arliss and Gladys Cooper. Among the clients of the New York studio were Mary Pickford and Lady Diana Manners. Photo Sculpture created interest on both sides of the Atlantic and it is likely that Henry provided substantial financial support for a considerable time, especially while Howard was setting up his studios; even in the 1920s, renting premises in Pall Mall and West 40th Street must have been a very expensive proposition, but no doubt Henry and Howard felt that the studios had to be located in fashionable areas where they were most likely to attract famous and wealthy clients.

Yet Photo Sculpture was not a commercial success. The history of invention is littered with ideas that were borne of great ingenuity and developed at great expense, but failed for the simplest of reasons. We do not know for certain why Photo Sculpture did not bring Howard and Henry the rewards they expected. Henry wrote the last chapter of his *Reminiscences* in March 1924, when his hopes for the process were at their highest. Neither he nor Howard left any account of the subsequent decline of the Cameograph business but an enlightened guess about what happened can be made, based on the few documents and profit and loss accounts that have survived.

On 10 September 1923, the board decided to raise more capital by issuing preference shares to its original shareholders (the register of shareholders has not survived, though Henry is likely to have had a major holding). The prospectus accompanying the offer reported that improvements to the Photo Sculpture process justified further expenditure on apparatus for the London studio, and that Howard Edmunds had produced high-class work in New York, although in England *'no commercial work has yet been done; that is to say, nothing has been made and sold for profit'*. On 1 January 1924, the business was restructured and the original company was taken over by the Cameograph Company Ltd, with an authorised capital of £75,000 in £1 shares, of which 61,652 were issued. The company's board of directors consisted of the Hon Philip Henderson (chairman), F Summers (managing director), Howard Edmunds (technical director) and Sir Edward Iliffe; Henry Edmunds did not join the board of the new company, but is assumed to have been a major investor. On 30 September 1925, office expenses during the preceding 21 months had exceeded £5000, £1500 had been spent on advertising and general expenses, and there was a trading loss of £2800 - equivalent to more than £60,000 in today's values. The New York studio was closed in April 1925, so that development of the process could be concentrated in London; business in Cameograph portraits was disappointing, though prospects were encouraging for portrait busts, Wedgwood plaques, medals and medallions.

On 31 March 1927, the company had liabilities of more than £66,000 and reported a loss of more than £7600 (equal to more than £170,000 today) during the preceding 18 months. On 7 September 1927, at the annual meeting of shareholders, the directors reported that accumulated losses came to £13,000; an attempt to revitalise the business in New York was showing *'a certain amount of success'*, and that a *'comparatively small amount of business'* had been done in the London studio *'at a very large expense'*. Sir Edward Iliffe resigned from the board, having sold his shares to Philip Henderson, who also took over a loan of £3500 that Sir Edward had made to the business. The company's auditors retired and did not seek re-election. From now onwards, the business just petered out, leaving only one question: why was it a failure?

Photo Sculpture was, perhaps, too much of a novelty; bas-relief portraits were an undoubted source of amazement and perhaps amusement, but not something that many people wanted, nor ever likely to have anything other than curiosity value. Perhaps Henry and Howard should have developed other applications for the process. Sir Edward Iliffe, in a letter to *The Times* dated 8 November 1923, suggested that it could be applied to the art of medal making. In its own brochure, the Cameograph Company described how portrait plaques had been made by cameography for Josiah Wedgwood & Sons' Jasper ware. These, perhaps, were two of the applications to which Henry and Howard should have devoted more effort.

There are several reasons why companies fail. They can be inadequately capitalised, they can have poor cash-flow, they can be badly managed, they can fail to show a profit on their activities or they can undertake activities which are commercially unsustainable. In the case of the Cameograph businesses, there appears to have been a combination of all these circumstances, and, despite the limited company status, Henry Edmunds was unable to protect his personal assets against the consequences of the collapse of the venture.

The accounts of the Cameograph Company Limited were prepared under the accounting conventions of the 1920s, when disclosure requirements and the regulatory regime were less stringent than now. At that time a company was only required to disclose minimal details of its affairs, which usually resulted in a Directors' Report, Balance Sheet and a Profit and Loss account being laid before the members and filed.

Two sets of accounts have survived. These cover the 21 months from incorporation to 30 September 1925 and the 18 months from 1 October 1925 to 31 March 1927. There is (in both cases) a Profit and Loss Account and a Balance Sheet, which show the absolute minimum required by law.

In both cases, the accounts show a gross profit from the trading account, *not* the turnover or *any* indication of how the profit was calculated. We have no idea of precisely how much money was coming into the business or of what the gross or net margins were. It may be that the company had a large turnover, although on the evidence, turnover was quite modest, if not non-existent at times. In both cases the directors reported that business had been disappointing, and appear to have taken the Micawber-like view that something would turn up. There were certainly accumulated losses of £13,068 over three years, which although equivalent to approximately £290,000 in modern money, in itself, may not have resulted in the business folding if it had been adequately capitalised.

Both Balance Sheets show that the cash required to carry such losses and to service the cost of any loans was inadequate, because £35,894 of shareholders funds had been applied to the purchase of non-productive intangible assets, the goodwill and patents. Even some of these transactions seem to have been illusory, because a block of 10,000 shares was issued to the inventor as consideration. These shares, with hindsight, appear to have had no real commercial value.

Patents and goodwill are only of any value if they are capable of producing an acceptable return for the investor, either by trading them or by passing them on to someone else. There is no record of any subsequent person or company making a living from this photo sculpture process. Henry Edmunds hoped, perhaps even expected, that the Cameograph would become as popular and successful as the Phonograph. Yet again, this time in partnership with his son Howard, he expected to become a successful pioneer and promoter of new and exciting technology. However, he seriously misjudged what the public's reaction would be, and to make matters worse, persisted when it was very clear that the idea was not catching on. In 1926, at the age of 73, Henry found himself in serious financial difficulties. This must have been a tremendous shock, since until then he had lived comfortably, maintained a large house, entertained his many friends and relations, and enjoyed long visits to the USA, travelling on luxury liners and staying at the best hotels

Unfortunately, most of Henry's personal papers have disappeared; when and how that happened is a mystery. The loss of documents that would tell us more about Henry's career and the last years of his life is undeniably regrettable but fortunately a few papers survive, and these give us some idea of the circumstances in which he was placed at the time when he became short of money.

From the Will he signed on 20 October 1920, it is clear that he had investments which, although unspecified, seemed likely to provide his wife, daughter and sons with an adequate income after his death. As we have seen, he also bequeathed an annuity of £100 to Edward John Pilcher, his confidential clerk, and appointed him one of his executors. However, in a codicil dated 26 May 1925 he revoked Pilcher's annuity and appointment, and instructed that if Ellen's income from his investments came to less than £500 a year his trustees could, if Ellen wished, make up the deficiency by selling some of his residuary estate. The codicil is the first evidence we have of Henry rearranging his financial affairs in the face of an uncertain future, but towards the end of 1926 his situation became more serious and he instructed a local firm of auctioneers and estate agents, Wilkinson, Son & Welch, to sell the remainder of his lease on Moulsecoomb Place. In 1913, Henry had leased the property for 21 years. In 1918 he signed a new lease for a term expiring in 1941, and in 1923 he obtained an option to purchase the property for £6525. Clearly, at that time he intended Moulsecoomb to be his home and that of his heirs for a long time to come; his decision, only three years later, to sell his lease must have caused the family much distress.

In a letter written on 7 December 1926, to James H Rothwell, town clerk of Brighton, Wilkinsons said that Henry thought that Brighton Corporation might be interested in purchasing his lease and option on Moulsecoomb. The letter continued:

> 'Our client has expended something like £5,000 or £6,000 upon the property, which has been greatly improved and is well maintained. Our client is asking a premium of 3,000 guineas to partly recoup himself for the large expenditure he has incurred, for the benefit of his lease and the valuable option to acquire the freehold - the usual tenant's fixtures and fittings; outdoor effects and the Organ-Orchestrelle with electric blower combination, to be taken by valuation.'

Negotiations continued during the winter and on 4 March 1927, Henry and James Rothwell signed an agreement transferring all Henry's interests in Moulsecoomb to Brighton Corporation. Henry received a premium of £1400, less than half the sum he had asked for. A few weeks later, on 25 and 26 March (a few days after his 74th birthday) his furniture, Organ-Orchestrelle, pictures and other valuables were sold by public auction. The catalogue of the sale, comprising 624 lots, has survived, although unfortunately all records of the sale - the buyers, and the prices they paid - have been lost. Henry and Ellen and Dorothy then moved to a flat at 19 Adelaide Crescent, a Regency town house near the sea front at Hove, the neighbouring resort to Brighton. The house was owned by Sir Park Goff, Conservative MP for the Cleveland Division of the North Riding of Yorkshire; Sir Park was probably one of the high-ranking friends that Henry made while living in Brighton, and whose help was sought or offered when Henry experienced his evidently sudden financial crisis.

Henry died at 19 Adelaide Crescent on 18 November 1927, after suffering a cerebral thrombosis. Howard Edmunds was in New York City and too far away to be able to travel to England in time to attend the funeral and burial service, which took place at Stanmer church, a few miles from Moulsecoomb, on Tuesday 22 November. Claud, who was by now vicar of St Augustine's, Leicester, was present at Henry's death and was one of the chief mourner, accompanied by Ellen, Dorothy and immediate relations. Among the old friends and business associates who attended were Edward Manville, Llewelyn Atkinson (representing the Cable Makers' Association), T O Callender (representing Sir Tom Callender and Callenders' Cable Company) and W J Crampton, whose difficulty in obtaining a car for Parsons' entry in the Side Slip Trials in 1904 had led Henry to borrow Henry Royce's first car and bring it to London. Rolls-Royce Ltd was not represented; Henry had, of course, outlived Charles Rolls, but Ernest Claremont and Claude Johnson had both died within the previous five years. Sir Henry Royce was now a semi-invalid, still designing cars and engines but living at Le Canadel, in the south of France, and isolated from his company's day-to-day affairs. It is unlikely, therefore, that any of Rolls-Royce's directors in Derby were aware of the significance, to their company, of the death of an old man in Hove. As the story of

From the catalogue of the auction of Henry and Ellen's property in 1927

Rolls-Royce's origins would not be fully researched and published for several years, historians had not yet delved into the rather obscure *M&C Apprentices' Magazine* in which the circumstances in which Rolls met Royce had been revealed, but only to a limited readership.

Perhaps unwittingly, Henry's family chose, for his gravestone, an appropriate epitaph for someone who had been a pioneer of electric lighting:

IN THY LIGHT SHALL WE SEE LIGHT

When Henry died he was heavily in debt. Ellen Edmunds died intestate only six months later. It took Claud Edmunds and the family's solicitor, A W Claremont, until 1929 to sort out the financial problems that blighted the last few years of Henry and Ellen's lives. Before she died, Ellen told Sir Edward Manville about Henry's debts and he gave her a cheque for £250, which she paid into Henry's estate. Later, Sir Edward told Claud that he had been *'only too glad'* to make his *'little contribution - your father was my oldest and I think I may say my dearest friend, and I am always regretting he is with us no longer'*. Sir Park Goff bought, for £68, the bedroom suite that Henry and Ellen had left at 19 Adelaide Crescent, and paid £50 (£10 for the contents of each of the flat's five rooms) for miscellaneous furniture. In April 1929, £750 was still owing to various creditors and it looked as though it would take the family another four years to pay the debts.

By now Claud and Dorothy had each received £500 from the estate and a similar amount was due to be paid to Howard. Claud proposed that each of them should return £250 to the estate, since this would be *'preferable to allowing the winding-up to drag on over several years'*. It is not certain that such drastic action was eventually necessary, but the fact that it had to be considered reveals that a life that had been full of much promise, and distinguished by more adventures and achievements than most of us enjoy, had ended in sad circumstances, not only for Henry but also for his family. This was, perhaps, the inevitable result of leading a life rich in enthusiasm for new inventions and full of encouragement for others, but lacking the judgement and prudence that would have left Henry and his heirs better rewarded for what he had achieved.

FAMILY TREES

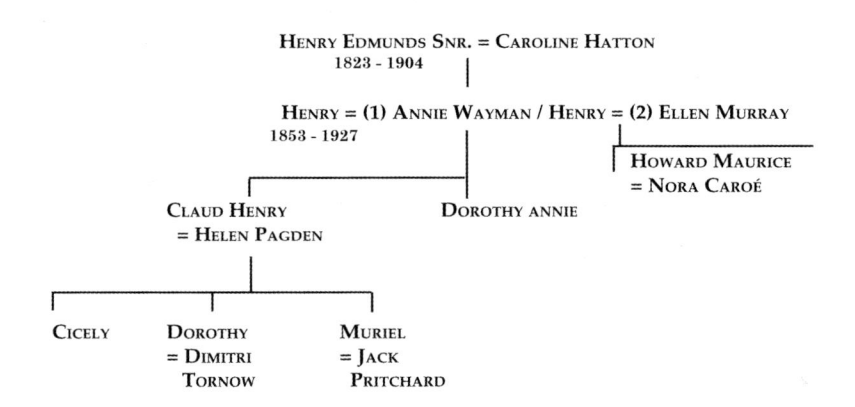

```
                    HENRY EDMUNDS SNR. = CAROLINE HATTON
                           1823 - 1904
                                |
              HENRY = (1) ANNIE WAYMAN / HENRY = (2) ELLEN MURRAY
              1853 - 1927                   |
                                            |    HOWARD MAURICE
                                            |     = NORA CAROÉ
        CLAUD HENRY              DOROTHY ANNIE
        = HELEN PAGDEN
              |
    ┌─────────┼─────────┐
  CICELY   DOROTHY    MURIEL
           = DIMITRI  = JACK
           TORNOW     PRITCHARD
```

Simplified family tree, showing Henry's parents, children and grandchildren.

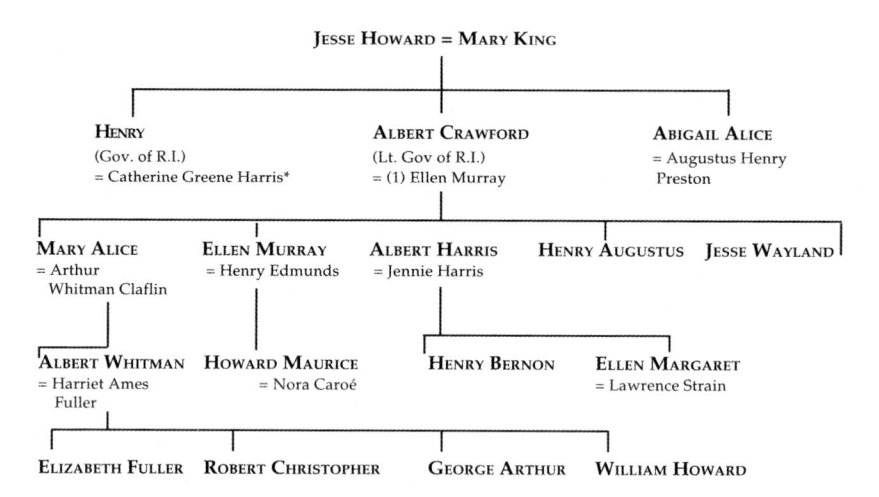

```
                    JESSE HOWARD = MARY KING
                              |
          ┌───────────────────┼───────────────────┐
        HENRY            ALBERT CRAWFORD        ABIGAIL ALICE
     (Gov. of R.I.)      (Lt. Gov of R.I.)      = Augustus Henry
     = Catherine         = (1) Ellen Murray        Preston
     Greene Harris*
```

MARY ALICE	ELLEN MURRAY	ALBERT HARRIS	HENRY AUGUSTUS	JESSE WAYLAND
= Arthur	= Henry Edmunds	= Jennie Harris		
Whitman Claflin				

ALBERT WHITMAN   HOWARD MAURICE   HENRY BERNON   ELLEN MARGARET
= Harriet Ames   = Nora Caroé   = Lawrence Strain
  Fuller

ELIZABETH FULLER   ROBERT CHRISTOPHER   GEORGE ARTHUR   WILLIAM HOWARD

Simplified family tree showing Henry's marriage to Ellen Murray Howard and how he was related to Rhode Island's distinguished Howard and Claflin families. The descendants of Albert Crawford Howard and his second wife, Jenny W Randall, are now shown; nor are the marriage and descendants of Henry Augustus Howard.

* Catherine Greene Harris was the daughter of Elisha Harris and Sarah Taylor. Elisha Harris was a Governor of RI.

EPILOGUE

The small wax-coated Graphophone cylinder was placed on the 'electronic phonograph' that had been built at the British Library's National Sound Archive to enable rare recordings made at and before the turn of the century to be reproduced with the aid of the latest audio technology. Peter Copeland, the NSA's conservation manager, gently lowered a stylus on to the cylinder. His witnesses - Benet Bergonzi, curator of artefacts and Stephanie Millard, the London Science Museum's curator of acoustics and sound reproduction - leaned closer to a loudspeaker that had been linked to the phonograph, and wondered whether they would soon hear a Royal voice that had been recorded on a Graphophone more than 100 years earlier.

Three separate bands of grooves were visible on the cylinder, suggesting that three recordings or attempted recordings had been made on it. Whilst the bands were being tracked with a series of styluses, and played at various speeds, the recordings were immediately transcribed on to magnetic tape, just in case the cylinder's fragile wax coating would withstand only one attempt to discover whether or not it retained any recording signals.

The surface noise - scratches, clicks and thumps - that emanated from the grooves was almost deafening, but when the transcriptions were replayed through electronic filters, a woman's voice - so faint as to be almost beyond the range of the human ear - could be heard. Of the thirty or forty words or syllables spoken, only a few phrases could be made out. The consensus of opinion among those present at the audition was that the only unambiguous words that could be heard were:

> 'Greetings ... the answer can be ... I've never forgotten.'

Subsequent monitoring added, in the opinion of one listener, three more words, giving:

> 'Greetings, Britons and everybody ... the answer can be ... I've never forgotten.'

When news of the discovery of the cylinder was reported in the media, the transcription was broadcast by television and radio stations all over the world and recorded by audio enthusiasts and historians. They tried, and are still trying, to discern the missing words. John Wrigley Jnr has put forward as complete an interpretation as it seems possible to get:

'Greetings, Britons everywhere ... the answer can be ... the phonograph is a wonderful thing. I have never forgotten ...'

More than a century had passed since Henry Edmunds introduced the tinfoil Phonograph and the Bell-Tainter Graphophone into Britain, and the chances of finding any of his sound recording apparatus were remote. Henry's Will was consulted, but it contained no references to recording machines or cylinders. After Henry died, his wife Ellen returned to Providence, Rhode Island. So far as is known, she did not take any of his recording equipment with her. She died on 21 May 1928. Henry's children, Dorothy, Claud and Howard, would have known what, if anything, Henry had kept in later life to remind him of the time when he had hoped to become a pioneer and promoter of sound recording, but they died many years before the research for this biography commenced (as did Claud and Howard's wives). Dorothy never married. Only Claud had any children - three daughters, Cicely Edmunds, Dorothy Tornow and Muriel Pritchard. By the time Henry's life was being researched, the few possessions of Henry and Ellen that still remained in their family belonged to Cicely Edmunds or to Dr Michael Pritchard, Michael being the oldest of Henry's six great-grandchildren. Neither Dorothy nor Michael knew whether Henry's recording machines or any of the recordings made on them had survived.

Fortunately, Leonard and Violet Simmons, who had worked for Henry and Ellen at Moulsecoomb, remembered that shortly before the contents of the house were auctioned in 1927, Henry sold a tinfoil Phonograph to a Mr John Hay, who had a gramophone and cycle shop in Brighton. By coincidence, this piece of information emerged at the same time as enquiries at the Science Museum revealed that a tinfoil Phonograph belonging to a Mr John Hay had been displayed at an exhibition held in 1977 to commemorate the invention's centenary. This was the machine that Henry once owned, and it now belongs to John and Peter Hay, the sons of the man who had bought it.

John recalls how, when he was about six or seven, he went to Moulescoomb with his father: *"I remember Henry showing [him] this weird machine. It meant absolutely nothing to me. I expect I fidgeted and was only anxious to leave this great house and its formidable occupant"*. John also remembers revisiting Moulscoomb after Henry died, and seeing several shelves of glass 'accumulators' (voltaic cells) which Henry had probably installed to generate current for electrical apparatus and experiments.

Henry's Edison tinfoil phonograph with John Hay,
whose father bought the machine in 1927 (Author's collection)

Although no longer in working order the Phonograph is virtually intact. In a drawer in its base there are a few tools, some sheets of tinfoil and an instruction manual, signed 'H.Edmunds'. Unfortunately the pieces of tinfoil are blank; if only Henry had left some recordings of his own voice and the voices of those to whom he demonstrated the machine! He did, however, hand down some interesting documents with the Phonograph, including a letter that says:

> *'The Phonograph which you have purchased from me is of considerable historic interest. I was in America in 1877 and first met Mr Edison at the house of a friend with whom I was staying in August. Later in December I called to see Mr Edison at Menloe [sic], New Jersey, at his laboratory. I found him experimenting with several of his assistants in connection with an apparatus consisting of a cylinder on which a spiral groove had been cut, which was covered with tin foil. Mr Edison had just spoken into a mouthpiece holding a tin diaphragm with a metal point which through a series of vibrations produced a series of impressions on the tin foil. When this was afterwards revolved, it spoke the words 'Mary had a little lamb'. Later in 1879, Mr Edison gave*

me the phonograph you have purchased - the first one to come to Europe - I brought it myself in 1879.

*Yours faithfully
Henry Edmunds MIEE, MInst CE'*

Henry was mistaken in thinking that his Phonograph was the first one to come to Europe. Other tinfoil Phonographs had been sent over in 1878. Henry's instrument, Phonograph No 205, was given to him by Thomas Edison when he met him for the third time, in 1879.

Another coincidence led to evidence of what became of some of the Graphophone apparatus used by Henry and his friend and solicitor, Sydney Morse, during their Graphophone venture in 1888. When told that Queen Victoria's voice had been recorded by Sydney Morse, John Hay wondered whether there was any connection between his solicitors, Waltons & Morse, and Sydney Morse. There was. Sydney had founded Morse & Co, which in 1975 had amalgamated with Waltons & Co. Documents in the company's files revealed that a few months after Sydney died in January 1929, a number of items of scientific interest that he had acquired during his career were offered to the Science Museum. Among these were the Graphophone recording machine that he had demonstrated to Queen Victoria, and a Graphophone recording cylinder. During the 1920s, Sydney often invited his friends and grandchildren to listen to the Graphophone, and played them the recording he had made of Queen Victoria in 1888.

The Science Museum did not accept the Graphophone recording machine, because several vital parts were missing. It did accept the cylinder, but due to an oversight at the time it was handed over, no one suspected that it might be the one on which, to quote Henry Edmunds' own words, *'the voice and speech of the celebrated Queen'* had been recorded.

It was not until 1980 that Dr D B Thomas of the Science Museum was told of the possible historic significance of the cylinder. No machine was available on which it could be played, but its tracks were examined under a stereo-microscope. The indentations or engravings formed by the recording stylus in the grooves of cylinders or disc records are usually visible when examined in this way, but no such marks could be seen on this cylinder. There the matter rested until 1991, but in the meantime the National Sound Archive had built its 'electronic phonograph' and an electronic process called Computer Enhanced Digital Audio Restoration ('Cedar') had been developed.

The circumstantial evidence acquired so far suggests that the voice on the cylinder is more likely than not to be that of Queen Victoria. The investigation continues.

Dr D B Thomas with the graphophone cylinder that once belonged to Sydney Morse (Author's collection)

Note:
A full account of Sydney Morse's demonstration of the Graphophone at Balmoral Castle, and the investigation into what became of the recording he made there, can be found in *The Lost Voice of Queen Victoria - The Search for the First Royal Recording* by Paul Tritton (Academy Books, 1991, ISBN 1 873361 11 4).

POSTSCRIPT TO THE FIRST EDITION

I started researching the life of Henry Edmunds in January 1980, when several anniversaries of great importance to Rolls-Royce were imminent. In September the 40th anniversary of the Battle of Britain was commemorated. As everyone knows, Rolls-Royce Merlin aero-engines powered the Spitfires and Hurricanes in which the gallant pilots of RAF Fighter Command fought and won that epic conflict. The anniversary was significant not only to Rolls-Royce plc, the aero-engine firm, but also to Rolls-Royce Motor Cars Ltd because its factory at Crewe, Cheshire, was originally built to manufacture Merlins. In September 1981 celebrations were held to mark the fiftieth anniversary of Britain's third successive victory in the Schneider Trophy air race, an achievement which allowed Britain to retain the trophy for all time. That victory was made possible by the incredible 'R' engine, developed by Sir Henry Royce for Reginald Mitchell's Supermarine seaplanes, precursors of the Spitfire. Both these anniversaries reawakened interest in the history of Rolls-Royce and so, encouraged by David Preston, editor of *Rolls-Royce Motors Journal,* I began trying to discover all that I could about the circumstances in which Rolls and Royce first met, and the man whose brief account of how he introduced them is quoted or paraphrased in all the authoritative books and articles on the origins of Rolls-Royce.

In 1984 Rolls-Royce enthusiasts looked back 80 years to that historic introduction in Manchester, after which the most famous partnership in business history was formed. On the foundations of that partnership, Claude Johnson built what became the world's most famous company. That reputation remains. Although two entirely separate enterprises are now responsible for producing Rolls-Royce motor cars and Rolls-Royce aero-engines, they share a common heritage. But what if Henry Edmunds' efforts to introduce the two men had failed, and Rolls and Royce had never met? Royce would have still become a great engineer, but would he have achieved commercial success as a motor car manufacturer without Rolls' and Johnson's encouragement, business acumen and, above all, their connections with the wealthy classes who were the natural market for Rolls-Royce cars? If Rolls and Royce had not met, the world would probably never have seen the succession of charismatic and beautiful cars that began with the Rolls-Royce '10' in 1904 and continues today with the Silver Spirit. And how would Britain have fared, in war and peace, without Rolls-Royce aero-engines? The immortal Merlin of the Second World War was a direct descendant of Royce's first aero-engine, the Eagle, designed in the First World War; without the Merlin, could Britain have built fighters of the calibre of the

Hurricane and Spitfire, and bombers with the destructive power of the Lancaster? Without supremacy in the air, the war would have been lost; that supremacy was due largely to Sir Henry Royce's pioneering work on high-performance piston engines in the 1920s and early 1930s. A jet age without Rolls-Royce aero-engines is also unimaginable - their performance is derived from technologies that would amaze even Sir Henry, but his disciplines and principles still guide today's Rolls-Royce engineers.

Unrelated and unlikely circumstances and events shape the destinies of men who emerge from different walks of life to meet, achieve greatness and make history together. Henry Edmunds, as I began to discover in 1980, was responsible for more than he had been given credit for. So after writing two articles about him for *Rolls-Royce Motors Journal* I continued my research into his personal and business life, hoping to unearth enough material to justify a full-length biography. This would involve an attempt to trace, some 60 years after Henry's death, his descendants, people who knew him (or knew of him) and anyone who had inherited his papers and other possessions; I would also have to locate the places where he lived, and do some research into the industrial scene around Hulme and Trafford Park, Manchester, at the time Henry Edmunds and Royce worked there. I began my search in Brighton and Hove, where he spent the last 14 years of his life, because that was where his most recent friends and acquaintances might be found. From there perhaps there would be an 'Edmunds trail' back to London and Halifax, and even to his relations in Providence, Rhode Island.

After Henry sold his lease on Moulsecoomb Place to Brighton Corporation, part of the house was used as an elementary school, the rest as offices of the council's parks department. Later, some of the upstairs rooms and the music room were converted into a public lending library. More recently the entire

Moulsecoomb Place: the garden entrance to the music room where Henry and Ellen entertained their friends (Author's collection)

building was taken over by Brighton council's parks and recreation department, except for what became known as the 'west wing', whose bottom floor was rented to Moulsecoomb Social Club. Upstairs, a flat was provided for a caretaker. Mr Woolven, the parks department's chief administration officer, found copies of the documents drawn up at the time Henry surrendered his lease, and during a visit to the property several reminders of his tenancy were discovered: the motif 'HE 1913' in coloured glass above the door from the music room to the garden; some old electric lamps that must have been there in Henry's day (perhaps he installed them); and the room where Howard installed his Cameograph machine and experimented with Photo Sculpture. Although Moulsecoomb is now hemmed in by new housing estates and, on its southern boundary by Brighton Polytechnic, its substantial grounds and lawns on its east and north sides, and an old walled garden, remain; it was easy to imagine Henry and Ellen strolling there in the sunshine with their family and friends.

Henry's grave in Stanmer churchyard near Moulsecoomb (Author's collection)

A colleague of Mr Woolven, J W F Markwick of Stanmer House in Stanmer Park (once the home of the Earls of Chichester and now a public park) had also heard of Henry Edmunds. Mr Markwick's father and Henry once had a mutual friend, whose widow had a colour photograph of Henry, taken a few years before he died. She also had one of Howard Edmunds' first Cameographs. Mr Markwick also directed me to Henry's grave; the inscription on its headstone gave me the dates of his birth and death and revealed that Ellen Edmunds died in Providence in 1928.

Several local newspapers published stories about my search for acquaintances of Henry Edmunds and I was also interviewed by BBC Radio Brighton. Among the readers and listeners who responded was Phyllis MacLiesh, a niece of the late Sir Philip Dawson, who put me in touch with his son, Captain P J Dawson. Soon afterwards, Leonard and Violet Simmons telephoned me from Peacehaven, with vital information about Henry's tinfoil Phonograph. Sadly, Mr Simmons died before I had a chance to have a long talk with him, but when I eventually met Mrs Simmons she told me that Henry and Ellen had been forced to sell up and move from Moulsecoomb Place because of financial problems that developed quite suddenly during the last years of their lives. Mrs Simmons gave me a copy of the catalogue of the auction held at Moulsecoomb in March 1927.

I had wondered whether I would find anyone in Brighton who had helped Henry and Howard build or operate the Cameograph machine at Moulsecoomb, but just when I had given up hope I heard from John A Cooper and Ronald Horton. Mr Cooper told me that as a boy he lived at Lewes Road Nurseries, near Moulsecoomb Place, and went to school with the children of the estate workers. When he left school Henry gave him a job in the Photo Sculpture workshop. Mr Cooper had photographs of himself operating the Cameograph machine, and of Howard's special camera. So far as Mr Cooper was concerned, Howard was last heard of working for Gerrard Gears Ltd. Mr Horton recalled working on the Cameograph machine with three other mechanics in 1924, and had photographs of the workshop, its staff, the Cameograph machine and of finished and partly finished Cameographs. With Mr Horton's help I located Betty Guy, a niece of the late Albert Lambourne. Lambourne had been a friend of Henry Edmunds and ran an engineering business at the Old Mill Works, off Dyke Road, Brighton, where he built 13 'Old Mill' 10 hp cars in the early 1900s. He won a City & Guilds of London Institute bronze medallion for motor car engineering in 1908 and a silver medallion in 1909. From his various papers and photographs, which were handed down to Mrs Guy, it seemed that he had been closely associated with Henry and Howard at the time they were developing Photo Sculpture. Mrs Guy showed me carbon copies and a mimeographed copy of a description of the Cameograph process, headed *'Caption sheet on exhibit in South Kensington Science Museum'*; photographs of Cameographs of the Prince of Wales, George Bernard Shaw. Lady Elizabeth Townsend, Oliver Nares and Lord Balfour; the Cameograph Company's brochure; and a carbon copy of the typescript of a poem entitled *'The Cameograph'*, dated 4 November 1923:

On the living form in a chamber dark
Shadows projected from a blazing arc
'Tween lines engraved on a crystal screen
Produce a chart which is plainly seen
Which is trapped on a camera's field
Whereon contours of features are revealed.
Following the chart with patient skill
The craftsman sculptor can at will

Direct a revolving carving drill
Which ploughs a curved furrow in marble fine
Revealing features line by line
Which doth create which the light did give
An image so true that it almost lives.

Beneath the poem are the words: *'The blank verse is by Mr Edmunds Senior, who financed the Cameograph venture. The patent was granted to his son, Howard'*.

Mrs Guy also produced two photographs of the Cameograph machine, one of which was captioned: *'N Duplex Cameograph photo carving machine (one head removed). Designed and built by Albert Lambourne at Old Mill Works, Brighton 1923. Original in South Kensington Science Museum'*. This answered a question that had been in the back of my mind all along: What became of the Cameograph apparatus? It now appeared that Albert Lambourne had acquired some of Howard's equipment and samples, perhaps in lieu of payment for building the machine. It also seemed significant that the photo caption credited him for designing and building a 'duplex' machine, which I took to be a development of Howard's original patent, capable of carving two Cameographs simultaneously. Albert Lambourne's memorabilia and the location of his business also appeared to shed some light on the patent for variable speed machine gears, filed in 1920 by H Edmunds and Messrs Banister, Grimes, McCarty and Thompson of 55 Dyke Road. Apparently, several others had been closely involved in the development of Photo Sculpture; were they, too, owed money by Henry and Howard?

Having gone over the ground in Brighton I was able to find Henry's homes in London quite easily, through a clue contained in *Reminiscences of a Pioneer*. Henry wrote of sending his chauffeur, Goody, out on his De Dion motor tricycle to collect some friends who were to dine at his home 'in Tulse Hill'. Captain Dawson told me how, in 1906, his father had motored over to Tulse Hill to show-off his new Daimler motor car to Henry, who lived in a *'detached house in its own garden, near a church with a yellow brick square tower'*. I thought it remarkable that Captain Dawson could remember an outing with his father nearly eighty years earlier, but obviously a journey in a brand new Daimler was an experience no schoolboy of the 1900s would forget.

The collection of Post Office Directories in the Guildhall Library in London revealed that Henry had lived at 71 Upper Tulse Hill, Streatham, London SW2; the district is now part of the London Borough of Lambeth. The church with the yellow brick tower was still there but, sadly, Number

71 (renumbered 131 in 1936) was not. It stood opposite Roupell Road, and its site is now part of the grounds of Tulse Hill School. Then, Miss M Y Williams of Lambeth's Minet Library, found out something that added an air of mystery to Henry's life at 71 Upper Tulse Hill. Nearly 30 years before he moved to that address, it was called Antron House. The name officially went out of use when the road was numbered in 1867. Henry, apparently, had called himself 'Henry Antron Edmunds' for a time while living in what had been Antron House; he also named his second Daimler motor car *Antrona.* What was behind all this, I wondered; did Henry discover the name *Antron* in the deeds of the house, or find it inscribed on the gatepost or above his front door, and decide to adopt it?

Members of the Edmunds family with friends and relations in the garden at 71 Upper Tulse Hill in the summer of 1904. Henry is sitting on the right, with his hands on the shoulders of his son, Howard. On Henry's right is his daughter, Dorothy, and on his left are his wife, Ellen, and her niece, Madge Howard. Behind Henry are his son, Claud, and Louisa Howard.

Henry's previous home was even easier to find. In his *Reminiscences* he said that the first house in which he and Ellen lived was in Streatham and called Rhodehurst. Kelly's Directories of 1883 to 1889 contain a house of this name, and an occupant named Henry Edmunds, in St Julian's Road, Streatham. In 1902 the road was renamed Leigham Court Road; Rhodehurst became No 108. It is now No. 288, and has been converted into flats. It was virtually 'round the corner' from Sir Henry Tate's home, Park Hill (now St Michael's Convent). While in

Streatham I drove along what I surmised was the route Henry took when he drove a 'self propelled vehicle' (his De Dion motor tricycle) in London for the first time: left out of Herne Hill Station yard into Norwood Road, second right past Brockwell Park into Trinity Rise, and straight across Tulse Hill into Upper Tulse Hill. Parked outside where his drive would have been, I imagined him setting off early one morning in May 1904 to meet Charles Rolls and catch the train to Manchester for their meeting with Henry Royce.

I next tried to find out what became of Henry's youngest son, Claud. Henry's death certificate told me that Claud's address in November 1927 was St Augustine's Vicarage, Leicester. No one of that name was to be found at the vicarage or anywhere else in Leicester but the present incumbent at St Augustine's, Rev Peter Folks and a member of his congregation, Miss M E Gee, told me that Claud had moved to the parish of St Paul's, Hemel Hempstead, in 1933.

With the help of Mabel Plumb and other parishioners, and the Diocesan Office at St Albans, I learned that Claud had retired in 1947 and moved to Bath to live with Cicely Edmunds, the oldest of his three daughters. He died on 7 April 1969; his wife Helen (nee Pagden), whom he had married in Ceylon in 1910, had died nearly 20 years earlier. Cicely showed me photographs from Henry's family album, his obituaries in newspapers and trade magazines, and a Cameograph of Edward, Prince of Wales, made on the Photo Sculpture machine invented by Claud's half-brother, Howard. She also produced three artefacts that her father had inherited from Henry and which have been the subject of some curiosity in the family for many years. One was a napkin ring on which is engraved 'HAE 1853' (the year of Henry's birth), the others were tiny silver-plated boxes - snuff boxes perhaps - engraved 'Antron 1898'. The napkin ring is thought to have been one of Henry's Christening presents but, if so, why is the letter 'A' included in his initials? I checked my small collection of his papers but found that his birth certificate gave him only one Christian name, that he always signed himself 'Henry Edmunds', and that his Will and the documents surrendering his lease on Moulsecoomb Place name him only as Henry Edmunds. The little boxes reminded me of Antron House, his car *Antrona,* and of the time when Henry called himself 'Henry Antron Edmunds'; the only important event in Henry's life in 1898 was the purchase of his De Dion motor tricycle, his first motor vehicle. If the boxes were made for him or given to him to mark this or some other occasion in 1898, why was the name Antron engraved on them? I never did discover why Henry's name and that of Antron House became so closely associated; perhaps there was no special reason for it, and Henry was motivated only by a whim?

At the time I met Cicely I did not expect to find any great (or great-great) nieces or nephews of Henry. So far as I knew then, he was the only child of Henry Edmunds Snr and Caroline (nee Hatton) and although Henry Snr remarried, two of his children by Sarah, his second wife William and Maria - died when only a few months old, and Alice Mary died after giving birth to her only child (who herself died at the age of 11 weeks). It was not until after I met Cicely that I came across the letter that Mary Hatton, Henry's grandmother, wrote to him in 1882, inviting him to bring his new bride, Ellen and *'your sister Edith'* to tea. In January 1992 Michael Pritchard searched through his Edmunds family papers and found that Edith married a Harry Latham. They had four children - Harry, Alice, Queenie and Ronald. Readers of this book named Latham, or having a Latham among their immediate ancestors, are invited to trace their ancestry back to the 1880s. They may find that they are descendants of Harry and Edith (nee Edmunds) Latham, and are therefore distantly related to 'the Godfather of Rolls-Royce'. They will belong to one of only two extant branches of Henry Edmunds Snr's family tree - the other branch consisting of the descendants of Claud and Helen (nee Pagden) Edmunds.

Before I met Cicely Edmunds, I knew that Henry's daughter Dorothy died unmarried and that Claud had two other daughters. At that stage in my research I was hoping that Henry and Ellen Edmunds' son Howard had some sons or daughters; it occurred to me that they would be more likely than anyone to possess any of Henry's papers that may have been handed down to Howard, but Cicely told me that although Howard had married (his wife, Nora, nee Caroé, worked on *Good Housekeeping* magazine in New York) they did not have any children. Howard died in New York on 9 January 1962. Sadly, Cicely died a few years after I met her, so at the time I finished writing this book I was sure that the only living descendants of Henry Edmunds were his grand-daughters Muriel Pritchard and Dorothy Tornow, and Muriel and Dorothy's children and grandchildren. When I met Dr Michael Pritchard, the oldest of the four children of Muriel and the late Professor Jack Pritchard, he showed me three letters written to Henry by Thomas Edison. He also had reprints of all except the first chapter of *Reminiscences of a Pioneer* and a manuscript, written by Henry that reads as follows:

These reminiscences were commenced in July 1919, a series of 20, and were finished March 1924. A total of about 90 pages in all including illustrations. They refer to personal experiences commencing in 1877 in connection with the beginning of electric lighting, which are mostly of considerable interest in pioneering the growth and development of electric undertakings in which the writer and his friends were interested during that period. This being the only complete set kindly return after perusal to Henry Edmunds, 19 Adelaide Crescent, Hove.

Michael also showed me Henry's narratives of his visit to America in 1877 and his voyage from New York to Liverpool on the *Coronia* in 1907. Both were in typescript (the former with dates inserted by hand) but it was not possible to tell whether they were Henry's original typescripts, or transcripts made from accounts written some time after (perhaps long after) the events described in them took place. To our frustration the 1877 script concluded without mentioning Henry's visit to Thomas Edison's laboratory to hear his first recording. We concluded that the visit was an unexpected addition to Henry's schedule, arranged after he had packed his notes in his luggage and was expecting to sail for England very shortly. Michael owns the only substantial collection of documents known to have survived the various upheavals of Henry's possessions and papers that occurred between March 1927 and May 1928. This was the period during which he moved from Moulsecoomb Place and died in Hove, and Ellen returned to Providence; it was around this time, I suspect, that what would now be valuable historic records were destroyed, including the most sought-after document of all, the letter book containing Henry's correspondence with Rolls and Royce.

9 Adelaide Crescent, Hove, where Henry died (Author's collection)

Cicely Edmunds and Michael Pritchard also told me about a trust fund that Thomas Wayman, the father of Annie, Henry's first wife, had set up for the benefit of Claud and Dorothy; Cicely and Michael understood that Henry was expressly precluded from having any control over the fund; evidently he was regarded as being incapable of handling money wisely.

From my meetings with Cicely and Michael there emerged some ideas for following-up Henry's connections with the Howards of Rhode Island, so I wrote to the Providence *Sunday Journal* asking any readers who were members of the family to contact me. An item appeared under the headline *'All you Howards'*. While waiting for responses I did some research in Halifax, West Yorkshire, to see if any traces could be found of him in the town where he had spent his early life, even though one hundred years had passed since he moved to London.

During my time in Halifax I came to realise that no one there knew that one of its sons had been an important motoring pioneer and the man behind the formation of Rolls-Royce; the town's recognised pioneers in the transport field were Michael Holroyd Smith and Percy Shaw (the inventor of the 'cat's eye' reflective road marker). I was a little annoyed when in May, 1982, the *Halifax Courier* published an article on Henry in which all the research I had done for *Rolls-Royce Motors Journal* was attributed to a local author, but the story did at least create interest in my subject among the town's librarians, archivists and historians, one of whom, Mr M E Corbett, Calderdale Central Librarian, helped me find Henry and his parents listed in street directories and census returns. I was then able to set off on a walk around the town to look for his birthplace and later residences.

The area where Henry Edmunds Snr lived and had his ironmongery business had long since been redeveloped, and as far as I could make out the Trustee Savings Bank now stands on the site of 2 Silver Street, Henry Jnr's birthplace. In the hope of finding a contemporary picture of the area in Victorian times I went to the West Yorkshire Folk Museum at Shibden Hall, on the outskirts of Halifax, where the Calderdale Museum Services' historical collection is kept. There, June Hill produced a print showing Henry Edmunds Snr's shop; later, from old trade directories, she traced the ownership of the shop from 1871, when Henry's father was its sole proprietor, to the 1880s, when he was joined by a partner, William James Hookway, and the business became 'Edmunds & Hookway'. The business's address is in some cases given as 2 Silver Street and in others as 3 Silver Street. *The Halifax Itinerary* of 1875 said 'the shop has been an ironmongers and silversmiths as far back as memory goes. It was owned by John Hudson, then Adam & Mitchell (from Cheapside), then Samuel Fowness, then Roper, then Roper & Edmunds. Mr Edmunds has it now'.

Southfield, the house in Stafford Road, Skircoat, to which the Edmunds family moved in the 1870s, is still standing; on the opposite side of the road there is an overgrown entrance to what were the grounds of Moorside, Skircoat Green, where Henry's friend Louis John Crossley and Michael Holroyd Smith had their experimental electric tramway. From an upstairs window at Southfield, Henry would have seen and heard the trams rattling around their track, and hurried across the road to take a closer look at what was going on.

The saddest occasion in Henry's early life was, of course, the death in childbirth on April 2nd, 1881, of his wife Annie. The scene of that tragedy was Henry and Annie's house in Heath Villas, a few minutes' walk from Stafford Road. I wanted to find their house but identifying it was, at first, difficult. In a street directory for 1881 Henry came fourth in a list of residents of Heath Villas. This suggested that his address was 4 Heath Villas but I could not assume that whatever house was at that address in the 1980s was there in the 1880s; the street may have been rebuilt or renumbered since then. Fortunately my research coincided with the release, after the statutory delay of one hundred years, of the 1881 census returns. These give the names of everyone living at every residence and institution in England and Wales at midnight on the day of the census, and contain valuable supplementary information such as the relationship of the people at each address to the head of the household, and their age at their last birthday. In the entry for 5 Heath Villas, the following people were listed:

Claud Edmunds, son
Dorothy Edmunds, daughter
Phebe Tetcombe, 55, professional nurse
Margaret Wardle, 16, servant
Elizabeth Beek, 17, servant

The 1881 census was for Sunday 3 April the day after Annie died and two days after Claud and Dorothy were born. You might wonder why Henry's name is not listed. He was at The Grove, the home of his father-in-law, Thomas Wayman, obviously sharing his grief with Annie's father and the rest of the family. The census had clearly identified Henry's home and from Calderdale Council I established that Heath Villas were built in the 1860s and that in 1885 No 5 bore the name Manor Royd. Heath Villas now consists of eight groups of handsome Victorian detached and semi-detached houses set back from an avenue off Free School Lane, opposite the Royal Halifax Infirmary. Manor Royd is still there; its rear entrance has access to the avenue but unlike all the other houses in Heath Villas its front entrance is in Heath Avenue, opposite Manor Heath and several streets away from Free School Lane. Manor Royd was clearly the most exclusive of all the houses in Heath Villas; originally, it probably had about an acre of grounds but part of Henry's garden is now occupied by new houses. His front lawn and carriage drive survive; I could imagine him rushing up to his front door on that dreadful day when he arrived at Halifax railway station and heard that Annie was seriously ill. I also pictured him setting off from Manor Royd on the journeys he made on Joseph Swan's behalf, to demonstrate incandescent lamps to shipbuilders and the Admiralty and organise the magnificent display of Swan lamps at the Paris Exposition.

Before visiting Halifax I had written to the *Halifax Courier*, asking any readers who knew anything about the Edmunds family to contact me. Mr J C Mansfield, Cemetery Registrar with Calderdale Council, responded and on a gloomy November afternoon took me to the Edmunds family graves at Stoney Royd Cemetery. In Section N we found the double grave (numbers 9A and 10A in Mr Mansfield's records) that Henry bought on the day Annie died; her gravestone bears the inscription *'He giveth his beloved sleep'* and the dates of her birth and death. Henry, we can be sure, intended that one day he would be buried beside her, not realising that he would soon remarry and live many miles from Halifax. Near Annie's grave we found one in which were buried Henry's step-sister, Alice Mary Milnes, and her baby daughter (also named Alice Mary) in the summer of 1880, and Henry's step-mother, Sarah, who died in October 1891. I remembered Henry's tribute to Sarah: *'She was a true foster mother to me, and I owe nearly everything to her kindly care and encouragement'*. From inscriptions on the gravestones and Mr Mansfield's research I discovered three interesting details about Henry's family and relatives: Alice Mary Milnes lived at Homeleigh, Lordship Road, London, immediately before her death; her daughter had died in Blackpool; and her husband, Alfred Stert Milnes, had died in Sydney, Australia, on 23 September 1882. Had baby Alice been a frail infant and sent, after the death of her mother, to a wet-nurse at the seaside, away from the damp climate and sooty air of the industrial West Riding? And was Alfred so grief-stricken at the death of his wife and daughter that he decided to seek a new life in Australia, only to die there of a broken heart? I also learned that Henry Edmunds Snr had died at Cheadle on 4 September 1904, and that the person who informed the Registrar of his death was Kendal Milnes, a member of the Cheshire family that owned a fashionable department store in Manchester.

With Mr Mansfield's help I also found the grave of Caroline Edmunds, Henry's mother, in Lister Lane Cemetery and discovered that the grave was re-opened after Caroline's death for the burials of William Milnes Edmunds, aged six months on 14 January 1858, and Maria Louisa Edmunds, aged seven weeks, on 3 March 1860. These were other children of Henry Snr and Sarah.

Lister Lane Cemetery resembled a setting for a Victorian Gothic drama when I first went there; later its undergrowth was cleared to reveal, for the first time for many years, memorials and inscriptions providing a wealth of information for biographers and family and local historians. An obelisk in the north-west corner marks the graves of Caroline and the two babies, and bears this inscription:

*IN MEMORY OF CAROLINE THE WIFE OF
HENRY EDMUNDS OF HALIFAX WHO
DIED MAY 26TH, 1853, AGED 29 YEARS*

All that remained for me to do to complete my research into Henry's Halifax background was to visit the Congregational church near People's Park where he married Annie Wayman; and Cromwell Street, where Annie was born. I then drove over the moors to see Stannary House, Stainland, his step-mother's childhood home.

Although Henry moved away from Halifax in 1882, after marrying Ellen Murray Howard, his career soon brought him back to the north of England, when he became a partner of Walter T Glover and a shareholder and (according to one source) a director of Royce Ltd in Manchester. What remained there, I wondered, of the places

The obelisk in Lister Lane Cemetry, Halifax, that marks the grave of Henry's mother, Caroline.
(Author's collection)

Stannary House, Stainland,
the childhood home of Henry's stepmother, Sarah.
(Author's collection)

314

where Henry worked and introduced Rolls to Royce? The Midland Hotel still stands, though much altered. Across the road in the City of Manchester Public Library I found a photograph of the hotel's grill room, taken at about the time the hotel opened, where the three men are most likely to have had lunch on that day in May 1904. Sadly, nothing remains of the tiny factory in Cooke Street, Hulme, where Royce built his first cars. The entire area has been redeveloped but enthusiasts can work out their own 'Rolls-Royce heritage trail' and find Royce Court (more or less on the site of his factory), Rolls Crescent, Royce Road, and a pub called the Sir Henry Royce. The achievements of Rolls-Royce plc and Rolls-Royce Motor Cars Ltd have overshadowed the story of Royce's original company, Royce Ltd, which moved to a new factory at Trafford Park, Manchester, in the early 1900s and built electric cranes there for another 30 years. Although badly damaged by fire in the 1970s it was rebuilt to its original proportions; inspecting it and the former Glover factory on the opposite side of the road, I was surprised at how similar the scene was then, to that depicted in another photograph that I had come across in the public library, showing the two factories in 1901. Cars and lorries had taken the place of railway wagons and horses and carts, of course, but even the lamp posts and a letter box outside the Royce factory were in the same positions as those of more than 80 years earlier.

Soon after I visited Manchester I started to receive replies from residents of Rhode Island who had read the item *'All you Howards'* in the Providence *Sunday Journal.* The first to write to me was Nancy Howard Landry of Riverside, a granddaughter of Governor Henry Howard's son, Charles. A few days later I heard from Molly Howard Mears of Warwick Neck, a daughter of Charles Howard. Both helped me find out more about the Howards and their influence on politics and business in Rhode Island, but neither Nancy nor Molly knew anything about Henry Edmunds. The only person in Rhode Island who did remember him was Harriet Ames Fuller Claflin of Providence, who wrote to tell me that as a young girl she frequently met Ellen Edmunds, 'Uncle Henry' and Howard Edmunds. Harriet's relationship with the Howard family was tenuous. Her late husband, Albert Whitman Claflin, was one of Ellen's nephews and a grandson of Ellen's father, Albert Crawford Howard. From Harriet's letter I could tell that the Howards, the Edmundses and the Claflins were close friends as well as relations; now, perhaps, I would be able to unravel Henry's American connections, and find out whether Howard Edmunds had passed on any relevant material to friends in Rhode Island? By this time I was not only interested in knowing more about Henry's Howard relations; I also wanted to verify his account of his visit to America in 1877, especially his claim to have witnessed Edison's first recording of the human voice. To do all those things, I decided to follow the 'Edmunds trail' from England to New York and Providence.

For every day that Henry Edmunds spent crossing the Atlantic by sea, travellers now spend less than an hour in the air, but they are denied the excitement Henry must have felt when he first caught sight of the New World from his ship the *Abyssinia* in July 1877. There was no point in trying to reconstruct Henry's arrival in Jersey City and his journey to the Fifth Avenue Hotel; the places he knew had been swept away by redevelopment. Nevertheless, I wanted to experience something approximating Henry's arrival in New York, and I did this by taking the ferry to Staten Island and the motor launch to Liberty Island, crossing the shipping channels used by the liners on which Henry travelled. Henry probably did not notice Liberty Island when he sailed past it in 1877, 1879 and 1882. It was then called Bedloe's Island and its only feature was a marine hospital. But when he returned in 1883, hoping to introduce Michael Holroyd Smith's electric traction system into the USA, he would have noticed that the hospital was being demolished to make way for the Statue of Liberty; as a lover of poetry and song, he had probably been moved by the sonnet by Emma Lazarus that in 1883 had been read in public for the first time at one of the events held to raise money to build the statue's massive pedestal:

> *Give me your tired, your poor, your huddled masses yearning to breathe free.*

As Henry's ship made its way through the Narrows when next he came this way, in 1887, he would have been confronted by the sight of the statue in all its pristine splendour, following its completion the previous year; the torch-bearing right arm that had been on show in Madison Square Park when he was in Manhattan in 1877 now soared more than three hundred feet above the waters of New York Harbour.

In one respect I was able to follow Henry's footsteps of 1887 almost literally, and this was by crossing the Brooklyn Bridge - though not along the precarious 'aerial pathway' that Henry used. On the much safer walkway that was completed six years after his visit I made my way to Brooklyn. Henry had looked down on an East River busy with 'various crafts and many ferry boats, with their assortment of vehicles, including brewers' wagons'. I looked down on several lanes of nose-to-tail motor vehicles (but no brewers' wagons) and an almost deserted river.

To find published sources of information relevant to Henry's first visit to America I went to the New York Historical Society's newspaper library at 170 Central Park West. Reports of Henry's demonstrations of the Jablochkoff electric lamp at Columbia College in the *New York Herald* and the *Daily Tribune* tallied with those that Henry had quoted in his *Reminiscences*. I found that the demonstrations had taken place on 26 October 1877. Henry had not given a definite date but the unpublished narrative in Michael Pritchard's possession enabled an almost complete day-by-day log of his travels to be constructed, and after seeing the original newspaper reports I knew exactly when Henry went to Columbia. The Society also had a collection of theatrical programmes and notices. These gave me details of Mary Anderson's performances at the Fifth Avenue Theatre in November and December 1877, and helped me confirm Henry's claim to have witnessed a far more important performance, that of Thomas Edison and his talking machine. My third discovery was a collection of old railroad timetables, including one for the New York to Providence service. This showed that it would have taken Henry anything from 5 hours 25 minutes to 7 hours 45 minutes to make the journey during his first visits to America; there was also a timetable that enabled me to work out how Henry had travelled from New York to Edison's laboratory at Menlo Park. There is no point in making such a journey today; in the last years of Edison's life his friend Henry Ford moved the laboratory and other Edison relics from Menlo to Dearborn, Michigan, for a huge museum of industry and invention. The Edison archives, however, are kept at the Edison National Historic Site at West Orange, New Jersey. Equipped with travel directions provided by George Frow, president of the City of London Phonograph and Gramophone Society, who had been helping me to research the history of the Graphophone, I took the PATH subway to Hoboken, the Erie Lackawanna Railroad from Hoboken to Orange, and walked to West Orange.

It took only a few hours to verify the authenticity of the letters Henry received from Edison and check Henry's account of the birth of sound recording against all the other documentary evidence of when and how the 'Mary had a little lamb' recording was made. Although the ultimate proof would be a document, written or signed by Edison or one of his assistants, saying that Henry was a witness, I was convinced that Henry's story was true. I also inspected Edison's several scrapbooks, containing press cuttings about platinum and price lists and reports published by various manufacturers, including Johnson Matthey. My hopes of finding confirmation that Edison had purchased platinum from Johnson Matthey for his early incandescent lamps and that Henry had been the 'middleman' were not realised, but what I saw confirmed that Edison was having great difficulties in obtaining the material locally and that Johnson Matthey was most likely to have been his supplier.

To complete my research I caught the *Benjamin Franklin Express* and went to Providence, travelling on the railroad on which, 105 years earlier, Henry had made his first journey to meet the Howards. I had an appointment with one of their relatives but first I went to the Rhode Island Historical Society's library on Hope Street, on the edge of the campus of Brown University, to read its collection of papers on many of the industrial pioneers to whom Henry was introduced by Governor Howard, including Brown and Sharpe, the celebrated gauge makers; James Brown Herreshoff, designer of the US Navy's first torpedo boat; and Armington and Sims, whose steam engines drove the generators at New York's first public electric power station, designed and built by Thomas Edison. Next day, in Harriet Claflin's Colonial-style timber framed house on Medway Street, College Hill, I was able to complete my story of Henry and Ellen's life together, their visits to Providence and the sad events surrounding his death. Tea was served, and Harriet's cat, 'Shadow', made herself comfortable on my lap. I placed my tape recorder on the tea tray and then, and to an accompaniment of intermittent purring from the cat and the steady beat of a 'banjo' clock on the wall, Harriet reminisced about life with the Howards 60 and more years earlier:

> "Albert Crawford Howard had built a double [semi-detached] house on Waterman Street for his two daughters. Alice, who married Arthur Whitman Claflin, lived on one side [No 190] and she had not only her husband but her three brothers living with her part of the time. The other house [No 192] was meant for Nellie [Ellen], her sister, but Nellie married Mr Edmunds and went abroad; she never lived in the house, but she still owned it. We youngsters used to go next door to the Claflins where there were always interesting games to play, and an instance of Uncle Henry Edmunds' sense of humour always stuck in my memory. We were trying to untangle a great ball of string - some kite string, perhaps - and when one after another of us kept asking 'Where is the end'. Uncle Henry suggested that the end had been cut off! In the summertime we lived in a cottage at Buttonwoods Beach, on Narragansett Bay, where there was generally a breeze, and it was very pleasant to sit on the piazza in the evenings. Henry had a repeater watch; when it was dark he would press the spring and the watch would chime the quarter hours and minutes and my future father-in-law would think it was the sound of a ship's bell out in the bay. Later Henry presented the watch to him, after having the words 'to Arthur W Claflin from Henry Edmunds' inscribed on the back cover. He carried it in his vest pocket for as long as he lived; he loved children, and more than one generation of them was shown the watch and how it worked. In 1926 my husband inherited the watch and after his death in 1956 I gave it to my son, George Arthur Claflin, who now lives in California."

The repeater watch that Henry gave to Arthur W Claflin.
It is still in working order. (George Arthur Claflin)

Harriet produced her family album and scrapbook and showed me a portrait of Henry Edmunds, a photograph of members of the Claflin, Howard and Edmunds families taken in the garden of 71 Upper Tulse Hill in 1904, and a report from the *Sussex Daily News* of the wedding of Madge Howard and Lawrence H Strain at Falmer. We digressed while Harriet told me that, like the Howards, her father, R Clinton Fuller, was involved in the pioneering telephone experiments that took place in Providence; he was a student of Professor John Peirce of Brown University in 1877:

> *"As children, when father showed us this extraordinary instrument, I asked if it was the first telephone made in Providence and he specified one of the first. My father was not allowed to finish college because on the death of one of his uncles my grandfather put my father in his uncle's place at the Fuller Iron Works. I was told that Professor Peirce pleaded with my grandfather to let my father continue his college course, to no avail."*

This reinforced the impression I already had of Henry Edmunds making his first visit to Providence at a time when it was a centre of great progress in science and engineering. I steered our conversation back to Henry, Ellen and Howard, and Harriet continued:

"It was so sad. When Mr Edmunds died, Nellie came over to spend the rest of her life with her sister. When she had been here for about three weeks she went down to New York City to visit Howard and go to the English chapel in the Cathedral of St John the Divine, where Howard had been married. She caught a dreadful cold on the train coming back and died of bronchitis just a week later. Her sister Alice died on the evening of her funeral. All papers and properties of importance were sent to Howard in New York."

"Did you get to know Howard?", I asked.

"We went down to see his Cameograph machine in New York, and his portraits of famous people. His wife, Nora, was a charming person; I think she worked for UNICEF at one time. Howard was distressed that the Cameograph did not do better. We did not see very much of Howard but when he was over he was a bit annoyed when we 'twitted' him for being half American. He didn't like that at all. I was told that he used to read aloud for an hour every day so that he wouldn't lose his British accent. He became awfully nervous after the war and he had to smoke. Smoking was anathema in the Claflin house and he was always itching to get out and smoke."

"Was he as clever as his father?"

"I don't think so. They seemed either to be on top of the world or sunk between inventions, or something of that sort. I think they were in difficulty often."

"What did Howard do when the Cameograph business failed?"

"I don't think he did anything, because I remember Nora saying he would walk up and down in their apartment, wringing his hands; he was just forlorn. He didn't seem to have anything else to do. I guess Nora supported him. His mother was disappointed that the Cameograph had failed ... she felt that everything she had left, she wanted to give to him, but she didn't have time to make another will."

Cicely Edmunds had told me that Howard died in New York on 9 January 1962; he was 78 and, like his father, had experienced great disappointment in his last years. Harriet told me that Nora had survived Howard but, as I expected, had died some years before my visit; she may have preserved some of Howard's or Henry's personal papers, but I realised that they were unlikely to have survived the disposal of her personal effects and that that line of enquiry was now closed. Harriet told me that Ellen, Howard and Nora were buried in Swan Point Cemetery, Providence, close to a group of Howard graves. There was nothing else I needed to know. I went to Waterman Street to see Alice and Ellen's house and then caught the train back to New York.

Harriet Claflin died in 1989. In 1990 her son William Howard Claflin found, among her papers, an invitation to Henry and Ellen's wedding, which took place at 190 Waterman Street. The invitation had been sent by Ellen's father, Albert C Howard, to Mr and Mrs George Lyman Claflin. William also found a collection of letters written by A C Howard while visiting the Edmunds family in Streatham. Some of the letters are headed with imprinted or hand-written addresses containing the name 'Antron' - proof that Henry retained the original name of his house, even though it had been given a number by the time he lived there. William also came across a letter written by Henry on 14 January 1926. It is a letter of condolence to his sister-in-law, Mary Alice Howard Claflin, who had sent Henry and Ellen a cablegram saying that her husband, Arthur Whitman Claflin, had died. In his letter, Henry told Alice that Ellen had fallen on a polished floor and injured her arm, so for the time being the doctor forbids her using her right hand, which greatly limits her in writing or sewing and other domestic uses. Henry added: *'We have recently had very severe weather, much rain and floods in many places ... and today quite a fall of snow and severe cold for Brighton'*. The year 1926 had begun badly for the Edmunds family. In the months to come Henry would have to start negotiating to surrender his lease, and realise that he would have to sell nearly all his personal possessions.

When I had completed my research I showed the first draft of this book to Michael Pritchard and asked him to summarise Henry Edmund's life for me:

> *"He died many years before I was born, and my information comes mainly from the text of this biography. The reader may therefore come to an equally well-informed opinion.*
>
> *Although Henry was not in the first rank of electrical or automotive pioneers, he was not among the many inevitable failures of that competitive era either. He was self-educated. He did not have the aristocratic and financial backing of Charles Rolls and, it must be admitted, he lacked the self-discipline and*

diligence of Edison or Royce He did however know a good thing when he saw it and wherever there was technical progress, Henry was on the scene. He enjoyed life to the full and would do anything as long as there was some new experience in it. His first trip to America is illustrative. He went at a moment's notice to sell the Jablochkoff Candle but ended up having an extensive sightseeing trip, including crossing the unfinished Brooklyn Bridge on a workman's catwalk, and came back to sell the patents of a rival lighting process. He was able to relate easily to all levels of society on both sides of the Atlantic, and although his contemporaries seemed to like him, at least in his younger days they appeared not to take him very seriously. His book-keeping was criticised several times and this neglect of the more mundane aspects of life in favour of new adventures was a fundamental part of his character. However he settled to become managing director of several important companies and his opinion became widely sought. Of his 150 patents, though, none was widely adopted or apparently developed further by Henry himself once the idea had been registered. The grass was always greener elsewhere.

He seemed to have remained popular all his life with a large circle of friends, and even fairly quarrelsome and touchy people like Edison still regarded him as a friend when they met many decades later. Henry even found time to give a 'recherché little dinner' in Manchester for the drivers of the One Thousand Miles Trial, so he took his social life seriously, even in strenuous situations.

There are two unanswerable puzzles. Firstly, the failure to go to Balmoral to demonstrate the phonograph to Queen Victoria is curious, as this must have been little less than a Royal Command. Perhaps his background and his admiration of technical progress and self-made men made him impatient of old fashioned Royalty. There is a family tradition that he refused a knighthood on the flimsy grounds that he would have to give larger tips, but perhaps he just was not interested. Secondly, was the Cameograph fiasco just bad luck or was Henry changing the habits of a lifetime for the sake of his son Howard? Instead of becoming associated with a project that was already successful, he put everything into a new and untried principle and was unable to stop pouring money into it until virtually bankrupt. Was this his first truly emotional commitment to an idea, which just happened to be in the wrong place at the wrong time?

Henry is an ideal guide to the exciting developments of the age. Never committed to any one person or idea to the exclusion of others; friend and confidant of all the great inventors of the day; an effective public speaker; always ready for a new adventure or idea, which would usually be dropped as the next one caught his attention; and a genuine zest for life's curiosity and variety. I am sure I too would have enjoyed his company."

Secrets of the locked trunk

Even as final preparations were being made to print this book, more information about Henry Edmunds and his family was being found in an unlikely location. When things like this happen, authors and publishers react with a mixture of delight and dread. Obviously, the discovery of hitherto hidden facts at the eleventh hour is welcome, but qualms and questions are inevitable. Will research that was originally regarded as reliable have to be revised? Will conclusions based on previous 'best evidence' have to be abandoned? Will whole sections of the story - entire chapters, perhaps - have to be unravelled and recast? Any major revisions to the foregoing chapters of this book would have strained an already tight production budget, and would have delayed publication until after the date on which the book trade was expecting its first deliveries.

What happened was that on 9 March 1992, while continuing to clear out his late mother's belongings from her house at 180 Medway Street, Providence, Rhode Island, William Howard Claflin finally gained access to a locked trunk in the back of the cellar. In the trunk he found a collection of pictures and papers, and as he sifted through them he became aware that they originally belonged to his great aunt, Ellen Murray Howard Edmunds, Henry Edmunds' second wife. Unrolling a coil of magazines, William was amazed to find a complete set of reprints of parts 2 - 20 of Henry's *Reminiscences of a Pioneer* from the *M & C Apprentices' Magazine* and a copy of the July 1919 issue in which the first instalment of Henry's memoirs was published. The trunk also contained photographs of houses, gardens, automobiles and machinery (including Henry's motor car *Antrona* and his son Howard's Cameograph); correspondence from Frank Hedges Butler, who was a motoring pioneer, balloonist and a founder of the Royal Aero Club; portraits and Cameographs of relatives and friends; packets of letters (including one marked 'from Howard'); Henry and Ellen's passport, dated 1921; and passenger lists and other souvenirs collected by them during their transatlantic voyages.

It appeared that Ellen had brought the trunk with her from England when she moved back to Providence after Henry died, and that at the time of her own death in 1928 many of her possessions were still unsorted. They remained unsorted following the death, a few days later, of her sister, Mary Alice Howard Claflin, William's grandmother. At this time William's mother, Harriet Ames Fuller Claflin, was pregnant (with William) and too preoccupied to find time to sort through family possessions. Ellen's trunk was taken from Ellen and Mary's house in Waterman Street, Providence, and placed in Harriet's cellar - where it remained unpacked for 64 years, until William stumbled across it.

Nothing in the trunk appears to contradict anything that has been written about Henry Edmunds in this book, but among Ellen's pictures and papers there are sources for two more stories that someone, some day, should write - a history of Photo Sculpture and the Cameograph; and a family history of the Howards and Claflins.

POSTSCRIPT TO THE SECOND EDITION

The foregoing pages comprise the first edition of *The Godfather of Rolls-Royce,* published in 1993. Although subsequent research has confirmed that my story of Henry Edmunds's life and career remains substantially correct, there have been some important recent developments that need to be reviewed in this second edition.

On 4 May 2004, celebrations were held at the Midland Hotel, Manchester, and elsewhere, to mark the 100th anniversary of Rolls and Royce's first meeting; 4 May 1904 having long been acknowledged as Day One in the history of Rolls-Royce.

Having researched the history of the company for many years, those of us who regard ourselves as authoritative Rolls-Royce historians (or are regarded as such by others) had become convinced by their own detective work, and by circumstantial evidence gleaned from various sources, that 4 May was the only day in 1904 on which the historic meeting could possibly have taken place.

I believe that Tom Clarke was the first to pinpoint this date, back in 1972. Ten years later, Michael H Evans of Rolls-Royce reached the same conclusion and published the results of his very detailed investigations into the company's origins in his book *In the Beginning – the Manchester origins of Rolls-Royce,* published by the Rolls-Royce Heritage Trust. More recently, Mike has delved even deeper and a second, and considerably larger, edition of his book was launched at the centennial celebrations. This sheds even more light on the events that occurred on and following Day One.

Nevertheless, despite everything we had done to prove our case, not one artefact or document had been discovered to confirm that, yes, Rolls and Royce really did meet for the first time on 4 May 4 1904. So there was always a chance, albeit a slight one, that a 'smoking gun' would be discovered to scupper our interpretation of the evidence.

As the anniversary approached, some of us became increasingly concerned that hitherto unsuspected or overlooked sources would suddenly come to our notice and oblige us to rewrite the history of the origins of Rolls-Royce!

Even to discover that the historic meeting had taken place just a day earlier or a day later than the one that had become set in stone (or at least engraved on some rather prominent and familiar plaques) would have been embarrassing (to put it mildly) to the hosts at the centennial gatherings.

Then, a few weeks after the tumult and the shouting had died, and the captains of industry and other guests had departed from the Midland

Hotel, a jewellery dealer in Wimbledon, south London, contacted a member of the Rolls-Royce Enthusiasts' Club and said, *'I have something that might be of interest to you'* (or words to that effect). That 'something' was a sterling silver matchbox, with a hinged lid inscribed:

FROM

CSR - FHR

4.5.1904 – 4.5.1909

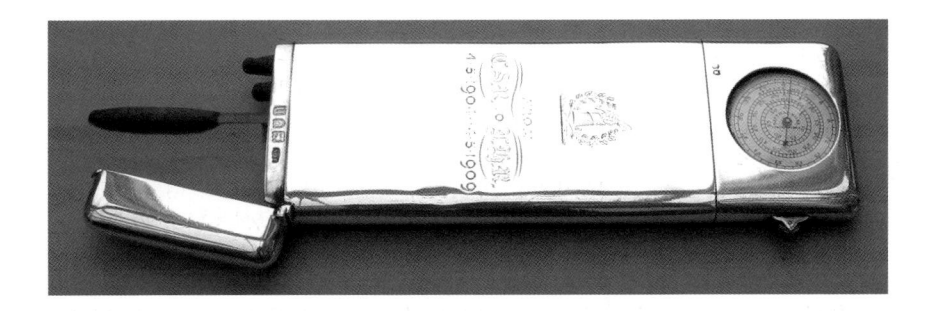

Face of the silver matchbox

The monograms are those of Charles Stewart Rolls and Frederick Henry Royce. Beyond all reasonable doubt, the matchbox was a present to commemorate the fifth anniversary of the day the two men first met, for why else does it bear these dates? Above the monograms there is a hallmark, believed to be that of J C Vickery of Regent Street, London. The London Assay Office has confirmed that it is genuine. A removable wheel and dial for measuring distances on a map (an opisometer) are attached to the matchbox, and inside there are three 'matches', left over from a supply of strikers that would have been used for lighting the carbide motor car lamps, as well as an occasional Edwardian cheroot. On the reverse side of the matchbox, the strike face, there is another inscription, similar in style to the other monograms, that reads:

FROM

FHR - GAP
WITH ALL BEST WISHES
FEBRUARY 6th 1932

Strike face of the silver matchbox

'GAP' was George A Palfrey of No 26 Mount Row, Carlos Place, London W1, who owned the largest hire fleet of Rolls-Royce motor cars in London and also, evidently, a butchery business in Derby. The date coincides with his purchase of a Rolls-Royce 20/25 GFT52 series Maythorn limousine. Palfrey was indeed honoured to be given an object of such intrinsic and sentimental value. In 1932 Royce became seriously ill and from the autumn of that year he was bedridden for many months. He died on 22 April 1933. Perhaps, by February 1932, he had started to put his affairs in order, and to pass on certain treasured possessions to those he considered would appreciate them most.

The matchbox's history from 1932 until 2004 is not known. We can only assume that it remained in Palfrey's ownership until he died and was subsequently inherited by friends or relatives, finally coming on to the antiques market in the summer of 2004 at the behest of the executors of someone's estate.

The matchbox is now on display at The Hunt House, Paulerspury, Northamptonshire, the headquarters of the Rolls-Royce Enthusiasts Club and the Sir Henry Royce Memorial Foundation. It forms part of a fascinating collection of Royce and Rolls-Royce memorabilia. Other recent acquisitions include the Henry Edmunds Hill Climbing Trophy (see Chapter 11), presumed to have been lost during or soon after the First World War, only to be found in a garage a few years ago; and various items of electrical apparatus made by Royce Ltd, some of which have cables and wires that may have been made by W T Glover & Co in the days when Edmunds was a director of that firm.

Among the remaining unfinished business in the Henry Edmunds story is the recording Queen Victoria made on a wax cylinder for Sydney

Morse, Henry's partner in the Graphophone venture, at Balmoral in 1888. When I wrote about this in the foregoing Chapter Eight and Epilogue, and in my book *The Lost Voice of Queen Victoria*, a few words and phrases in barely audible voices, muffled by surface noise, had been transcribed from the cylinder at the British Library's National Sound Archive.

Those of us who held our breath when, on 11 June 1991, for the first time for more than 60 years, a stylus was applied to the delicate cylinder, subsequently had to become resigned to the opinion of Peter Copeland, the NSA's conservation manager, that it would be ten years before advancements in electronics and computer technology would enable a clearer transcription of the voices to be obtained. After the ten years had passed, I assumed that interest in the cylinder amongst those who conserve ancient cylinders, and develop electronic transcription processes, had waned, until Chris Goddard of Plymouth University drew my attention to this report by Peter Day in the 18 July 2004 issue of *The Sunday Times*:

> The voice of Queen Victoria may soon be heard, thanks to an invention designed to decipher a recording made more than 100 years ago. Victoria is believed to have delivered a brief message at Balmoral during a demonstration of Thomas Edison's Graphophone, an early recording machine. The wax cylinder with the message scratched into its surface was kept at the Science Museum in London for decades without its significance being realised. A new laser-based reader should allow the recording, to be heard as part of a British Library project. "It is not like using a record stylus. It is more like a satellite plotting the contours of the earth," said John McBride, professor of instrumentation and measurement at Southampton University, who leads the team making the device. "We create a map and use numerical techniques to convert it into sound."

Nigel Bewley, of the British Library Sound Archive, said:

> "(Victoria) would have had to use a speaking tube and something similar to an anaesthetist's gas mask and shout like the clappers. She was a game old bird but there must have been a question of whether it was beneath her dignity."

Thanks to Joe Pengelly, a colleague of Chris Goddard, *The Sunday Times* subsequently corrected an important error in this report: Thomas Edison invented the Phonograph; the inventors of the Graphophone were Chichester Bell and Charles Sumner Tainter.

On 27 July, *The Times* published this report from James Bone in New York:

> Queen Victoria will speak again thanks to science. Eminent Victorians such as Alfred Tennyson, Florence Nightingale and even the unamused Queen herself might soon speak again to modern ears. Scientists at the Lawrence Berkeley National Laboratory in California are turning technology developed for tracking sub-atomic particles to the task of decoding unplayable sound recordings from the late 19th and early 20th centuries. The work of Carl Haber and Vitaliy Fadeyev could bring back to life tens of thousands of voices recorded on tin and wax cylinders that are now too damaged to play, as well as hundreds of thousands of 78rpm discs.
>
> "With our current technology, we are going to be able to get the scan time for a cylinder down to a few hours," Dr Haber said yesterday. "It's still not minutes, but for a particularly valuable cylinder, say something with Queen Victoria on it, these kind of scan times are acceptable."
>
> The Queen's voice is believed to be preserved on a wax cylinder that was rediscovered in 1991 at the Science Museum in London. It is thought to have been made by the Queen in 1888 at Balmoral during a demonstration of the 'graphophone' invented by the telephone pioneer Alexander Graham Bell. The 14-second recording contains about 40 words, but only a few are recognisable: "Greetings...the answer must be...I have never forgotten."

Here again, a correction is needed: Alexander Graham Bell was not the inventor of the Graphophone.

The project mentioned in the above reports is a spin-off from leading-edge metrology studies at Southampton. The method of reproducing mechanical recordings that Carl Haber and John McBride are developing is in its infancy, but is now probably sufficiently advanced to allow an experimental transcription of the cylinder to be made.

Nigel Bewley told me, *"I suspect that the noise reduction algorithms are not sufficiently powerful to make an appreciable improvement in the sound, and are likely to remain so for the foreseeable future, given the poor signal to noise ratio of the original. I think we should all bear in mind that this new scanning method, whilst a welcome and important development, will not provide a philosopher's stone for mechanical recordings with resultant miraculous results, but I'm hopeful that it can be used to great effect once a working and practicable prototype has* been developed". Carl Haber told me, *"Of course if such a cylinder [recorded by Queen Victoria] exists, one could imagine applying this technology to it. I expect there are certain logistical issues, such as getting access to it."*

The cylinder is the property of the Science Museum in London, who would have to decide whether to take the risk of sending the cylinder to Berkeley or wait until Southampton University's process is up and running. At the time of writing, it seems likely the latter course of action will be preferred. Whatever is gleaned from the cylinder next time it is played is unlikely to reveal, one way or the other, whose voice or voices were recorded on it. And even if the statement, *"This is Queen Victoria speaking,"* emerges, the question 'Is this a hoax?' will have to answered! So whilst I hold my breath, more in hope than in certainty that in 1991 I found Queen Victoria's lost voice, readers can keep up to date with developments in this project, and research into archive sounds in general, at the following web sites:

www.taicaan.com

www.mech.soton.ac.uk/archivesound

http://tinyurl.com/6f5om

http://www.bbc.co.uk/radio4/aboutradio4/diary/04.shtml

http://www.sfgate.com/cgi-bin/article.cgi?file=/c/a/2004/07/12/MNGJP7JRC21.DTL

http://palimpsest.stanford.edu/byform/mailing-lists/arsclist/2003/06/msg00133.html

www.webrarian.co.uk

Also recommended for further reading is *Aural History: Essays on Recorded Sound*, published as a hardback book and on CD-ROM in September 2001 by British Library Publishing (ISBN: 0712347410), with a chapter by Peter Copeland entitled *Forensic evidence in historical sound-recordings*.

Some other aspects of Henry Edmunds's family history and business and motoring career need to be reviewed as a result of research conducted since 1993 by Catherine Pritchard (whose husband, Michael, is Henry's great grandson) and Tom Clarke. In Chapter One, writing about Henry Edmunds Snr, I surmised that his father, Richard (1793-1872), had moved from Northamptonshire to Halifax and that the family had probably been in the West Riding for 50 years. In fact Richard married Alice Page from Broughton, near Banbury in 1818 and raised his family in Banbury, where he also had a business as an ironmonger and corn merchant. He defected from the Church of

England to Methodism and all members of the family were raised as active members of the Methodist Church. He was also active on the local political scene and became Capital Burgess of Banbury. His four sons Frederick, Richard, Henry (1823-1904) and William (there were also three others who died in infancy) were all sent to a Methodist boarding school at Oxhill in Warwickshire, but were at work in their early teens. Catherine is not sure how Henry Snr met Caroline Hatton but has come to the conclusion that there may have been links through the Methodist Church. Richard's sons were Methodist local preachers and Frederick was ordained as minister. Caroline's family came from Lightcliffe, near Halifax, where there was the same strong Methodism. She was living in Islington with her grandmother (her father Joseph having died in 1845) and the marriage took place on July 26, 1849 at St Paul's Church, Islington. They set up their first home in Banbury and in the 1851 census are registered as living at Bridge St North; his occupation is given as ironmonger. They moved to Halifax in 1852 or 1853 as Henry was born there on March 19, 1853.

Henry Snr probably moved north because of Caroline's family links and business opportunities in the thriving industrial town. Caroline died on 26 May 1853, two months after the birth of Henry, and the cause of death was 'asthenia, paralysis and marasmus'. This means a combination of general 'wasting away', paralysis and debility. Her illness could have been caused by a pregnancy condition or tuberculosis, or a combination of both.

Henry Snr was a lay preacher at South Parade Methodist chapel. He met Sarah Hannah Walker and married her on 1 June 1854. She was from Stainland near Halifax and one of a family of 10, the children of Samuel Walker, a woollen manufacturer at Bankhouse Mill. They must have been fairly comfortably off. The 1851 census shows he was a worsted spinner and employer of 65 men, 17 women, 58 boys, 39 girls; and also a farmer of 35 acres employing one labourer.

The rest of the Edmunds family remained in Banbury and became important local figures in their own right as brewers, mayors and JPs. Henry was not alone in having the drive to be successful. The family seemed to have their fingers in all sorts of pies! The Banbury links remained strong. Thomas Wayman (father of Annie Edmunds, nee Wayman, Henry's first wife) also retired to Banbury to be near his other daughter Kate, who had married Frederick Ellis Edmunds (Henry Snr's nephew and son of William Edmunds). Thomas and Sarah Wayman, both from Halifax, are buried in Southam Road Cemetery Banbury.

In my Epilogue I cited Kendal Milne as the informant of the death of Henry Snr in 1904. This now seems to have been family legend. The actual informant was Arthur Sidney Latham, the husband of Edith

Milnes Edmunds, his daughter by Sarah Hannah Walker. They lived at 'Ashlea', Cheadle, near to South Bank where Henry lived after he retired. Interestingly, James Milne (a partner in Kendal Milne's store in Manchester) was a neighbour and it is known that the families were fairly close friends and attended the same parties. More information about the Edmunds family and its relations are on Catherine's website, www.mypritchardfamily.co.uk.

Tom Clarke has found references in contemporary issues of The Automobile Club Journal to Henry's 1897 De Dion tricycle and trailer and De Dion Quad; and to his ownership of a Faugere Ochin & D'Angleterre electric phaeton; a Krieger electric car, and 7 hp and 10 hp Daimlers built in 1899. According to Henry's obituary in The Motor on 29 November 1927 (page 929) he was also involved in the development of the Hedgeland axle, a system that aimed to do away with the rear differential and use a ratchet instead.

Tom has also had access to documents related to the public flotation of Rolls-Royce in 1906, and to what has been established as Volume 10 (1905–1907) of the ledgers of Claremont Haynes (see Chapter 11), solicitors to Royce Ltd, Rolls-Royce, Henry Edmunds and the Claremont and Punt families. The flotation documents indicate that the number of shares involved in the exchange of Royce Ltd and W T Glover & Co Ltd shares agreed by Henry and Ernest Claremont some time before 4 May 1904 (see Chapter Twelve) could have totalled 15,000. As the owner of such a large stake in Royce's company, Henry had a compelling incentive to introduce Rolls to Royce and ensure that their business succeeded.

The ledger, which is untitled, is another important find, since the archives of Claremont Haynes (now Claremont Smith) were thought to be complete. The ledger must have been taken away by a member of staff and become lost. Within it there are intriguing entries that confirm that Henry was associated with granite and stone-splitting businesses and a combustion engine development of some kind. There are also references to agreements for land bought by Rolls-Royce for its factory at Derby, and the acquisition by Rolls-Royce of Charles Rolls' company, C S Rolls & Co.

Clearly, this book, and Mike Evans and Tom Clarke's publications, will not be the last words on the history of Rolls-Royce and its Godfather.

Paul Tritton
November 2004

Photographs by courtesy of Roger Varney

THE AUTHOR

Paul Tritton was educated in Canterbury, England, and began his writing career in the 1950s, as a newspaper reporter on the *Kentish Gazette* and the *Poole & Dorset Herald.* From 1960 until 1964 he was Press Officer at the late Sir Alan Cobham's company, Flight Refuelling Ltd. During that time he became interested in the lives and achievements of those who pioneered swift and convenient air, sea and land transport.

Other books by the author are:

John Montagu of Beaulieu - Motoring Pioneer and Prophet, which won the Society of Automotive Historians' 1986 Award of Distinction.

The Lost Voice of Queen Victoria - the Search for the First Royal Recording.

Historical Series

1. *Rolls-Royce - the formative years 1906-1939*
   Alec Harvey-Bailey, RRHT 2nd edition 1983
2. *The Merlin in perspective - the combat years*
   Alec Harvey-Bailey, RRHT 4th edition 1995
3. *Rolls-Royce - the pursuit of excellence*
   Alec Harvey-Bailey and Mike Evans, SHRMF 1984
4. *In the beginning – the Manchester origins of Rolls-Royce*
   Mike Evans, RRHT 2nd edition 2004
5. *Rolls-Royce – the Derby Bentleys,* Alec Harvey-Bailey, SHRMF 1985
6. *The early days of Rolls-Royce - and the Montagu family*
   Lord Montagu of Beaulieu, RRHT 1986
7. *Rolls-Royce – Hives, the quiet tiger,* Alec Harvey-Bailey, SHRMF 1985
8. *Rolls-Royce – Twenty to Wraith,* Alec Harvey-Bailey, SHRMF 1986
9. *Rolls-Royce and the Mustang,* David Birch, RRHT 1997
10. *From Gipsy to Gem with diversions, 1926-1986,* Peter Stokes, RRHT 1987
11. *Armstrong Siddeley - the Parkside story, 1896-1939*
    Ray Cook, RRHT 1989
12. *Henry Royce – mechanic,* Donald Bastow, RRHT 1989
14. *Rolls-Royce - the sons of Martha,* Alec Harvey-Bailey, SHRMF 1989
15. *Olympus - the first forty years,* Alan Baxter, RRHT 1990
16. *Rolls-Royce piston aero engines - a designer remembers*
    A A Rubbra, RRHT 1990
17. *Charlie Rolls – pioneer aviator,* Gordon Bruce, RRHT 1990
18. *The Rolls-Royce Dart - pioneering turboprop*
    Roy Heathcote, RRHT 1992
19. *The Merlin 100 series - the ultimate military development*
    Alec Harvey-Bailey and Dave Piggott, RRHT 1993
20. *Rolls-Royce – Hives' turbulent barons,* Alec Harvey-Bailey, SHRMF 1992
21. *The Rolls-Royce Crecy, Nahum,* Foster-Pegg and Birch, RRHT 1994
22. *Vikings at Waterloo - the wartime work on the Whittle jet engine by the Rover Company,* David S Brooks, RRHT 1997
23. *Rolls-Royce - the first cars from Crewe,* K E Lea, RRHT 1997
24. *The Rolls-Royce Tyne,* L Haworth, RRHT 1998
25. *A View of Ansty,* D E Williams, RRHT 1998
26. *Fedden – the life of Sir Roy Fedden,* Bill Gunston, RRHT 1998
27. *Lord Northcliffe – and the early years of Rolls-Royce*
    Hugh Driver, RREC 1998
28. *Boxkite to Jet – the remarkable career of Frank B Halford*
    Douglas R Taylor, RRHT 1999
29. *Rolls-Royce on the front line – the life and times of a Service Engineer*
    Tony Henniker, RRHT 2000
30. *The Rolls-Royce Tay engine and the BAC One-Eleven*
    Ken Goddard, RRHT 2001
31. *An account of partnership – industry, government and the aero engine,*
    G P Bulman, RRHT 2002

32 *The bombing of Rolls-Royce at Derby in two World Wars – with diversions,* Kirk, Felix and Bartnik, RRHT 2002
33 *Early Russian jet engines – the Nene and Derwent in the Soviet Union, and the evolution of the VK-1*
    Vladimir Kotelnikov and Tony Buttler, RRHT 2003
34 *Pistons to Blades, small gas turbine developments by the Rover Company,* Mark C S Barnard, RRHT 2003
35 *The Rolls-Royce Meteor – Cromwell and other applications*
    David Birch, RRHT 2004
36 *50 years with Rolls-Royce – my reminiscences,* Donald Eyre, RRHT 2005
37 *Stoneleigh Motors - an Armstrong Siddeley company,*
    Alan Betts, RRHT 2006

Technical Series

1 *Rolls-Royce and the Rateau Patents,* H Pearson, RRHT 1989
2 *The vital spark! The development of aero engine sparking plugs*
   K Gough, RRHT 1991
3 *The performance of a supercharged aero engine*
   S Hooker, H Reed and A Yarker, RRHT 1997
4 *Flow matching of the stages of axial compressors*
   Geoffrey Wilde OBE, RRHT 1999
5 *Fast jets – the history of reheat development at Derby*
   Cyril Elliott, RRHT 2001
6 *Royce and the vibration damper,* T C Clarke, RRHT 2003
7 *Rocket development with liquid propellants*
   W H J Riedel, RRHT 2005 (translated by John Kelly 2004)
8 *Fundamentals of car performance*
   Hives, Lovesey, Robotham, RRHT 2006

Specials

* *Sectioned drawings of piston aero engines,* L Jones, RRHT 1995
* *Hall of Fame,* RRHT 2004
* *Rolls-Royce Centenary Luncheon,* M H Evans, 2005
* *Rolls-Royce Armaments,* D Birch, RRHT 2000

ROLLS-ROYCE
HERITAGE TRUST